THE REGULATORY C

THE REGULATORY CHALLENGE

Edited by

MATTHEW BISHOP
JOHN KAY
COLIN MAYER

OXFORD UNIVERSITY PRESS
1995

Oxford University Press, Walton Street, Oxford OX2 6DP
Oxford New York
Athens Auckland Bangkok Bombay
Calcutta Cape Town Dar es Salaam Delhi
Florence Hong Kong Istanbul Karachi
Kuala Lumpur Madras Madrid Melbourne
Mexico City Nairobi Paris Singapore
Taipei Tokyo Toronto
and associated companies in
Berlin Ibadan

Oxford is a trade mark of Oxford University Press

Published in the United States
by Oxford University Press Inc., New York

British Library Cataloguing in Publication Data
Data available

Library of Congress Cataloging in Publication Data
The regulatory challenge / edited by Matthew Bishop, John Kay, and Colin Mayer.
Rev. of: Privatization and regulation, 1986, which was split into 2 works: The regulatory challenge and Privatization and economic performance, both being published in 1994.
Includes index.
1. Privatization—Great Britain. 2. Deregulation—Great Britain. I. Bishop, Matthew, 1964– . II. Kay, J. A. (John Anderson) III. Mayer, C. P. (Colin P.) IV. Title: Privatization and regulation.
HD4145.R39 1994 94–29639
338.941—dc20
ISBN 0–19–877341–2
ISBN 0–19–877342–0 (Pbk)

Set by Hope Services (Abingdon) Ltd.
Printed in Great Britain
on acid-free paper by
Biddles Ltd.,
Guildford & King's Lynn

PREFACE

In 1986 Colin Mayer, David Thompson, and I edited a collection of readings *Privatization and Regulation: The UK experience.* At that time, privatization was still a novel idea and Britain's new style of utility regulation was only two years old. Now, privatization is a policy which has aroused not only interest but imitation around the world, and we have learnt that regulation introduces many new problems as well as solving old ones. The explosion of what was then a very limited literature in the field has now justified two separate volumes on Privatization and Regulation respectively. The articles they contain have been written and revised at various dates, and while some authors have brought their analysis or conclusions up to date at the time of going to press, others have preferred to leave their views as they stood.

J.A.K.

The editors are indebted to Barbara Lee for assembling the material and putting together the manuscripts. David Thompson provided valuable comments and advice in the early stages of editing this volume.

CONTENTS

FIGURES

TABLES

CONTRIBUTORS

MARK ARMSTRONG:	Gonville and Caius College, University of Cambridge
WILLIAM BAUMOL:	Professor at the C. V. Starr Center for Applied Economics, New York University
MICHAEL BEESLEY:	Professor of Economics at the London Business School
MATTHEW BISHOP:	Journalist at *The Economist*, formerly at Centre for Business Strategy, London Business School
MARTIN CAVE:	Dean, Faculty of Social Sciences, Brunel University
EVAN DAVIS:	Economics correspondent at the BBC. Previously a Research Fellow at the Centre for Business Strategy, London Business School
RUTH DODSWORTH:	Previously a Research Assistant at the Centre for Business Strategy, London Business School
SIMON DOMBERGER:	Professor at the Graduate School of Business, University of Sydney
STEPHANIE FLANDERS:	Previously a Research Assistant at the Centre for Business Strategy, London Business School
PETER GRINDLEY:	Center for Research in Management, University of California, Berkeley, Calif.
PAUL GROUT:	Professor of Economics, University of Bristol
NORMAN IRELAND:	Professor of Economics, Department of Economics, University of Warwick
JOHN KAY:	Chairman of London Economics, and Professor of Economics at the London Business School
BRUCE LAIDLAW:	Managing Director of BMP International, a telecommunications consultancy
JOHN MCELDOWNEY:	Professor at the School of Law, University of Warwick
FRANCIS MCGOWAN:	School of European Studies, University of Sussex
COLIN MAYER:	Professor of Economics and Finance at Warwick Business School
ALAN MAYNARD:	Professor of Economics and Director of the Centre for Health Economics at the University of York
RAY REES:	Professor of Economics, Department of Economics, University of Guelph, Guelph, Ontario
LAURA ROVIZZI:	Previously a Research Assistant at the Centre for Business Strategy, London Business School

PAUL SEABRIGHT:	Churchill College, University of Cambridge
AVROM SHERR:	Alsop Wilkinson Professor of Law at the Faculty of Law, University of Liverpool
DAVID THOMPSON:	Previously a Senior Research Fellow at the Centre for Business Strategy, London Business School
JOHN VICKERS:	Professor at the Institute of Economics and Statistics, University of Oxford
THOMAS WEYMAN-JONES:	Senior Lecturer, Department of Economics, Loughborough University
ANN WHITFIELD:	Previously a Research Assistant at the Centre for Business Strategy, London Business School
PETER WILLIAMSON:	Professor at the Department of Strategic and International Management, London Business School

Introduction

MATTHEW BISHOP,* JOHN KAY,† AND COLIN MAYER‡

1. INTRODUCTION

The last decade has witnessed the introduction of an elaborate system of regulation in the UK. In part this has been an adjunct to the privatisation programme which is the subject of the companion volume, *Privatization and Economic Performance,* in this series. However, in some areas, most notably financial services, regulation has been introduced where little or none previously existed. Whole segments of British industry are now operating under the supervision of regulatory bodies whose powers and importance are not dissimilar from those of the government departments which they were designed to replace. This introduction evaluates the UK's programme of regulatory reform in the utilities and financial services. It describes the motivation behind establishing regulatory organizations, the function that they perform, and the way in which they operate. It considers the reasons why regulation is needed in privatized companies, the scope of regulation in the UK and the form that it has taken. It then considers the performance of regulation in the UK. It discusses the advantages of the combination of privatization and independent regulation over state ownership and the problems that have been encountered.

The article draws four main conclusions. The first is that the form of regulation of the privatized utilities has been dictated by the structure of the privatized industries. The task of regulation has been made very much more onerous than it need have been by the inadequate levels of restructuring that occurred before privatization. In particular, the scope of regulation has been broader than it should have been and regulators have in many cases been faced with the impossible task of trying to compensate for the deficiencies of inappropriately structured private sectors.

This problem has not been restricted to the privatized utilities. The second conclusion is that a similar problem of inappropriate industrial structure and therefore regulation occurs elsewhere, in particular financial services. A cumbersome and costly system of regulation has been

* Journalist with *The Economist*.

† Chairman of London Economics, and Professor of Economics at the London Business School.

‡ Professor of Economics and Finance, Warwick Business School.

established that is failing to provide adequate investor protection. This reflects the fact that the primary sources of market failure have not been identified. The solution is neither more nor less but different regulation.

The third conclusion is that, while most of the problems of the UK regulatory system are structural in nature, there have also been difficulties of conduct. The relation between the regulator and the firm is best thought of as a contract. However, the contract between regulator and company was loosely specified at the time of privatization. As a consequence, a great deal of discretion was left in the hands of regulators. This has created considerable uncertainty about the precise form of regulation and the way in which regulators can adjust the basis on which companies are rewarded.

The fourth conclusion concerns the system of arbitration between utilities and regulator. Acrimonious conflicts have emerged that can only be resolved through a cumbersome arbitration procedure involving the Monopolies and Mergers Commission.

The main lessons therefore to be learnt from regulation in the UK are:

1. Regulatory failures are most in evidence where the form of privatization has been incorrect. Notable examples are water where the basic structure of the industry is inappropriate, electricity where the structure of the industry was unduly influenced by concerns over nuclear power and gas which was privatized as a monopoly.
2. Regulatory failure is also in evidence where the main causes of market failure have not been identified in advance, for example in financial services.
3. The UK did not specify regulatory rules with sufficient precision prior to privatization. Considerable uncertainty has thereby been created about the way in which regulation is being implemented.
4. Procedures for adjudicating disputes between regulators and companies are cumbersome. However, regulation can never be an exact science, and disputes between regulator and regulated will often not be resolved to the satisfaction of both parties. When there is a choice between regulating and making markets more competitive, the market route should be preferred. That may hold true even if the market shows some signs of failure: regulators, too, can fail, and often do.

Section 2 of the paper considers the theoretical justification for regulation of utilities and financial services; Section 3 describes the activities that are regulated; Section 4 discusses the regulatory process in the utilities; Section 5 describes the organization of regulation and Section 6 evaluates its performance. Section 7 discusses how regulation is related to the structure of industries and the way in which structural changes could have improved the operation of regulation. Section 8 concludes the article.

2. WHY REGULATE?

The paper considers two areas in which the introduction of regulation has been most pronounced: the utilities and financial services. The regulation of other professions has been subjected to less dramatic changes. The introduction of widespread regulation in the UK was an adjunct to the structural changes that took place in industries. In the utilities the dominant force was the shift of industries from public to private ownership. In finance it was a product of the changing way in which the City organized its activities and in particular the arrival of Big Bang.

Utilities

The most powerful economic justification for public intervention is the correction of market failure. The companion volume documented how privatization is in part a response to the observation that public-sector regulation, particularly through direct ownership, has been largely ineffective in reducing the impact of market failure. Also, the market failures which provided the *raison d'être* of public ownership mostly related to small parts of the industries concerned. In those cases, public ownership of the entire industry was unjustifiable. A far better solution was private ownership combined with regulation targeted directly on the identified source of market failure.

The main form of market failure in utilities is monopoly. The privatization of gas created a private-sector monopoly out of a state-owned monopoly. Competition in airports and telecoms is limited. In electricity and water several private-sector firms were created but competition has been inhibited by geographical segmentation of the national market in the form of regional monopolies. Throughout the privatized utilities competition has therefore been limited and regulation has been required to prevent abuse of a dominant position.

Financial services

Regulation of financial services, education, and health have different underlying rationales. The ability of market mechanisms to elicit appropriate outcomes is inhibited by limited information on the part of consumers. Evaluating quality of the provision of services is difficult and costly for consumers that may have little expertise and incentive to collect information. Regulation is required to correct the market failures arising from imperfect information.

While market failure may provide a prima facie case for regulation, public-sector or regulatory failure may more than offset its benefits.

Thus regulation that is designed to avoid the distributional consequences of monopoly pricing may dampen incentives to pursue improvements in efficiency and undertake long-term investments. Regulation to improve the provision of information to consumers may impose excessively high costs on the providers of services and discourage innovation in new forms of service. It is therefore important in evaluating the merits of regulation to examine its overall effects on consumer welfare.

3. WHAT IS REGULATED?

This section examines the different aspects of firms' activities that are regulated. It discusses financial returns, quality, and quantity, first in relation to utilities and then financial services.

Financial returns

The most obvious response to possible monopoly abuse is to regulate prices. In fact, the traditional form of regulation in the US has been to regulate rates of return on capital employed rather than prices. The argument for rate-of-return regulation rather than prices is that utilities require adequate rates of return to encourage them to invest. The avoidance of monopoly requires that the rates of return that utilities earn should not be excessive. The problem that has emerged with rate-of-return regulation is twofold. First, by offering utilities a fixed rate of return, regulation provides little incentive to improve efficiency. If improvements in operating efficiency provoke lower prices to achieve target rates of return then utilities will have no incentives to improve efficiency in the first place. Secondly, since rates of return are computed on the capital base of the firm, by expanding the value of assets employed, utilities can earn higher profits. Rate-of-return regulation therefore provides undue incentives to invest. The UK has attempted to avoid these deficiencies of rate-of-return regulation by regulating prices directly. Instead, of setting rates of return, the regulators of UK utilities set prices for specified periods. The principle behind this is that by fixing prices, utilities are provided with appropriate incentives to reduce costs and raise profits. In contrast to rate-of-return regulation, price regulation allows firms to retain the benefits of efficiency improvements. Furthermore, since price regulation caps the earnings of firms, it does not distort firms' choices between different factors of production. Increases in both capital and current costs reduce returns to investors.

Quality

The utilities

Consumers are affected by the quality as well as the price of services. Quality takes quite different forms in different industries. In some industries, such as telecoms, it is primarily concerned with speed and reliability of delivery. In others, such as water, there are also environmental considerations. In the professions, quality is a more nebulous concept. A successful diagnosis or operation may restore a patient to health but some forms of treatment may be more comfortable and durable than others. Likewise, the quality of financial advice should reflect the particular circumstances of the individual concerned. Price regulation on its own would result in inadequate quality of services. As a consequence, quality is specifically regulated in the utilities. The regulator of electricity is concerned about the reliability of supply. The regulator of water has to oversee the implementation of drinking-water standards imposed by the UK government and the European Commission. The regulator of telecoms is concerned with the reliability of connections, the number of telephone boxes that are out of service, and the way in which customer enquiries and complaints are handled.

Financial services

Quality is the primary concern of regulators in the professions. Competition between firms limits scope for excessive pricing but consumers are frequently imperfectly informed about the quality of services that they purchase. The competence and diligence of the providers of professional services are difficult to determine in advance and even after the event performance of professionals is not easy to evaluate. There are poor benchmarks against which to measure performance of doctors, accountants and financial institutions and highly technical assessments are required to establish whether poor performance is attributable to negligence, or incompetence, or simply bad luck.

Financial institutions in the UK are expected to offer their clients 'best practice'. This involves consideration of how financial institutions handle clients' securities and monies, the type of advice that they offer clients and the accounting procedures that financial institutions practice. In other professions, less attention is paid to the quality of outputs than inputs. The regulation of doctors, lawyers, and accountants is primarily concerned with the training that they receive. The completion of training qualifications is often an arduous task. In contrast, beyond controlling for malpractice, there is much less attention given to the quality of service offered. Lawyers are not required to follow prescribed procedures in representing a client in court. Indeed, the notion of a true profession is intimately associated with pre-screening of members rather than the regulation of behaviour.

Quantity

The final element of regulation that relates primarily to the utilities concerns quantity. A utility provides a necessity that consumers cannot readily forgo. As part of their licence condition utilities are frequently subject to obligations to supply, e.g. universal service obligations. The clearest example of this relates to the Post Office: everyone has the right to have access to postal delivery and collection. To a greater or lesser extent this also applies to electricity, gas, water, and sewerage. This means that in contrast to most private-sector suppliers, utilities do not have complete freedom to choose which customers to supply.

4. THE REGULATORY PROCESS

This section considers the way in which the regulatory process operates. It begins by describing the regulatory contract in utilities and then considers the operation of regulation in financial services.

The regulatory contract in utilities

As part of the procedure of privatizing utilities independent regulatory offices were created. These are responsible for overseeing the regulation of particular privatized industries as set out in broad terms in an Act of Parliament and slightly more detail in the Licences that were conferred on privatized utilities. There were two central components to the initial privatization process. The first was the structure of the industry, i.e. whether the public-sector monopoly was sold off intact, regionalized, split up by function, or broken into competing companies. This was discussed in the companion volume. The second was the terms on which the utilities were initially regulated.

The best way of thinking of the regulatory process is as a contract between the government on the one hand and the companies on the other. The government acts on behalf of consumers and local communities in the case of industries where environmental considerations are of importance, for example in relation to sewage disposal. The contract lays down certain conditions that privatized firms have to satisfy: the provision of services of certain quality for particular groups of consumers, for example domestic as against industrial consumers.

In return for an obligation to meet these targets utilities are rewarded by being offered certain revenue streams which are in general specified as maximum price caps. Given projected levels of demand, the price caps determine expected levels of earnings. The duration of a contract in principle corresponds to that of a regulatory period. For example, when the water companies were privatized they were subject to a regulatory formula which was supposed to last for either five or ten years. In fact, the regulator of water services decided to review the regulatory formula after five years and, as we will discuss shortly, regulatory formulas have not in general been able to survive even this period.

The price cap

The way in which the price cap is in principle determined is as follows. A variety of financial models is used to establish the *cost of capital* of the industry. This is the minimum return that investors require to induce them to invest in the industry. This rate of return is then applied to the value of *capital assets* employed in the industry. The product of the cost of capital and the value of assets is the *minimum profits* that the business requires to reward shareholders adequately. An estimate of the *operating costs* of the business is added to this minimum profits to determine the *required revenue* of the firm. Finally, a projection of demand is used to convert a revenue stream into a price cap.

Operating costs

As will be discussed below, each stage of this process is in practice fraught with difficulties. One of the first problems to be encountered was the determination of minimum operating costs. It was clear that nationalized utilities were not being run efficiently. There was a great deal of slack that could be eliminated. The problem was determining the precise extent of possible efficiency gains. An unduly pessimistic view of potential efficiency gains would permit utilities to earn excessively high earnings at the expense of consumers; an unduly sanguine prediction of efficiency savings could undermine the financial condition of companies. As it was, the government opted for caution in giving the utilities the benefit of the doubt and setting quite loose constraints. This provided greater assurance of the success of the privatization process and raised the revenues that were earned from the sales.

Comparative efficiency

Where there is more than one firm operating in an industry then minimum operating costs can be ascertained with a greater degree of precision. Instead of setting prices on the basis of the actual or expected costs of particular firms, cost information on all firms in the industry can be used. On the assumption that similar factors influence the costs of firms operating in an industry then all firms should be able to attain the same lowest costs of production. In that case prices should be set in relation to the lowest costs in the industry. The use of minimum rather than actual costs provides firms with appropriate incentives to minimize their own costs of production.

More generally, costs can be related to the exogenous factors which firms are unable to control. For example, the costs of a distribution company are influenced by, *inter alia*, the density of the population that it serves, the age of its capital stock and the distribution of its customers between industrial and domestic users. Companies with dispersed populations cannot be expected to attain the same level of costs as those supplying large urban conurbations. In principle, there are econometric techniques that allow the frontier of lowest costs of production to be identified.

The regulation of financial services

The regulation of financial services does not have the feature of a contract between government and firm. The existence of competition means that prices do not have to be regulated. Instead, regulation is concerned with ensuring that the nature of services purchased by clients is transparent. The way in which this has been done is to impose (minimum) standards of conduct which all firms are expected to meet. Since the standard is supposed to conform with best practice there is little room for discretion. The significant difference between financial services and utilities is that consumer choice in many utilities is constrained and the regulator is therefore required to elicit consumer preferences that then form part of the regulatory contract with consumers. Financial services are not natural monopolies and therefore in principle it should not be necessary to impose quality or quantity restrictions on suppliers.

5. THE ORGANIZATION OF REGULATION

The privatization of utilities has involved a shift in control from government departments to independent regulators. The Acts of Parliament and the Licence place the operation of the privatized utilities under the control of a Director General of Regulation. Each privatized industry is controlled by a separate regulatory office, for example OFTEL the regulator of telecoms, OFGAS the regulator of the gas industry and OFFER the regulator of the electricity industry. These regulatory organizations are concerned with economic regulation.

In water and sewerage, other bodies are concerned with environmental regulation (for example, the National Rivers Authority) and the standard of drinking water quality (HM Inspectorate of Drinking Water).

Some of the standards are set by the European Commission as part of the process of harmonization across Member States. Either the regulator or the companies can refer points of dispute to the Monopolies and Mergers Commission (MMC). Rulings of the MMC only have the status of advice to the Secretary of State who is empowered to enact or reject it. Alternatively, either party can take legal action against the other party in relation to specific violations of the Licence. Thus far, little resort has been made to either the MMC or the courts to arbitrate over disputes.

6. AN EVALUATION OF THE PERFORMANCE OF THE REGULATORY PROCESS

This section considers the merits and deficiencies of the UK system of utility regulation. There are some distinct merits of the combination of regulation and private ownership:

The process is more transparent

Previously the control of utilities had been undertaken in the depths of some government department. Nationalized industries were accountable to a government department, the relevant Secretary of State and ultimately Parliament. The process by which decisions were arrived at was opaque. A succession of White Papers attempted to clarify the criteria by which prices were set and investments were evaluated. In fact, control was subject to arbitrary intervention by the government to meet some additional (frequently macroeconomic) objectives. Now public sector interventions by the regulator are subject to direct negotiation between companies and the regulator. The regulator has specific objectives as set out in the Licence and the process of intervention is subject to scrutiny by the MMC and the courts.

Regulation can be limited to specific areas of market failure

As noted above nationalization was in general a response to problems of monopoly. The innovation of privatization plus regulation is to establish the principle that control of monopoly abuse can be achieved through very specific actions, namely control of prices and possibly quality. Elsewhere, public control is not necessary or desirable. A good illustration of this distinction is telecoms: transmission and interconnection are regulated while the provision of value-added network services is unregulated.

Price regulation can provide incentives to efficiency

Choice of price regulation as against rate-of-return regulation has provided incentives to pursue operating efficiency gains. By setting prices, utilities can raise profits by cutting costs. As the companion volume recorded, privatization has been accompanied by substantial rationalizations and reductions in costs. Share prices provide a good guide to the performance of firms. High equity returns can be attributed to lax regulation or the achievement of large efficiency gains. Where there is more than one firm in an industry then market values are a particularly valuable source of information on corporate performance. Set against these advantages is a substantial list of problems that have arisen in practice.

Regulatory uncertainty

Most points of dispute to date have concerned prices and rates of return to utilities. As noted above, regulation of utilities is subject to periodic review after, for example, five or ten years in the water industry. The principle of price regulation expounded above is that firms should be able to retain profits made during a regulatory period. At the end of the regulatory period prices are reset on the basis of best estimates of future costs and costs of capital. In practice, there is a strong tendency for both companies and regulators to intervene between regulatory reviews. Companies wish to pass on unanticipated costs that arise between reviews. Regulators wish to claw back unduly generous prices. Regulatory interventions between reviews have proved irresistible in most privatized industries (for example, electricity, gas, and water). The principle of setting prices for a five year period is particularly difficult to sustain where there are large investment programmes. In water, the degree of uncertainty surrounding capital expenditure programmes required to meet particular quality standards is substantial.

The UK regulatory process deliberately eschewed the legalistic approach of the US and is not derived from the application of formal rules. Regulators are not required to set out the basis on which they arrive at a decision. As a consequence, while in principle resort can be made to the courts, UK regulation is not readily open to judicial review. This has the merit of making the system more flexible and potentially less costly than a rule-based system. On the other hand, it places a great deal of discretion in the hands of the regulator. Even if individual regulators do not wish to abuse this discretion, one generation of regulators is unable to bind the next to any particular regulatory principle. Therefore, utilities have little certainty as to how regulation will operate at any date beyond, at most, a ten-year period. This gives rise to what has been termed regulatory uncertainty, namely uncertainty engendered by the future behaviour of regulators. It is thought to have created significant increases in the cost of capital over and above those arising from normal economic uncertainty, but the precise scale of such effects remains unclear.

Costly disputes between regulators and firms

Privatization has created a new activity in the UK: the formation of regulatory departments that are concerned with achieving the best outcomes for companies from negotiations with regulators. Companies become embroiled in 'regulatory games' in which they attempt to outmanœuvre the strategy of the regulator. In general, companies are at an advantage in so far as they can afford to spend more on such activities than the public-sector funded regulatory offices. On the other hand, where there is more than one firm in an industry the regulator is able to play companies off against each other. Since firms are in general more concerned about relative than absolute performance, 'divide and rule' can be achieved by the more astute regulators.

The area in which the cost of regulation has been most in evidence is in relation to the regulation of financial services. As noted above, regulation of financial services extends beyond that of the utilities in requiring firms to follow 'best practice'. In response firms have been forced to create substantial compliance departments. These are particularly damaging for small firms and have acted as a significant barrier to entry. In the case of utilities it could be argued that some of the regulatory costs are not deadweight costs in so far as firms are encouraged to collect information that is in any event relevant to their activities. Thus regulators require information about costs, investments, quality, levels of service and customer complaints. Much of this is information that well-run companies should assimilate in any event. In contrast, regulation of financial services may require conduct that is not well suited to the activities of firms. For example, companies that expose clients to little financial risk through separating clients' funds should not be required to hold capital. Since capital is regarded as being something that well-managed investment firms should hold, UK regulation requires all investment companies to hold capital.

In addition, to the direct costs of regulation there have been several indirect costs. Regulation has encouraged firms to (i) use transfer pricing (pricing at other than marginal cost) to take revenue out of and load costs into the regulated business from unregulated businesses; (ii) to expand, in particular through acquisition, into unregulated activities; (iii) to use the regulated business as a method of subsidizing the funding of unregulated activities; and (iv) to transfer costs to those regulated businesses that enjoy a more liberal arrangement for passing on costs to consumers (for example, the supply businesses of the RECs).

Poor bench-marks against which to measure performance

One of the most serious problems that regulation has encountered has been the determination of bench-marks against which to measure performance. The principle of price determination described above was that costs of capital were combined with asset valuations to determine profits which were then used with comparative-efficiency exercises to establish minimum costs and therefore revenues and prices. In fact, each and every one of these stages has encountered serious difficulties.

First, there has been a great deal of disagreement about the appropriate measure of the cost of capital. Reference has been made to the standard approaches to the determination of costs of capital (for example, the Capital Asset Pricing Model and the Dividend Growth Model). However, even where there has been agreement over the appropriate model, the value of the parameters that should be used in the models has been the source of considerable controversy. Much of this has centred around the appropriate level of the risk premium of equity returns above riskless government securities. The utilities and the regulators have referred to estimates that differ by as much as 6 per cent.

Secondly, it was originally thought that the value of assets would simply be taken from the accounting valuation shown in utilities' books. In fact, in most cases these valuations bear little relation to the underlying economic valuation of the companies' assets. This is most clearly seen in the case of the water companies where the book value of the companies' assets on a current-cost basis exceeds their market value (as recorded by their stock-market valuations) by a factor of ten. Were current-cost valuations to be used as the basis for determining reasonable levels of profits then this would imply substantial increases in prices. Instead, it has been necessary to devise alternative methods of valuing assets based on their market valuations at the time of privatization.

Thirdly, comparative efficiency exercises have proved much harder to perform than was originally envisaged. The principle of comparative efficiency is that information on the costs incurred by firms in a particular industry can be used to identify the minimum costs at which any firm should be able to operate. In fact, for companies operating in regionally segmented parts of the country (for example, water companies and the Regional Electricity Companies) the underlying determinants of costs differ appreciably. The costs incurred by a firm are sensitive to a large number of factors, some of which can only be measured imprecisely. Incorporating all the relevant factors in an econometric regression involves the use of a large number of independent factors with a small number of observations. Furthermore, it is unclear precisely how many of these factors are really exogenous to companies as against being choice variables. For example, leakages in a water system are clearly in part a function of the age of the inherited pipes but are also determined by the care with which repairs and maintenance are carried out.

Finally, even if it is possible to go through the process of determining minimum profits and revenues then in some cases regulation is constrained by the requirement that businesses should have adequate revenues to fund their activities. In the case of high-investment industries, in particular water, prices have had to be set at such a level to ensure not an adequate rate of return to investors but a sufficient cash flow to meet capital expenditures. In effect, the customer has been called upon to act as a source of funding for the companies on terms which have never been made precise.

A poor system of arbitration

As noted above, the MMC is supposed to act as the arbitrator of disputes between regulator and the regulated. In fact, the MMC is a very cumbersome system of arbitration. Investigations by the MMC are protracted affairs, involving the provision of detailed information by both sides. The terms of reference of the MMC are frequently wide-ranging, extending beyond those of the immediate cause of dispute. The composition of members of a MMC panel differs between cases. As a consequence, panels can come to quite different conclusions. Recommendations by the MMC do tend to influence future panels but there is no formal process of precedent binding one MMC panel's decisions to those of the next. There is therefore a great deal of uncertainty about the conclusions to which any panel may come. Furthermore, as a recent reference involving British Gas has illustrated, MMC decisions can readily be overturned by the Secretary of State.

Reference to the MMC is regarded as an action of last resort for adjudicating in serious instances of disagreement, not a natural forum in which complex issues can be resolved. This is a serious deficiency as many of the regulatory questions that have arisen have been technically complex and would have benefited from independent analysis. The MMC could in principle have introduced a degree of consistency into the approaches taken by different regulators. As it is, regulators and companies have been reluctant to refer matters to the MMC. There therefore remain wide discrepancies in the approaches that different regulators take to similar issues. For example, currently the regulator of telecoms is suggesting equity-market risk premia in the cost of capital 5 per cent higher than those proposed by a number of the other regulators.

Regulatory uncertainty, costly disputes between regulator and company, poor bench-marks for judging performance, and poor systems of arbitration are serious deficiencies of the UK regulatory process. However, they are probably a symptom of a more fundamental underlying problem.

7. REGULATION AND MARKET STRUCTURE

The introduction to the companion volume noted that the privatization of UK utilities has in virtually every case created inappropriate industrial structures. Monopoly nationalized industries have been converted into monopoly private-sector utilities and opportunities for introducing competition have been missed.

The first privatization of telecoms created a duopoly. Entry of other new firms was deliberately impeded as a way of nurturing the competitor to the dominant supplier, British Telecom. British Gas was transferred directly from public to private ownership without any attempt at industrial restructuring. The privatization of electricity was dominated by concern about privatizing the nuclear industry. In the end, this had to be abandoned but not before irreparable damage had been done to the structure of the electricity-generating business.

The structure of the privatized water industry was based on river basins. This created ten regionally separated water and sewerage companies together with a large number of much smaller water-only companies. Regional separation has made direct competition between water companies virtually impossible. Instead, reliance has to be placed on yardstick competition to provide any form of inter-company comparisons at all. Concerns about pricing have been heard most clearly in this industry. Here a major contributory factor has been the large scale of investment programmes. Some of these are required to meet European Community regulations, others to satisfy national water quality and pollution standards. One alternative that could have been used to the river-basin structure of England and Wales is to retain assets in local or regional ownership and put out the running of the assets to franchise. This is a procedure that has been suggested in Scotland and it is close to the approach that operates in France. The advantage that this approach has over ownership of assets by water companies is that it allows water and sewerage companies to compete for franchises. The drawback is that long franchises may be required to provide incentives to undertake large investment programmes efficiently. In that case, competition between water companies might have been limited.

The failure to create adequate competition has considerably complicated regulation. Only the national and regional transmission systems are natural monopolies in gas. The trading of gas and the provision of domestic appliances are readily open to competition. Regulation of gas should therefore have been primarily concerned with the determination of transmission prices. Prices in the tariff and industrial market could both have been determined by competition between suppliers.

Similarly a competitive electricity-generation market would have significantly reduced the extent to which regulatory intervention in electricity was required. Much of the criticism of electricity since privatization has concerned pricing by the generators. The question has arisen as to whether the two generators have been exerting market power in setting prices. Since there are few economies of scale involved in operating more than one generating plant, the possibility of market dominance should have been largely eliminated by the creation of several competing generators.

The consequence of the failure to give adequate attention to the structure of industries prior to privatization has been that regulation has not been able to realize one of the advantages that it should have had over public ownership—careful targeting on market failures. The areas of market failure in most utilities are quite narrow. In contrast, the scope of regulation in all cases has been very broad, encompassing entire industries. As a consequence, the job of regulators has been made impossible by the nature of the task that they have inherited, namely the stewardship of whole industries.

One industry in which inappropriate regulation is particularly in evidence is the financial sector. As previously described the nature of the market failure afflicting financial services is imperfect information. In fact, on closer examination there is one form of failure that is by far and away the most important and that is fraud. Most regulation of financial services is concerned with the avoidance of fraud. Other types of failure, for example, negligence and incompetence can be dealt with in other ways such as through insurance. Once the primary role of financial services regulation is understood to be the prevention of fraud then the appropriate response becomes much clearer. It is not necessary to subject the entire financial services sector to regulation concerning the way in which they conduct their business. The imposition of regulation regarding best practice is a serious interference with the operation of financial institutions. Instead, attention should be focused on those areas where there is greatest risk of fraud occurring. Risks of fraud occur where institutions handle clients' monies and assets. The response of some regulatory authorities (for example, the Germans) is to treat all institutions that handle monies and assets as banks and subject them to stringent regulation. Other institutions, such as portfolio managers, that do not handle monies or assets are subject to little or no regulation.

The UK approach of regulating all financial institutions leads to both over- and under-regulation. It over-regulates those institutions where there is little risk of fraud and it provides insufficient protection against risks of fraud. As a consequence, the UK regulatory authorities have been given the unenviable task of protecting against fraud with inadequate tools. It would instead have been better to use custody of clients' monies and assets as a method of limiting the number of institutions that are subject to risks of fraud and concentrate regulation in these areas. Elsewhere, regulation could have been directed to the improvement of information flows to investors rather than the imposition of conduct of business rules.

8. CONCLUSIONS

Privatization and regulation have distinct advantages over public ownership. They allow market processes to operate and regulation to be concentrated in areas where market failures are most pronounced. Privatization in the UK has failed to realize these benefits to the full. The reason for this is that the UK privatization programme has not introduced competition where it could have done. As a consequence, regulation has had to be broader in scope than it need have been.

The most important feature of regulation is that there should be as little of it as possible. This involves identifying the precise sources of market failure in industries and targeting regulation specifically on these. Financial services in the UK are a good example of an industry in which market failures have been ill-defined and regulation imprecisely and ineffectively directed.

There are in addition a number of specific aspects of the design of regulation that could be improved. First, the absence of rules to guide the regulatory process has introduced an excessive level of uncertainty about the effects of regulation. The procedure by which prices are determined at regulatory reviews needs to be set out with greater precision. There should be more consistency in the way in which different regulators set prices and the criteria by which the performance of firms is judged. Secondly, regulators should be required to provide clearer guidance of the basis on which they come to regulatory decisions. These decisions should be open to scrutiny and, where thought appropriate, open to challenge by companies in the courts. This in turn would have led to a simpler system of arbitration between regulators and companies. The current system of arbitration through the MMC is too lengthy and costly. Instead, a body that is explicitly concerned with regulatory cases should be constituted and should be able to provide expert analysis of the particular issues that confront regulated firms. To build on the progress made so far in British regulation, then, strenuous efforts must be made to further identify and reduce the problems not just of market failure but also of regulatory failure.

1

Express Coaching: Privatization, Incumbent Advantage, and the Competitive Process

DAVID THOMPSON* AND ANN WHITFIELD†

1. INTRODUCTION

The deregulation of express coach services, implemented in October 1980, has resulted in profound changes in this industry—some of them expected but some almost wholly unexpected. The significant scale of market entry which followed immediately after deregulation, and the associated reduction in real price levels, can both be counted as expected outcomes. More surprising has been the success which the main incumbent—National Express—achieved in fighting entry, the large share of the deregulated market which it was able to sustain, and the rising trend in real price levels after 1982. These unexpected outcomes have been examined in several studies (see Jaffer, for example, Jaffer and Thompson 1986; Davis 1984) and these point to various advantages of incumbency which enabled National Express (NE) to successfully meet the threat of market entry. Such advantages included exclusive access to major coach terminals, an established brand name, an extensive marketing network, and a weak bankruptcy constraint, arising from NE's status as a subsidiary of the public-sector National Bus Company (NBC).

Since 1987, however, legislative changes, and in particular the privatization of the NBC, have acted to reduce the importance of these entry barriers. Access to the major terminals has become easier whilst the separation of NE from the rest of the NBC, upon privatization, can be expected to have strengthened the bankruptcy constraint which it faces.

* Previously a Senior Research Fellow at the Centre for Business Strategy, London Business School.

† Previously a Research Assistant at the Centre for Business Strategy, London Business School.

Helpful comments on an earlier draft of this paper came from Evan Davis, John Kay, David Starkie, and Peter White. We are also grateful to Stephen Glaister and Richard Smith of London Regional Transport for providing data on the characteristics of travellers using Victoria Coach Station. The financial support of the Gatsby Foundation is gratefully acknowledged. The usual disclaimer applies.

Our purpose in this paper is to examine whether these recent policy initiatives have resulted in changes to entry and to market performance and to assess, on this basis, the implications for regulatory policy in this sector.

The plan of the paper is as follows: in Section 2 we briefly recap on the implementation of deregulation and the development of the coach market up to the mid-1980s. The main unexpected outcome has been the high market share which National Express continued to hold following deregulation. We consider the incumbent advantages which enabled NE to protect its position and we compare NE's experience with that of companies in the Scottish Bus Group which enjoyed fewer advantages of incumbency. This comparison suggests that NE continued to hold significant market power in the years immediately after deregulation.

In Section 3 we outline the recent policy initiatives which have acted to reduce the incumbent advantages enjoyed by NE, in particular the establishment of common-user access rights to major coach terminals and the privatization of the NBC. Section 4 examines the pattern of entry and exit since these changes were implemented and Section 5 looks at measures of market performance—in particular the level and structure of prices and measures of service quality. The analysis shows that there has been no significant entry following the recent policy initiatives. Whilst their introduction was followed by a small reduction in the real level of prices charged by NE this has subsequently been overlaid by a larger real increase. However, prices remain significantly lower, on average, compared with the period immediately prior to deregulation although these findings also suggest that NE continues to benefit from some advantages of incumbency.

In Section 6 we analyse NE's financial performance, using added value as our measure of assessment in order to take account of the special organizational features of the industry. The results complement our analysis of price trends in that they show that NE has been able to earn substantial rents. However, our results suggest that the 'height' of residual barriers to market entry is now comparatively modest—estimated to be equivalent to a price premium of between 6 and 8 per cent. In the final section we draw together the results of our analysis and set out our conclusions.

2. DEREGULATION AND ITS IMMEDIATE CONSEQUENCES

Prior to 1980, the UK express coach industry had been subject to the regulatory controls introduced under the Road Traffic Act of 1930. This regulation comprised both quality controls, relating in particular to vehicle safety and the competence of the driver, and 'quantity' controls. These latter required companies to obtain Road Service Licences (RSLs) before they could operate a service. Licences were issued by the Traffic Commissioners, a quasi-judicial body, if the service was deemed to operate 'in the public interest'. Existing RSL holders on the proposed route, and also British Rail, were allowed to register objections. In practice this meant that the requirement to hold a RSL acted as a barrier to entry by new operators and so gave incumbents an effective monopoly on each route (see Glaister and Mulley 1983). It was also difficult for coach operators to compete effectively with British Rail, because changes to fares or timetables had to be deemed 'in the public interest' by the Traffic Commissioners and, as we have noted, British Rail had a right to object. Prior to deregulation, the incumbent operator on the majority of routes in England and Wales was National Express, the coaching subsidiary of the publicly owned National Bus company. On routes within Scotland, and on the express routes between London and Scotland, the incumbents were the regional subsidiaries of the nationalized Scottish Bus Group (SBG).

The 1980 Transport Act aimed to 'encourage new private operators' (as outlined in the 1979 Conservative Party manifesto) and to enable new services to develop. Quality regulation was retained but quantity regulation was abolished. In place of the previous requirement to hold a RSL, operators now merely have to notify the Traffic Commissioners twenty-eight days before commencing a new service. From 1 October 1980, entry into the UK express coaching industry became, in effect, deregulated.

The events immediately following deregulation have been well documented (see, for example, Davis 1984; Robbins and White 1986; Jaffer and Thompson 1986; and Douglas 1987). Express coaching appeared to be a business in which entry costs could be expected to be low, in particular because there already existed a large, unregulated—and highly competitive—market in the provision of contract coach services from which cross entry seemed likely. This proved to be the case. A consortium formed from ten of the larger existing private-sector coach companies, British Coachways, entered the market on the 6 October 1980, providing a comprehensive network of low-priced services. Other entrants operated on a relatively smaller scale, typically just between London and their regional base. This significant scale of entry was associated with rapid product innovation (new services provided meals and in-journey videos) and significant changes to the level and structure of prices. NE's prices on the main trunk routes out of London were reduced by a third with corresponding, although less substantial, reductions on other trunk routes.

Thus far the outcomes of deregulation can be classed as expected, although perhaps exceeding the expectations of the authors of the legislation. Less expected was the lack of success enjoyed by the entrants. In 1981 it is estimated that the independent operators carried just over 10 per cent of traffic on routes out of London. This was not enough to sustain the British Coachways consortium. Once NE had matched its low prices it held few other advantages and it began breaking up as early as mid-1981, finally ceasing business in January 1983. Many of the smaller entrants lasted only a few weeks, but those that did survive appeared to do so by differentiating their product to offer higher quality services aimed at a sector of the market which NE did not initially cater for. The consequence of this significant scale of exit through 1981 was that NE became once more the dominant operator on routes within England and Wales, and fares began to increase on these routes during 1982. A different picture emerged on the routes within Scotland and between London and Scotland, where companies in the SBG were incumbent prior to deregulation. On these routes more entrants (in particular Cotters in 1980 and Stagecoach in 1981), again offering high quality services, were able to successfully establish themselves in the market.

Several sources of incumbent advantage have been suggested to explain NE's success and the relatively less successful experience of companies in the Scottish Bus Group. NE benefited from a brand name and marketing network established during the regulated era: replication by entrants would require significant sunk costs. By contrast the various companies in the SBG did not establish a single brand name for their express coach services until three years *after* deregulation had taken place. NE also benefited from a weak bankruptcy constraint as a consequence both of being a public-sector company and also a subsidiary of a larger group whose main business lay in regulated local bus markets; this same advantage favoured the SBG companies although to a smaller degree. These 'innocent' barriers to entry (following Salop's (1979) distinction) provided the basis and incentive for strategic action to deter potential competitors. NE acted to deny rivals entry to city-centre coach terminals which it controlled (in particular Victoria Coach Station in London) thus facing potential entrants with the choice of using inferior facilities or incurring the sunk costs of establishing comparable facilities (see Davis 1984). NE also invited selected competitors into joint-ventures (see, for example, White 1983 on the London–West Country market). Finally it followed a pricing strategy in which it systematically matched the prices offered by entrants. In contrast, the SBG companies allowed their prices to be undercut by between 10 and 20 per cent. The product of these various 'innocent' and strategic entry barriers enabled NE successfully to protect its market position. By 1984, a significant difference in price levels could be identified between those routes where NE had been incumbent and those where incumbent SBG companies had been less successful in deterring potential competitors (see Jaffer and

Thompson 1984). However, recent policy developments have removed the basis of some of these incumbent advantages and in the next part we outline the nature of these before considering their effect on market performance.

3. POLICY DEVELOPMENTS—TERMINAL ACCESS AND PRIVATIZATION

Previous studies have noted the difficulty which independent operators faced in gaining access to city-centre coach stations, in particular Victoria, the major central London coach station. Table 1.1 shows that, in 1983, most entrants' service made use of car-parks or street-side stops. Access to coach stations is potentially important for operators for three separate reasons. Terminals provide an important information point on the service available, they provide opportunities for connecting journeys (although only 14 per cent of all passengers arriving at Victoria change there to continue their journey) and finally terminals provide amenities, such as waiting-rooms and refreshments. Denying entrants access to major terminals raises entry costs in two ways. First, there are the sunk costs involved in building a competing terminal; costs which are incurred in locating a suitable site, and in obtaining the necessary planning permission; and in carrying out the construction work. Second, there are the further costs in making the public aware of the new terminal's existence. Existing coach terminals, like incumbent coach companies, benefit from established product awareness.

In the period after deregulation, the majority of coach stations in England were controlled by the NBC, which, as we have noted, adopted a policy of denying access to operators attempting to compete with its coach subsidiary—National Express. A similar situation existed in

TABLE 1.1. Percentages of services terminating at a bus or coach station, coach- or car-park, or in a street

Company	Station to station	Station to park	Station to street	Park to park	Park to street	Street to street
National Express and Scottish Bus Group	83	2	13	0	2	0
Private companies	5	7	17	5	29	37

Source: Barton and Everest 1984.

Scotland, where the SBG owned and controlled the major terminals. As Table 1.1 shows their competitors were generally forced to utilize road-side bus-stops and, in London, temporary sites, lacking any passenger facilities. There were, however, some exceptions. Some entrants, particularly those serving the London–Scotland routes, used hotel car-parks and arranged for their passengers to use the hotel's facilities. One company, Flights, a Birmingham operator specializing in up-market services connecting the major English airports, introduced its own terminal in Birmingham, when it began operating in October 1980. And from 1983 coaches were allowed to operate from Wilton Road bus station, owned by London Buses, a subsidiary of London Regional Transport (LRT), and close to Victoria. Only a very few services operated from here, however, and it is probable that lack of space prevented it being a viable option for the majority of independent operators.

Since 1985, legislative changes and the privatization of National Express have resulted in increased ease of access to terminals for independent operators, whilst increasing road congestion in central London appears to have simultaneously decreased the importance of terminal access there. The 1985 Transport Act established common-user access to publicly owned bus stations. Section 82 states that local authorities or Passenger Transport Executives (PTEs) shall not discriminate against any holder of a Public Service Vehicle (PSV) licence with respect to the provision, operation, and charges imposed for the use of bus stations and their associated facilities. The Act also brought privately owned terminals within the scope of the Competition and the Fair Trading Acts, by extending the definition of the services covered by those acts to include 'the making of arrangements for the use by public service vehicles . . . of a parking place which is used as a point at which passengers on services provided by means of such vehicles may be taken up or set down'.

These legislative changes were tested in 1987 when the Office of Fair Trading investigated the refusal by the Southern Vectis Omnibus Company Ltd. to allow competitors to use their bus station at Newport, Isle of Wight. The decision to investigate was announced by the Director General of Fair Trading on the 16 June 1987 and the report, published in February 1988, found Southern Vectis's behaviour to be anti-competitive. The investigation concluded that the major entry barrier faced by small operators is in establishing awareness amongst the public of the existence of their services and that refusal to allow access therefore prevented independent bus operators from competing effectively. Following the publication of the report, Southern Vectis undertook to change their policy and to allow access, in order to prevent referral of the case to the Monopolies and Mergers Commission. The implication of the report for the issue of terminal access in general was further spelt out in the press release announcing OFT's decision, in which the Director General expressed the hope that 'other companies owning bus stations elsewhere will similarly agree to admit other bus operators to those stations, where they have not already done so'.

Privatization of the NBC further improved the prospect for terminal access by placing Victoria Coach Station, a separate subsidiary of NBC, in the hands of London Regional Transport from October 1988. David Mitchell, the then Transport Minister, announced in August 1987 that Victoria should remain in the public sector until long-run strategic decisions had been made on the future of London's coach services, so as not to close any of the options in advance. By remaining in the public sector Victoria was therefore subject to the common-user access clause of the 1985 Transport Act, whilst transfer to LRT meant that Victoria was no longer owned by the main incumbent in the express coach business.

National Express itself was subject to a management buy-out completed on 17 March 1988. This included three coach stations in Birmingham (Digbeth), Manchester (Chorlton St.), and Leeds (Wellington St.) as well as the central marketing activities, following the NBC decision that NE needed security of tenure with respect to the major coach-stations it currently enjoyed access to. The other terminals were sold with their respective NBC subsidiaries, except those judged to have high potential redevelopment values, notably the London Country bus terminals, which were marketed separately, with leasing arrangements.

Following these changes, terminal access does appear to have become easier for independent operators. Cotters, who operated one of the successful London–Scotland services in competition with Scottish Citylink, the SBG coaching subsidiary, gained access to Victoria from February 1987, having previously been forced to use the Royal National Hotel, Bedford Place, as their Central London set-down and pick-up point. At the same time they also gained access to the major Glasgow and Edinburgh terminals, where previously they had on-street stops. Scottish Citylink already had access to all these terminals. Flights gained access to Manchester's Chorlton St. coach station in January 1989, after previously operating from a bus lay-by in Chorlton Street itself. Moreover, their Birmingham–London service, launched in April 1990, operates from Victoria. Armstrong Galley, who run the 'Clipper' Newcastle–London service gained access to the main coach station in Newcastle in 1988, although in London they still operate from Vauxhall Bridge Road, near Victoria. Excelsior, operating between Poole, Bournemouth, and London, via Heathrow, began operating from Bournemouth's Travel Interchange from December 1988, where both its and the rival NE service are displayed equally on TV display screens. Previously Excelsior utilized roadside stops in Bournemouth, and they still terminate at King's Cross in London.

However, Halcrow Fox and Associates, in a market-research study conducted on behalf of London Regional Transport, found that Victoria was still seen as a National Express terminal, since in 1989 60 per cent of all movements at Victoria were by NE. Entrants felt that the disadvantage of exposing their passengers to NE marketing outweighed any advantage they could obtain by informing travellers at Victoria of their service. This situation is also exacerbated by the layout of the ticketing offices at Victoria: one office caters exclusively for NE, whilst the other deals with all other companies with no accessible information about what services are available. It has also been suggested that Victoria grant a discount on terminal charges for large operators, i.e. NE and Scottish Citylink, and so the incumbent operators probably still receive preferential access rates. Since terminal charges are one of the reasons independent operators give for preferring roadside stops—such charges typically constitute 1 per cent of passenger revenue on long-distance routes, and 10–14 per cent on shorter routes—this preferential treatment could still constitute an entry barrier.

However, increasing congestion in central London, adding to journey times and hence operators' costs, has meant that the issue of terminal access, in London at least, has become less important. Berry's, a Taunton-based operator running between London and Somerset, now terminate next to the Underground stop in Hammersmith, in an attempt to avoid the worst congestion, and operators who are catering mainly for day-trippers coming to London prefer to terminate close to Oxford Street, or to the West End, as these are the destinations most people require, and as this gives them an advantage over rail services.

Therefore, even if the legislative changes and the transfer of Victoria to LRT have not succeeded in ensuring completely equal access to terminals, taken together with increasing congestion in central London the overall situation appears to indicate that, if terminal access did once act as a significant entry barrier, then this should have been substantially eliminated in the years since 1987.

The divestment of NBC subsidiary companies on their privatization can be expected to have further reduced entry barriers to express coaching by reducing the potential financial strength upon which the incumbent National Express could draw. This divestment has also created a new source of potential entry in the form of the former subsidiary bus companies of the NBC. The NBC was created by the Transport Act 1968, by combining various existing express and stage services. NE was formally created in October 1973, as a central organization responsible for the planning, marketing, and provision of express coach services. Prior to 1986, NE carried out its operations on a co-operational basis with the other NBC subsidiaries, who actually owned most of the coaches, provided most of the staff and received the profits. However, the 1985

Transport Act directed the NBC to draw up proposals for its transfer to the private sector and to change its organizational structure so as to promote sustained and fair competition between its own present subsidiaries, former NBC subsidiaries, and independent operators. This led to the NBC acting, in effect, merely as a financial holding company from April 1986, with its subsidiary companies being given a large degree of autonomy. For the first time, NE obtained the coaches to operate its services by means of formal contracts. Companies were invited to submit quotations for regular work-cycles for which they would receive a fixed sum per journey. The contracts required the bidder to provide vehicles which were of the specific type and standard required by NE, and which were decorated in NE livery. They also had to provide uniformed staff, and to comply to a specified code on maintenance, safety, and staff training. In this way NE aimed to maintain quality standards whilst introducing competition between subsidiaries, and any independent operators, which could be expected to reduce costs. NE carried out the planning and marketing of express services, determining the design of the network and service frequencies, and it registered and licensed each service. NE was thus responsible for the ultimate financial performance of express services, with the contracting suppliers of the coaches being guaranteed a fixed sum regardless of revenues.

The NBC's disposal programme was approved in May 1986. Its 72 subsidiaries were to be sold off separately. The first, National Holidays, was sold in May 1986, and by the end of March 1987, 27 former NBC subsidiaries had been transferred to the private sector. There were six bids for NE, and it was finally subject to a management buy-out, for an undisclosed sum, on the 17 March 1988. By April 1988, all of the NBC's subsidiaries had been transferred to the private sector.

Following the privatization of the NBC, the SBG has also been privatized. The Transport (Scotland) Act was passed by Parliament in 1989, with the directive that, as with the NBC, the SBG's subsidiaries should be sold individually. There were four bidders for Scottish Citylink, including NE, whose bid, however, was disqualified by the Scottish Office, almost certainly on competition grounds. Citylink was finally sold to its management-employee buy-out team on the 4 September 1990, reputedly for less than £500,000, after the team was given 'preferred bidder' status by the Scottish Office.

4. MARKET ENTRY AND EXIT

As we noted earlier, NE had by the mid-1980s re-established its predominant position on most of the routes on which it had been incumbent at the time of deregulation. There is little evidence of significant market entry subsequently. Following privatization, the newly independent, former NBC bus companies may themselves have been expected to constitute a new wave of entrants into the express coaching market. Many of these companies already operated coach services under contract for NE, and so would have had the necessary assets and operational experience to enter the market. However, the lack of such entry indicates that the former NBC companies have preferred to continue operating services for NE. One reason for this is that, since 1986, these companies have faced deregulation of their local bus markets and the competitive tendering of their subsidized bus services, as well as privatization. Diversification into the coach business is unlikely to have had high management priority in these circumstances.

As well as a lack of entry from former NBC subsidiaries, there has not been any significant entry post-privatization from independent operators. However, it is likely that the privatization of the NBC has made entry easier for such operators to enter the coach market in another sense, notably in providing services for NE. In 1988 NE obtained 950 coaches on contract from 60 different operators, the majority of whom were NBC subsidiaries. Whilst hard data is not available, it is the opinion of those working close to the industry that the numbers of contracts awarded to independent operators has increased. Certainly if those operators believed that NE would fight entry if they began to operate services in their own right, thus not allowing them to make a positive return on the sunk costs involved, then they might in these circumstances prefer to operate under contract to NE, and thereby receive a less risky return.

On many routes the pattern has been one of further exit rather than of new entry. For example, Roman City, who began operating between London and Bath in January 1984 were taken over by Badgerline, who also operated the same service under contract to NE. Badgerline operated both services in parallel for a while before dropping the independent service. Len Wright, who ran the 'London Statesman' service between London and Manchester from December 1982 suffered from financial difficulties and sold the service to Skyliner International Ltd., who themselves suffered from a lack of publicity, and collapsed in March 1989. One of the few successful independent operators active before deregulation, Barton, offered a London service as part of the British Coachways consortium, which ceased with the collapse of British Coachways. However, Barton continued to operate several services in the north Midlands, until taken over by Trent in the Autumn of 1989, who now operate the Barton routes under contract to NE.

Some of the original entrants are still operating. Bere Regis (London–Devon), Swanbrook (Tewkesbury–Oxford–London), Elsey's (London–Peterborough–Boston), Primrose Motors (London–Gloucester–

Leominster) offer very limited competition on some routes. Brylaine, a local bus company, bought Hogg International in 1990, and are continuing to operate the London–Boston–Skegness route.

A more effective challenge to NE can also be found on only a few routes. The 'Londonliner' service, originally started in March 1986 and operated jointly by London Buses and West Midlands Transport, between Birmingham and London, is still running although London Buses no longer have any involvement. Competition increased further on this route with the entry of Flight's 'Royale' service in April 1990. Competition also remains on routes in the West Country. Berry's, whose London–Somerset service began in March 1983 are still operating, though they now terminate in Hammersmith. Bakers (London–Avon, London–Bristol), and Arrow (Bristol/Bath–London) are also still operating. The London–Newcastle route also continues to be one on which NE face strong competition—from Blue Line and Armstrong-Galley—as are those in the rapidly growing market for services to airports.

Overall, then the picture on routes on which NE was incumbent is one of almost no entry in recent years, piecemeal exit by some of the smaller players who were challenging NE in the mid-1980s, albeit at the fringes, and of sustained competition on only a handful of routes. In contrast to this pattern, the one major route within England where NE was not the main incumbent (London–Oxford) has seen intense competition in recent years. Thames Transit's 'Oxford-Tube' service began in March 1987, entering into fierce competition with City of Oxford Motor Services Ltd.'s existing 'Oxford Citylink' service. This latter incumbent operator was the newly privatized former-NBC bus company. Both operators offer very high frequencies, each running every twenty minutes throughout the day. In 1989 return fares were £2.97 on each service, compared with NE's fare of £5.00. NE only operate two services a day on the route.

The picture on the trunk routes between London and Scotland—where companies competing with the incumbent Scottish Citylink were well established by the mid-1980s—is also very different to that on routes where NE was incumbent. Here one of the three main players, Cotters, has been forced into receivership followed by its take-over in 1987 by the other main entrant, Stagecoach. Subsequently, in mid-1989, Stagecoach sold out to NE. Thus for the first time the two main incumbents from the regulatory era have come into head-to-head competition. The geographic scope of this competition has been extended by NE's decision to terminate an agreement with Scottish Citylink, following the threat of OFT action, in which services between provincial English cities and Scotland were operated on a co-operative basis. Similarly, Scottish Citylink have, during 1990, started to operate services in England in competition with NE (for example, London–Birmingham). NE have also expanded Stagecoach's previous operations within Scotland. At the end of 1988 a further entrant started a 'low-cost' service between London and Glasgow and this has resulted in both existing companies—Scottish Citylink and Stagecoach (now NE)—setting up rival low-cost operations. Overall, competition on routes where Scottish Express is the incumbent has continued to be intense, with no single dominant operator.

5. MARKET PERFORMANCE

We will start by considering two important dimensions of service quality—service frequency and journey time—and then consider the level and structure of prices. We will distinguish separate categories of routes to reflect the different competitive conditions identified in our earlier discussion:

- Routes where National Express was incumbent: the main trunk routes from London and routes between English provincial cities.
- Routes where companies in the Scottish Bus Group were incumbent: both between London and the main Scottish cities and within Scotland.

Frequencies

To measure changes to service frequencies over the period we collected data from timetables on absolute frequencies and used this to construct indices measuring average frequencies on the separate groups of routes. Whilst the published frequencies do not necessarily correspond to the numbers of coaches actually run, due to the practice of running duplicate services when demand is expected to be high, these figures reflect the range of alternative departure times available to the consumer.

Figure 1.1 shows that frequencies increased substantially in the years following deregulation. However, frequencies on routes where National Express was incumbent increased by less (on average 70 per cent) than on routes where SBG companies were incumbent. The particularly rapid growth in frequency of services within Scotland reflects their relative underdevelopment—many routes were characterized by weekend-only services—at the time of deregulation.

Journey times

Using data collected from timetables we also calculated an index of journey times. Figure 1.2 shows a substantial reduction in journey times over the period since deregulation—by between 5 and 25 per cent. This results both from faster routings (fewer stops and more motorway

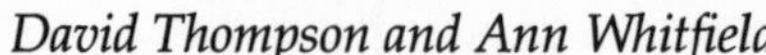

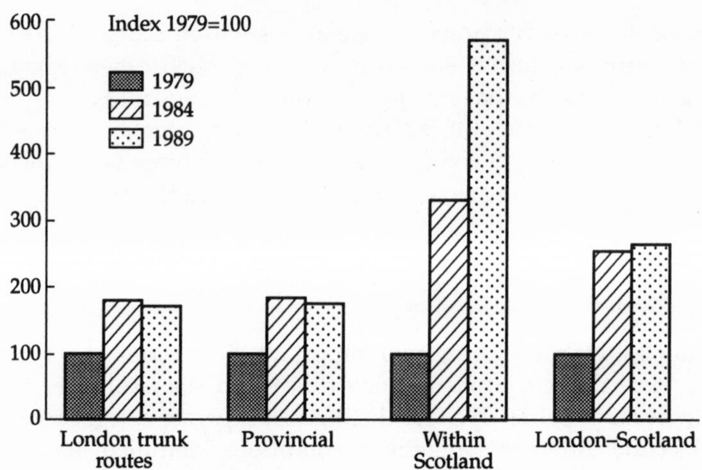

FIG. 1.1. Average service frequencies

mileage) made possible by the removal of British Rail's veto on the development of coach services, and from the introduction of coaches with on-board refreshment facilities. By 1989, almost two-thirds of the main trunk routes out of London were served by coaches providing higher quality in-vehicle facilities; generally these coaches were not operated on shorter distance routes, however.

Over the period since deregulation, NE moved from a finely differentiated peak–off-peak pricing structure, through to a much more coarsely differentiated structure (see Table 1.2). At the same time, however, they have increased the degree of price discrimination between different

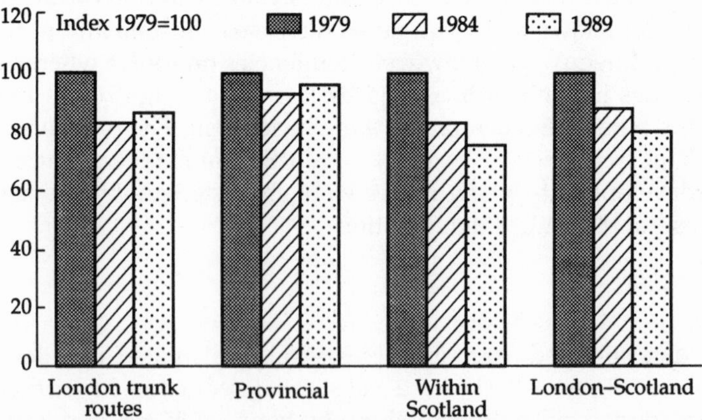

FIG. 1.2. Average scheduled journey times

TABLE 1.2. Fare structure (summer): fare products offered

1979	S		DR			OPR	PR
1980	S		DR			OPR	PR
1981	S		DR			—	PR
1982	S		DR			OPR	PR
1983	S		DR			OPR	PR
1984	S		DR			—	PR
1985	S	=	DR			OPR	PR
1986	S	=	DR			OPR	PR
1987	S	=	DR	=	MR	OPR	PR
1988	S	=	DR	=	MR	OPR	PR
1989	S	=	DR	=		OPR	PR
1990	S	=	DR	=		OPR	PR

Key: S = Single; DR = Day return; MR = Mid-week return; OPR = Off-peak return; PR = Period return.

Note: MR was introduced for the winter period since 1983.

types of passenger. Prior to deregulation, four different types of fare were available:

- A single.
- A day-return.
- An off-peak return.
- A period return.

The off-peak return was valid for travel except on the peaks of Fridays and summer Saturdays, when period-return fares applied. The effect of deregulation was to alter this pricing structure to just three fare types: single, day-return, and a comprehensive period return. All these fares were offered at especially low rates (marketed under the brand name 'beeper'). From 1982 an off-peak return was reintroduced but this was only valid for travel on Monday through to Thursday. In the winter of 1983 a new fare-type, a 'midweek return', valid for travel on winter Tuesdays and Wednesdays only was introduced, at a lower rate than the off-peak return. The first move to simplify the by-now complicated fare structure, came in the summer of 1984, when single and day-return fares were set at the same level. In 1985 the off-peak return was reintroduced with its 1979 definition. In 1987 the midweek return was introduced all year round, at the same level as the single and day return. Finally, in 1989 the midweek return was abolished, and the off-peak return was brought down to the level of the single and day return. This structure has continued into 1990. Hence, from four separate types of fare product in 1979 NE have altered their price structure to now offer only two types of fare product. It appears that this simplifying measure was undertaken in order to make it more comprehensible for passengers.

Whilst the peak structure of prices has been simplified, in the period following deregulation segmentation of the market between different types of passenger has become more complex. Prior to deregulation children under 5 travelled free and children between 5 and 16 paid half-fare. This discount was abolished on deregulation, when NE offered very low 'Beeper' fares to all passengers. Child discounts were reintroduced for summer 1981 at the lower level of one-third, with students also able to claim one-third off on production of valid ID. In September 1983 this discount was further extended to include senior citizens. In October 1984 the student discount became conditional on the holding of a NE 'student coachcard', but for the first time discounts were available for children, students, and senior citizens on high quality 'Rapide' services too. Finally, in October 1989, the 'student' discount was expanded to include all 16–23-year olds, as well as students, although it was still conditional on possession of the appropriate card.

The fare structure on routes within Scotland has remained stable since summer 1984, with single, day-return, and period return fares all being offered; prior to summer 1984 there was no day-return. Children have had a 50 per cent discount since 1979. During summer 1984 a discount of one-third was introduced for students, conditional on possession of a coachcard. Senior citizens also received a discount at this time, although the amount depended on which of the regional companies was operating the service, and they were only available on single fares. In 1989 the average OAP discount amounted to 83p, compared with an average single price of £5.38, i.e. approximately 15 per cent.

The fare structure on routes between London and Scotland has also changed over the period. Up to 1984 only single and period return fares were offered. During 1985 and 1986 off-peak returns, valid for travel except on Fridays and summer Saturdays, were introduced. These were replaced in 1987 by the midweek return, which was only valid on journeys on Tuesdays and Wednesdays. This was still available in 1990. Children were entitled to a regional discount in 1980. In 1984 this discount was reduced to one-third. Students became able to claim one-third discount, conditional on possession of a coachcard, also in summer 1984. Senior citizens had gained a one-third discount by 1987.

Changes in the level of prices

We have constructed price trends for express coach services over the last decade by collecting data on the prices of the main types of fare product and then weighting these together. The data we have used relates to summer fares charged by the incumbents: comprehensive data on entrants' fares is not available.

London trunk routes

The results for the London trunk routes, shown in Figure 1.3, express the average level of single and period return fares, in real terms, as an index with 1979 as the base year. Each route is given an equal weighting in the results shown in the figure, but we have confirmed that these results are robust to weighting our sample according to service frequency; we found that this made less than 2 per cent difference, using sample data from Steer, Davies, and Gleeve 1986.

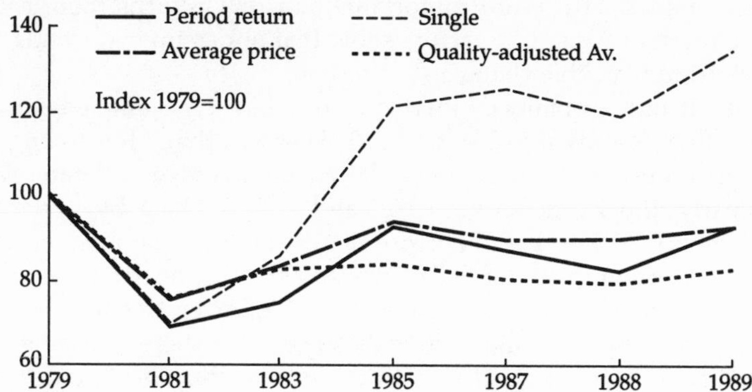

FIG. 1.3. Trend in real prices, London trunk routes
Note: The weighted average price includes allowance for the introduction of discount fares for children, students, and senior citizens; the quality-adjusted average price includes allowance for the price differential associated with the faster journey times and improved in-journey facilities available in the latter part of the period.

To establish the impact of the changes to the structure of prices which we have discussed, we used data from a market-research study carried out by Halcrow Fox and Associates (HFA) on behalf of London Regional Transport in 1989. The survey found that 22 per cent of passengers qualified for an OAP discount and that 13 per cent of passengers had received a student discount and that only a 'very few' children were travelling in the parties which they interviewed. In order to estimate this percentage we used Cross and Kilvington's 1986 study which put the figure at just 3 per cent.

The final adjustment was to weight the different fare types together. The index for single fares has risen at a substantially faster rate than the period return. The off-peak return didn't exist at all in 1987, and fell over the period 1983–9, whilst the indices for the other two types of fare increased. As well as these three fare types, a day return has also been available throughout the period. Comprehensive data relating to the importance of each ticket type is not available. However data from the HFA report, relating to the number of vehicle departures from Victoria each day during a typical summer week, enabled us to estimate the split between the proportion of people travelling at peak times, and those travelling off-peak. The ratio obtained was in the order of 1 : 2, and this is consistent with data collected in the 1978/9 National Travel Survey. Weightings for the different off-peak fares were estimated using findings from Cross and Kilvington 1986. The weighting factors used in the analysis are 20 : 30 : 15 : 35 (single : period return : day-return : off-peak return), since Cross and Kilvingtons' analysis has shown that single fares were numerically more important than day returns. Sensitivity tests with different weighting factors show that our estimated trends are highly robust to plausible changes.

The overall index obtained, following our fare type and passenger type weighting, is shown in Figure 1.3. This shows that, after falling by 25 per cent immediately after deregulation the average real fare paid rose by nearly 20 per cent between 1981 and 1985, fell back by 5 per cent over the period 1985–8, but then rose again slightly. The average real fare paid on London trunk routes in 1989 still stood at nearly 10 per cent below its level in 1979, prior to deregulation. Moreover, this trend in the real-price level disguises the fact that, since 1985 there has been an improvement in product quality, with the introduction of 'Rapide' services offering faster journey times and a washroom and hostess service on the majority of routes in our sample. This innovation has typically commanded a price premium of around 15 per cent, and once this is allowed for we find the increase between 1981 and 1985 to be reduced to just 10 per cent, and the 1989 (quality adjusted) value to be a more substantial 20 per cent below the pre-deregulation level of fares.

Provincial trunk routes

Figure 1.4 shows the results of a corresponding analysis which covers eighteen routes connecting the major provincial cities in England and Wales. Period-return fares fell by 19 per cent after deregulation, and have since increased steadily, to stand only just below their pre-deregulation value in 1989. Single fares have increased significantly in real terms. The weighted-average price trend, allowing for a passenger-type weighting, shows a level in 1989 which is broadly 20 per cent lower, in real terms, to that prior to deregulation; only a small minority of these routes had high quality in-vehicle facilities.

Scottish routes

Real-price trends for fifteen routes connecting Scottish cities are shown in Figure 1.5. Various concessions were introduced throughout the period, and the different fare types exhibited different trends, and so

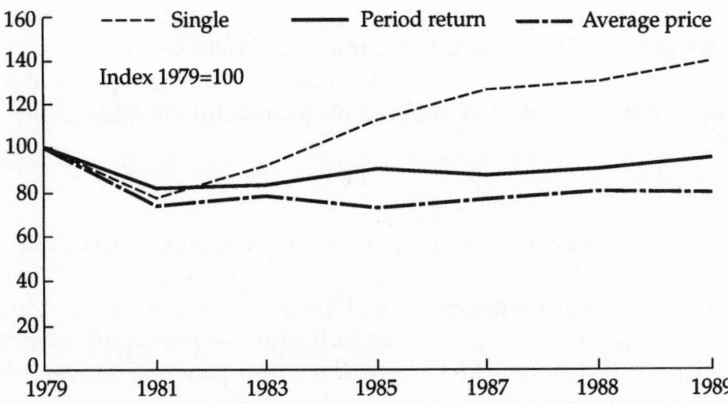

FIG. 1.4. Trend in real prices, provincial routes

again we have estimated a weighted-average price trend. However, few of these routes were operated with 'Rapide' vehicles and so no adjustment has been made for in-vehicle quality. The results show the weighted-average price falling by almost 30 per cent over the period.

London–Scotland routes

The final sample consisted of just three routes, connecting London to the major Scottish cities—Glasgow, Edinburgh, and Aberdeen. Figure 1.5

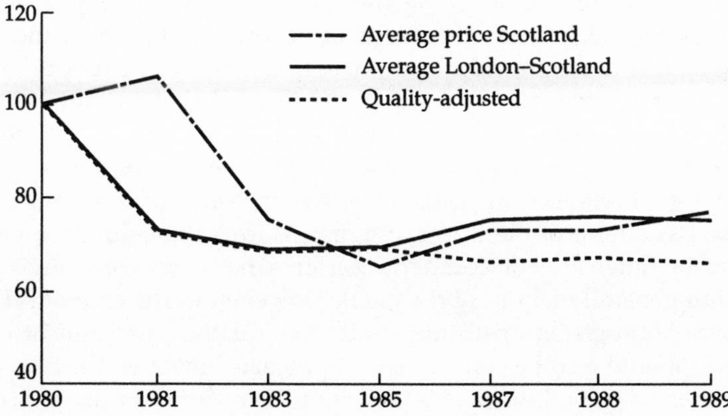

FIG. 1.5. Real-price trends, routes within Scotland and London–Scotland

Note: The weighted average price and quality-adjusted price both include allowance for the introduction of discount fares for children, students, and senior citizens. The 'quality-adjusted average' makes allowance for the price differential associated with the faster journey times and improved in-journey facilities available in the latter part of the period.

shows the average real-price trend; we again weighted the data using figures from the HFA report. We found that prices fell nearly 30 per cent between 1980 and 1981, and then stabilized at around 68 per cent of their pre-deregulation level after making allowance for changes in in-vehicle quality.

6. ANALYSIS OF RENTS EARNED BY NATIONAL EXPRESS

An extensive literature has examined the issues which arise in the use of financial performance measures as indicators of monopoly power (see, in particular, Fisher and McGowan 1983, and Kay and Mayer 1986). A particular issue, in the case of National Express, arises from its methods of organizing its business. The re-structuring of the National Bus Company in preparation for privatization required National Express to contract the physical operation of its services—the supply of vehicles and drivers—from other bus and coach companies. One consequence of this is that NE owns few tangible fixed assets; the result is that the most familiar measure of financial performance—return on capital employed—can be expected both to be high, because the denominator is small, but also to be a misleading measure of performance for this reason.

Instead of returns on capital employed we therefore use an alternative measure developed by Davis and Kay 1990. This measures the ratio of 'added value' to the value of the company's own inputs, or value added. Added value is defined as being the amount by which the value of a company's output exceeds the value of all the inputs which the company uses. It is therefore calculated by subtracting from operating profit a rental charge for the capital employed in the business, estimated by multiplying a measure of the capital stock (tangible assets plus stocks) by a bench-mark, normal, return on capital employed. In order to account for differences in firms' size, the measure of added value is expressed as a ratio of the firm's own inputs (or value added) to yield a measure of 'intensity' of company performance. The company's own inputs are generally labour and capital. However, in the case of NE, the risk borne through its operating contracts—for the provision of coach services—should also be considered. In practice, however, the operating contracts are specified in ways which shift the majority of this risk on to the companies supplying the coach services, and NE's own inputs can therefore properly be regarded as capital and labour.

Table 1.3 sets out the results of our analysis. Prior to 1984 National Express was not required to prepare separate accounts; however, contribution statements prepared by the National Bus Company suggest that profitability was low up to this point. More recently, our results suggest

TABLE 1.3. Measures of the financial performance of National Express

Year	Profit (£000)	Return on capital (%)	Added value (£000)	Intensity (%)
1984	888	164	838	44
1985	4019	131	3972	94
1986	3925	462	3851	71
1987	–3983	–130	–4056	–152
1988 (*a*)	3531	129	3375	60
1988 (*b*)	5652	96	5496	96

Notes: Results for 1987 are reported for the first 24 weeks of the year. 1988 (*a*) shows reported results for 52 weeks to 18 June. 1988 (*b*) shows reported results for 41 weeks to 31 December. Changes in reporting periods are associated with privatization.

Sources: National Express Annual Accounts and authors' calculations.

that NE has been able to achieve a substantial level of rent generation, although results for 1987 and 1988 are distorted by NE's privatization in March of the latter year. For example, the intensity ratings shown in Table 1.3 can be compared with Davis and Kay's findings, which show the main supermarket chains achieving intensity ratings around 10 per cent. The organizational structure adopted by NE means that its capital stock is relatively low; the measures of rent intensity shown in Table 1.3 are thus highly robust to alternative measures of the normal rate of return used in the calculations. Only limited comparison can be made with other companies in the express coach market. Scottish Citylink did not prepare separate financial results whilst in public ownership, although privatization proceeds of £0.5m. are indicative of low profitability. Similarly its main rival, Stagecoach, has not produced separate financial results for its coaching activities; again the relatively small goodwill payment realized on the sale of this business is indicative of low rent intensity.

To bench-mark the estimated rents earned by NE, we have estimated the change to its prices which would be implied in reducing the intensity rating to 15 per cent, a figure which appears closer to competitive levels on the basis of Davis and Kay's analysis. The results of this calculation are shown in Table 1.4 which details the relatively simplified range of assumptions made on the relevant demand and cost functions. The analysis suggests that a reduction in NE's prices of between 6 and 8 per cent would reduce its rent intensity to 15 per cent.

TABLE 1.4. Estimated price reduction associated with alternative rent intensity

Cost elasticity	Price elasticity		
	zero	−0.35	−1.15
0.75	−6.3%	−6.8%	−8.0%
1.0	−6.3%	−6.2%	−5.9%

Notes: Price elasticities are drawn from Halcrow Fox 1990 and Douglas 1987: their analysis suggests a figure of −1.15 on the basis of stated preference analysis and −0.35 on the basis of revealed preference.
Cost elasticities show alternative assumptions on the ratio of marginal costs to average price (see Douglas 1987 for a review of empirical findings).
Simulations are based on turnover and profit data for the 41 weeks to 31 December 1988 and show price changes required to reduce rent intensity to 15%; elasticities are assumed constant over the relevant range.

7. INCUMBENT ADVANTAGE AND THE COMPETITIVE PROCESS

Our analysis of developments following the deregulation of express coach services in 1980 show significant changes in both services and to the level and structure of prices. In summary:

- On NE's trunk routes out of London (which account for two thirds of their services) average prices are nearly 10 per cent lower than their pre-deregulation levels. Quality of service has improved over this period, both because journey times are shorter and because in-journey service is better; we estimate that these quality improvements are equivalent to a price premium of between 10 and 15 per cent. There has also been a significant increase in service frequencies.
- On routes between the other provincial cities in the UK, fares are broadly 20 per cent below deregulation levels, with some small improvements in in-vehicle quality and significant increases in service frequencies.
- On the trunk routes between London and Scotland, and on routes between Scottish cities, average prices are substantially lower in real terms (by approximately 25 to 30 per cent) than prior to deregulation. Again journey times, in journey service and frequencies have all shown significant improvement.

Overall these results suggest that consumers have benefited significantly from the changes that have followed from deregulation, although the pattern of price changes has varied between different types of route (see also Barton and Everest 1984). However, there have been a small number of losers. On some very minor provincial routes, not included in our analysis, prices have not been reduced and frequencies have fallen (for an analysis of these routes see Robbins and White 1986). Equally changes to the structure of prices mean that the young, old, and off-peak travellers have gained more substantially than others.

Our results also suggest some surprises. Most striking is the very different pattern of market performance between routes where NE was incumbent prior to deregulation and routes where other companies (primarily these in the Scottish Bus Group) were incumbent. We suggested that differences in the pattern of prices observed in the mid-1980s corresponded to differences in both the significance of barriers to entry and the actual incidence of successful entry. Thus we argued that NE benefited from various 'innocent' entry barriers to a greater degree than did the other incumbents, in particular a well-established brand name, a network of marketing outlets, and a weak bankruptcy constraint. These important barriers would allow NE to engage in prolonged entry-deterring activity. In particular, we noted that NE denied its rivals access to city-centre coaching terminals and it pursued an aggressive pricing policy. The outcome was that entry was successfully sustained most commonly, although not exclusively, on routes where companies other than NE had been incumbent prior to deregulation.

We suggested in Section three that various legislative changes introduced in the 1985 Transport Act would act to reduce the importance of the 'innocent' entry barriers that benefited NE, in particular, the provision for common-user access rights to bus and coach terminals, the separation of NE from the rest of the National Bus Company, and, on its privatization, the separation of the ownership of Victoria Coach Station from NE.

However, our analysis suggests that NE has continued to exercise market power since it re-established its dominant market share in the years immediately following deregulation. Analysis of National Express's financial performance shows that significant rents are being earned. These results are consistent with findings from analysis which we have carried out of the determination of prices and market structure. These findings suggest that barriers to entry, associated with information and reputation effects, have enabled prices to be sustained above competitive levels (see Thompson and Whitfield 1992). In general, although not exclusively, NE has benefited to a greater degree from these entry barriers and this observation explains, in part, the differential pattern of successful entry.

These findings raise two questions in particular. The first relates to the continuing sources of incumbent advantage from which NE continues to benefit, and the reasons for the absence of significant entry into its markets. The second relates to the policy implications of this observation; is NE's predominance likely to be sustained into the future and, if so, does this suggest that intervention by the competition authorities is desirable?

Of the entry barriers which we have discussed, it is NE's product name and its established marketing network which have endured the policy changes implemented over the last five years. NE's continuing high market share suggests that these barriers are of some significance. That is not a surprising observation; NE has a large network of retail outlets, around 3,000 in the UK, a well-established brand and it is able to exploit economies of scale in advertising. A part of NE's exceptional financial return might reasonably be regarded therefore as a return to the intangible assets of brand and product reputation. NE also developed a reputation for fighting entry in the years immediately following deregulation. Whilst recent policy changes have removed some of the advantages which enabled this reputation to be established—preferential terminal access and a weak bankruptcy constraint—it is likely that the reputation will only be eroded if, or when, NE accommodates entry.

Given the existence of these entry barriers, the absence of any significant entry into NE's markets in the years since privatization is less surprising. Over this period the most plausible entrants (those facing the lowest costs of cross-entry) have been the former NBC subsidiary companies. But over this period they are likely to have been more concerned with protecting their existing core business in the face of local bus deregulation than with diversifying into the express coach market. Similarly, potential new entrants are likely to have perceived greater profit opportunities in the local bus market, following deregulation in 1986, than in entering the express coach market in competition with an incumbent renowned for its success in defeating entrants. Perhaps the most immediate example is the decision in 1989 by Stagecoach, the most successful entrant into the coach market, to pull out and re-focus its business upon local bus markets. If this company, with costs already sunk in coaching, perceived greater returns in the local bus market then this would be true to an even greater degree for other potential entrants.

What are the implications for policy of these findings? Our analysis suggests that whilst the entry barriers which we have discussed have been important in sustaining National Express's predominant market share their 'height' is now comparatively modest. We estimate from our analysis of NE's financial performance that they are equivalent to a price premium of between 6 and 8 per cent. Our expectation is that as the local bus market adjusts to the consequences of deregulation then the threat of entry into coaching will rise; and if NE's reputation for aggressively fighting entry diminishes (as we expect) then this threat is more likely to be acted upon.

If correct, this assessment does not suggest a case for further policy intervention. We have noted some changes in the organization of terminals which might facilitate entry and the application of competition policy will, of course, remain highly relevant. In general, however, we expect that the residual barriers to entry will diminish for the reasons which we have discussed, and that prices will approach the levels achieved on routes where competition is already more effective. The advantages associated with indivisibilities in brand and marketing suggest that market structure will remain concentrated but the absence of significant entry costs suggests that performance will not diverge significantly from the contestable bench-mark.

We started this section by noting the significant changes which have followed express coach deregulation and we concluded that consumers (with some exceptions) have benefited significantly. Our analysis suggests that some further, although modest, benefits may be achievable as residual entry barriers diminish. Whilst it is quite likely that coach markets will remain highly concentrated, our findings suggest that the scope for exercising market power is already quite limited and will diminish further as the residual entry barriers are reduced.

References

Barton, A. J. and Everest, J. T. (1984), 'Express coaches in the three years following the 1980 Transport Act', TRRC Report, 1127.

Beesley, M. E. (1990), 'Collusion, predation and mergers in the UK bus industry', *Journal of Transport Economics and Policy* (Sept.), 295–310.

Benoit, J. P. (1984), 'Financially constrained entry in a game with incomplete information', *Rand Journal of Economics*, 15: 490–9.

Cross, A. K. and Kilvington, R. P. (1986), *Deregulation of Express Coach Services in Britain*, Oxford Studies in Transport, Gower.

Davis, E. (1984), 'Express coaching service 1980: Liberalisation in practice', *Fiscal Studies*, 5/1: 76–86.

—— and Kay, J. A. (1990), 'Assessing corporate performance', *Business Strategy Review*, 1/2: 1–16.

Douglas, N. J. (1987), *A Welfare Assessment of Transport Deregulation*, Gower.

Fisher, F. M. and McGowan, J. J. (1983), 'On the misuse of accounting rates of return to infer monopoly profits', *American Economic Review*, 73: 82–97.

Glaister, S. and Mulley, C. (1983), *Public Control of the British Bus Industry*, Gower.

Halcrow Fox and Associates (1990), 'Market research study into coach demand: Final report'.

Jaffer, S. M. and Thompson, D. J. (1986), 'Deregulating express coaches: A reassessment', *Fiscal Studies*, 7/4: 45–68.

Kay, J. A. and Mayer, C. P. (1986), 'On the application of accounting rates of return', *Economic Journal*, 96: 199–207.

Levine, M. E. (1987), 'Airline competition in de-regulated markets: Theory, firm strategy and public policy', *Yale Journal of Regulation*, 4: 393.

Nelson, P. (1970), 'Information and consumer behaviour', *Journal of Political Economy*, 78: 311–29.

Office of Fair Trading (1988), 'Southern Vectis Omnibus Company Limited', report by the Director General of Fair Trading, OFT, 1988.

Robbins, D. K. and White, P. R. (1986), 'The experience of express coach deregulation in Great Britain', *Transportation*, 13/4.

Salop, S. (1979), 'Strategic entry deterrence', *American Economic Review*, 69/2: 335–8.

Schmalensee, R. (1974), 'Brand loyalty and barriers to entry', *Southern Economic Journal*, 40: 579–88.

Steer, Davies and Gleave Ltd. (1986), 'Study into coach terminal facilities in London'.

Thompson, D. J. and Whitfield, A. (1992), 'Regulatory reform and incumbent advantage: The case of express coaches', Centre for Business Strategy working paper, London Business School.

Vickers, J. S. (1985), 'Strategic competition among the few: Some recent developments in oligopoly theory', *Oxford Review of Economic Policy*, 1/3: 39–62.

Waterson, M. (1984), *Economic Theory Of The Industry*, Cambridge, Mass.: MIT Press.

2

Conflicting Regulator Objectives: The Supply of Gas to UK Industry

EVAN DAVIS* AND STEPHANIE FLANDERS†

INTRODUCTION

The British government appears to have pursued two conflicting policies towards the gas-supply industry. On the one hand, it privatized British Gas as a single, integrated company. In doing so, it sacrificed the opportunity to foster competition in gas supply to the pragmatic requirements of its privatization programme. On the other hand, it has consistently encouraged competition in the supply of gas to large users.

The outcome of this ambiguous policy stance provides an interesting case for studying post-privatization experiences: in early 1992, British Gas accounts for nearly 90 per cent of the contract gas market; a figure which it has agreed must fall to 40 per cent by 1995. Judged against past performance, that will be no easy feat. Whether or not the policy succeeds, there are some useful implications for policy-makers.

It is typically supposed that the difficulties faced by entrants into utility industries relate to the naturally monopolistic nature of a transmission network and discriminatory actions by incumbents. As a result, regulatory attention has tended to focus on measures that ensure common carriage and fair interconnect provisions and non-discriminatory trading practices.

There is every reason to believe that if a competitive market results from these measures, economic efficiency (in static and dynamic terms) is enhanced. In the industrial gas case, however, competition did not result. The dominant incumbent's advantages included not only its vertical integration over a naturally monopolistic transmission network, but also the horizontal extent of its activities. This confronted the regulators

* Economics Correspondent at the BBC. Previously a Research Fellow at the Centre for Business Strategy, London Business School.

† Previously a Research Assistant at the Centre for Business Strategy, London Business School.

The authors were both at the Centre for Business Strategy when much of the work on this chapter was conducted. The work was completed when both were at the Institute for Fiscal Studies, London. They would like to thank David Thompson, Catherine Price, Graham Shore, and Carl Bakker for helpful comments. The usual disclaimer applies.

with a dilemma as to how far they should go in inducing new competition where its natural emergence was unlikely.

This chapter is divided into two sections. Section 1 briefly describes the history of the industrial gas market since 1982, including an account of why regulators wished to see competition in the market after British Gas was privatized, and the measures which they took to achieve this. For various reasons, the early vision of the regulators was not fulfilled.

Section 2 draws lessons about regulation from the industrial gas experience, concentrating on two striking features of the gas case, that the advantages of the incumbent were not all based on its rent-seeking abilities; and that those advantages varied in significance depending on the segment of the market to which they were applied. While it is hard to outline any very satisfactory means of regulating a monopolist in this situation, we do conclude that a more consistent approach to regulation of the industrial gas market might have resulted, had this feature of British Gas's presence in the industrial gas market been recognized earlier.

1. THE HISTORY OF BRITISH GAS AND ITS INDUSTRIAL GAS MONOPOLY

The UK Gas Market

There are two main ways of selling gas in the UK: by tariff and by contract. The contract sector is made up of approximately 21,000 customers, the vast majority being industrial and commercial users. The tariff sector consists of everybody who uses less than 25,000 therms a year, residential users, half of Britain's commercial firms, and about 13 per cent of industrial users. It is a sector that is regulated and monopolized by British Gas. Figure 2.1 breaks the entire market down into its component sub-markets.

The contract sector comprises about 38 per cent of British Gas's gas sales volume and about 26 per cent of its revenue (Annual Report 1990/1). Contract customers can be subdivided again into those who, like tariff customers, receive firm supplies of gas which British Gas cannot interrupt (other than in exceptional circumstances), and those who are supplied 'interruptible' gas by British Gas. Interruptible contracts give British Gas the right to cut supplies, usually for up to 63 days a year, although in practice interruptions occur rather less than this. Interruptible supplies account for about half of all contract sales in volume terms.

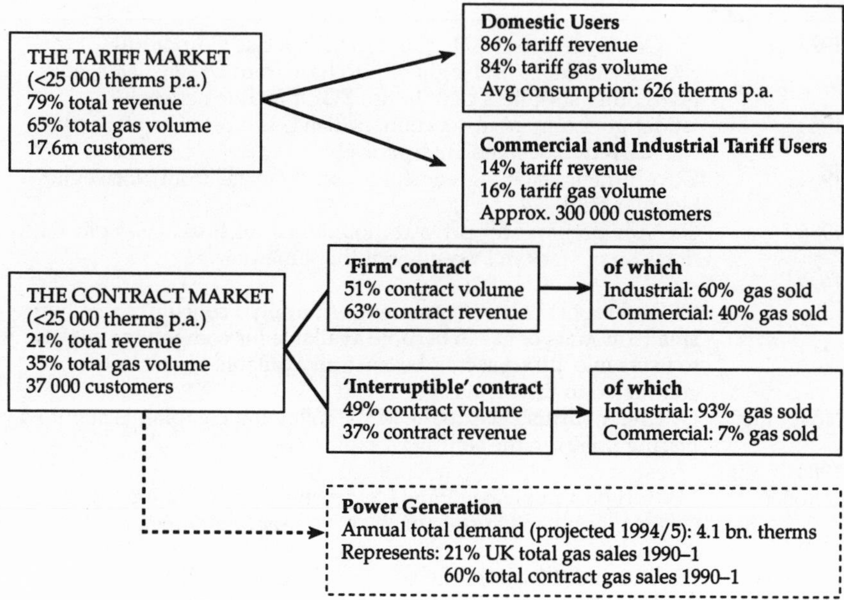

FIG. 2.1. The UK gas market
Source: Monopolies and Mergers Commission.

Motivations For Competition and Privatization

It is the contract market which has been the focus of government hopes for a competitive gas supply industry. As early as 1982, it was envisaged that independent suppliers would use British Gas pipelines under common carriage arrangements which were first included in the Oil and Gas (Enterprise) Act of that year. These arrangements, reiterated and extended in the 1986 Gas Act, liberalized the pipeline system and allowed independent suppliers to make use of the network on payment of a 'reasonable' fee to British Gas. The history of common carriage, along with the other key events concerning British Gas since 1982, are outlined in Table 2.1.

In a report of 1987, OFGAS identified gas producers operating in the North Sea as those most likely to want to enter the UK gas-contract market in competition with British Gas. First, they could hope to sell gas at a higher price than they received from British Gas, given the significant margin which existed between British Gas's industrial contract prices and the supply price which they paid to producers, even after accounting for transportation costs and overheads. Second, direct sales of gas to industrial users might be more attractive to producers because demand

TABLE 2.1. Chronology of events

1982	Oil Gas (Enterprise) Act: removes British Gas Corporation (BGC's) statutory first-right of purchase from UK gasfields, and gives other suppliers right to use BGC pipeline network.
1983	Under government instruction, British Gas North Sea oil assets transferred to become Enterprise Oil.
1984	Government vetoes agreement to purchase gas from Norwegian Sleipner field.
1986	Gas Act: prepares for privatization of BGC as British Gas plc, with flotation of stock in December of the same year.
1987	
July	OFGAS report ('Competition in Gas Supply') concludes that only small amounts of gas to become available for competitive supply to users in contract sector, because all available gas already contracted to British Gas.
November	OFT refers British Gas to the MMC following complaints about its pricing policy in the contract sector.
1988	
October	MMC report published. Finds 'extensive discrimination' by British Gas in pricing and supply of gas to contract customers.
1989	
February	OFGAS and British Gas agree changes to British Gas's Authorisation, including the requirement to publish price schedules.
April	Government announces terms of 90 : 10 obligation.
May	First price schedules introduced.
June	British Gas first publishes details of carriage terms and illustrative charges.
December	British Gas publishes new contract-price schedules, following extensive criticism of May schedules.
1990	
February	Quadrant (an Esso/Shell joint venture) sign first gas transportation contract with British Gas.
March	Quadrant begins delivering gas to a small number of industrial/commercial users. BP Gas Marketing follow suit one month later.
August	British Gas signs first 'swap' deal with Mobil. Gas advanced from Camelot (available from October 1990) in exchange for gas from the Beryl reservoir.
September	British Gas's common carriage charges further reduced.
December	OFGAS warns that 'time is running out for British Gas'. Proposes target of 30 per cent competitive market share to be reached by October 1993.
1991	
March	British Gas announces 35 per cent rise in price of interruptible supplies to large gas users. OFGAS imposes injunction to protect at least one independent power-generating company from the price hike until a new deal can be reached. British Gas says it will loan more of its gas from existing contracts to independent competitors. The first deal following the announcement is with Quadrant Gas, signed 15 March.

April	OFGAS and British Gas agree new pricing agreement for the tariff sector, pegs price increases to RPI-5 for period April 1992–7.
June	British Gas survey finds that only 11 per cent of contract customers had some contact with alternative suppliers. A smaller survey by the Major Energy Users Council over the same month finds that 10 per cent of members now use a third-party supplier for at least some of their needs.
July	British Gas agrees amended price schedule with independent power generators affected by March price rise.
August	British Gas concludes two more swap deals with competing suppliers, making a total of seven deals with different companies since June 1989.
October	Completion of OFT progress report on market for industrial gas supply. MMC enquiry threatened unless British Gas and OFGAS agree compromise on Report's proposals by the end of 1991. Peter Lilley announces that government plans to introduce competition to tariff sector by 1996.
1992	
January	OFGAS and British Gas reach a compromise on the OFT's proposals; MMC report averted. John Wakeham announces government is to lift ban on gas imports.

from such users was subject to less seasonal variation than the residential market which British Gas was committed to supplying. A smaller seasonal 'swing factor' implies lower supply costs because less investment in capacity is required to meet a demand pattern which is more consistent over time. Lastly, producers might have been able to bring a given field on-stream more quickly by supplying direct to users, if British Gas's demand was increasing at a slower rate than that with which gas was becoming available from new fields (OFGAS 1987, 8).

In the same report, OFGAS also expressed the hope that competition would come from buyers in the existing market. Large gas customers could act together to buy direct from gas producers, arranging for conveyance of the gas themselves. Gas producers would be able to approach users with combined gas/transportation contracts which undercut British Gas's existing prices. Clearly with an eye to developments following gas deregulation in the United States, OFGAS also saw a place for 'entrepreneurial gas marketing companies who would enter into contracts with both producers and consumers and would arrange with British Gas for use of the pipeline system' (OFGAS 1987, 18).

There were several motives behind privatization of British Gas and the drive towards competition. Obviously, the government had confidence in the general efficiency gains to be derived from private provision of gas. In fact, the value added of British Gas was a smaller proportion of its total turnover than in some other privatized firms (see Figure 2.2), and in some sense this meant that British Gas itself was less responsible for the delivery of the final product to consumers than, say, British Telecom, which was more vertically integrated. A percentage gain in efficiency at British Gas therefore, would lead to smaller changes in its retail prices than in some other industries. Another potential benefit to private control, however, related to the incentives and effectiveness of British Gas to buy and sell gas at efficient prices.

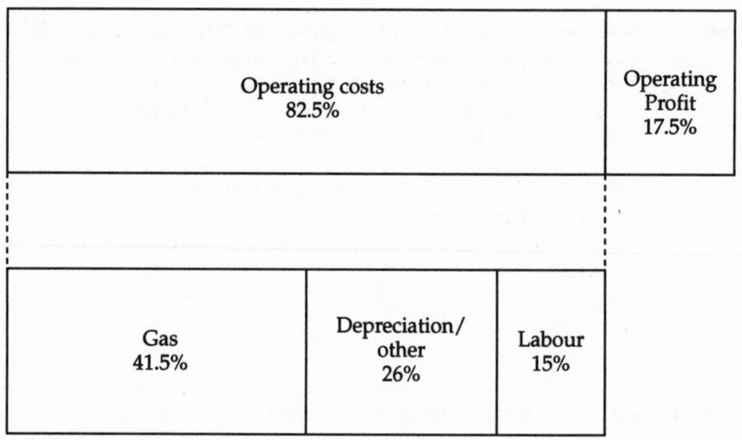

FIG. 2.2. A breakdown of British Gas turnover (1991: £9,491m.).
Source: British Gas 1991.

The third and most prominent reason for promoting a change in the structure of the industry was to reduce British Gas's market power, a power it had displayed a consummate skill in exploiting. It was highlighted by an MMC report in October 1988.

The MMC's report found 'extensive discrimination' by British Gas in the pricing and supply of gas to its contract customers. It was very clear that in its pricing decisions, the company faced no constraint other than the presence of suppliers of other fuels, which are not always a good substitute for gas.

The core of British Gas's policy appears to have been pricing the supply of gas in each case according to the cost to that customer of using alternative fuels. The price offered would depend on not only the price of competing fuels but also on the relative ease with which a given company could switch to these in the short to medium term. On average, higher prices would be charged to clients who had little or no feasible alternative to gas as a source of energy. Thus, no set-price formula was applied by British Gas in its sales of contract gas. The only published prices were maxima, which the company had to make public under the terms of its Authorisation. This meant that contract prices were unpredictable, and customers would find it difficult to compare the prices they were charged with those paid by other users.

The form of British Gas's supply contracts was designed to buttress their price discrimination. For example, each contract had to specify the purposes for which the gas was to be used, and British Gas reserved the right to inspect premises in order to validate this. This stipulation allowed British Gas to gather the information which discrimination between customers requires, namely the ease and cost with which the customer could switch to another fuel, as well as the precise nature of this alternative (i.e. gas oil, electricity, coal, etc.). Customers whose alternative to gas was a relatively costly fuel, such as gas oil or electricity, or could only switch from gas after considerable time and expense, were generally obliged to pay higher prices than users with greater flexibility. In particular, British Gas would often refuse to supply such customers with the much cheaper interruptible gas, unless they installed the equipment for using alternative fuels.

Customers with easy and cheap alternatives to gas supply were not only offered lower prices in general by British Gas; the price they were charged was also more responsive to changes in the price of competing fuels, especially oil. As the MMC said, 'the range of prices for firm gas contracts has widened since the fall in oil prices in 1986. British Gas reduced the prices to those customers well placed to switch to potentially cheaper fuels . . . but maintained its prices to other customers' (MMC 1988, para. 8.30).

Both OFGAS and the MMC attributed a dual significance to the MMC's Report. In the first place, British Gas had abused its dominant position in the industrial market, exploiting the fact that many customers had few alternatives to gas as their main source of energy, having sunk highly specific investments into receiving gas. Secondly, it provided evidence of both the breadth of British Gas's market power and the factors which preserved it, deterring others from entering the market. Neither regulator felt that the arguments to suggest that price discrimination can be welfare-enhancing—by allocating fixed costs of delivery to customers whose behaviour is least sensitive to price—justified the behaviour of British Gas.

Regulatory Action I: Preventing Abuse

The MMC made four main recommendations in its report. The first two proposals were directly intended to prevent British Gas from price discriminating, primarily to prevent it from abusing the monopoly position it enjoyed. The third and fourth recommendations were directly intended to address the factors which they considered to have impeded competition from developing.

The first two recommendations were:

- that British Gas should be required to publish a schedule of prices at which it is prepared to supply firm and interruptible gas to contract customers and not to discriminate in pricing or supply;
- that British Gas should not be allowed to refuse to supply interruptible gas on the basis of the use made of the gas or the alternative supply available.

The first ensured transparency, to the extent that each customer would pay, and be seen to pay, the same price as other firms with the same supply requirements, regardless of their relative ability to use other fuels. The second reinforced this: British Gas had to make interruptible gas available to users with a demand of over 25,000 therms, again, regardless of their position with regard to other fuels.

New price schedules, taking effect in May 1989 (although later amended on account of initial controversy) represented British Gas's compliance with the MMC's first two recommendations. Schedules of reference prices were published for the supply of both firm and interruptible gas, with various volume bands in both categories. Under the banding system, prices depend on the customer's consumption, with larger users paying less than smaller ones. Firm customers are allowed to aggregate their consumption on different premises so as to move to a higher volume band and pay a lower unit price, provided that each site consumes more than 25,000 therms per annum. Interruptible gas was available to all customers using more than 250,000 therms a year. British Gas initially refused to lower this threshold, on grounds of operational efficiency, but the revised December schedules did bring it down to 200,000 therms. The later schedules also permitted aggregation of consumption with respect to interruptible supplies, which had not previously been granted.

The pricing packages introduced in 1989 ruled out the first degree price discrimination which British Gas had previously pursued. Contract customers were offered the schedules regardless of their situation *vis-à-vis* alternative fuels. The reference prices themselves could be changed at intervals of no less than 28 days, to take account of movements in competitive fuel prices and general market conditions. Consumers could choose between this system (contract prices according to the schedule), a fixed-price contract (at extra cost), and an index-linked contract, related to the Producers Price Index and gas oil prices.

Regulatory Action II: Promoting Competition

The requirement to publish schedules was at least partly aimed at improving the entry conditions for competing suppliers, who face a much reduced prospect of post-entry predation by British Gas as long as the schedules are in force. There were fears however, that in forbidding the company's previous pricing policies the authorities would merely eradicate the most obvious symptom, and not the cause, of British Gas's continued market dominance. The MMC's third and fourth recommendations attempted to promote competition more directly. These were:

- that the company should publish further information on common carriage terms, providing sufficient details for potential customers to make a reasonable estimate of the price they would be charged for the service;
- that British Gas initially contract no more than 90 per cent of any new gas field.

Most entry hopes had been pinned on the gas producers, yet despite the attractions, take-up of the competitive opportunities was low. By the end of 1988, no gas producer had actually concluded an arrangement for the transportation of their gas with British Gas under the terms of the two acts.[1]

In line with the third MMC requirement, British Gas established a 'one-stop' Gas Transportation Services Department in October 1989. The new department was to deal with all requests and negotiations relating to common carriage. It was the result of British Gas's undertaking to the Secretary of State that it would 'expeditiously co-operate in setting up and conducting negotiations for the securing of rights to have gas conveyed in its pipelines under Section 19 of the Gas Act 1986 (common carriage). In particular British Gas (would), within four weeks of any application . . . provide to the applicant a full response thereto setting out the terms and conditions offered by it for the exercise of such rights' (OFT 1991, Annex 1).

Details of the new service, including proposed charges were published soon afterwards. The level at which they were set was controversial, however. Associated Gas Supplies (AGAS), a potential competitor to British Gas, complained that British Gas had proposed prices in both its published tariffs and in individual quotations which appeared to be 'two to three times higher . . . than those charged by pipeline operators elsewhere in the world' (House of Commons Energy Committee 1989–90).

[1] Prior to 1982, British Gas had concluded such a deal with one company, but this concerned a gas producer which sold most of its output to British Gas, with the remainder carried by British Gas for use in the producer's own plant (MMC 1988, 24, para. 3.34).

In September 1990, British Gas published prices for the conveyance of gas which were significantly lower than the previous schedule. At the same time, the demand for common carriage quotations rose significantly; from fewer than 500 per month early in 1990 to approximately 3,500 quotations in May 1991. Nevertheless, a number of specific grievances have continued to arise, including the time it takes British Gas to conclude a contract, and the company's apparent inflexibility when it comes to contract terms (OFT 1991, 17, para. 70).

Regulatory Action III: Managing the Market

While the need to ensure common carriage and non-predatory pricing have been considered important in other deregulated industries, there was a strong feeling that this was not going to be enough in the gas-supply industry. Attention increasingly focused on the MMC's fourth recommendation, which had, in effect, placed a quota on British Gas's share of new supplies.

The Secretary of State decided to implement the fourth MMC recommendation in a modified form. He demanded that 10 per cent of the *total* amount of gas coming from new fields after May 1989 (as opposed to 10 per cent for each new field) had to be marketed by suppliers other than British Gas. The Secretary of State also made it clear that a limited number of large deals would not constitute the development of adequate competition in the industrial and commercial market. In fact, British Gas applied the 90 : 10 rule to each new field that they purchased from early 1989 onwards, as the MMC originally suggested, apparently, so that no blame could be attached to them in the future if insufficient deals were made.

The implementation of the 90 : 10 rule released a significant amount of gas for independent supply. At last, a number of contracts for direct sale to consumers were obtained through 1989–90. These included joint ventures by Associated Heat Services and Elf (AGAS), Shell and Esso (Quadrant Gas), and Conoco and PowerGen (Kinetica). Nevertheless, doubts continued as to whether 10 per cent of new production would be sufficient for a real penetration of the market by new suppliers. Both BP and AGAS stated that the 90 : 10 rule would not make gas available to third-party suppliers in significant volumes until after 1992 (House of Commons Energy Committee 1989–90).

Those who doubted whether the 90 : 10 rule would bring in effective competition were further convinced by a separate development; the surge in the demand for gas from an entirely new segment of the market. The combination of electricity privatization and greater environmental awareness proved a powerful stimulus to UK gas demand in the late 1980s. Concerns about sulphur emissions from power-stations made gas increasingly popular, as a relatively 'green' fuel, just as a number of private generators were entering the market following privatization of the British electricity supply industry. Most of the new independent power generators planned to make extensive use of combined-cycle gas turbine generators, which set off a period of unprecedented growth in the demand for gas.

The impact of the electricity generators' 'dash for gas' was considerable. In the year ending June 1990, a full 99.5 per cent of newly contracted gas was destined for power generation, with the sector still accounting for 85 per cent the following year (OFT 1991, 4, para. 13). Estimates vary as to the future size of the market. Nevertheless, one commentator has suggested that the total gas contracted for power generation over the past three years is roughly equivalent to one-third of today's total UK gas demand. It will take years for all the gas to come on stream. But when it does, power generators may account for 25 per cent of annual UK gas consumption (Ball 1991: 6). OFT and industry figures on recent contracts for power generation are included in Tables 2.2 and 2.3 respectively.

TABLE 2.2. Gas flows from contracts concluded, June 1989–May 1991

	1990	1991	1992	1993	1994	1995	1996	TOTAL
Share of gas flows from 1989–91 contracts (%)								
Excluding non-British Gas power generation								
British Gas	0	0	33	87	99	100	101	93
Non-British Gas (industrial/ commercial)	100	100	67	13	1	0	–1	7
Including non-British Gas power generation								
British Gas	0	0	27	59	68	69	69	65
Non-British Gas (industrial/commercial)	100	100	55	9	1	0	–1	5
Non-British Gas (for power generation)	0	0	18	32	31	31	31	30
TOTAL NON-BRITISH GAS	100	100	73	41	32	31	31	35

Notes: No gas will actually flow from the contracts covered in the Table until 1992, and then only in small amounts. The OFT reached the figures above by including flows from 'swaps' of gas between British Gas and the independent suppliers. Thus, the independents received supplies from BG in 1990 and 1991 which, in theory, have to be repaid in future years from gas contracted in the 1989–91 period. These repayments explain the negative percentage share indicated for independent suppliers to the industrial and commercial sector in 1996. The OFT concluded that 'in the absence of new supplies of gas there is insufficient gas contracted to non-British Gas suppliers to allow for repayment of swap gas beyond 1994' (OFT 1991, 5).

Source: Produced from OFT (1991) figures by Henderson Crosthwaite Ltd.

TABLE 2.3. Total gas contracted in Britain by primary buyer groups, June 1989–May 1991

Source	Primary purchasers			
	British Gas	Independent marketers	Power	TOTAL
UK Southern Basin (bn. m³)	5	22	30	57
UK Central North Sea (bn. m³)	110	10	55	175
UK Northern North Sea (bn. m³)	35	8	—	43
TOTAL UK (bn. m³)	150	40	85	275
Share (%)	55	15	30	
Split British Gas/ Others (%)	55	45		
Norway (bn. m³)	—	—	30	30
TOTAL UK + NORWAY (bn. m³)	150	40	115	305
Share (%)	49	13	38	
Split British Gas/ Others (%)	49	51		

Notes: Volumes show rounded estimates of total committed reserves. The categories list the *primary* purchasers of gas from producers; thus, for example, the 'power' category excludes gas which was first sold to a gas marketer. The OFT figures listed in Table 2.2 excluded the various contracts for imported gas which were awaiting government approval at the time when the report was written. Table 2.3 includes these contracts, since they now look set to go ahead. It should be remembered that the figures above are estimates of *total* reserves committed in contracts agreed over the June 1989–91 period. The percentages on the table should not be taken as alternative approximations of market share. Rather, they give an indication of the relative future claims which the parties have to gas contracted over the past two years, but due to be delivered over an extended time horizon.

Source: *Gas Matters*, 30 September 1991.

The gas which became available whilst the 90 : 10 rule was in operation was always going to take a long time to come on stream, and growth in the independent share of the market correspondingly slow. But demand from the power-generation industry had the effect of diluting even the long-term impact of the rule in terms of the development of genuine competition with British Gas. Independent generators were snapping up the new supplies of gas, leaving little left over for those firms wishing to compete with British Gas in the non-power-generating sector.

OFGAS tried to address the problem of the long lead times for new gas supplies at the end of 1990. The regulator demanded that British Gas play a more active role in the development of competition, setting a target for independent suppliers of 30 per cent of the firm contract market by the end of 1993, about 15 per cent of the total contract market. That would entail growth of sales to some 1.2 billion therms, compared to the 200 million therms that non-British Gas suppliers provided in 1991. In order to achieve this, Sir James McKinnon announced that British Gas, 'being the sole source of competition [must] be called upon to come to a series of arrangements whereby quantities can be made available to competitors on an interim basis'. The statement came with a clear threat that structural reform of British Gas would get serious consideration if the company did not act in this way to free up supplies.

British Gas duly responded, concluding a number of 'gas swap' deals with competing suppliers over the following months. Contracts with a total of seven companies had been concluded by August 1991. The terms required payment of the gas with similar supplies in the period 1992/3 to 1996/7, in addition to the payment of a small facility fee per therm of released gas.

These measures did nothing to reduce the demand for gas from the power-generating sector, which continued to absorb much of the newly freed gas. Indeed, the fact that most of the new gas contracts were being snapped up by that sector cast doubt on the other independent suppliers' ability even to repay all the swapped gas, let alone build up gas supplies of their own. In 1991 the OFT predicted that the non-British Gas share of gas supplied to this sector would peak at only 8 per cent in 1992, before falling to less than nothing if gas repayments to British Gas are made on schedule (see Table 2.2).

One long-term solution to the gas supply problem rested in the liberalization of imports of gas, finally proposed by the Secretary of State early in 1992. OFGAS, meanwhile, had moved further towards total management of market shares of different providers. British Gas provisionally submitted to a 1991 OFT proposal, to halve its market share in the contract market.

Despite the efforts to encourage competition, both before and after privatization, British Gas continues to account for virtually all the gas supplied through pipes to industry and commerce in the UK. It remains to be seen whether the agreed market share quotas will have to be renegotiated.

2. THE REGULATION OF BRITISH GAS IN THE INDUSTRIAL GAS MARKET

The Regulatory Task

There has been a tendency to view regulators as having two objectives: to prevent abuse of a monopoly and to promote competition (see, for example, Beesley 1991). This gives rise to the familiar dilemma between tough regulation, which diminishes the attractions of new entry into an industry, and light regulation, which allows more exploitation of monopoly power than might be considered ideal.

This provides a stylized presentation of the challenges facing a regulator. One could imagine, for example, setting a level of regulated prices and profits that provide reasonable returns to the incumbent, and merely waiting to see whether competition emerges. If it does, the regulation could be allowed to become obsolete. If it does not, then the regulation remains binding.

That regulators feel a conflict between promoting competition and promoting reasonable prices or profits signifies a lack of trust in market forces as a means of determining the overall level of competition that should prevail. The industrial-gas case probably provides a more contrived promotion of competition than that which has been seen in any British privatized utility. Is there a better way of viewing the task of regulators, one which provides an escape from the dilemma they believe themselves to be in? A more refined way of distinguishing their goals might be to state them in terms of the rent-generating assets owned by the regulated company.

One can place the intangible assets that firms possess into two categories. These are reminiscent of, but not identical to, Salop's distinction between 'innocent' and strategic entry barriers (Salop 1979). Assets in the first category are purely benign. They may be acquired by the investment or good luck of the owner; reputations, patents, well-developed systems, or production skills are all possible examples. Alternatively, they may have been inherited rather than created by the current owner. An example would be incumbency in a market in which there is only room for one operator. It would be inefficient to develop competition, but there may be little reason to believe that this incumbent is much better than other potential operators. In this case, the asset is equivalent to some sort of licence. The important feature of these assets is that there is no social cost to their being exploited. There may be doubts as to who should receive the benefits, but not to their existence.

Assets in the second category are those that are not socially useful, which might be labelled 'strategic assets'. A firm may have privileged access to a valuable source of supply for a market; or it may have access to sufficient funds from operations in one market to predate or fight unfairly in another. Unless there is an established property right over the asset in question, it pays to confiscate away these advantages—which are rent-seeking rather than rent-creating—in order that no one destroys social welfare by exploiting them.

On this view, the two regulatory tasks are not so much to promote competition or cap the profits to be made from a dominant position but, first, to regulate the profits that accrue from the benign competitive advantages (in order to prevent them generating rents disproportionate to the effort of creating them); and second, to remove the rent-seeking kind of assets completely. In other words, to let competition flourish where it is due, and cap profits of incumbents where it is not.

Regulatory Success: British Gas's Strategic Advantages

In the early years, policy to British Gas was motivated by the idea familiar from other industries that incumbents have more strategic advantages than competitive ones. In particular, they have a large advantage in owning or running a distribution network and in the ability to price discriminate in a way that deters entry.

British Gas's pricing policies have been discussed in some detail above. They were considered both an abuse of a dominant position and a means of deterring entry. The strategic importance of the company's ability to price discriminate was that it gave it the means to predate entry by offering cheaper prices to those customers, and only those customers, whom it knew were about to be offered better deals by new entrants. The imposition of the price schedules following the 1988 MMC Report raised the stakes of such predation, by ruling out selective price-cuts.

Ownership of the national transmission network is a strategic asset for British Gas in a number of ways. Most important, it gives British Gas a central role in determining any competitor's entry cost, as well as privileged access to information which could be used to undermine an entry attempt. The negotiations which occur prior to entry give British Gas a clear warning of impending competition, as well as the power to delay entry by protracting the process. By engaging in secretive behaviour, British Gas has the power to increase the risk of entry, by raising the variance of entry costs facing potential competitors.

When it was decided that British Gas should retain the pipeline network after it was privatized, the authorities did try to address the problem of ensuring open access to the network. Under Condition 9 of its Authorisation, British Gas was required to provide a statement of guidance about common carriage, including examples of the prices which it would expect to be paid in typical circumstances, and the principal matters which would be subject to negotiation. Although such a statement was published in 1986, it was sufficiently vague to keep users in the dark over what they might expect. It was not possible for them to determine the relationship between price and distance from the statement, nor did it specify the costs of using the local distribution system. This rendered it impossible to close negotiations with customers. But at the same time, British Gas maintained that the costs of transmission were so variable, that it could not specify a final price until the exact location of the company being supplied had been revealed. This meant that prior to completing a contract with a customer, the competitor faced the possibility that British Gas would itself make a competitive response. Whether or not British Gas used this information was probably secondary in its effect to the fear that it might, which on its own could provide a serious deterrent to the new entrant.

At the time of the MMC report in 1988, there was thus a strong perception that British Gas had been uncooperative on common carriage. After the Report, British Gas undertook to provide more information on common carriage, to enforce 'Chinese walls' and to provide quotations for specific carriage arrangements within four weeks of application. One aspect of the Chinese walls policy was the establishment of the Gas Transportation Services Department within the company in March 1989 (see above, 51).

Despite British Gas's investment of resources, the OFT, in its later report, referred to a number of complaints about the time it took British Gas to conclude contracts, and the fact that British Gas refused to contemplate contracts that depart from a rather narrow norm: for example, British Gas would not allow interruptible contracts. In addition, British Gas insisted on the installation of a data-logger—at a cost of about £1,000 per site—for monitoring gas usage at sites which were transferred to competing suppliers, although it did not have a similar policy for itself.

The continued grievances about British Gas's treatment of competitors eventually led the OFT to insist that the distribution network be hived off as an independent subsidiary. The likelihood is that this will help competitors. Indeed, the move represents an important step in the removal of British Gas's main strategic advantages.

Regulatory Failure: British Gas's Competitive Advantages

In dealing with British Gas's strategic advantages, the objective of policy is unambiguous. The regulatory dilemmas really started to emerge because it became apparent that the early measures adopted to eradicate these advantages were not sufficient to generate the envisaged intensity of competition. If competition, in itself, is the overriding objective, this is a problem that needs to be resolved.

It is interesting to investigate why competition did not emerge. Experience tells us that as quickly as new industries are deregulated, so new forms of incumbent advantage are discovered. In judging regulator performance, it is important to know whether the precise source of monopoly power being regulated is benign. For British Gas, there is a good case to suggest it is.

The three most important of British Gas's competitive strengths lay in the following: its ability to exploit its size and horizontal extension to stabilize the flows of gas; the advantages resulting from its size in concluding new gas deals with suppliers; and its inherited structure of contracts to supply gas to it that left the company with enough gas to serve much of the UK market for the early years after competition was supposed to enter.

As the OFT commented in their 1991 Report, 'competition is limited by the ability of competitors to balance their supply and demand . . . British Gas has an inherent advantage in balancing the supply of and demand for gas by virtue of its size and its large portfolios of both suppliers and customers' (OFT 1991, 12). Market solutions can be found to this problem, and indeed, have been adopted in the electricity-supply industry, because one expects that spot markets for gas would allow any supplier to obtain gas at any time at some price. Whether it is transaction costs that prevent this solution being adopted, or whether it is the existence of a dominant player who would keep out of the market to prevent entry is unclear.

Nevertheless, if it is the former, it is not obvious that we would wish to throw away British Gas's advantage. Its monopoly in the domestic market, which has peaks that differ from those of the commercial market, is very helpful. Interruptible gas customers can be served very cheaply because even at this price, gas provided on these terms is less costly than the extra storage facilities which would be required if all users signed up for firm supplies.

The sheer size of British Gas's presence, both across and within markets, also has benefits upstream. British Gas's history as the sole purchaser of gas from the UK continental shelf (UKCS) is still an advantage when it comes to negotiating contracts to buy gas with the big producers. In the past, they complained that British Gas abused its monopsony buying power. Nevertheless, that there are distinct advantages to dealing with British Gas has been illustrated by the extent to which producers, given the choice, still seem inclined to favour British Gas over other buyers.

Gas exploration involves huge investments up front, with lead-times of five years or more before the gas comes on stream. The pipeline will usually be specific to a given field, and again involves a lot of highly specific investment before the producer sees any return. These and other features of the gas production business favour long-term contracts with the primary gas purchaser, involving a more or less solid commitment to take up the available supplies well into the future. British Gas itself has commented on the 'large degree of mutual interdependence between the two parties to a gas purchase contract' (House of Commons Energy Committee 1986–7, 44). Minimum-take conditions, for example, spread the production and market risks over both suppliers and consumers, allowing for a more efficient long-term operation of the gas market. Without such guarantees 'the development of some higher cost or less flexible reserves would never be undertaken' (Boucher and Smeers 1987: 4).

Evidence that this argument has some validity is the fact that new power-generation contracts concern supplies from particular gasfields to particular power-stations. The generator does not just have a contract to buy gas, but to buy a particular field of gas. That reflects the benefit, or necessity, for both buyer and seller, of having a stable purchase contract.

If the preferred form of contract is one for 100 per cent of a field, with a steady flow of gas, then British Gas it at an advantage in this area because its wide customer base and storage facilities enable it to give a credible guarantee of steady take-off. The power-generating sector has been quite successful in concluding supply deals with gas producers, indicating that they are more able than smaller users to contract large enough amounts of gas to rival British Gas. Nevertheless, there have been clear signs even here that producers place a higher risk premium on such contracts.

The above indicates that there may always be a role for a company with British Gas's size if gas producers are to be encouraged to recover all available gas supplies in the UKCS. As new fields become more difficult to exploit, British Gas may be the only company able to promise the steady off-take which such conditions require. As long as other forms of gas are not being artificially blocked from the market, there are clear gains to British Gas's position as an attractive—but none the less hard-bargaining—long-term partner for gas producers.

British Gas's third competitive advantage, albeit a diminishing one, is the large number of outstanding gas-purchase contracts which it has inherited, some of which stem from agreements drawn up in the 1960s and 1970s. Although the price which British Gas pays for such gas is linked to complex escalator clauses (see MMC 1988, 22–3), geological factors mean that the gas from earlier fields is far cheaper to extract. Thus, British Gas has a significant cost advantage over entrants, even despite recent price reductions. For example, in the year to March 1990, British Gas paid 11.5 pence per therm for gas from the Old Southern

Basin, compared to 19 and 26 pence per therm for New Southern Basin and Frigg area gas, respectively (Barclays de Zoete Wedd, 1988).

On top of the preferential prices paid for old gas relative to new is the fact that of the gas sold in 1992, the vast bulk would have been contracted prior to 1989. Table 2.4 provides an indication of the vintage structure of British Gas's gas supplies. The effect that this exerts on the market can only be transitory, however. The output from the older fields is falling off rapidly; gas from the Old Southern basin, for example, now covers only 30 per cent of British Gas's annual requirements, compared to 51 per cent eight years ago. Gas from the Frigg field is set to fall even more sharply in the next few years.

TABLE 2.4. Profile of source of British Gas supplies, 1983–1991

Source of supply	Contract start	Percentage of total British Gas supply		
		1983–4	1986–7	1990–1
Old Southern Basin	1968–72	51	43	30
Frigg Field (N. Basin)	1973	39	33	20
New Southern Basin	Early 1980s	—	8	33
Other	1973 onwards	9	13	17

Source: British Gas.

With all these factors in mind, it was not surprising that new competition did not emerge for the bulk of the market for industrial and commercial customers. There could only be a limited independent sector, on account of the shortage of supplies, and the only segment in which British Gas's other advantages were not substantial was that for power generation, where large purchases of a guaranteed mind prevailed, and where historic contracts had not pre-determined all sales.

The regulatory response to the lack of competition was to demand it. If it did not emerge on its own, then British Gas would have to provide it regardless of whether there were good reason or bad for the lack of competition. This was particularly necessary given that there was no effective price regulation in the gas-contract market. An alternative policy would have been to accept the level of competition that emerged as in some sense the efficient level of competition. It is true that would probably only have emerged after several years, as the advantages that British Gas enjoyed depreciated with time. It may also have been that some price regulation would have been needed as a substitute for competition for the intervening years, but the advantage of the alternative policy would be the protection of any socially advantageous assets of British Gas.

One could certainly interpret the *ad hoc* and reactive regulatory response to British Gas's domination of the gas market as a sign of the regulators' difficulties in grappling with the dilemma between promoting competition and capping monopoly abuse. In the absence of price regulation to cap monopoly abuse, the promotion of competition became the overriding goal.

Regulatory Failure: The Problem of Market Definition

If we accepted the promotion of competition as the overriding goal, and we accepted that extra help was necessary to stimulate such competition into existing, the British Gas case highlights another problem. A difficulty arises in attempting to apply a single regulatory regime across a number of different markets in which very different competitive conditions prevail. Competition may be very likely in one market, but not in another. In this case, the adoption of a single regulatory regime may lead to competition in one market, but excessively light regulation in the other; or no competition in either market, even when, in one at least, it would have been appropriate. For example, it is possible to imagine a 'merit order' of customers, ranked by British Gas in order of the incremental cost advantage it has over rivals in serving them. Just as British Gas would like to price discriminate between such customers, so might discriminatory regulatory regimes be applied.

For all these purposes, the 'contract-gas market' turned out to be far too wide a definition. There are numerous sub-segments which offer differing likelihoods of competitive entry. A policy of promoting competition has the effect of stimulating competition in one segment—in the gas case, it was the power-generation segment—while doing nothing to alleviate the problems of monopoly exploitation in the rest of the market.

Setting quotas for market share does nothing to provide a solution to the problem. While the outcome of this policy has yet to be observed, we have every reason to believe that it will have the same effect as that which has been observed already. British Gas will face more competition, but this will be in those particular markets in which its competitive advantage is weakest. It will be able to carry on exploiting the remaining markets. Indeed, if one was to ask what British Gas should do, faced with the demand to cut its overall market share, it would be to retreat to the customers that are least attractive to new entrants and exploit them as much as it can without promoting new entry.

So what else could the regulator have done? The first-best option would have been to adopt a reasonable uniform level of regulation (in preference to the lack of price regulation that existed), to impose a 'no discrimination' rule on British Gas, and to have merely accepted the level of competition that emerged. It would emerge in those markets where competitors stood a chance of competing and would not emerge in the others, where regulation would be effective in capping monopoly abuse. This policy would be consistent with a market-oriented determination of the level of competition that exists.

The second-best policy, consistent with the prevailing view that the regulator should determine the level of competition, would be to treat the contract sector not as one market, but as several distinct markets, crafting different regulatory regimes for each one. Competition could be promoted where it might be expected to emerge, with no sacrifice in regulation in the markets where it was not likely to emerge.

The view underlying this second-best approach is that when a firm's rent-generating assets are deployed in different markets, the value of these competitive advantages should be assessed with respect *to every different market in which they can be exploited*. And markets, for these purposes, should be defined in the narrowest possible terms. An asset, such as a reputation which allows one producer to charge more for an equivalent product than a rival, may be very valuable in one market segment, but not very valuable in another. We should classify customers as belonging to different markets if the assets of the incumbent have a differential impact on them.

Thus, within each market, British Gas would have a different competitive advantage. The appropriate regime would balance regulation and competition market by market. If British Gas has a strong advantage in one market, the level of regulation consistent with promoting competition in that market needs to be very light. In another market, where British Gas has a strong advantage over potential rivals, competition would only be provoked at price levels which might be considered excessive. In these markets, tighter regulation is necessary to prevent abuse.

Such a policy would require a very clear notion of distinct markets, but it is not hard to see what notion should apply. Two customers should be considered as being in distinct markets if the British Gas's opportunity-cost advantage of serving one (over the best potential entrant's opportunity cost of serving that one) is significantly different from British Gas's opportunity-cost advantage of serving the other. For example, a small residential customer in Filkins with extremely variable demand would be very expensive for the independent to serve, but not expensive for British Gas. A large power generator in the Midlands can be served at equal cost by both British Gas and the independents, so the small residential user and the power generator should be considered as occupying different market segments. This is because British Gas's cost advantage is much larger in the one case than the other.

This discussion is reminiscent of the issue of what services should be included in a regulated-price basket. The most important difference is that it is not only different product lines that should determine what is included, but also different types of customer. Markets have to be defined in terms of both dimensions: product types and customer types.

Suppose that we did wish to disaggregate the markets further. Customers could be attributed to different markets on the basis of size, usage pattern, and, possibly, location. It was in the first two of these that the power generators presented such a contrast with the rest of the market, and were thus so much more attractive to independents. The same factors would be important in ranking the attractiveness of other customers as well.

There are two reasons why the regulators might have been reluctant to adopt this level of disaggregation. First, they do not have a confident idea of the boundaries of market segments. Second, there is the ubiquitous problem of joint costs. The incremental cost of serving one particular segment depends on what decisions have been taken about serving other segments. If the others are going to be served anyway, the incremental costs of serving a new one are low. If the segment under consideration is the first to be chosen, the incremental cost of serving it is enormous. The problem of looking at each market individually on an incremental or opportunity-cost basis is that the overall return across markets may not be efficient or equitable.

In deciding the number of separate regimes to impose, regulators therefore face a trade-off: leaning towards disaggregation will help them select the precise regime which is appropriate for each market segment. But grouping markets together will obtain a fair overall return.

In the gas case, the regulator initially treated the contract market as homogeneous; this became unsustainable when a very obvious division emerged between power generation and other contract sales. We shall have to see whether further subdivisions within the contract market emerge in future, as British Gas and the regulator attempt to meet the ambitious competition targets which have now been agreed.

CONCLUSION: AN ASSESSMENT OF THE REGULATORY RESPONSE

If we look at the whole regulator response to the assets that allowed British Gas to dominate all segments of the British gas market our overall assessment must be mixed. The unambiguously appropriate policy goal was to remove the strategic assets which impeded entry. This was largely started in the 1988 MMC report, and has been pursued sensibly since. These strategic assets were a substantial advantage to British Gas in all segments of the gas-supply market. On the other hand, removing them has not done much to generate competition in most of those segments. It clearly *was* enough in the power-generation market, where the market share of new entrants may be significant by 1993, but it was not enough in the rest of the firm-contract market.

The first choice is whether we should just live with British Gas domination of the markets they dominate. If they win the game on a level playing-field, is there any reason to worry? If we are not willing to accept this situation, a preferable option to administering market shares would be a policy of setting regulation market by market. That, in turn, requires that one decide how many different regimes are necessary. Clearly, if competitive conditions were homogeneous—which they are not—there would be one. The more heterogeneous different segments are, the harder it will be to establish a sensible means of allocating joint costs and overall return. And the less willing the regulator will be to separate disparate markets from each other, whatever the benefits of such well-tailored regulation. Indeed, it is here that the dilemma between competition and regulation truly emerges. Regulation that is too stiff encourages excessive competition into those segments that are attractive to new entrants, while regulation that is lax leaves some customers who face no choice of supplier being exploited.

If one has to impose one regime, the cost-benefit analysis of imposing tough regulation is not straightforward. It depends on the size of the relative segments and the costs of leaving a given number of them with an inappropriate policy regime. It may also depend on the magnitude of the potential dynamic benefits to competition, which could render static efficiency costs worthwhile.

The regulator's bias towards competition in the gas case had costs. First, it is costly to dispense with the genuine economies of scale that British Gas might have if they are important; the managed market may result in excessive entry. Second, the policy that tells British Gas to reduce its market share imposes large negative incentive effects on British Gas which has little reason to be efficient, little reason to price competitively, and every reason to confine its attention to the market segments in which its monopoly power is likely to be most enduring. The customers in that group are not likely to enjoy the transition to competition. Third, the job of managing the market distracts from and conflicts with the task of regulating prices (or profits) in those market segments that are never going to be competitive. That British Gas have lost market share in the supply of gas to large customers is of little consolation to an exploited small contract customer facing unregulated prices in a less contestable market.

References

Ball, J. (1991), 'Power showdown exposes UK government supply blockade', *Gas Matters*, 30 Sept.: 1–10.

Beesley, M. (1991), 'Price regulation and competition', lecture for the Centre for Business Strategy Series on Regulation, London Business School, 18 Apr.

Barclays de Zoete Wedd (1988), *After the MMC: British Gas Plc.*

Boucher, J. and Smeers, Y. (1987), 'Economic forces in the European gas market: A 1985 perspective', *Energy Economics*, 9/1, 2–17.

British Gas (1988), *Contract Gas After the MMC: A Commentary by British Gas.*

—— (1990), *Gas Transportation Services from British Gas.*

—— (1991), 'Financial and Operating Statistics', Suppl. to the *Annual Report and Accounts.*

Kleinwort Benson Securities (1992), *Drill Bits: British Gas—to Review or not to Review*, 17 Jan.

Monopolies and Mergers Commission (1988), *Gas: A Report on the Matter of the Existence of a Monopoly Situation in Relation to the Supply of Gas through Pipes in the Contract Sector*, Cm 500, London: HMSO.

Office of Fair Trading (1991), *The Gas Review* (summary version), OFT.

Office of Gas Supply (1987), *Competition in Gas Supply.*

Office of Gas Supply (1990), *Annual Report.*

Salop, S. (1979), 'Strategic entry deterrence', *American Economic Review, P&P*, 69: 335–8.

Spring, P. (1991), *Regulation and the UK Gas Supply Division*, Henderson Crosthwaite Institutional Brokers Ltd.

3

Reforming the NHS

ALAN MAYNARD*

INTRODUCTION

The problems that characterize the performance of health-care systems are very similar despite great differences in their structure and level of funding. In all health-care systems there is a failure to define the nature of the problems that precipitate the political decision to reform, in particular cost inflation, unproven and probably inefficient resource use and inequity, and a reluctance to target policy changes to facilitate the resolution of these problems. This was evident in the 1989 reforms of the British NHS: the government failed to define clearly what the problems were that initiated the reform process and the selection of remedies was poorly targeted and proved difficult to implement and maintain. What are the problems the British reforms sought to address and did the development of 'competition' in health-care markets improve the efficiency of resource allocation in the UK National Health Service?

COMMON PROBLEMS IN HEALTH-CARE MARKETS

Inadequate information

It is commonplace for health-care policy to be formulated and executed in a data-free environment! The information needed to inform resource-allocation decisions in health-care markets are largely absent. There is a dearth of data about costs (inputs), process (activities), and outcome (health gains).

Few health-care systems have cost data which reveal the value of what society gives up when patients pass through a treatment episode. The UK has cost systems designed to facilitate the achievement of macro-economic financial control, i.e. the meeting of cash limits. The US health-care system has price data but prices do not necessarily reflect opportunity costs for particular activities, let alone for complete

* Professor of Economics and Director of the Centre for Health Economics at the University of York.

treatment episodes. UK NHS and US price-cost data are not linked and consequently primary-care, hospital-care, community-care, and household-production information are collected in a fragmented manner. As a result it is difficult to cost a treatment episode (e.g. for a heart attack) from onset in the home through primary care, to the hospital, back to the household, and back to the resumption of everyday work and leisure.

Data about activities and outcomes vary in quality. Generally some activity data are available in most health care systems, for example diagnostic-related group systems provide both financial and diagnostic volume data (DRGs are a system of fixed prices for clearly specified diagnostic-treatment categories). However these data are rarely related to outcomes and totally inadequate as a basis to inform efficient resource-allocation decisions. Thus, to test the 'quicker sicker' hypothesis, the Rand group had to collect specific linked and limited outcome data to demonstrate that reduced lengths of stay, induced by the DRG system, did not induce adverse outcomes in terms of mortality (Kahn *et al.* 1990).

The absence of routine outcome data has been recognized for hundreds of years. For instance the Prince of Wales's physician in 1732 advocated the collection and publication of outcome data:

> In order, therefore to procure this valuable collection, I humbly propose, first of all, that three or four persons should be employed in the hospitals (and that without any ways interfering with the gentlemen now concerned), to set down the cases of the patients there from day to day, candidly and judiciously, without any regard to private opinions or public systems, and at the year's end publish these facts just as they are, leaving every one to make the best use he can for himself. (Francis Clifton 1732)

The editor of the *Lancet* in 1841 argued that:

> All public institutions must be compelled to keep case-books and registers, on a uniform plan. Annual abstracts of the results must be published. The annual medical report of cases must embrace hospitals, lying-in hospitals, dispensaries, lunatic asylums, and prisons. (*Lancet* 1840/1: 650–1)

The *Lancet* debate influenced the formation of legislation: the Lunacy Act 1844 required all public psychiatric hospitals to measure outcome in terms of whether patients were dead, relieved, or unrelieved. This distinction was adopted by a UK nursing reformer, Florence Nightingale, who argued:

> I am fain to sum up with an urgent appeal for adopting this or some uniform system of publishing the statistical records of hospitals. There is a growing conviction that in all hospitals, even in those which are best conducted, there is a great and unnecessary waste of life. In attempting to arrive at the truth, I have applied everywhere for information, but in scarcely an instance have I been able to obtain hospital records fit for any purpose of comparison. If they could be

obtained, they would enable us to decide many other questions besides the ones alluded to. They would show subscribers how their money was being spent, what amount of good was really being done with it, or whether the money was doing mischief rather than good. (Florence Nightingale 1863)

Mortality outcome measures are limited (they ignore the quality of survival) and may be ambiguous (small sample size may mean variations are explained by case severity, social-class differences, and/or the skills of the surgeon and the anaesthetist). The appropriate measure of outcome is enhancements in the length and quality of the patient's (and carer's) life. Data about survival duration are few and fragmented, i.e. there is an absence of record linkage and follow-up through the separate stages of the treatment process and back into the activities of everyday living in the community. Instruments to measure the quality of life are crude and experimental and whether such data can be combined to produce a single measure of outcome (for instance a quality-adjusted life-year or healthy-year equivalent) is a matter of fierce debate.

Variations in practice

The few data that are available show that there are significant variations in costs, clinical activities, and outcomes (i.e. mortality). These variations in medical practice are observable between clinicians in primary care and in the hospital system. Similar patients with breast cancer may have radical surgery (mastectomy), minor surgery (lumpectomy), and an array of different regimes of chemotherapy and radiotherapy. For given presentations cancer specialists offer a wide range of services (Priestman 1989). The treatment process in terms of what treatments patients receive, may be determined by to whom they are referred: clinicians within a particular hospital, district, or region offer very different treatment regimes to 'remedy' similar diagnoses. The causes of these variations have been studied quite thoroughly by Wennberg in the USA and McPherson in the UK. McPherson (Anderson and Mooney 1990) offers some explanations of the variations which occur in different parts of the health-care system and it can be seen that differences in clinical practice are an important explanation of these variations (see Table 3.1).

In many areas of clinical practice there is little consensus about 'best practice' and clinicians 'experiment on the job'. Where there is uncertainty systematic experimentation is sensible, provided it is conducted with agreed protocols in large trials. Unfortunately the experimentation is often discretionary, for small numbers of patients, and poorly evaluated. Such behaviour perpetuates uncertainty about the efficiency of interventions and is dubious from the ethical point of view. Inefficient practices deprive potential patients of care from which they could benefit and such behaviour is unethical.

Table 3.1. Plausible causes of variation at different levels of aggregation

Variation between:	Morbidity	Supply	Clinical	Demand
GPs	S	O	L	S
Districts	M	M	L	S
Regions	L	L	S	M
Countries	L	L	L	L

Key: L = large; M = medium; S = small; O = no effect relative to others in row.
Source: McPherson, in Anderson and Mooney (eds.) 1990.

Ignorance of outcomes

One explanation of this absence of consensus about 'best practice' is that the ignorance about input–output relationships in medicine is acute. There are few treatments where outcomes are known and certain and these are scarce islands of rationality in a sea of uncertain health-care practices. Cochrane (1972) argued that the majority of health-care therapies in use in the 1960s were unproven. Fuchs (1984) argued that 10 per cent of health-care expenditure reduced health status, 10 per cent had no effect, and 80 per cent improved patient health. The problem, he argued, was that no one knew which therapies were in the 10 and 80 per cent categories! Black (1986) argued that 10 per cent of treatments were proven whilst researchers at the Rand Corporation in the USA assert that 30 per cent of health-care activities have no effect on health. In the evaluation of clinical practice narrow outcome measures have often been used and failed to evaluate systematically 'health gains', i.e. whether treatments produce enhancements in the length and quality of life of patients. There are no agreed outcome measures and little scientific knowledge about the efficiency of health care.

Perverse incentives

In the few areas of health-care activity where there is some knowledge of input–outcome relationships it is often not used to improve practices. For some procedures, for instance open-heart surgery and organ transplants, the relationship between surgical volume and mortality outcomes may be such that, if surgeons do not carry out some minimum volume of activity, they are likely to kill their patients (see e.g. Hughes, Hunt, and Luft 1987). It is evident that there are major differences in patient (hospital) mortality. Some of these differences may be explained by case severity and other factors, but others may be related to variations in the efficiency of surgeons and anaesthetists (Kind 1988, and 1990).

Such knowledge is often ignored by managers and clinical decision-makers: knowledge is not translated into practice (Woodward and Stoddart 1990). One reason for this is perverse incentives. Patients and producers in public and private health-care systems do not bear the financial consequences of their decisions because of moral hazard and third-party payers (either the government or insurers), and consequently have few incentives to economize and use resources efficiently.

The fragmentation of all health-care systems creates incentives for cash-limited decision-makers to shift patients and hence costs from their budgets on to those of other component parts of the health-care system. Thus in the NHS a manager with a cash-limited hospital system may shift drug costs on to the primary-care system. With the hospital buying in bulk and using cheap generic drugs, and the primary-care GP prescribing expensive brand-named drugs, this behaviour may increase the NHS drug bill with no significant benefits in patient outcome.

Summary

In the UK in the 1980s the political consensus, by which the government left resource allocation to the discretion of the medical profession provided it left funding decisions to the politicians, broke down (Klein 1983). The government was confronted by evidence that much of what was going on in the NHS was of unknown efficacy and did not yield demonstrable 'value for money'. This recognition of the unknown efficiency of the NHS was heightened by deliberate parsimonious funding of the service: rationing decisions became more explicit and the basis for explicit rational choice between treatments competing for funding was absent. As a consequence the system created more 'disturbance' (e.g. media attention) for politicians and the search for the 'Holy Grail' of a 'quick fix' was resumed.

THE UK NHS REFORMS

Resource allocation in the NHS

The tax-financed budget of the UK NHS is determined by Cabinet with separate budget allocations to England, Scotland, Wales, and Northern Ireland. The funding level is modest in international terms, and cash-limited. These budgets are unequal and if allocated on the basis of population weighted by need (proxied by mortality as in each national resource-allocation formula) would reduce Scottish and Ulster funding by 18–25 per cent, with gains to the English NHS (Ludbrook and Maynard 1980; Birch and Maynard 1988).

Each budget is allocated by formula in each country. In the case of

England this results in the budget being allocated to fourteen Regions which then reallocate most resources to constituent Districts; some 'top slicing' takes place to fund regional specialties in cancer, kidney dialysis, and other services. Prior to 1991 the District Health Authorities were the purchasers and the providers of hospital care and required to keep within their cash-limited budgets each year. Treatment decisions are taken by clinicians, who are autonomous, and audited weekly both by peers and NHS managers. Thus the system uses centrally provided resources at the discretion of clinicians and there is neither information nor management capacity to question clinical choices and determine whether resources are used efficiently. Patient care is largely free at the point of delivery with co-payments for dentistry and prescriptions.

The failure to manage this expensive health-care system was recognized by the Conservative government in the early 1980s. Instead of decrying 'bureaucratic administrators', management was transformed from group consensus (often lowest common denominator) to chief executives on short-term performance-related contracts which were reviewed annually.

Managerial reform took place against a background of little real resource growth in the hospital system, increasing patient demand, and the need to restructure treatments to take account of technological change (e.g. enhanced possibilities for day-case surgery). It was these factors, enhancing the visibility of previously implicit rationing, that created the political pressures for the review of the NHS and the 1989 reforms. With increased public criticism before and after the 1987 election, the Prime Minister was embarrassed by accusations of privatization and media stories about untreated patients.

The reform process

The decision to reform the NHS was taken unilaterally by the Prime Minister, Mrs Thatcher, and announced, to her Cabinet colleagues' surprise, on BBC TV in January 1988. The discussion of the reasons and the options for reform took place in a small group controlled by the Prime Minister which met in secret. After six months, during which the focus was on demand-side reform (e.g. increased private insurance and the greater use of co-payments), the Health Minister was replaced and the focus of reform switched to the supply side. This process of policy formation was influenced by the academic debate (e.g. Enthoven 1985; Maynard 1985). The focus of change was the maintenance of public funding of the NHS and reforms to inject competition and greater efficiency in resource allocation on to the supply side.

The proposals

The reforms were to produce 'competition' but the White Paper defined it imprecisely. For competition to be established and thrive it is necessary for alternatives to be available—excess capacity facilitates choice—and for the parties concerned to strive for market share (Bevan *et al.* 1988). To create competition the government proposed seven reforms in the acute-care sector (Department of Health 1989*a*, p. 4).

1. delegation of decision-making to the local level to make the NHS responsive to patient needs;
2. creation of NHS Trust hospitals with greater managerial discretion;
3. funding to follow the patients i.e. patients could be treated anywhere in the NHS or in the private sector at cost;
4. reduction of waiting times and improvement of the quality of service;
5. improvement of patient services, general practitioners applying for their own budgets to purchase diagnostic and a small group of (non-emergency) surgical procedures from hospital;
6. reduction in size of managerial bodies and reformation 'on business lines';
7. audit of medical practices to ensure quality and value for money.

Inherent in these reforms was the creation of an explicit market, i.e. the separation of the supply and demand sides of the market and the creation of a network of buyers (purchasers) and sellers (providers). The purchaser (e.g. the District Health Authority) has a cash-limited budget to buy care for its resident population. It is required to (a) measure the health needs of the local population, and (b) identify the cost-effective treatments to meet these needs. It can 'contract' with providers in the public or private sectors through agreements which are explicit but not binding in law.

The NHS Trusts were created in groups over time. The first group, some fifty-seven hospitals, became Trusts in April 1991, with a second group of ninety-nine given this status from April 1992. Thus many Health Authorities remain, with their purchaser and provider function continuing to be executed by the one body: the District Health Authority. However with 'contracting' there is some greater openness in setting the volume of activities. Initially (1991–2) the contracting was for blocks of services and expenditure; with price/volume contracting emerging only at the margins, e.g. regional specialties such as transplantation, renal dialysis, and cancer treatments. In 1992–3 it was planned to increase the extent of price/volume contracting. Even in 1991 the prices emerging for particular treatments showed large variations between Districts, indicative not only of accounting practices but also variations in doctor behaviour.

In addition to the reform of the acute hospital system, the government also reformed primary care and community care. The GP budget-holding arrangements were implemented in annual groups (or 'waves'). After some initial opposition by the medical profession there was much greater enthusiasm for this reform amongst doctors than for the hospital reforms. Their budgets covered pharmaceuticals, diagnostics, in-patient diagnosis, and in-patient care for a range of non-emergency surgical procedures. In addition the GP's contract was reformed radically from April 1990 with a set of core services identified, and with strong financial incentives to provide these services. Most of these core services are of unproven cost-effectiveness (Scott and Maynard 1991).

Community care, which provides care for the mentally ill, the intellectually and physically disabled, and the elderly is to be reformed separately from April 1993 (Department of Health 1989*b*). This involves the identification of a local government social services purchaser who will be responsible for ensuring that appropriate care packages are defined for all clients and that support is then purchased from competing public and private providers. Preparations for the implementation of these reforms in April 1993 are slow and uncertain because of funding uncertainties, but their development is essential if acute-sector bed blockages are to be avoided.

Potential advantages

The acute-care-sector reforms were untested and operated without any significant evaluation since April 1991. In principle they should have enhanced the efficiency with which NHS resources are used by the twin processes of 'glasnost' and 'perestroika'. The clear identification of trading roles makes it easier to identify what services are being traded, by whom, at what price and quality. In principle this glasnost should enhance the accountability of managers and clinicians.

The information created by the processes of trading should make it easier for traders to identify opportunities for gain by manipulating trading relationships. If market contestability can be created and sustained, substantial welfare gains may be achieved. The pace of this process, once created, is uncertain but its effects may be significant, obliging managers to restructure the supply side in a fashion which reflects not only current market demand rather than past history, but also the cost-effectiveness of competing providers and treatments.

Another potential advantage of the reforms is the greater integration of primary and hospital care. General practitioners are free to refer their patients to any hospital. The local purchaser has to make contracts with the chosen providers and then ensure that GP's patients go to these providers. If they do not, and patient 'traffic' goes to providers who are not contracted to the local purchaser, NHS money follows the patients and the District Health Authority will have financial difficulties. Thus the reforms require that purchasers identify and meet GPs' requirements. Consequently, for the first time, purchasers have a strong incentive to be responsive to the needs of the GPs.

Some problems with the reforms

Defining property rights

A market is a network of buyers and sellers. How they interact and the scope for competition in any market is determined by the rules which govern transactions between purchasers and providers. Property rights determine:

(a) how resources *can* be used (e.g. there can be short-term contracts for newly recruited doctors in NHS Trusts);
(b) how resources *cannot* be used (e.g. the NHS Trusts' ability to borrow capital and sell assets is constrained);
(c) the use and exchange rules for assets.

In principle, a competitive market with transferable property rights would lead to 'survival of the fittest' with inefficient managers, clinicians, and institutions being driven out of the market-place. Adam Smith's early writings epitomized these arguments.

> It is not from the benevolence of the butcher, the brewer and the baker, that we expect our dinner, but from their regard to their own interest. We address ourselves, not to their humanity but to their self-love, and never talk to them of our necessities but of their advantages. (Smith 1776 (1976), i. 26–7)

This view of competition 'red in tooth and claw' is the epitome of the liberal ideology espoused by Thatcher, Reagan, and other politicians in the 1980s. But is competition concerned with conflict or collaboration? (Sen 1987). The predominant textbook view of competition is that it is a process which produces survival of the fittest. However Adam Smith, in his book *The Theory of Moral Sentiments*, contradicted this view and his better-known arguments in *The Wealth of Nations* thus:

> Those general rules of conduct when they have been fixed in our mind by habitual reflection, are of great use in correcting the misrepresentations of self-love concerning what is fit and proper to be done in our particular situation . . . The regard of those general rules of conduct, is what is properly called a sense of duty, a principle of greatest consequence in human life, and the only principle by which the bulk of mankind are capable of directing their actions. (Smith 1790, ch. 4, para. 12; ch. 5, para. 1, pp. 160–2)

The sense of duty and moral obligation to colleagues and clients is clearly important and the crude application of so-called market principles may not enhance the efficiency of resource allocation. Contracting in many markets is a long-term, collaborative undertaking which reflects the self-interest of the purchaser, who requires an assurance of a reliable supply of good quality services and merchandise, and the provider, who requires the assurance of a reliable market for her output. These relationships are evident in many markets and dominate market transactions in Japan (Sen 1987; Maynard 1991). Such trading relationships are not short-term expedients which reflect transient market advantages. They reflect the mutual self-interest of purchaser and provider which may be best enhanced by long-term contractual relationships which reflect their interdependence and their duty to each other.

So, is the issue the clear definition of roles and the sharpening of incentives to use resources efficiently, or the creation of 'free' competition? Unrestricted competition has never existed because, *inter alia*, capitalists are the enemies of competition. The relevant issue for reform of health-care markets is the nature of their regulation; crude competition may damage doctor–patient relationships if Smith's 'sense of duty' is eroded. Whilst 'spot contracting' may be useful at the margin, long-term trading relationships may be more efficient in many areas of health care.

Why regulate competition?

(i) By their very nature some hospitals are local monopolists or, if members of an oligopoly, can formulate 'agreements' to divide the market and manipulate prices. Such power has to be regulated by government with some form of agreed rules which review and limit provider choices.

(ii) There is some evidence from the United States (e.g. Robinson and Luft 1988) that competition in health-care markets is based on quality rather than on price, i.e. sellers compete for market share by emphasizing the quality of the health care processes, usually measured by the luxury of their carpets and the shininess of machines rather than superior health outcomes! Quality competition is also evident in the pharmaceutical market where, like the health-care market more generally, price competition is difficult to create let alone sustain.

(iii) The market power of providers and quality competition may create cost inflation. These effects may be enhanced by the erosion of the monopsony power of the NHS as wage bargaining in a very labour intensive industry (e.g. hospitals typically spend 35–40 per cent of their budgets on nurses) is dencentralized and the pay of workers is decided at the local level. In a cash-limited NHS, these forces may lead to the delivery of declining service volumes at reduced levels of quality in terms of service process and patient outcome. The UK government cannot ignore the potentially inflationary effects of these factors on public expenditure.

(iv) The UK government is attracted by the idea of productivity gains but fears the effects electorally of inefficient providers being driven out of business. Faced by a general election the government tried to maintain a 'steady state' in market transactions. This process often involved tacit advice to purchasers to maintain existing contracting relationships rather than allocate them in relation to comparative advantage. Additionally the government prevented the closure of two or three teaching hospitals in London which were surplus to market needs by the classic 'Yes Minister' mechanism of setting up a government commission to investigate London hospital needs and report after the election! London hospital closures have been 'delayed' for 80 years! (Rivett 1986)

How has competition been regulated?

The 1989 White Paper was a general statement of intent by the government. As ministers began to put 'flesh on these bones' they recognized the difficulties of creating and sustaining competition. The influence on the politicians of the arguments in favour of regulation was significant as they and their advisers sought to constrain market freedoms to create a 'smooth take off' for the reforms in an election year (1992–2). Thus:

(i) To inhibit the use of monopoly power, a 6 per cent rate of return on assets was set as a maximum (i.e. prices are controlled in aggregate).

(ii) Use of the capital market was constrained. For instance NHS Trusts were not permitted free access to capital markets because if they were, they would, in the view of HM Treasury, be given preferential rating in the financial markets. If, as government agencies, they could access capital at lower interest rates, there was a risk of 'over-capitalization'. To avoid this risk, volume controls (quotas) for capital for Trusts were introduced. Trusts also cannot sell assets in excess of £1 million without government agreement.

(iii) Faced by labour-market organizations of considerable political and economic power (such as the British Medical Association), the government both failed to define some general rules (e.g. in principle GPs are free to refer their patients, but in practice purchasers limit this freedom by demanding prior authorization of referrals of cold-elective patients), and defined other rules too restrictively (e.g. setting centrally junior-doctor staffing levels in Trusts to achieve training and other goals which are not consistent with market goals).

The government sought to constrain, by the narrow and imprecise definition of property rights, the working of the market mechanism.

Outstanding regulation issues

The Conservative government changed its health-care policies radically, in terms of setting rules, over the period 1989–92. It left major issues unresolved:

(i) *Consumer views*: the role of the consumer in the reformed health-care market of the UK was limited. The purchaser, be she the District Health Authority manager or the GP budget-holder, is the guardian of the patients' interests. Whilst the purchasers might seek to reflect consumer preferences by reacting to the results of market research, the incentives for this to happen were limited. The patient's freedom to shift her custom to alternative suppliers was limited because of the nature of the health-care market—an asymmetry of information between patients and providers, and the exploitation by providers of the consequent agency relationship to induce patient demand. For the consumers' 'voice' to affect resource allocation, purchasers and providers have to be made accountable by creating both appropriate information about patients' preferences and suitable incentive mechanisms to ensure the information affects their behaviour.

(ii) *Capital*: whilst the reforms set out a clear declaration to produce more efficient allocation of capital, there has been little progress (Mayston, in Culyer, Maynard, and Posnett (eds.) 1990). With the quality of the capital stock of the NHS seriously depleted by poor investment in maintenance, the comparative advantage of competing hospitals is determined by history and luck. Since April 1991 all capital stock has been valued and interest is paid by providers to the Regional Health Authority. Whilst this may induce greater economy in the use of the existing capital stock, it does not provide an efficient means of augmenting it. How should capital resources be allocated in the NHS? The 1989 reforms offered no answer to this central resource-allocation service.

(iii) *Information*: the behaviour of consumers, purchasers, and providers is determined, not only by the property rights and the resultant incentives, but also by information. The price data that are emerging in the UK NHS are crude and show considerable variations within therapeutic categories. These variations, as much as seventeenfold in some specialties, are a product of accountancy practices and variations in hospital length of stay. The publication of these data is focusing attention on variations in practices.

These variations may be the product of patient-case severity, reflect a better quality of care, or be indicators of inefficiency in resource allocation. A central piece of information for trading is information about the quality of care in terms of process (was the hospital clean and were post-operative infections as low as possible?) and outcome (the duration and quality of life). Outcome data is needed to facilitate contracting; enabling purchasers to identify good providers, and enabling providers to demonstrate their cost-effectiveness. Without such data the system may be cost-driven, to the detriment of patient outcomes. This problem exists in all health-care systems and, without improved outcome data, resource management will remain crude.

Outcome data are also central to the process of prioritization. The purchaser has a central role in identifying the relative costs of producing a desired health outcome from alternative treatments. She has to identify and buy those treatments which meet the local population's health needs (defined earlier as the ability of different patients to benefit from care). However, how can the purchaser build quality assurance into the contracts with providers? Information about post-infection and recurrence rates are relevant, but mortality data are poor, with little record linkage to identify survival duration. The measurement of the quality of survival in terms of physical, psychological, and social functioning is possible (there are many competing quality-of-life instruments (see e.g. Spilker 1990) but such techniques are little used in clinical trials and health-care management.

The quantity and quality of information needed to enable a market to function efficiently is not available. The government's Audit Commission in its annual report (Audit Commission 1991) has noted the weakness of NHS information systems and Sir Roy Griffiths (1991) has also focused on the inadequacy of existing cost, process, and outcome information. Efforts to remedy these inadequacies have not always been well managed. Some of the investment appears to have been spent unwisely, e.g. there has been a failure to define core data sets, to facilitate national collection of data, and a failure to regulate the supply of hardware, which would have produced economies of scale: lower prices and fewer 'cowboys'!

(iv) *Equity and efficiency*: the process of implementing the reforms has been rapid and uneven. What is their purpose? Mrs Thatcher argued at the Conservative Party Conference in October 1982 that: 'The principle that adequate health care should be provided for all, regardless of their ability to pay, must be the foundation of any arguments for financing the health service.'

This apparent rejection of the liberal objective, and the use of willingness and ability to pay as the means of allocating health-care resources, necessitates careful definition of the non-price alternative. If resources are to be allocated on the basis of need, what is need? One definition of need involves two steps:

1. a technical judgement: which patients would benefit most from care in terms of enhanced duration and quality of life (e.g. quality-adjusted life years or QALYs) per unit of cost?
2. a social judgement: is it worthwhile to treat patients? (How much is society (or its political representatives) prepared to pay to purchase an additional QALY?)

This definition means that purchasers will target resources at those patients who can benefit most: resource allocation will be efficient. It is likely that the capacity of different social groups to benefit will differ. As a consequence whilst resources may be used to maximize health gains, they may increase inequalities in health. How much is society prepared to use resources inefficiently to achieve equity goals? The equity effects of developing competition on the supply side are important but ignored. The achievement of greater technical efficiency (allocating resources in relation to the marginal product of health care) may disadvantage vulnerable and marginal groups. How are efficiency gains and equity to be traded off? How is equity to be defined?

(v) *Creating and sustaining a market*: the NHS has been cheap to administer—less than 5 per cent of total costs were spent on NHS management in the NHS in the 1980s, compared to in excess of 15 per cent in the USA and in the UK private sector. In the first few years of the reforms it is 'guesstimated' that an additional £1,000 million has been spent on information technology and increased managerial inputs. That the cost-effectiveness of this expenditure is as unknown as the opportunity cost (in terms of patient care) is obvious.

CONCLUSIONS

It is very difficult to determine whether the 1989 Conservative reforms of the NHS were successful, particularly as no attempt was made to evaluate them systematically. Thatcher's Government was confused about its policy goals and provided little guidance about how it would judge the 'success' of the reforms. Many of the reforms were structural, with imprecise definition of process and outcome effects.

What has been the impact of each of the reforms proposed in the 1989 White Paper?

Reform proposed	*Achievement*
1. Delegation of decision-making to the local level.	Local management feels empowered but constrained by advice to limit competition (retain in a 'steady state' rather than switch expenditures to reflect comparative advantage).
2. Creation of NHS Trust hospitals with greater managerial discretion.	Trusts were created with discretion which was restricted (e.g. capital) and left these bodies better managed but with little more freedom than managers of other NHS hospitals.
3. Funding to follow the patients.	It did, but with its policy of 'steady state', the government

	tired to limit patient movements so reducing the incentive for providers to be efficient.
4. Reduction of waiting times and improvement of the quality of service.	Waiting times remain a major problem. All purchasers reduced waiting time to two years maximum by April 1992 by central management dictat and increased poorly targeted funding.
5. Improvement of patient services, GPs applying for their own budgets.	GP budget-holders were created in 1991 and 1992. The 'patient pool' may be inadequate to manage the population risks and these agencies duplicated the purchaser role. Consideration was given of extending these budgets to cover maternity and community nursing services. There was little monitoring of performance and the funders were funded liberally to ensure initial viability.
6. Reduction and reform of managerial bodies.	The reform has had unknown benefits but has apparently increased managerial time to focus on resource allocation and improving performance.
7. Medical audit of cost, process, and outcome.	Little is known of the effects of audit. It is suspected that it is focused on process and there is some reluctance to share audit information with managers. There were significant investments in audit (e.g. £48 million in England in 1991–2).

There has been a shift in power with management becoming potentially more influential in resource allocation. However no attempt has been made to evaluate this major social experiment, let alone set criteria by which its 'success' can be measured. The reformed structures of the NHS have inherited their management personnel and they are of uneven quality, unassisted by systematic investment policies in human capital (training and education). The NHS, following the disbandment of the Red Army, may be the largest employer in Europe. This key resource is both poorly trained and ill-informed, thus ensuring that the likely benefits of any reforms will be limited. Such defects may be remedied in time but the politicians are anxious for immediate benefits ('a quick fix') which, if absent, may generate demand-side reform and the erosion of the UK NHS.

There appears to be an international consensus, seen in the USA, the Netherlands, the UK, and elsewhere that 'the problem' is a supply-side issue which can only be resolved by 'competition'. The US term for this approach is 'managed competition'. In the UK, the Conservative reforms created regulated competition. A change of government may remove the word 'competition' but continue the focus on management. Whether decision-making is centralized or decentralized, decision-makers need information and incentives to improve resource allocation and better match inflating health-care needs with limited health-care provision. Central to the task of management is outcome measurement. These data are central, not only to inform provider and purchaser choices, but also to assist with prioritization. Cost and outcome data, together with vigorous management and incentives to induce the adoption of efficient practices throughout the NHS, are the way forward regardless of which political party forms the government.

Some progress towards this goal was made by the 1989 reforms. However this progress was limited. Furthermore what appeared to be very radical reforms, were watered down. Perhaps the net effect of these efforts has been modest but this is a familiar outcome, as one of the Roman Emperor Nero's administrators pointed out:

> We trained very hard, but it seemed that every time we were beginning to form up into teams, we would be reorganized. I was to learn later in life that we tend to meet any new situation by reorganizing, and a wonderful method it can be for creating the illusion of progress, while producing confusion, inefficiency and demoralization. (Caius Petronius (AD 66))

References

Anderson, T. F., and Mooney, G. (eds.) (1990), *The Challenge of Medical Practice Variations*, London: Macmillan.

Audit Commission (1991), *Report and Accounts for the Year Ended 31st March 1991*, London: HMSO.

Bevan, G., Holland, W., Maynard, A., and Mays, N. (1988), *Reforming the UK Health Care System to Improve Health*, York: Centre for Health Economics (York) and St Thomas's (London).

Birch, S., and Maynard, A. (1986), 'The RAWP review: RAWPing primary care: RAWPing the United Kingdom', Discussion Paper 19, Centre for Health Economics, University of York.

Black, A. D. (1986), *An Anthology of False Antitheses*, Rock Carling 1984 Fellowship, London: Nuffield Provincial Hospitals Trust.

Cochrane, A. L. (1972), *Effectiveness and Efficiency*, London: Nuffield Provincial Hospitals Trust.

Culyer, A. J., Maynard, A., and Posnett, J. (eds.) (1990), *Competition in Health Care: Reforming the NHS*, London: Macmillan.

Department of Health (1989*a*), *Working for Patients*, Cmnd 555, London: HMSO.

—— (1989*b*), *Caring for People: Community Care in the Next Decade and Beyond*, Cmnd 849, London: HMSO.

Enthoven, A. C. (1985), *Reflections on the Management of the National Health Service*, Nuffield Provincial Hospitals Trust, Occasional paper 5, London.

Fuchs, V. (1984), 'Rationing health care', *New England Journal of Medicine*, Dec. 18.

Griffiths, R. (1991), 'General Management in the NHS: 7 Years of Progress', Audit Commission Lecture.

Hughes, R. G., Hunt, S. S., and Luft, H. S. (1987), 'Effects of surgeon volume and hospital volume on the quality of care in hospitals', *Medical Care*, 25/6: 489–503.

Kahn, K. L., Keeler, E. B., Sherwood, M. J., Roger, W., Rubenstein, L. V., Reinisch, E. J., Draper, D., Kosecoff, J., and Brook, R. H. (1990), 'Comparing outcomes of care before and after the implementation of the prospective payment system', *Journal of the American Medical Association*, 264: 1969–73.

Kind, P. (1988), The design and construction of Quality of Life measures, Discussion Paper No. 43, Centre for Health Economics, York: University of York.

—— (1990), Outcome measurement using hospital activity data: Deaths after surgical procedures, *British Journal of Surgery*, 77/12: 1399–402.

Klein, R. (1983), *The Politics of the National Health Service*, London: Longman.

Ludbrook, A., and Maynard, A. (1980), 'Applying the resource allocation formulae to the constituent parts of the UK', *Lancet*, 1: 85–7.

Maynard, A. (1985), 'Performance incentives', in G. Teeling-Smith (ed.), *Health, Education and General Practice*, London: Office of Health Economics.

—— (1991), 'Incentive contracts', in G. Lopez-Casanoves (ed.), *Incentives in Health Systems*, Berlin: Springer.

Priestman, T., Bullimore, J. A., Godden, T. P., and Deutsch, G. P. (1989), 'The Royal College of Radiologists fractionation study', *Clinical Oncology*, 1: 39–46.

Rivett, G. (1986), *The Development of the London Hospital System 1823–1982*, London: King's Fund.

Robinson, J., and Luft, H. (1988), 'Competition and the Cost of Hospital Care, 1982–86', *Journal of the American Medical Association*, 260: 2676–81.

Scott, A., and Maynard, A. (1990), 'Will the new GP contract lead to cost effective medical practice?', Discussion Paper 82, Centre for Health Economics, University of York.

Sen, A. K. (1987), *On Ethics and Economics*, Oxford: Basil Blackwell.

Smith, A. (1776) (1976), *An Inquiry into the Nature and Causes of a Wealth of Nations*, Oxford: Clarendon Press.

—— (1790) (1976), *A Theory of Moral Sentiments*, Oxford: Clarendon Press.

Spilker, B., Molinek, F. R., Johnston, K. A., Simpson, R. L., and Tilson, H. H. (1990), 'Quality of Life, bibliography and indexes', *Medical Care*, suppl., 28 Dec., 12.

Van de Ven, W. (1989), 'A future for competitive Health Care in the Netherlands', NHS Occasional Paper No. 9, Centre for Health Economics, University of York.

Woodward, C. A., and Stoddart, G. L. (1990), 'Is the Canadian health care system suffering from abuse: A commentary, *Canadian Family Physician*, 36: 283–9.

4

Regulatory Reform in Higher Education in the UK: Incentives for Efficiency and Product Quality

MARTIN CAVE*, RUTH DODSWORTH,† AND DAVID THOMPSON‡

1. INTRODUCTION

The last decade has seen a series of significant changes in the funding, organization, and regulation of higher education in the UK. Whilst the objectives and motivations of the changes in higher education have been multifaceted (see, for example, Kogan and Kogan 1983), it seems clear that they share some common goals with the wider programme of public-sector reforms—goals motivated by concern with the contribution which the (then) public-sector institutions could make to the health of the UK economy and shaped by a belief that these institutions were failing to perform effectively (see, for example, Moore 1983). It was suggested variously that the public-sector bodies were poorly managed, lacked clear objectives, or had been captured by their work-forces.

Similarly, in relation to higher education, the minister then responsible, William Waldegrave, argued in November 1982 that the origin of the changes in funding at the beginning of the 1980s 'lies in the failure of the higher education sector over the last 13 years, and more, to demonstrate decisively its claim to protected share of taxpayers' money', whilst in the 1985 Green Paper (*The Development of Higher Education into the 1990s*) the government set out the basis for its policies in the following terms: 'the government believes that it is vital for our higher education to contribute more effectively to the improvement of the performance of the economy.'

* Dean, Faculty of Social Sciences, Brunel University.

† Previously a Research Assistant at the Centre for Business Strategy, London Business School.

‡ Previously a Senior Research Fellow at the Centre for Business Strategy, London Business School.

Helpful comments on an earlier draft of this article (in *Oxford Review of Economic Policy*, 8/2) came from Peter Dolton, John Kay, Tim Jenkinson, Ken Mayhew, and Daniel Storey. The authors are grateful to the Gatsby Foundation for financial support and to Ken Cooper for research assistance: the usual disclaimer applies. The article covers events to 1992.

Our objective in this article is to examine these changes in higher education policy using methods drawn from the extensive literature on economic regulation, as it applies to enterprises in either public or private ownership (see, for example, Vickers and Yarrow 1988, or Cave 1991*a*). We will be particularly interested in considering the consequences of the reforms for incentives to efficiency in the production of education services—given the government's apparent concern that the sector has been underperforming—and we will also be concerned with incentives to maintain the quality of output, which has attracted widespread interest and concern in higher education and, more recently, in other publicly provided services. It should be noted that we will not be directly concerned in this article with either the level of funding for higher education or the breakdown of funding between public and private sources.

It may be useful at this stage to summarize our basic argument. We characterize the behaviour of higher education institutions (HEIs) as emerging from the interaction between the institutions' objectives (themselves not uniform across any institution), the market framework within which HEIs operate, and the regulatory constraints to which they are subject. We show that these latter have changed considerably over the past decade, with the expansion of competition for private funding of higher education and the introduction of (quasi) competition for public funding, and that these shifts in regulation have been associated with changes in the internal structure of institutions. We expect these changes to have a positive impact upon productivity, and in the article we consider what evidence exists of such effects.

Accordingly, the plan of the article is as follows. Following this introduction, we begin in Section 2 by considering the objectives of higher education institutions. As non-profit-making organizations their behaviour will be determined both by the objectives of their staff, and by the external constraints imposed by the market conditions and the regulatory conditions which they face. These external constraints are the subject of Section 3. The reforms in higher education can be characterized—very loosely—as progressively increasing the competition which universities face in generating income from the outputs which they supply. This has arisen as a result both of changes in the composition of output—with marketed courses increasing in importance—and of changes in the product market conditions faced in supplying particular outputs (for example, in relation to research grants). In parallel the system of financial regulation has—again very loosely—shifted from one which accommodated differing levels of costs—through deficit funding—to one which offered lower-cost institutions positive rewards by facilitating their expansion.

The economic theory of regulation predicts that these regulatory changes would be followed both by changes to universities' internal organizational structures and by changes in performance, and this is the subject of the next two sections of the article. In Section 4 we consider internal structure and, in particular, the specific policy initiatives which have sought to change the way in which the institutions organize their affairs. Section 5 considers the costs of supplying higher education services. We begin by considering economies of scale. Although the evidence is weak, it is likely that most UK universities are operating at, or above, minimum efficient scale. To this extent, the opportunities for realizing unexploited scale economies are probably limited, although there are no doubt individual departments which are below efficient size. Correspondingly, the changes in financial regulation will probably result in only limited restructuring. The implications for X efficiency are likely to be more material. Evidence on this is extremely sparse. However, cross-sectional studies of institutions' costs, adjusted for output mix, show some considerable variation, suggesting prima facie scope for efficiency improvements.

Analysis of trends in the aggregate levels of costs and productivity in the UK university sector shows that productivity growth has been comparatively slow over the decade to 1988/9. However, in 1989/90 (the most recent year for which complete data is available) there has been a significant reduction in real unit costs. Together with forecasts which indicate a similar shift in 1990/1, these results suggest that the most recent regulatory reforms have had their intended effect.

However, central to any assessment of universities' performance must be consideration of the quality of their output. Whilst there is no direct evidence of quality being eroded as productivity has been increased—in fact the proportion of graduates achieving first-class degrees has progressively increased—we note in Section 6 that existing methods of quality control in the universities are essentially self-regulatory. We contrast these methods with the greater degree of external regulation in the polytechnics and colleges. We argue that the introduction of incentive mechanisms which exert a more powerful motivation to reduce costs will make self-regulation of quality an increasingly less appropriate solution.

The final section draws together our discussion and considers its implications.

2. THE OBJECTIVE FUNCTION OF HIGHER EDUCATION INSTITUTIONS

Universities in the UK are independent self-governing organizations whose autonomy is guaranteed by a variety of individual Charters and Statutes. They are, however, subject to parliamentary accountability as far as public money is concerned, and depend on the State for substantial funds for teaching and research. Internally they are governed by

Councils, which include a majority of lay representatives, and Senates, comprising academic staff. In most cases the Council is formally the superior body and Senates concentrate on academic matters.

Until 1989, polytechnics and colleges were under the direct control of local authorities, although much of their revenue came from central government. Since 1989, with the establishment of the Polytechnics and Colleges Funding Council, these institutions too are governed by Councils or Boards of Governors. For reasons of convenience, some institutions of both types have chosen to set themselves up as companies limited by guarantee, but this variation does not make much essential difference to modes of decision-taking or incentives.

HEIs in the UK are thus a variant of the familiar not-for-profit organization (NPO) (James and Rose-Ackerman 1986). There is no residual claimant on their profit stream with an incentive to maximize the gap between revenue and costs. Instead, like other NPOs, their behaviour is the result of interaction between the market conditions and regulatory environment which they face and the objectives which flow from the internal management or bargaining structure of the organization.

There is an extensive literature devoted to NPOs, which provides a basis for modelling higher education institutions as either labour-managed co-operatives or as public enterprises pursuing managerial goals. In each case we first assume a 'team' model in which all members of the institution share the same objectives. The model is then widened to embrace differences of objectives among organizational subdivisions—departments.

Labour-managed co-operatives have been the subject of much economic analysis following the original work by Benjamin Ward (1958) on the firm in Illyria. The application of the concept to HEIs originates with James and Neuberger (1981), although the same analysis has been fruitfully applied to health care, with hospitals regarded as physicians' co-operatives (Pauly and Redisch 1973). When applied to firms selling a tradable output, the convention has been to adopt maximization of net revenue per head as the co-op's objective function. This maximand yields now well-known results: persistent income differences among firms when barriers to entry (and exit) exist; where they do not, a long-run convergence to the perfectly competitive equilibrium, as new firms enter industries where net incomes are above average and drive down the price of output; perverse short-run responses, including downward-sloping supply curves; and sensitivity of the results to assumptions made concerning the capacity to monitor effort (Bonin and Putterman 1987).

In the UK, the notion of a labour-managed HEI finds its most obvious reflection in Oxbridge colleges, where the fellows are typically self-governing both in law and in practice. As such institutions operate on different pay scales from the rest of the system, we observe the expected equilibrium wage differences. But James and Neuberger, in application to the United States, argue that all HEIs (and not just those which are formally self-governing) are effectively captured by their academic staffs, who run them in their own interests. To employ a phrase used at the foundation of another co-operative (United Artists), the lunatics have taken over the asylum.

With given pay scales, it is, in most instances, impossible for academic staff to divide among themselves the net revenue of the institution. Like all employees with objective functions which differ from the preferences of their enterprise's managers or owners, they can, however, take rents associated with their employment in other forms. One familiar route is through discretionary expenditure; for example, by excessive expenditure on travel and entertainment or by employing excessive numbers of auxiliary staff such as secretaries. Another obvious form of dividing surplus product is through shirking. With its long time horizons, much academic work is difficult in principle to monitor from day to day, and few institutions rigorously seek to measure the input of working time. Instead, attempts are made—often rather unsuccessfully—to monitor outputs.

However, James and Neuberger attach relatively little weight to this phenomenon and treat distortion of the output mix as the dominant form of conduct in a labour-managed university. They assume that academics have a fairly uniform preference ordering over the various parts of their activity, preferring research to teaching. Moreover, within teaching they prefer graduate courses or small advanced undergraduate courses. They also prefer higher-quality students. The effect of labour management is thus to entrench a preference for research over teaching within the institution.

The extent to which this preference can be taken depends upon relative prices, the strength of preference for research and advanced teaching over basic teaching, the reward system within the institution, and the degree to which an individual's inputs can effectively be monitored. Clearly if the institution received the same revenues irrespective of how many students were taught, then a labour-managed university of the kind postulated by James and Neuberger would admit no students and devote itself entirely to research and leisure. Equally, if it were impossible to monitor individual teaching contributions, then a rational faculty would do no teaching. Although there have been instances where universities in the UK have continued to receive revenues in respect of students which they have not recruited, this is the exception rather than the rule. And many departments adopt an egalitarian 'points system' for measuring input of teaching and administrative hours in order to prevent shirking of teaching responsibilities.

However, in the USA the market for undergraduate and graduate students is relatively competitive. In these circumstances it might be expected that if students paid more than the stand-alone cost of teaching to mixed output (i.e. teaching and research) universities, then the latter would lose market share to specialized teaching-only institutions; this follows from the definition of cross-subsidy proposed by Faulhaber (1975). The fact that they do not implies that Faulhaber cross-subsidies do not apply (see Rothschild and White 1991). Moreover, any apparent cross-subsidies may fail to reflect the fact that research may benefit teaching, either directly, or by attracting better-quality staff, or by signalling a better quality of graduate.

In contrast, in the UK the major part of universities' income comes from government funding. This suggests that the regulatory controls which govern this funding will be important to understanding institutions' behaviour. Recent developments in public enterprise theory—in which the enterprises are essentially characterized as managerially driven firms subject to a set of market and regulatory constraints—provide a basis for predicting the incentives associated with alternative regulatory regimes (see, for example, Rees 1984, or Bos 1988). Following this approach we would characterize the institutions' objectives function in terms of the usual range of managerial goals—concern with the size of the institution, the scale of resources commanded, preferences for particular types of output, disinclination for certain types of efficiency-enhancing activity, etc.—and behaviour would be determined by the interaction of these objectives and the relevant regulatory constraints.

To be more precise, a model of a public firm can be constructed in which its maximand has arguments reflecting output (entering positively) and effort (entering negatively). In addition the enterprise is required to make a specified profit (which might be framed as a required rate of return on its assets). Information asymmetries between institutions and regulators mean that the severity of the budget constraint will depend in part upon the institution's actual levels of costs and investment. Thus a firm which accumulates a high capital stock or builds up a history of inefficient performance may benefit in terms of receiving a less rigorous profit target. In the term introduced by Kornai (1980) there will be a soft budget constraint.

A public enterprise regulated in this way will, on normal assumptions, respond to a tightening in the budget constraint by increasing cost-reducing effort. The regulator can also influence the institution's input of effort if it can credibly refuse to relax the profit target as the capital stock rises or as it accumulates observations reflecting a low level of effort. Here, access to comparative observations of similar institutions enables the regulator to introduce yardstick comparisons (see Shleifer 1985) and thus enhance its information and hence the credibility of its bargaining position.

Whilst extremely stylized, these models capture some of the essential features of the changes made to the regulatory arrangements over the last decade. It is to discussion of these changes that we now turn.

3. CHANGES TO THE FINANCIAL REGULATION OF HIGHER EDUCATION

In discussing the evolution of the regulatory framework we will find it useful to distinguish three separate periods: the framework operating at the end of the 1970s, the present framework, and the period of transition in the 1980s between the two. For a more detailed account of this evolution (see Becher and Kogan 1992).

1970s Structure

Universities engage in multiple activities which are not all subject to the same market conditions. The two main activities are education (teaching) and research. In addition they engage in consultancy work, offer short courses, and provide conference and library facilities (see Table 4.1). Universities educate students to varying levels of attainment (such as first degree level, Ph.D., etc.) in many different subjects. In the UK final consumers (i.e. students) do not in general purchase the product directly. Instead places are bought for them by funding councils and then allocated to institutions. But this mode of distribution, increasingly common in the UK public sector, permits some degree of competition among suppliers in a 'quasi-market' (Le Grand 1991; Glennerster 1991).

However, in the 1970s education was (largely) non-marketed. There was some non-price competition in attracting students (as each student generated fees for the institution) and competition for staff in the academic labour market. For students this competition was probably based on a mixture of reputation, required entry standards, and location, as well as other factors. Reputation also played a part in recruiting academic staff together with opportunities to conduct research and to gain promotion, etc. Salaries were fixed according to a national pay scale and contained few discretionary elements within each scale.

Research was also largely non-commercial. The majority of funds for research came from the block grant received from the government. Universities could compete for additional funds in the form of grants, mainly from Research Councils, but also from other sources such as charitable bodies and government departments. However, these additional funds formed only a small proportion of the income used for research.

Universities engaged in some commercial activities, such as provision

TABLE 4.1. General recurrent income by source (percentages of total)

Year	Total recurrent income (£m)	In real terms (1988/9 prices) (£m)	Exchequer grants	Fees, full-time		Fees, part-time	Research training and other support grants	Endowments, subventions	Computer board grants	Other general recurrents	Research grants and contracts	Other services rendered
				Home rates	Other rates							
1975/6	708	2,096	82.0*	—	—	—	—	1.0	—	2.0**	12.0	3.0
1978/9	1,003	2,112	62.5	14.2	2.8	0.4	0.3	1.0		1.5	12.7	2.6
1981/2	1,720	2,507	59.1	14.7	4.2	0.4	0.3	0.9	0.8	3.3	12.9	3.4
1985/6	2,295	2,710	57.2	7.2	5.4	0.6	0.4	1.2	0.8	3.8	17.9	5.5
1988/9	3,081	3,081	52.6	6.4	5.6	0.7	0.3	1.5	0.7	5.0	20.4	6.9

* No distinction. ** Other. Data for more recent years is not available on a comparable basis.

Source: *University Statistics*, vol. 3, *Finance*, various issues, Universities Funding Council/ University Grants Committee.

of conference facilities, consultancy work, short courses, library services, and selling gifts. However, these formed only a small proportion of an institution's total recurrent income (see Table 4.1), the vast bulk of which came from the government in the form of a block grant which could be spent as each institution wished.

The University Grants Committee (UGC) was responsible for distributing the total grant the government made available for the university sector. The distribution was largely made on the basis of planned student numbers for each university, which in turn was based to some extent on the capacity of an institution's buildings (at least in the period 1972–7). Although research was financed through a dual-funding system which consisted of the proportion of UGC block grant allocated to research and Research Council grants—the latter were relatively small-scale (see Table 4.1).

Two aspects of this funding system are particularly relevant. First, although the UGC issued guidelines as to how the grant should be spent, universities were not required to take such advice. Second, under this system, small and financially weak institutions received a higher proportion of grant than their student numbers would otherwise justify. The UGC (1984), in advice to the government in September 1984, described the resulting system as follows: 'In other words, it was a deficiency grant.' A five-year planning period (the quinquennial system) was used and the grant 'reduced to take account of universities' "other income" over the previous five years'.

Thus in the decade beginning in the mid-1960s as continued expansion of the university sector took place, financial controls from the centre were weak. Most university activity was grant-supported, the grant being related to both institutions' achieved costs (the 'deficiency' aspect) and their expected output (student numbers). Given this *ex post* elastic regulatory framework, we would expect that incentives to X efficiency within the universities would be weak and that there would be considerable discretion in allocating resources between teaching and research.

Transition

The quinquennial grant-allocation system collapsed in the late 1970s in the face of inflation and problems in accurately forecasting student demand. From 1975 onwards financial constraints were placed on the university system in line with the constraints in funding across the public sector. Hopes for level funding were not fulfilled, as dramatic cuts in government funding were announced in 1981 and finance remained tight throughout the decade.

As a result, universities sought income from other sources, and the balance between sources of income and the nature of university activities shifted. As the overall level of exchequer grant was reduced in real terms, the proportion of grant-supported and non-marketed activities decreased, while more commercial sources of income increased proportionately. Similarly, income from research grants and contracts significantly increased, raising the competitiveness of the conditions under which research was conducted. The proportion of income from commercial activities such as short courses more than doubled for the university system as a whole between 1981/2 and 1988/9 (see Table 4.1). Educating overseas students also became a more commercial activity as the exchequer subsidy was ended: from the academic year 1980/1 increased levels of tuition fees could be charged to overseas students. Overall exchequer funding fell from 82 per cent to 60 per cent of total recurrent income between 1975/6 and 1988/9, whilst income from industry, overseas student fees, and research grants rose from 15 per cent to 33 per cent of total recurrent income between the same years.

Furthermore, the financial stringency led to the basis of the exchequer grant allocations becoming, of necessity, more selective. The 1981 cuts were made on a selective basis, but little information was disclosed concerning the criteria adopted. This created a demand from universities for clearer information about the basis used for allocating the grant. By the mid-1980s it was made clear that practice had switched from a system of deficiency financing to one of core funding. The grant remained a block grant and funds for teaching and research were not explicitly distinguished. But from the mid-1980s they were allocated on separate identifiable bases (although the first year for which this is clear is the academic year 1986/7).

In 1985/6 the UGC carried out a research selectivity exercise which involved the determination of a research rating for each subject group or cost centre in every university. Although the method for arriving at the research ratings was severely criticized, from the 1986/7 allocation onwards these ratings became progressively more important in calculating the research component of the block grant. Another research selectivity exercise was conducted in 1989, and a third round is being conducted in 1992. In the second half of the 1980s account was taken of external sources of research finance, as it had under the quinquennial system, but with the switch from the concept of deficiency financing to core funding, the ability to attract outside funding was positively, though weakly, rewarded in the UGC allocation.

In calculating the teaching allocation the process was more one of systematization than of transition to (quasi) competition. Although there was agreement that judgements of teaching quality should be used in the allocation process, no satisfactory quantifiable performance indicator was developed for this purpose. The teaching component continued to be allocated on a student load basis, weighted by cost centre, and the main change was that this became more clearly transparent. Value for money and efficiency were stressed and the clamour for indicators to measure performance was met by the publication by the UGC and the Committee for Vice-Chancellors and Principals (CVCP) of annual volumes of management statistics and performance indicators (Cave *et al.* 1991). More detailed, comparative information was thus collected but the data were published in an opaque form and it is unclear what systematic use was made of it.

With the realization that extra exchequer funds would not be forthcoming, universities had greater incentives to cut costs (or to degrade quality—an issue to which we will return) in order to continue their activities. The financial control framework was severely tightened from the later 1970s, and as such, we would expect incentives to efficiency to have increased throughout the period.

The Current System and Prospects for Change

The Education Reform Act of 1988 replaced the University Grants Committee with the University Funding Council (UFC). The UFC has split the grant allocation into funding for teaching and funding for research. Although the grant remains a block grant, which individual universities can distribute as they wish, we note in Section 4 below that universities are increasingly adopting decentralized or divisionalized internal financial procedures in which allocations to departments or faculties depend upon their outputs.

In relation to research, the UFC is continuing selective allocation of this component of the block grant. The proportion of research funds allocated selectively (that is, with reference to the research rankings) is being increased overall relatively to the remainder which is allocated largely by reference to student numbers. However, a proportion of research funds is allocated according to income earned from contract research, rewarding with extra funds those who attract a lot of such research; this proportion is being increased to encourage further income generation from commercial sources. Finally, the balance of resourcing in the dual-funding system has been altered. Fewer research funds are allocated through the block grant and a greater proportion than before will come from the Research Councils and will thus be directly subject to competition between institutions.

In relation to teaching, the first important change has been a substantial increase in tuition fees, with a corresponding decrease in the block grant unit of teaching resource. In 1989/90 about 92 per cent of the total public funding of undergraduate tuition in the UK came from the block grant, with 8 per cent provided through tuition fees. In 1991/2, the block grant constituted only about 70 per cent of this total. Tuition fees are now broadly differentiated by subject, although the new increased tuition fees are still less than the average cost of tuition. The increase in the relative level of tuition fees makes possible the second important change—a move to a more competitive system of grant allocation.

The UFC's first attempt to introduce competition into the supply of student places in universities operated through a tendering system. In 1990 all universities were asked to submit tenders for the number of student places in each cost centre which they would undertake to provide in 1994/5. The tender could take the form of offering to supply *X* places at £*Y* per place, and *Z* further places at £*W* per place, where it was assumed that £*Y* would be at most a 'guide price' set by the UFC, on the basis of average costs, and £*W* would be less than £*Y*. The UFC's intention was to allocate student places for 1994/5 in accordance with tendered prices, subject to a check on quality and subject to an undertaking not to impose upon any institution larger reductions in places and funding than it could assimilate. A gradual transition to the 1994/5 allocation would be made over the years 1991/2 to 1994/5.

In adopting competitive tendering, the UFC was following in the footsteps of the Polytechnics and Colleges Funding Council (PCFC), which introduced competitive tendering in 1989. But whereas the PCFC proposed that tendering should cover a comparatively small proportion of its allocations, the UFC intended that—subject to the qualifications noted above—its full allocation of teaching funds would be allocated competitively.

In the event, the universities responded by declining to tender competitively. Following some encouragement towards collusion by the UFC, 93 per cent of all student places were tendered at the guide price, and only a small number of institutions were prepared to discount those prices. Some possible reasons for this outcome are discussed in the Annex. As a result, the UFC rejected the tenders and chose to adopt a different form of quasi-competitive allocation.

In 1991/2, universities received a specified level of funded student numbers in each cost centre and received grants in respect of these at the guide price. They could if they wished recruit additional students on a 'fees only' basis, but if they failed to fill their funded numbers they might be subject to clawback and to reductions in funded numbers in later years. The UFC has stated that any increases in funded numbers in following years would be made on the basis of each university's relative performance in attracting 'fees only' students in the relevant subject group. The decision process for an institution in deciding whether to exceed its funded numbers was thus a complex one. The institution had to compare the costs of admitting a 'fees only' student with the benefits, both in terms of the initial fee income and any consequent increase in funded student numbers in later years. The latter benefit had to be estimated using both a time discount rate and an allowance to take account of possible changes in the allocation system. Moreover, as universities were to be judged on the basis of their relative performance in each area, they were trying to beat a yardstick the value of which they did not know.

Thus, as we noted in the introduction, the system which emerged had some characteristics of yardstick competition. Competition operates at two levels—in terms of average costs, which determine the guide prices, and in terms of the relative growth in output. The guide price, which determined the grant allocated to a university for a funded student place in a particular subject, was based broadly upon average costs. For each institution the guide price could be treated as exogenous, even though collectively they determined its level. Universities with above average costs would thus be penalized, while those with below average costs would be rewarded.

The second dimension of yardstick competition was in terms of growth rates through the recruitment of unfunded students. The mechanism proposed for adjusting funded student places was intended to reward institutions which offered above average levels of fees-only places. Note that, because this second dimension of yardstick competition was in quantities rather than prices, the prospects for collusive behaviour were more limited.

The general aim of yardstick competition was to generate a set of costs, quantities, and prices which would emerge in a competitive market (Shleifer 1985). However, it should be noted that the system which we have described departed from classical yardstick competition in several respects. In particular, institutions could not be assumed to be profit maximizers and the UFC retained a safety net intended to preserve the position of universities with particularly high costs. The outcome of this process determined the UFC's allocation of resources for 1992/3. The process is, however, likely to be changed in subsequent years.

We have thus described three phases in the regulatory relationship between universities and their funding body. The transitional phase of the 1980s introduced evaluation and accountability into the allocation system. The system implemented for the 1990s introduces elements of competition—both direct and yardstick. The success of these changes depends to a considerable degree upon the internal management structure of universities, and in particular whether the system of incentives and rewards imposed by the funding authority can be translated into corresponding incentives applying to faculties, departments, or individuals. Thus in the next section we discuss the changes which have been made in the internal management structures of higher education institutions.

4. CHANGES TO INTERNAL GOVERNANCE ARRANGEMENTS

An extensive literature, stemming initially from the work of Coase and Williamson, has examined the relationship between firms' organizational relationships and their business performance (see, for example, Thompson and Wright 1988). Two aspects of internal structure which appear particularly relevant are organizational form and management remuneration.

Thus in relation to the former, interest has focused upon the ways in which management responsibility is decentralized and accounted for in large organizations and the comparative merits—of structures which decentralize financial responsibility to business units (the multi-division—or M form—of company organization) and those which centralize decision-making in a unitary or U form. There is a presumption in favour of the former in most, but not all, circumstances (see Cable 1988, for a review). As far as remuneration goes, interest focuses upon the role of incentive pay in attenuating the agency problem which results once ownership and control are separated.

Evidence from the UK's nationalized industries suggests that the organizational arrangements suggested by theory and private-sector practice had been slow in adoption under traditional methods of public-enterprise regulation. However, the regulatory reforms of the last ten years have resulted in a significant shift in organizational arrangements toward those suggested in the literature (see Bishop and Thompson 1992*a*).

In higher education there is also a further issue of importance—the relative power exercised by each institution's management and its academic staff. The *locus classicus* of moves to relocate power in universities is the *Report of the Steering Committee for Efficiency Studies in Universities* (The Jarratt Report, CVCP 1985). This Committee was established to promote and co-ordinate a series of efficiency studies for the management of universities and to report to the Committee of Vice-Chancellors and Principals and the University Grants Committee. Its membership included the Prime Minister's adviser on efficiency.

The aspect of its recommendations of the greatest present interest concerns arrangements for the exercise of power within universities. The Committee proposed a new relationship between university Councils and Senates:

> the decades of expansion up to 1981 placed Senates in the ascendancy in those relationships. It does seem to us that the relative decline in the exercise of influence by Councils has increased the potential for Senates to resist change and to exercise a natural conservatism . . . It may well be that a degree of tension between (Senate and Councils) is necessary in the circumstances now facing universities, and can be creative and beneficial in the long run. That can only happen if Councils assert themselves. (para. 3.51H)

The Committee also emphasized the role of the Vice-Chancellor:

> To enable the institution at least to survive and to seize the opportunities open to it in the future, the Vice-Chancellor will have to adopt a clear role as the executive leader as well—and to have the necessary authority to carry it out. (para. 3.16)

Again:

> The tradition of Vice-Chancellors being scholars first and acting as chairmen of the Senate, carrying out its will rather than leading it strongly, is changing. The shift to the style of chief executive, bearing the responsibility for leadership and effective management of the institution, is emerging and is likely to be all the more necessary for the future. (para. 3.58)

One of the further major recommendations of the Committee, now widely implemented, was the creation of a Planning and Resources Committee, of strictly limited size, reporting to Council and Senate with the Vice-Chancellor as Chairman and with both academic and, in some cases, lay members. Combined with the development of better procedures for monitoring output and budgetary delegation to departments held responsible to the Planning and Resources Committee, this has recentralized the administrative structure and removed at least some of the power of the academic co-operative.

A second, and more conventional, change in internal management in universities in recent years has been the development of financial decentralization—'cost or profit centres'—typically faculties or departments. We are not aware of any systematic study of this change, but observation and anecdotal evidence suggest that many or most universities now practice financial accountability at the level of individual departments. Arrangements differ from institution to institution in the extent to which resources (such as space) are allocated on an internal market, the degree to which internal allocation procedures mimic external payments to the institutions, and the scope for safety nets or cross subsidies. None the less, there is evidence of a clear trend towards use of financial decentralization in internal control.

The final route by which the government has sought to recast internal relations within HEIs is by alterations to the employment structure and the labour contract (Cave 1991*b*, Keep and Sissons 1992). Since 1989 a proportion of the salary settlement for university academics has taken the form of discretionary payments, intended to enable institutions to give further increases to individuals at the discretion of local management, to reward exceptional performance, and to recruit or retain exceptionally scarce or valuable staff. In the first year of operation of the system, 1 per cent of an overall settlement of 7 per cent was allocated in this way; in the second year (1991) a further 1 per cent is discretionary. Results of the first round show that between 10 per cent and 39 per cent of university staff benefited from the discretionary element. In future pay settlements this is to be larger, with the clear intention of establishing better procedures to reward, and implicitly to punish, individual performance.

Simultaneously, attempts have been made to loosen the tenure of academics. The Education Reform Act of 1988 carried a provision that, subject to agreement of appropriate Statutes, university academics appointed or promoted after November 1987 would no longer be immune from redundancy in the event that the institution no longer had need of their services. This would be in addition to the traditional, but rarely used, grounds for dismissal such as incompetence, moral turpitude, etc.

In addition, an attempt has been made to test in the courts the right to tenure enjoyed by those appointed before November 1987. Each university has a different employment contract which confers different benefits upon its academic staff. For this reason, a general assessment of the value of tenure cannot be given. None the less, in the case of one university, the Court of Appeal has recently ruled that the university did not breach its statutes or contract in making a philosophy lecturer redundant. The issue has not been settled yet, as an appeal to the House of Lords is likely. None the less it is clear that as grant mechanisms carrying more powerful incentives are introduced more institutions may take measures of this kind.

Tenure is one of the key analytical concepts involved in labour co-ops. Attempts to make suppliers of labour the residual claimant on net income are undermined by the possibility of dismissal. The partial abolition of tenure neatly illustrates the decline of the co-operative tradition in HEIs in the UK.

5. THE COST OF SUPPLYING HIGHER EDUCATION SERVICES

The consequences of the various changes in regulatory controls which we have outlined will be determined by the cost characteristics of the supply of higher education services. We begin by considering economies of scale and scope; the existence of unexploited economies will condition the effects which the opportunities (and incentives) for expansion provided by the new grant arrangements will have upon the structure of the university sector, in terms of the numbers, size, and specialization of institutions. Next we consider X efficiency and the incentives provided by the new grant arrangements.

There is an extensive literature which suggests the existence of economies of scale in the teaching function in universities; little evidence exists for scale economies in research, although intuition suggests that these may also exist. However, evidence on the minimum efficient scales of HEIs (that is, the size at which no further economies of scale can be realized), shows quite widely varying results. Thus Radner and Miller (1975) found, for undergraduate-only institutions, economies of scale up to enrolment levels of 3,000 to 4,000 students. Applying such evidence to UK universities would suggest that the vast majority operate at, or beyond, minimum efficient scale. However, De Groot, McMahon, and Volkwein (1991) find evidence of scale economies at higher levels of enrolment whilst Cohn, Rhine, and Santos (1989) conclude that the minimum efficient scale for an HEI is an enrolment level of about 30,000 full-time equivalent (FTE) students with research grants of $80 to $100 million. If correct these results suggest significant unexploited scale economies in UK universities. However, the findings are not consistent with much of the US literature. Neither are they consistent with studies based on UK data. Thus Johnes and Taylor (1990) find that differences in unit costs between universities are unrelated to the size of the institution. Similarly, Verry and Davies (1976) find that marginal costs for both graduate and undergraduate students in the UK were generally constant over enrolment levels. The implication is that there are probably few significant scale economies which remain to be exploited at most UK universities although no doubt there are individual departments which are below optimum size and individual universities which have (unplanned) spare capacity.

Theoretical work has identified the conditions under which scope economies between teaching and research might arise (see Nerlove 1972) but empirical results are generally inconclusive. However, Cohn, Rhine, and Santos (1989) show findings which suggest economies of scope exist between teaching and research.

Perhaps the most interesting question relates to evidence on the X efficiency of HEIs. It is often argued that institutions are not cost-minimizers. The polar case of this view is the so-called revenue theory of cost expounded by Bowen (1980). Essentially, in this view HEIs are characterized as raising as much revenue as possible and then undertaking expenditure up to the level set by their revenues. There are, however, obvious objections to this extreme characterization of cost-maximization and there is little empirical evidence to support it.

In respect of UK universities we will first consider evidence on the cross-sectional variation in cost levels between institutions and then consider trends in the level of costs and productivity over the period when the regulatory controls have been subject to change. In the study mentioned earlier, Johnes and Taylor (1990) provide measures of average unit costs for universities for the years 1980/1 to 1987/8. Their measure is defined as 'general expenditure on academic departments' divided by the numbers of full-time equivalent students. This cost measure comprises about 40 per cent of universities total revenue-account expenditure and is the identifiable expenditure category most closely associated with teaching.

They find that unit costs vary widely across institutions although they are relatively stable for institutions over time; for example in 1985/6 from just over £2,000 in some cases to around £4,000 in others (see Table 4.2). Johnes and Taylor found that 70 per cent of this variation could be attributed to differences in subject mix between institutions; unit costs differ significantly between subjects. In Table 4.2 we reproduce the results of an analysis in which they standardize for subject mix. 'Expected cost per student' standardized in this way is compared with universities' actual costs. The comparison shows significant variation, between +25 per cent (UMIST) and –15 per cent (York); however, almost half the universities had a deviation from the average of less than 5 per cent.

This difference between expected and actual cost levels could be interpreted as reflecting differences in efficiency between universities, but obviously this is not the only possibility. Johnes and Taylor test a number of other factors. These include student mix (the proportion of postgraduate students to undergraduate students, the former being potentially more expensive), the type of degree taken (honours or ordinary, undergraduate or research postgraduate, etc.), the age structure and status mix of staff (in general, both the older and the more qualified the greater is the cost), student : staff ratios (SSRs), the level of research activity, and the size of the institution. Johnes and Taylor found only one factor (SSRs) to be unambiguously significant, with the others either insignificant or, for student mix, not robust with respect to small changes in the sample coverage.

Whilst the lack of significance of these other explanatory variables strengthens the interpretation of differences between actual and expected unit costs as differences in efficiency, there remain other factors which could not be included directly in the analysis. One example is the so-called special factors which the guide-price mechanism explicitly takes account of (relating to factors such as the operation of museums, or in some cases nuclear reactors, by individual universities). Another possibility relates to quality considerations—a high negative deviation of actual from expected unit costs could reflect lower quality rather than greater efficiency. Extending the notion of quality to a wider 'quality of life' concept has the same implication. The consequence is that if quality is important in explaining differences between actual and expected unit costs, use of the guide-price mechanism could penalize the worthy. This observation emphasizes the relevance of quality regulation—an issue we turn to in Section 6.

Another possibility relates to the time-scale over which expenditure

TABLE 4.2. Universities average unit costs, 1985/1986

Universities (Great Britain)	Actual cost per student (£)	Expected costs per student (£)	Percentage variation (Actual–Expected)
Aston	2,636	2,946	–10.5
Bath	2,869	3,110	–7.8
Birmingham	3,305	3,293	2.0
Bradford	2,681	2,932	–8.6
Bristol	3,544	3,356	5.6
Brunel	2,885	3,107	–7.1
Cambridge	3,036	2,970	2.2
City	3,150	2,771	13.7
Durham	2,529	2,688	–5.9
East Anglia	2,787	2,584	7.9
Essex	2,305	2,495	–7.6
Exeter	2,534	2,554	–0.8
Hull	2,507	2,465	1.7
Keele	2,487	2,522	–1.4
Kent	2,148	2,375	–9.6
Lancaster	2,776	2,498	11.1
Leeds	3,381	3,307	2.2
Leicester	3,045	3,007	1.3
Liverpool	3,342	3,561	–6.1
London	3,979	3,646	9.1
Loughborough	2,819	3,086	–8.7
Manchester	3,310	3,229	2.5
UMIST	4,006	3,205	25.0
Newcastle	3,274	3,407	–3.9
Nottingham	3,036	3,255	–6.7
Oxford	2,910	2,854	2.0
Reading	3,048	2,958	3.0
Salford	2,786	3,088	–9.8
Sheffield	3,248	3,265	–0.6
Southampton	3,206	3,164	1.3
Surrey	3,325	3,202	3.8
Sussex	2,652	2,740	–3.2
Warwick	2,573	2,497	3.0
York	2,387	2,787	–14.4
Aberdeen	3,202	3,156	1.5
Dundee	3,443	3,466	–0.7
Edinburgh	3,389	3,217	5.3
Glasgow	3,235	3,440	–0.6
Heriot-Watt	2,895	3,161	–8.4
St. Andrews	2,413	2,790	–13.5
Stirling	2,438	2,478	–1.6
Strathclyde	2,637	2,911	–9.4
Wales	2,972	2,941	–2.8

Note: 'Expected costs per student' standardize for subject mix; the calculations show the result if each university supplied its particular subject mix at the UK average level of costs for each subject.

Source: Johnes and Taylor 1990.

TABLE 4.3. Expenditure as a percentage of total recurrent expenditure

Financial year	Total recurrent expend. (£m.)	In real terms (1988/9 prices £m.)	Academic depts.		Academic services		General educational expend.	Admin. and central	Maint. and running	Staff and student facils.	Pensions	Capital expend.	Other recurrent expend.
			General	Specific	General	Specific							
1975/6	696	2,056	62.0*	—	8.0*	—	2.0	7.0	17.0	2.0**	—	2.0	—
1978/9	1,026	2,159	46.4	14.6	8.0*	—	2.5	6.3	17.1	1.6**	0.8	2.0	—
1981/2	1,687	2,459	45.5	15.0	7.4	0.8	2.4	5.7	16.3	2.5	2.3	1.3	0.7
1985/6	2,301	2,716	42.0	20.7	7.1	1.2	2.2	5.6	15.4	2.2	0.8	1.7	1.1
1988/9	3,035	3,035	39.8	24.3	6.6	1.3	2.2	5.7	12.8	1.9	2.6	1.9	0.9

* No distinction. ** Student facilities only. Data for more recent years is not available on a comparable basis.

Source: *University Statistics*, vol. 3, *Finance*: various issues, Universities Funding Council/University Grants Committee.

TABLE 4.4. Higher education: Unit public funding (1981/2 = 100)*

Institutions	1981/2	1982/3	1983/4	1984/5	1985/6	1986/7	1987/8	1988/9	1989/90	1990/1**	1991/2†	1992/3†
Universities (GB)	100	103	104	103	101	100	100	101	98			
Polytechnics and colleges (England)	100	96	91	88	85	87	83	81				
Universities (GB)									100	93	88	86
PCFC									100	92	86	84

* With the introduction of the PCFC sector in 1989/90 a new index has been calculated. ** Provisional. † Estimate.

Source: Government Expenditure Plans: various years.

decisions are evaluated. Managers interested in the long-term welfare of the university will have incentives to look at the long-term costs and benefits of projects, but short-termism may lead some managers to cut costs improvidently. Differences in time-horizons may once again impair the effectiveness of the guide-price mechanism.

It will thus be clear that caution is required in interpreting the observed differences between expected and actual unit costs. However, the results show that these differences are substantial; and, if explained by variations in efficiency, the results suggest considerable scope for efficiency improvement.

Consideration of the trends in universities' expenditures over time (see Table 4.3) shows that these have been shaped by the changes in the composition of output which we discussed in Section 3. We can see a move towards expenditure related to specific services in both departmental and services expenditures, although the trend is most pronounced in the former. Proportionately less seems to be being spent on staff and student facilities, and there has been a reduction in the proportion going to maintenance and running costs. Administration and central services expenditure has remained stable; a possible explanation for this is the increased administration required to provide specific services.

Trends in unit public funding in universities and polytechnics are published in the government's Expenditure Plans, as shown in Table 4.4. For the universities unit public funding is measured as a 'division of total UGC/UFC recurrent grant and tuition fee income for home and EC students by the financial year average of relevant FTE student numbers', whilst for polytechnics the measure is 'a division of their aggregate expenditure by financial year FTE student numbers'. On these measures (real) unit public funding for universities remained at broadly the same level through the period up to 1988/9; in the two most recent years, however, it has fallen—in total by broadly 8 per cent—and further reductions are forecast. For the polytechnics there has been a substantial reduction in real unit costs—broadly 20 per cent over the 1980s—with further reductions projected. Over this period there has also been a substantial increase in enrolment levels from an average of broadly 2,000 to 3,400. Our discussion of scale effects suggests that many polytechnics may have been able to exploit economies of scale over the last decade.

The measures of unit public funding for the universities have been calculated using a measure of income which has fallen as a proportion of the total over the period. In Table 4.5 we consider two alternative measures of the universities' cost performance. The first is based on the measure used by Johnes and Taylor (1990)—departmental recurrent expenditure from general income. As noted earlier this measure reflects broadly 40 per cent of total expenditure. To examine the robustness of these results to cost-allocation procedures we have also considered a

TABLE 4.5. Average unit costs and productivity (1978/9 = 100)

	1978/9	1981/2	1985/6	1988/9	1989/90
First cost measure:					
Real average unit costs (unadjusted for subject mix)	100	107.4	111.5	109.4	101.9
Real average unit costs (adjusted for subject mix)	100	106.9	111.9	111.6	105.2
Ratio of inputs to student numbers (adjusted for subject mix)	100	96.8	98.0	94.6	88.9
Second cost measure:					
Real average unit costs (adjusted for subject mix)	100	104.9	107.4	105.6	104.3
Ratio of inputs to student numbers (adjusted for subject mix)	100	94.7	93.8	87.5	88.0

Source: Authors' calculations using data from *University Statistics*, vol. 3, *Finance*: various issues, Universities Funding Council/University Grants Committee.

second, broader, measure which represents nearer two-thirds of total expenditure. In this, specific income and other fee rates are subtracted from total expenditure. If it can be assumed that income from these services reflect their costs, then this might be regarded as a measure of the stand-alone cost of teaching services. Output is measured by the numbers of full-time equivalent students; as in the case of the cross-sectional comparisons between universities, adjustment is required for changes in the mix of subjects offered.

For each cost definition Table 4.5 shows trends in real unit costs. This is measured as the ratio of the relevant expenditure category to the numbers of full-time equivalent students, expressed at constant prices using the GDP deflator. Also shown is the (inverse) ratio of student numbers to factor inputs; under familiar assumptions (see Muellbauer 1986) factor inputs can be estimated by dividing expenditure by an index of input prices and the universities pay and prices index has been used for this purpose.

The results in Table 4.5 show that over the decade to 1988/9, real unit costs increased by 9.4 per cent, before making allowance for changes in subject mix. Consideration of the latter shows that less expensive courses have increased in importance. When allowance is made for this, average unit costs are estimated to have increased by almost 12 per cent in real terms over the decade. However, the results also show a significant reduction in real unit costs, of broadly 7 per cent in 1989/90, the most recent year for which full data is available. The results for the ratio of inputs to outputs show an essentially similar pattern. Over the course of the decade measured productivity growth has been relatively slow; again there is a more substantial increase in 1989/90. Consideration of results based on our second cost measure shows essentially similar changes in costs and productivity over the period as a whole.

These results suggest two observations. First, there is little to indicate any significant changes in universities' efficiency in the decade leading up to 1988/9. To interpret the changes in measured productivity shown in Table 4.5 as reflecting changes to efficiency we would need to be confident that:

(a) no significant scale economies have been exploitable as a consequence of increased output (broadly 10 per cent over the decade to 1988/9, with a further 6.5 per cent in the year following);
(b) technical change has been slow; and/or
(c) quality changes not captured in measured output have been positive.

Whilst the first of these is consistent with our earlier discussion of likely levels of minimum efficient scale there is only limited evidence, either way, on the latter. Second, however, the results for 1989/90 show a significant increase in measured productivity (and an associated reduction in real unit costs). The data on real unit public funding (Table 4.4) suggests a further significant productivity increase in 1990/1. To the extent that the guide-price system, announced in 1989, and introduced in 1990/1, has been associated with reductions in real unit costs then it can be considered a success. The important issue which this raises, however, is whether quality levels have been maintained as costs have been reduced. It is to discussion of the regulation of quality which we now turn.

6. QUALITY FAILURE AND ITS REGULATION

The issue of 'quality' is pervasive in discussions of higher education policy. Yet what is meant by quality in these discussions often varies with the context. It is useful to distinguish three separate dimensions of quality. The first relates to the final product, that is whether the quality of the degree and its class can be considered reputable and comparable across institutions. The second relates to the quality of the tuition received—that is the process by which undergraduates are brought to a particular level of achievement. The third dimension relates to horizontal quality variation—differentiation in the contents of the course—concerning such things as which combinations of topics are covered. We will begin by considering why higher education institutions may fail to deliver services of appropriate quality. Next we will consider the applicability to higher education of several generic solutions to quality failure before considering the characteristics of the regulatory policies which have been adopted in practice.

Under familiar conditions, competitive markets yield goods and services of appropriate quality (see, for example, Waterson 1984). Failure to provide appropriate quality arises where these conditions are not met—in particular, where there are information asymmetries or where there is imperfect competition. With higher education the key problems are imperfect observability and infrequent purchasing. The significance of these depends, in turn, on the objective functions of the decision-makers in universities. Provided that those concerned seek to maximize an objective function which includes the quality of students' qualifications (that is, if the objective function is motivated by a professional ethic as discussed by Matthews (1991)), then incentives to undersupply quality will be attenuated. However, if the production of undergraduate and graduate degrees is regarded essentially as a business activity which generates a source of revenue then there will be obvious incentives to degrade quality in order to finance research or other preferred activities. A key issue is then whether prospective students can identify this behaviour—by assessing quality—prior to choosing between institutions.

The first dimension of quality, provenance of the degree awarded, can only be judged on the basis of experience. However, the provenance of degrees awarded to previous cohorts of students by different institutions can, in principle, be observed, although the search costs here are likely to be significant. Similar considerations apply to the quality of tuition; whether the tuition provided enables particular students to achieve the class of degree, or realize the career opportunities, of which they are capable, can only be assessed from experience. Again, however, previous cohorts can be observed; failure rates can be studied, as can the class of degrees awarded. However, value added is more difficult to assess, and the prospective student will face high search costs in determining the likely quality of tuition *ex ante*. Furthermore, because each student's progress will depend upon his individual characteristics and effort even *ex post* verification of the quality of tuition received is also problematic.

Our third dimension of quality, that of the construction of the course, is more readily observable prior to purchase. Even here, however, the relative merits of a course for a particular individual are less easily evaluated, although employers will be better able to make an assessment.

The literature suggests a range of solutions to information failures of this type. In the absence of regulation to certify product quality, reputable product brands are likely to become more important in determining consumer choice (see Shapiro 1982). In the university sector this obviously exists in some cases (Oxbridge and LSE are examples).

However, higher education is largely a 'one-off' purchase (or ' twice-off' for those progressing to higher degrees) and the incentives offered by repeat purchasing—in which the purchaser can punish the supplier if quality falls below that expected—are largely absent. Furthermore, there are no clear property rights to established reputations; this means that the usual incentives for incumbent management to protect established reputations—their interest in the value of the business—are absent. To the extent, furthermore, that reputations can be established this will also raise entry costs—because these will now include the sunk costs of establishing a reputation—and these costs are likely to be higher where purchasing is infrequent.

Another familiar solution is the provision of warranties to signal quality and to share the risks of failure between suppliers and purchasers. In higher education, however, there are evident dangers of moral hazard and, as already noted, difficulties in *ex post* verification to establish liability—an observation which also applies to legal redress. Another solution is the establishment of consumer groups (e.g. The Consumers' Association) to measure and report on the quality of goods and services for which consumers have imperfect information. However, there is a problem of gaining unbiased expert opinion and the usual free-rider problem applying to information products exists.

If market mechanisms are unlikely, as this discussion suggests, to resolve satisfactorily the information failures, then this suggests a case for regulatory intervention. This conclusion is reinforced when we consider the distributional issues which arise; information failures in higher education may result in disproportionately high disbenefits to particular individuals.

Regulation could take a number of forms. It may involve requirements for information provision to enhance observability and facilitate the testing of reputation. However, specific expertise may be required to act upon certain types of information whilst some dimensions of quality have experience characteristics. Regulatory intervention could otherwise take the form of establishing standards, for instance for every class of degree, or of validating institutions' processes of quality control. Alternatively, intervention could take the form traditionally adopted for many professional services in the UK—the development of a professional ethic, emphasizing the quality of services supplied, under the umbrella of protection from the competitive or commercial pressures which would otherwise make this unsustainable (see Matthews 1991).

Regulation in Practice

It is this last approach which has been followed in the UK until very recently. Internal self-regulation is the dominant procedure for regulating the quality of university degrees. By its charter and statutes, a university is responsible for its own academic standards, i.e. its judgement of the levels reached by its students. For undergraduate degrees especially, the Reynolds Report shows that there are a large number of examiners, providing some check on standards within universities. Consistency in standards between universities is provided by the external examiner system.

External examiners are appointed as full members of the relevant board of examiners and have two functions: to ensure comparability in similar subjects between institutions (whilst recognizing that courses differ in content), and to provide assurance that the evaluation procedure is fair, i.e. that the students receive the class of degree their examined work deserves. If the former function is performed satisfactorily the problem of distinguishing between degrees awarded by different institutions is eliminated. However, external examiners have a narrow basis for comparison—both the 1984 UGC code of practice and the Council for National Academic Awards (CNAA) recommend that an individual should take on no more than two external examinerships because of the workload involved. Moreover, the external examiner system is uncoordinated and its effectiveness depends in large part upon those appointed as external examiners.

In 1990 the CVCP established an Academic Audit Unit (AAU) with part of its remit to keep under review the external examiner system. In their first Annual Report (AAU 1992) the unit noted that the external examiner system 'is beginning to come under strain'. The unit was particularly concerned as to whether the system could be effective in maintaining consistent national standards and they concluded that 'the time may be approaching when a general inquiry into the working of the external examiner system will be desirable'.

A more formal approach to assuring the quality of the final product has been operated in public-sector higher education. All degree-level courses have to be validated by the Council for National Academic Awards (CNAA) or a university, except that some polytechnics have delegated powers. The Business and Technical Education Council (BTEC) validates sub-degree level courses. The main purpose of CNAA validation is to ensure comparability. An external examiner system also operates in the public sector, although external examiners are only appointed with the CNAA's approval. In those courses validated by a university, standards should in principle be equivalent to those reached in that university, although the identity of the examiners is likely to be different.

The recent Government White Paper *Higher Education: A New Framework* (DES 1991) proposed that polytechnics, on the whole, should become degree-awarding. So, while to date the public sector has had a greater guarantee of comparability from a more centralized system than that of universities, it now appears to be moving towards the universities' structure of self-regulation.

Methods for ensuring the quality of tuition are largely internal, and those outside bodies in existence which have a role in this area concentrate more on checking that the internal mechanisms already in place in universities for this purpose are adequate rather than judging the actual quality of tuition. Under the UGC self-regulation was supplemented by visits from subject subcommittees whose job it was to ensure that departments had the capacity for the work they were programmed to carry out. They could also suggest changes to teaching methods based on comparisons with other institutions. However, the committee system has been criticized as ineffective and, with the advent of the UFC, subject committees were replaced by single academic advisers. Throughout the decade guidance and codes of practice have been produced and initiatives on staff training, development, and appraisal initiatives begun, but direct assessment by outside bodies of the quality of tuition has not been introduced. The recently established AAU comes the closest to this. Its explicit objectives are to judge universities' internal mechanisms for maintaining and monitoring the quality of tuition and in so doing to maintain national standards. A visit to the university is an essential part of the audit.

This audit procedure, however, still falls short of the assessment of the quality of tuition carried out in the public sector by Her Majesty's Inspectorate (HMI). HMI evaluation of the quality of tuition in public-sector institutions is an ongoing process which results in the production and publication of broad gradings for the quality of tuition for each course in each institution. During their evaluation HMI visit the institutions and sit in on classes and lectures and thus use their own qualitative judgements, as well as considering indicators which are quantifiable, such as building space and capital resources. HMI advise on teaching practices and draw their authority from a wide experience of different learning environments and from familiarity with the system.

The CNAA also played a role in this area. It performed a quality-audit function similar to the AAU, monitoring the adequacy of the institutions' internal quality-control mechanisms. Thus, self-regulation of the quality of tuition has quite a substantial role to play in the public sector as well as in the university sector. The difference in the public sector is that there is more external scrutiny. However, as a consequence of the Lindop Report (April 1985), the CNAA adopted a policy of accreditation of the stronger polytechnics. This essentially involved agreeing self-evaluation procedures with the accredited polytechnics. Thus in some polytechnics there is self-regulation of quality in departments/courses by internal mechanisms, with the CNAA reviewing the procedures for quality control within the institution as a whole. This, too, has begun to resemble the university structure, and will do so more closely as the CNAA is abolished and more polytechnics and colleges validate their own degrees.

It is perhaps in ensuring the quality of the structure of the course that universities differ most obviously from the systems employed in the public sector. The system employed in universities has been described as threshold control. This is essentially a high amount of scrutiny in the selection (of both courses and academic staff) but, if implemented or accepted, a trust in those selected, i.e. a lack of scrutiny from then on. Conversely, in the public sector HMI scrutiny, plus the need to obtain and retain external validation of courses, leads to continued review of the course from then on. For instance, any proposed change to a course validated by a university must be notified to that university and approval for it must be sought.

It is clear that methods of quality control adopted by the universities and in the public sector have differed greatly in the degree of external regulation applied, but that they are now moving closer together. In the regulation of the final product universities rely mainly on self-regulation with an external examiner system now backed up by the AAU. Polytechnics and colleges essentially have external validation of courses. Informal peer judgements remain the external check on a reduction in the quality of tuition in the university sector now supplemented by AAU assessment of control procedures. For polytechnics there is more detailed HMI investigation, and there has been CNAA monitoring or accreditation.

The striking feature about all aspects of quality control in the university sector is the limited role of external regulation and corresponding reliance on self-regulation, especially prior to the establishment of the AAU. However, reliance on professional ethics is likely to become increasingly ineffective as a method of assuring quality as the policy reforms erode the protection from competitive and commercial pressures which once sustained this approach. In the new market environment which universities face, the absence of external regulation is likely to result in a greater reliance on quality brands, with associated costs of entry. Furthermore, the 'once-off' nature of most purchasing decisions, and the absence of clear property rights to an established reputation, is likely to mean that quality brands are only a highly imperfect solution. This observation has obvious implications for economic efficiency but in higher education quality failures may also have quite severe distributional consequences.

Both considerations suggest a case for an external structure of quality regulation. Our discussion suggests that this should comprise both external certification (in relation to the provenance of degrees awarded by different institutions, for example), required information provision (to inform prospective students and test reputation), and external assessment of procedures for quality control.

The recent White Paper proposes to establish a single quality unit for universities, polytechnics, and colleges, which will be independent of the new funding councils, and whose job will be to ensure that institutions have adequate control mechanisms in place. In addition, the White Paper proposes the establishment—with funding councils—of a quality assessment unit which will 'evaluate the quality of what is actually provided'. The exact balance which emerges from these proposals—between self-regulation, auditing of internal control procedures, and external comparison of outcomes—still remains to be determined.

7. CONCLUSIONS

Our objective in this article has been to examine the fundamental changes in higher education policy over the last decade, drawing insights from the literature on the regulation of public enterprises. In particular, we have suggested that the changes in the nature of the regulatory system for higher education imposed since 1980 have much in common with concurrent changes made in the system for financing and controlling public enterprises. On this reading, the government has sought to remould the system for regulating higher education according to a model used widely in other areas of the market or non-marketed public sector. The changes which have been implemented, or are in the process of implementation, include in particular:

(a) the introduction of elements of competition in the higher education market (or quasi-market), both through the increasing importance of commercially marketed services and also through competition in the allocation of public funding for research;

(b) a switch from a discretionary (and largely opaque) basis for funding institutions to a transparent model of resource allocation; in relation to research this has involved both the separate identification of universities' funding and explicit measurement or ranking of the research outputs of institutions. In relation to teaching, funding allocations are being implemented through a variant of yardstick regulation in the universities; in the polytechnics, competitive tendering has been used to allocate funds at the margin;

(c) a recasting of internal management arrangements within institutions, intended to remove decision-taking power from academics in favour of chief executives, accompanied by a revised system of financial accountability within institutions and changes in the basis upon which individual academics are paid.

We have argued that these various changes could be expected both to limit any distortion of the output mix in favour of discretionary research activities and also result in incentives to reduce X inefficiency in the supply of services by universities and polytechnics. Certainly cross-sectional studies of the costs incurred by individual universities show a wide range of unexplained variation suggesting prima-facie support for the view that efficiency gains remain to be realized. Productivity growth in the university sector over much of the last decade has been comparatively modest, reflecting the relatively limited opportunities of technical change. However, in the two most recent years, corresponding to the announcement of a new funding regime and its introduction in the 1990/1 academic year, there have been significant reductions in the levels of real unit costs and corresponding increases in measured productivity.

These observations raise three groups of issues in particular. The first relate to the (quasi) yardstick system of guide prices. Measured against the immediate consequences for costs and productivity, this must be rated a considerable success, mirroring the consequences of the analogous shifts in nationalized industry regulation (see Bishop and Thompson 1992*b*). However, if it is to be effective in securing further productivity change then this will require both the progressive phasing out of safety nets for individual institutions and also the sequential adjustment of the guide prices to reflect observed changes in the average level of costs in each subject area. Furthermore, to avoid perverse outcomes the 'special factors' built into the grant calculations for each institution should be capable of reflecting exogenous factors not directly captured in the guide price.

It is also important that cost reduction is not achieved through (unintended) quality shaving and the second group of issues relate to the regulation of quality. The changes in financial regulation, as they act to incentivize cost reduction, are equally likely to place strain on existing—essentially self-regulatory—methods of assuring quality. This point is recognized in the first report of the CVCP's Academic Audit Unit. We consider that the development of more formal external regulation will be essential both to securing the effectiveness of the changes in financial regulation, but also to informing (prospective) students' choices in what will become, increasingly, an education system which is demand driven.

This leads to the third group of issues. Whilst our focus in this article has been upon the consequences of the various policy reforms for productive efficiency, it will be clear that they also have allocative implications. Most obviously these relate to the levels of public expenditure on higher education, an issue discussed in the Assessment. But the policy changes which we have discussed also have implications for the determination of research priorities—which will become increasingly determined through the allocation of specific funding—and for the mix of subjects studied, which will become increasingly driven by the preferences of prospective students. The important issues which this raises relate to the forms of public policy intervention considered most appropriate in what may turn out to be, at least in the first instance, highly imperfect markets.

ANNEX: WHY DID THE UFC TENDERING EXERCISE FAIL?

We noted in the text at Section 3 the abandonment of the UFC's attempts to introduce competitive tendering for student places in universities following the receipt of (almost) uniform bids. In contrast the PCFC, which put 5 per cent of its budget out for competitive tender for 1990/1 and 10 per cent for 1991/2, received bids which diverged very substantially. Indeed, so successful was the scheme that in its third year of operation, the polytechnics and colleges sought relief from the rigours of competitive bidding. (For a review of the PCFC scheme, see London Economics 1991.) This annex considers possible explanations for the difference in outcomes.

One major difference between the two schemes relates to their size and scope. The UFC proposed putting all student places out to tender from 1994/5, subject to safeguards concerning quality of output and speed of adjustment. The PCFC, on the other hand, assigned only a small proportion (5 per cent or 10 per cent) of its funds to competitive tendering, and explicitly tempered the rigours of price competition by making allowance for quality differences and by providing for an adjustment path. The process thus assumed considerably more significance for the universities, the very existence of some of which appeared to be threatened. It was thus rational for some universities to devote time and resources to seek to neutralize its effects.

Within this atmosphere of concern and hostility, opportunities for collusion multiplied. These operated at various levels. There was no unanimity at the UFC concerning the merits of the scheme, and some of its officials encouraged the placing of bids predominantly at the guide price—a figure published by the UFC for each discipline and based loosely on average cost. This formed a natural focal point for collusive behaviour. At the same time, the Committee of Vice-Chancellors and Principals encouraged an information exchange. Universities were asked to indicate anonymously in advance the size and level of their intended bids. Finally, attempts were made at the level of individual cost centres and subject groups to oppose competitive tendering. Many of these relied upon moral suasion, but in some cases the possibility of sanctions was invoked. For example, a professional organization responsible for accrediting degrees wrote to university departments indicating that any discounting of the guide price might provoke an examination of the quality of teaching provided, possibly leading to withdrawal of accreditation.

A second reason relates to the relative complexity of the UFC scheme, which involved tendering at two separate prices. Had the UFC decided to minimize the costs of providing a given number of places, or of matching its demand curve, its decision rule would have been simply to find the university which offered the lowest average price on the total number of student places which it offered, and contract for them all. It would then find the university with the next lowest average price and contract for all of those, too. The process would continue until the average cost of contracting with an additional university in that subject exceeded the Council's valuation of an extra graduate. If this policy had been adopted, the two-part nature of the tender would have had no significance. But the UFC's commitment to avoid excessive adjustments imposed upon universities the task of anticipating the Funding Council's response to its bids. The difficulty of this task may have encouraged uniform bidding.

A third possible explanation relates to the scope for efficiency savings in universities, as perceived by the institutions themselves. The data in Section 5 above show that average unit cost per student in terms of public funding was remarkably constant throughout the 1980s. The UFC's guide prices were set broadly to equal average cost for each subject group. Accordingly, institutions may have taken the view that the scope for cost cutting was limited, and this may have discouraged competitive tendering.

Finally, as Johnes (1992) has shown, in an auction of the UFC kind, in which bids are required in the form of both price and quantity, in certain circumstances it will be rational for universities to bid the expected market-clearing price (possibly the guide price) and respond to any differences in their cost structures by varying the quantities which they bid.

References

AAU (1992), *Annual Report of the Director, 1990/91*, Academic Audit Unit.

Becher, T., and Kogan, M. (1992), *Process and Structure in Higher Education*, 2nd edn., London: Routledge.

Bishop, M., and Thompson, D. J. (1992*a*), 'Privatization in the UK: Internal organization and productive efficiency', *Annals of Public and Co-operative Economics*, 2.

—— —— (1992b), 'Regulatory reform and productivity growth in the UK's public utilities', *Applied Economics*, 24: 1181–90.

Bonin, J., and Putterman, L. (1987), *Economics of Co-operation and the Labour-Managed Economy*, London: Harwood.

Bos, D. (1988), 'Recent theories on public enterprise economics', *European Economic Review*, 32: 409–14.

Bowen, H. R. (1980), *The Cost of Higher Education: How Much Do Colleges and Universities Spend Per Student and How Much Should They Spend?*, San Francisco: Jossey Bass.

Cable, J. R. (1988), 'Organizational form and economic performance', in R. S. Thompson and M. Wright (eds.), *Internal Organization, Efficiency and Profit*.

Cave, M. (1991*a*), 'Recent developments in the regulation of former nationalized industries', GES Working Paper No. 115.

—— (1991*b*), 'Breaking the mould: Academic contracts in Europe and the US—the UK case', EEA Paper, mimeo.

—— Hanney, S., and Kogan, M. (1991), *The Use of Performance Indicators in Higher Education*, London: Jessica Kingsley Publishers.

Cohn, E., Rhine, S., and Santos, M. (1989), 'Institutions of higher education as multi-product firms: Economies of scale and scope', *Review of Economics and Statistics*, **71**: 284–90.

CVCP (1985), *Report of the Steering Committee for Efficiency Studies in Universities* (The Jarratt Report).

De Groot, H., McMahon, W. W., and Volkwein, J. F. (1991), 'The cost structure of American research universities', *Review of Economics and Statistics*, **73**/3 (Aug.).

DES (1985), *The Development of Higher Education into the 1990s*, Green Paper on Higher Education, Department of Education and Science.

—— (1991), *Higher Education: A New Framework*, Department of Education and Science.

Faulhaber, G. (1975), 'Cross-subsidization: Pricing in public enterprise', *American Economic Review*, **65**: 966–77.

Glennerster, H. (1991), 'Quasi-markets for education?', *Economic Journal*, **101**/408.

James, E., and Neuberger, E. (1981), 'The university department as a non-profit labour co-operative', *Public Choice*, **36**: 585–612.

—— and Rose-Ackerman, S. (1986), *The Non-Profit Enterprise in Market Economics*, London: Harwood.

Johnes, G. (1992), 'Bidding for students in Britain: Why the UFC auction "failed"', *Higher Education*, 23: 173–82.

Johnes, J., and Taylor, J. (1990), *Performance Indicators in Higher Education*, Oxford: Oxford University Press.

Keep, E., and Sisson, K. (1992), 'Owning the problem: Personnel issues in higher education policy-making in the 1990s', *Oxrep*, 8/2: 67–78.

Kogan, D., and Kogan, M. (1983), *The Attack on Higher Education*, London: Kogan Page.

Kornai, J. (1980), *The Economics of Shortage*, Amsterdam: North Holland.

Le Grand, J. (1991), 'Quasi-markets for social policy', *Economic Journal*, **101**/408.

London Economics (1991), *The PCFC Funding System: A Summary Report*, London.

Matthews, R. C. O. (1991), 'The economics of professional ethic: Should the professions be more like business?', *Economic Journal*, **101**: 737–50.

Moore, J. (1983), *Why Privatize?*, HM Treasury Press Release, 190/83.

Muellbauer, J. (1986), 'The assessment: Productivity and competitiveness in British manufacturing', *Oxford Review of Economic Policy*, **2**/3 (Autumn).

Nerlove, M. (1972), On tuition and the costs of higher education: Prolegomena to a conceptual framework', *Journal of Political Economy*, **80**.

Pauly, N., and Redisch, M. (1973), 'The Not-For Profit hospital as a physicians' co-operative', *American Economic Review*, **63**: 87–99.

Radner, R., and Miller, J. (1975), *Demand and Supply in US Higher Education*, New York: McGraw Hill.

Rees, R. (1984), 'A positive theory of the public enterprise', in M. P. Marchand et al. (eds.), *The Performance of Public Enterprises*, Amsterdam: North Holland.

Rothschild, M., and White, L. (1991), 'The university in the market place: Some insights and some puzzles', *NBER Conference on the Economics of Higher Education*.

Shapiro, C. (1982), 'Consumer information, product quality and seller reputation', *Bell Journal of Economics and Management Science*, **13**: 20–35.

Shleifer, A. (1985), 'A Theory of Yardstick Competition', *Rand Journal of Economics*, **16**: 319–27.

Thompson, R. S., and Wright, M. (eds.) (1988), *Internal Organization, Efficiency and Profit*, Oxford: Alden Press.

UGC (1984), *A Strategy for Higher Education Into the 1990s: The UGC's Advice*, London: HMSO.

Verry, D., and Davies, B. (1976), *University Costs and Output*, Amsterdam: Elsevier.

Vickers, J., and Yarrow, G. (1988), *Privatization: An Economic Analysis*, London: MIT Press.

Ward, B. (1958), 'The firm in Illyria: Market syndication', *American Economic Review*, **48**: 566–89.

Waterson, M. (1984) *Economic Theory of the Industry*, Cambridge: Cambridge University Press.

5

The Impact of Competition on Pricing and Quality of Legal Services

SIMON DOMBERGER* AND AVROM SHERR†

The legal profession in England and Wales has held an effective monopoly over conveyancing services since the beginning of the nineteenth century. Conveyancing is the term which describes the legal work associated with buying and selling real estate property. It covers the investigation and transfer of title as well as the legal formalities in connection with mortgage finance and has always been a highly profitable activity for lawyers.[1]

Any threat to the conveyancing monopoly would have a significant impact on the profession and was likely to be fiercely resisted. Yet such a threat did emerge during the 1970s and 1980s. Its origins can be traced to increasing consumer dissatisfaction with the high cost of conveyancing and the length of time required to complete a typical transaction. The conveyancing monopoly came to be viewed with increasing hostility by aspiring home-owners and by a government committed to greater competition.

After several years of intense public debate the British government finally gave an undertaking early in 1984 to liberalize the provision of conveyancing services by removing the state-supported monopoly. Although the precise form of new competition in the conveyancing field and its date of implementation had not been decided at the time of the policy announcement, the response of the profession to the threat of new

* Professor at the Graduate School of Business, University of Sydney.

† Alsop Wilkinson Professor of Law at the Faculty of Law, University of Liverpool.

This research was supported by a Nuffield Foundation Social Science Grant 181 (1472). We are grateful to the Consumers' Association for their co-operation in the collection and processing of the necessary data, and to Saadet Toker for expert research assistance. John Cubbin, Robert Fraser, Peter Gist, and Ian Walker made constructive comments, as did seminar participants in London, Warwick, and Sydney. We are also grateful to a referee of this Journal whose suggestions were particularly helpful in improving the final version of the paper. The usual disclaimer applies.

This paper first appeared in *International Review of Law and Economics*, 9: 41–56, June 1989. Permission has been obtained from the publishers, Butterworth-Heinemann to republish.

[1] The legal profession in England and Wales is divided into two branches: solicitors and barristers. It is only the former who have had a monopoly over conveyancing.

entry was swift. Reports of reductions in conveyancing charges first appeared in 1984. In October of that year the Law Society relaxed the restrictions previously imposed on advertising by lawyers, and this further assisted the spread of price competition which had begun within the profession. By May 1987, when new entry finally took place in the form of non-solicitor, licensed conveyancers, the pricing of conveyancing had already been transformed.

The breaking up of the conveyancing monopoly in England and Wales constitutes a unique, uncontrolled experiment in the liberalization of the supply of legal services. In this paper we analyse the economic consequences of that experiment, with particular reference to the pricing of conveyancing services and the clients' perceptions of quality of service provided. The analysis of fees is based on transaction data, that is, on information supplied by clients derived from their records of fees actually paid to their lawyers.

The paper is organized as follows: Section 1 will discuss the institutional background to the conveyancing monopoly and the chronology of recent developments. Section 2 will consider the theory relating to the pricing of professional services with special emphasis on the conditions facilitating price discrimination. Section 3 will outline the empirical framework including the econometric model, the data, and estimation methods. Section 4 will report and discuss the regression estimates of the determinants of conveyancing charges and the impact of the policy initiatives post-1984. Section 5 will report our findings on clients' perceptions of quality of service over time, and, finally, Section 6 will contain some concluding remarks and a brief evaluation of our results.

1. THE LIBERALIZATION OF CONVEYANCING SERVICES

The legal profession in England and Wales is divided into two branches: solicitors, of whom there are some 45,000–50,000, and barristers of whom there are some 4,000–5,000. Solicitors deal with the day-to-day running of the legal affairs of their clients, with whom they have direct contact. Barristers' work consists mainly of court appearances on behalf of clients and the provision of specialist advice. Their lay clients are referred to them only through solicitors. Recent estimates suggest that over 50 per cent of solicitors' earnings come from the fees for the conveyancing of residential property. In some cases, smaller firms still earn between 70 and 90 per cent of their income from this source. Conveyancing has always been regarded as profitable work for lawyers.[2]

[2] Details of the sources of income and size distribution of law firms in England and Wales were given in the Royal Commission on Legal Services in England and Wales (1979), *Final Report*, (I and II), Cmnd 7648, London, HMSO.

The solicitors' monopoly over conveyancing for fee or reward dates back to the Stamp Act of 1804. It was granted by William Pitt to alleviate the effect, on the income of the profession, of a tax on legal documents which had been imposed at that time. The first official investigation into restrictive practices among professional groups, including lawyers, was by the Monopolies Commission in 1970.[3] Although the Commission was not unduly concerned about the conveyancing monopoly, and recommended only that the scale of fees be abolished, persistent pressure from consumer organizations continued during the 1970s and early 1980s. Underlying these developments was the substantial rise in home-ownership in the United Kingdom since the end of the Second World War and increasing geographic mobility of the home-owning population as a result of changing economic conditions.[4]

The Law Society, the solicitors' governing and representative body, mounted a strong defence of the conveyancing monopoly. In the Law Society's view a house purchase or sale was probably the largest transaction which a lay person was likely to undertake during his/her lifetime. The laws of title and estate were complex, and conveyancing, therefore, necessitated a fully qualified professional to handle such matters. Furthermore, if the monopoly over conveyancing were to be lost, the provision of other legal services would suffer because many such services were unprofitable as compared with conveyancing. The essence of this argument was that a number of legal offices would close down if the monopoly was removed because many of these were only economically viable in their current location as a result of their conveyancing activity.

In the beginning of the 1983–4 parliamentary session, Austin Mitchell, a Labour Member of Parliament, put forward a Private Member's Bill. This was the appropriately named House Buyers' Bill which proposed, amongst other things, to end the solicitors' monopoly on conveyancing. Despite protestations from the Law Society the government agreed in February 1984 to implement legislation which would liberalize conveyancing. Following this undertaking by the government, the House Buyers' Bill was withdrawn. From this time onwards the Law Society, under pressure from its membership, relaxed the solicitors' rules of conduct in order to allow greater competition. Restrictions on advertising by solicitors were significantly reduced in October 1984, and from January 1985, solicitors were permitted to provide real-estate agency services. In October 1985 legislation was passed creating a para-profession

[3] Monopolies Commission (1970), *A Report on the General Effect on the Public Interest of Certain Restrictive Practices so Far as They Prevail in Relation to the Supply of Professional Services*, Cmnd 4463, London, HMSO.

[4] The proportion of dwellings under owner-occupation in the United Kingdom rose from 42.7% in 1961 to 61.9% in 1985. For further details see *Annual Abstract of Statistics*, London, HMSO.

of licensed conveyancers who would compete with solicitors. The first licensed conveyancers began to practise on 1 May 1987.[5]

2. PRICING OF CONVEYANCING SERVICES: THEORETICAL CONSIDERATIONS

Economists have traditionally associated price discrimination with the provision of professional services. The classic article by Reuben Kessel (1958) investigated the means by which the American Medical Association (AMA) was able to induce its members to engage in price discrimination and to refrain from competitive behaviour.[6] Most of the subsequent work on the incidence of price discrimination has been confined to the medical profession. Relatively little, by comparison, has been written on the pricing of legal services, perhaps because of the divergence that exists not only between countries but also between different types of legal services which makes generalization difficult.[7]

The nature of price discrimination in conveyancing services can be understood by reference to the profit-maximizing decision of a representative lawyer who sets his fee under uncertainty. Let C_{ij} be the fee quoted by lawyer i to client j for a conveyancing service. Assume that the marginal cost of conveyancing is F_j and that the maximum which the client is willing to pay for the service is given by r_j. This reservation price cannot be observed by the lawyer. Personal characteristics such as income and the propensity to search for low-cost conveyancing can be inferred from information revealed by the client. These factors, together with other unobservable personal characteristics of client j (but with a distribution known to the lawyer from past experience) jointly determine the level of r_j. The lawyer is thus able to estimate the probability that $C_{ij} \leq r_j$. Let this probability that client j buys from lawyer i be P_{ij}.

Clearly, P_{ij} will be inversely related to the fee, *ceteris paribus* ($dP_{ij}/dC_{ij} < 0$). The probability that $C_{ij} > r_j$ is therefore $(1-P_{ij})$, and the solicitor's expected profit from this transaction is:

[5] Another proposal put forward was that lenders of mortgage finance, e.g. banks, be allowed to provide conveyancing services to their clients in competition with solicitors. However, this competitive threat was rendered harmless by allowing legal services to be offered only in cases where the institution concerned was *not* the lender of mortgage finance.

[6] Reuben Kessel (1958), 'Price discrimination in medicine', *Journal of Law and Economics*, 1: 20–53.

[7] See P. J. Halpern and S. M. Turnbull (1982), 'An economic analysis of legal fees contracts' in R. G. Evans and M. J. Trebilcock (eds.) *Lawyers and the Consumer Interest*. Toronto, Butterworths. Also, an interesting discussion of fixed-fee versus hourly rate pricing for certain legal services is given in J. Kiholm Smith and Steven R. Cox (1985), 'The pricing of legal services: A contractual solution to the problem of bilateral opportunism', *Journal of Legal Studies*, 14: 167–83.

$$\pi_{ij} = P_{ij}(C_{ij} - F_{ij}) + (1 - P_{ij})0 \tag{1}$$

Assuming that the objective is to maximize expected profit from conveyancing, the first-order condition for the maximization of (1) with respect to C_{ij} is given by:

$$\frac{d\pi_{ij}}{dC_{ij}} = P_{ij} + C_{ij}\frac{dP_{ij}}{dC_{ij}} - F_j\frac{dP_{ij}}{dC_{ij}} = 0$$

Multiplying through by C_{ij}/P_{ij} and rearranging terms yields:

$$\frac{C_{ij} - F_j}{C_{ij}} = -\frac{1}{\epsilon_j} \tag{2}$$

where $\varepsilon_j = \frac{C_{ij}}{P_{ij}}\frac{dP_{ij}}{dC_{ij}}$ is the elasticity of the probability of purchase by client j with respect to the conveyancing fee. Expression 2 is equivalent to the 'Lerner index' and reflects the degree to which the fee quoted to an individual client can be raised above cost given the probability of loss of business. If it can be assumed that the marginal cost of a transaction does not differ significantly between clients (an assumption which will be considered further in Section 3) and if the elasticity for client k is ε_k such that $\varepsilon_j \neq \varepsilon_\lambda$, then the optimal ratio of fees for clients j and k is given by:

$$\frac{C_{ij}}{C_{ik}} = \frac{1 - 1/\epsilon_k}{1 - 1/\epsilon_j} \tag{3}$$

C_{ij} is greater than, equal to, or less than C_{ik} as ε_k is greater than, equal to, or less then ε_j. Expression 3 is analogous to the familiar formula for third-degree price discrimination between two sub-markets with different demand elasticities. However, in the present context the pricing rule suggests first-degree price discrimination given that ε is expected to differ between individual clients. This accords well with the observation that solicitors' conveyancing fees vary between clients and tend to be closely correlated with the value of the property being transacted. The special role which the price of the house plays in the setting of conveyancing fees will be examined below.

For price discrimination to be effectively sustained at the level of the individual practitioner, four important conditions have to be fulfilled. The first is the impossibility of arbitrage: in the case of conveyancing, this condition always holds because each transaction is unique to an individual client. A more stringent requirement is that entry be restricted to prevent outsiders, that is, non-qualified persons, from supplying identical or similar services at lower prices. Effectively, the profession as a whole must be able to protect its monopoly position over the activity in question. This protection was, until recently, guaranteed by law: statutory restrictions on unqualified persons (The Solicitors Act 1974) meant that conveyancing by a non-solicitor, that is, someone who does not hold a practising certificate issued by the Law Society, constituted an offence liable to criminal prosecution.

Such restrictions, through licensing and certification, are widespread among professions such as medicine and law and have been extensively discussed in the literature.[8] They are commonly justified on the grounds that they protect the client from unscrupulous and incompetent 'quacks'. The reason for imposing minimum standards of competence is that clients are unable to judge for themselves the quality of the service being provided. Markets for professional services are characterized by asymmetric information: the practitioner is typically better informed about the level of quality being supplied than the recipient of the service. Certification and licensing undoubtedly help by reducing the probability of fraudulent behaviour and incompetence. However, restricting entry in combination with other restrictions on the behaviour of those already qualified effectively ensures that price discrimination can be sustained.[9]

This brings us to the third requirement for price discrimination, namely, that individual lawyers should not engage in price competition. This is an important issue for a profession comprising large numbers of heterogeneous members. It is an issue that was carefully considered by Kessel (1958, 25) who argued that enforcement of non-competitive behaviour was conditional on 'the availability and willingness to use powerful sanctions against potential price cutters' by the relevant professional organization. The Law Society in England and Wales, like the AMA in the United States, has at its disposal such sanctions, the most powerful of which is its ability to revoke a lawyer's licence to practise. Such extreme action would normally only be taken in cases of 'serious professional misconduct', but it is the potential to revoke the licence which constitutes a powerful disciplinary mechanism. Until 1973, price competition was discouraged and price discrimination positively encouraged through a recommended scale of fees issued by the Law Society. The scale had the interesting, if not surprising, feature that the fees charged for conveyancing rose with the price of the house being transacted. In addition, advertising by lawyers was effectively prohib-

[8] For a detailed discussion of this issue in the context of the American medical profession, see K. Leffler (1978), 'Physician licensure: Competition and monopoly in American medicine', *Journal of Law and Economics*, 20: 165–86.

[9] For a theoretical analysis of entry and the emergence of legal 'para-professionals', see A. Shaked and J. Sutton (1982), 'Imperfect information, perceived quality, and the formation of professional groups', *Journal of Economic Theory*, 27: 170–81.

ited by the Law Society, and those who disregarded this ruling could be found guilty of serious professional misconduct. The implications of such an indictment on the lawyer's reputation would be severe, and, hence, the penalty constituted a strong incentive to comply.

The ban on advertising had the effect of stabilizing individual lawyers' shares of conveyancing business in the long run, by restricting the availability of information about alternative suppliers. Recent analysis of the effect of advertising in routine legal service markets confirms this view.[10] The stability of the client–lawyer relationship was reinforced by the fact that clients do not typically shop around among solicitors but rely either on personal recommendations or previous acquaintance. This behavioural characteristic reflects in part the client's uncertainty about the quality of service associated with an 'unknown' solicitor. Given the client's reluctance to switch lawyers, the incentive to secret price cutting by the lawyer is reduced because the scope for gaining additional business in this way is strictly limited.[11] The combined restrictions on entry and competitive behaviour, enforced through the threat of powerful sanctions by the professional organization, thus resulted in effective collusion by the legal profession.

Finally, lawyers require a mechanism that will identify a client's ability and willingness to pay for the service. The price of the house being transacted is a useful and obvious indicator of both. A client faced with costly conveyancing has essentially the following alternatives: search for a lower-priced solicitor or do-it-yourself conveyancing.[12] Both of these would require much of the client's time, because given the collusive behaviour of legal professionals, the search is likely to be extensive and do-it-yourself conveyancing, while feasible, would be time-consuming and risky to the non-specialist. Given that the opportunity cost of time is highest for the high income client, we would expect that such a client would be least likely to pursue either of these options. And since income and wealth tend to be closely correlated, it follows that the price of the house which is an indicator of the client's wealth, will be a reliable proxy

[10] The empirical analysis of Schroeter *et al.* suggests that advertising in routine legal-service markets has strong pro-competitive effects. See J. R. Schroeter, S. L. Smith, and S. R. Cox (1987), 'Advertising and competition in routine legal service markets', *Journal of Industrial Economics*, 36: 49–60; see also Lee Benham (1972), 'The effect of advertising on the price of eyeglasses', *Journal of Law and Economics*, 15: 337–51.

[11] In 'A theory of oligopoly', *Journal of Political Economy*, 72: 44–61 (1964), George Stigler argues that perfect collusion is achieved when no buyer changes sellers voluntarily. Restrictions on advertising make it more difficult for clients to identify potential price-cutters, and thus reduce the incentive to engage in price competition. By banning advertising, the Law Society effectively secured long-term contractual relations between client and lawyer.

[12] Do-it-yourself conveyancing is, and always has been, permitted in England and Wales. What was proscribed by law was conveyancing for fee or reward by a non-solicitor on behalf of another.

for the fee that can be charged without inducing search for alternatives and reducing the probability of purchase.[13]

These considerations help to explain why the observed fee structure remained essentially unchanged following the abolition of scale fees for conveyancing in 1973 by the Law Society. The factors which facilitate price discrimination by lawyers had not altered in any way. What did cause them to change was the prospect of new entry by non-solicitors (licensed conveyancers) and the removal of certain restrictions on advertising. The latter had the effect of reducing search costs and thus increasing the elasticity ε for any individual client. These developments would be expected to reduce the level of fees and the degree of discrimination, as solicitors began to compete amongst themselves in anticipation of new entry into the field.

3. EMPIRICAL FRAMEWORK

Quantitative and Qualitative Data

The data used in this study were obtained from a questionnaire survey of members of the Consumers' Association (CA) who had changed address between 1983 and 1986.[14] The vast majority had bought and/or sold a property, the only exception being those moving to and from rented accommodation. Obtaining information directly from clients has two important advantages. First, the information on the fees charged represents actual remittances made to the lawyer, and price data obtained from buyers rather than sellers are generally considered superior because they represent actual as opposed to 'list' prices. Secondly, having access to clients, allows us to ask questions about qualitative aspects of the transaction which is particularly relevant in the context of price discrimination. Discrimination only arises where significant variations in prices do not reflect differences in the cost of provision. If it turns out that some clients demand and obtain greater service quality in terms of time spent with the lawyer, for which they are charged correspondingly higher fees, then clearly the nature and cost of the service differs across clients. This would weaken any evidence in support of price discrimination.

[13] Masson and Wu show that the elasticity of demand for physicians' services is likely to be inversely related to patients' income. The argument is based on the plausible assumption that the opportunity cost of search is higher for the rich than for the poor. See R. T. Masson and S. Wu (1974), 'Price discrimination for physicians' services', *Journal of Human Resources*, 9: 63–79.

[14] The Consumers' Association is a voluntary, non-profit-making organization based in London, whose objectives are primarily to inform consumers about products and services and generally promote the consumers' interests.

The questionnaire was devised jointly by the authors and the CA and contained some seventy-five separate questions on many aspects of house purchase/sale. Eighteen of these questions related specifically to the legal side of buying and selling a property. In addition to the central questions on the fees charged for buying and selling transactions (net of disbursement, duties, and taxes), others covered aspects such as whether the solicitor was asked for an estimate of the fee before receiving the client's instructions, how much time elapsed between receipt of instructions and exchange of contracts between the parties, whether the property concerned was registered or unregistered, leasehold or freehold property. The significance of these characteristics stems from the fact that they have implications for the amount of work associated with a given transaction which could be reflected in the lawyer's fee. There were also four specific questions concerning the client's perception of the quality of the service provided. These covered the time the conveyancing took, the quantity and quality of information provided by the solicitor to the client, access to the solicitor (was he/she available when required), and, finally, was the service given judged to represent 'good value for money'. Thus the data allow us to test whether clients receiving particularly good service by one or more of the criteria defined above are also those who tend to pay more for their conveyancing.

The sampling frame was made up of CA members who had notified the Association of their change of address over the period January 1983 to August 1986.[15] From this population of 'movers' 2,500 were identified by means of random systematic sampling. The response rate was 57 per cent, yielding a total of 1,434 completed questionnaires.[16] However, the number of observations that identify purchase and sale transactions independently was considerably less than the total because some respondents only reported the aggregate fees and others did not answer all the relevant questions. Thus the usable samples comprised 771 and 580 observations for purchase and sale transactions respectively.

Econometric Specification

Our analysis of the impact of policy developments on conveyancing fees is based on an econometric pricing model estimated for the years 1983–6 inclusive. The crucial policy announcement was made early in 1984, and

[15] Approximately 10% of the 600,000 members of the Consumers' Association change their address every year. Although it would have been desirable to collect observations prior to 1983, problems with response rates and data reliability ruled out sampling earlier years.

[16] The CA membership is representative of the house-owning segment of the population in the United Kingdom, with 51% of CA members classified as upper-middle or middle class, and another 35% as lower-middle class.

consequently 1983 is treated as the bench-mark, that is, the pre-competition year against which subsequent developments are recorded in terms of changes in the relevant parameters of the pricing model. The specification incorporates the main factors that could account for differences in fees charged between clients which are related to the type of legal work involved. It is specified in simple linear form as follows:

$$C = \alpha_1 + \beta_1 PH + \beta_2 LEASE + \beta_3 UNREG \tag{4}$$

$$+ \beta_4 ESTIMATE + \beta_5 TIME + \sum_{i=84}^{86} \alpha_i D_i + \sum_{i=84}^{86} \beta_i D_i PH + e$$

where:

C	conveyancing fee (in £)
PH	price of house being transacted (in £000)
$LEASE$	dummy variable taking the value of 1 for leasehold properties and 0 otherwise
$UNREG$	dummy variable taking the value of 1 if the property is unregistered and 0 otherwise.
$ESTIMATE$	dummy variable taking the value of 1 if the client asks for an estimate from the solicitor whom he instructs and 0 otherwise.
$TIME$	variable measuring the number of weeks (in approximately two-week intervals) taken between the instructions being received and contracts exchanged.
D_i	dummy variable taking the value of 1 if the transaction occurred in year *i*, and 0 otherwise.

A linear specification has the advantage of distinguishing statistically between fixed percentage pricing, in which case $\alpha_1 = 0$, and charging that involves a fixed element ($\alpha_1 > 0$) plus a discriminatory component (β_1) which is related to the price of the house. The dependent variable (C) is the conveyancing charge associated with a given transaction. The price of the house (PH) is the key variable determining the extent of discrimination in the fees charged, and, following the discussion in the previous section, we expect the coefficient β_1 to be positive.

Equation 4 was estimated as a 'moving cross-section', that is a cross-section regression for each of the years from 1983 to 1986. The *LEASE* variable identifies leasehold as opposed to freehold properties and *UNREG* refers to unregistered properties.[17] In both cases the work and hence the cost involved is somewhat greater for properties of this type because of the more complicated legal title to be deduced. The *ESTIMATE* variable identifies clients who ask for a quotation before autho-

[17] Registered properties are dwellings, the title to which is registered at the Land Registry. The ownership of such properties is guaranteed fully or partially by the State and this simplifies the legal searches required for conveyancing.

rizing the solicitor to proceed with the conveyancing. By doing so, they effectively signal that they are price-sensitive and possibly that they may be searching, that is 'shopping around' among solicitors. We would expect solicitors confronted by such clients to respond by quoting a lower fee than that which would be charged to clients who had not inquired about the cost.[18] Hence we expect $\beta_4 < 0$. The variable *TIME* measures the length of time elapsed between receipt of instructions and 'exchange of contracts'. The latter is the point at which the parties concerned enter into an irrevocable commitment to complete the transaction. It is during this period that difficulties and delays tend to emerge, and, hence, solicitors could be justified in charging more for conveyancing which took longer time to complete.[19] Hence we expect $\beta_5 > 0$.

Finally, the dummy variables $D_i(i = 84 \ldots 86)$ classify transactions to the year in which they took place and allow for changes in the intercept (α_i) and slope (β_1) relative to the base year, 1983. The use of yearly dummy variables to capture the effect of competition synchronizes well with the timetable of policy developments. The first crucial step was the government's undertaking to implement legislation to liberalize conveyancing in February 1984. By the end of that year, the tight restrictions on advertising by solicitors were substantially relaxed, allowing them to advertise their services and prices, albeit under carefully specified guidelines. This ushered a new phase of competitive behaviour in 1985, by which time solicitors could also act as real-estate agents. Finally, in October 1985, the Administration of Justice Act was passed, formally constituting the Council of Licensed Conveyancers who were going to be competing directly with solicitors at some future date.

In the light of this chronology, we would expect competitive behaviour to take effect as of 1984 and to intensify in subsequent years. Greater competition generally implies lower fees and reduces the scope for price discrimination by individual lawyers. Empirically, this means that the difference in the fee charged for high and low value transactions

[18] It is evident that not all respondents inform themselves about the cost of conveyancing prior to instructing the solicitor. Consequently for some clients the actual fee charged may exceed r_j, as attested by occasional complaints of overcharging to the Law Society. It follows that the sample observations will lie on either side of r_j, thus avoiding sample selection bias.

[19] House purchase in England and Wales (not Scotland) involves the purchaser making an offer 'subject to contract'. That means that although the buyer and seller may agree on a transaction, neither party is committed until contracts have been 'exchanged'. Contracts will not be exchanged until surveys, title-search, and mortgage finance are resolved. Particular problems arise with house-buying 'chains', that is, where a succession of purchases and sales are interlinked with a first-time buyer at one end and a seller only at the other. A breakdown anywhere along the chain can cause the whole chain to collapse unless somebody is prepared to 'bridge'. That means someone is effectively financing two properties at the same time.

will narrow considerably, and this implies that the estimates of β_{84}, β_{85}, and β_{86} should have a negative sign.[20]

Analysis of Service Quality

Quality of service provided to clients or, more precisely, their perceptions of it was investigated using two-way analysis of variance (see also Section 5). For each completed transaction we have the client's ranking on a scale from 1 to 4 regarding the four qualitative aspects of the service that were outlined previously. A rating of 4 represents a 'very satisfied' client and 1 represents 'not at all satisfied'. Each qualitative observation was classified according to the year in which it took place (1983 through to 1986) and the fee that was charged. The six fee-bands used for classification purposes were as follows: £0–£100, £100–£200, £200–£300, £300–£500, £500–£1,000, £1,000+.

The analysis of variance essentially compares the cell means, that is, the satisfaction ratings across fee-bands and years. It allows us to test for significant differences in the perceived quality of service between clients paying low fees and those paying higher fees. It also allows us to test for significant changes in service quality over the years during which competition intensified and, in addition, permits analysis of interaction effects between years and fee-bands (for example whether service quality improves only for higher fee-bands in later years). Such behaviour could be consistent with attempts by solicitors to differentiate the service and provide the more demanding segment of their clientele with a better service and to charge them correspondingly higher fees.

4. THE DETERMINANTS OF CONVEYANCING FEES: REGRESSION RESULTS

Table 5.1 reports the sample means by year and by type of transaction of the dependent variable (*C*) and for house prices (*PH*). It is evident that house prices have been rising substantially and consistently between 1983 and 1986. The mid-1980s was a period characterized by rapidly rising house prices, particularly in the south-eastern region of the United Kingdom. As for conveyancing fees, their movement does not suggest a consistent pattern between purchases and sales: over the period under investigation fees fall somewhat for purchases but rise a little for sales.

[20] Note that both monetary variables *C* and *PH* are measured in current prices. Deflating *C* and *PH* by a common inflation index would leave the slope coefficients unchanged. Using different deflators for *C* and *PH* would make it difficult to interpret the results, and, more fundamentally, it seems hard to believe the lawyers' conveyancing fees are based on 'real' rather than nominal house prices.

TABLE 5.1. Sample means

	1983	1984	1985	1986
Purchases:				
House price (£000)	44.07	47.66	53.32	55.56
Conveyancing fee	363.96	339.00	328.67	329.94
Sales:				
House price (£000)	36.61	43.26	46.71	50.38
Conveyancing fee	290.08	330.77	301.12	313.91

Source: Consumers' Association

These figures also provide some indication of differences in the *level* of fees charged on purchases and sales, and, consequently, Equation 4 was estimated separately for the two types of transactions.

The merit of disaggregation becomes apparent when we examine the ordinary least squares regression results reported in Table 5.2. These allow for the simultaneous influence of the relevant factors on conveyancing fees and show the major changes which have affected the pricing structure since 1983. The first interesting feature is the difference in the degree of price discrimination between purchases and sales in the base year—£4.65 compared with £8.17 respectively for every additional £1,000 on the price of the property. This suggests that solicitors found it easier to charge higher fees on sales, perhaps because the proceeds of the latter typically embody substantial capital gains to the client, who may thus be less sensitive to high bills. However, when taken together with the estimated intercept terms, it is evident that fees charged on sales rise above those on purchases only when the value of the property transacted exceeds £50,000.

The coefficients on the *LEASE* and *UNREG* variables are positive, but not statistically significant. These results indicate that the important differences in the work involved in executing transactions of this nature are not, on average, passed on in higher fees. However, the coefficient on the *ESTIMATE* variable is negative and highly significant. Clients can save £49 and £47, respectively, on purchases and sales simply by asking for an estimate of the cost before instructing the solicitor to go ahead. This is an interesting finding which would indicate that clients requesting this information in advance succeed in creating the impression that they may be searching for low-priced solicitors. The latter respond by lowering their quoted fee, relative to what would be charged to a client who made no enquiries beforehand. This result goes some way towards confirming the important role of search in creating conditions which are inimical to price discrimination. The length of time taken to get the formalities completed from issuing instructions to exchanging contracts

TABLE 5.2. Regression results, 1983–1986

Independent variables	Purchases	Sales
PRICE OF HOUSE	4.65	8.17
	(.65)	(.63)
LEASEHOLD PROPERTY	14.70	3.85
	(17.41)	(16.61)
UNREGISTERED PROPERTY	20.7	2.51
	(14.10)	(27.64)
ESTIMATE	–49.28	–47.34
	(11.46)	(13.56)
NO. OF WEEKS TO EXCHANGE	3.86	8.33
	(2.63)	(3.12)
INTERCEPT Dummy 1984	–28.75	77.64
	(40.76)	(39.07)
INTERCEPT Dummy 1985	–49.91	73.85
	(37.23)	(38.79)
INTERCEPT Dummy 1986	–70.98	110.06
	(38.62)	(39.71)
SLOPE Dummy 1984	–.27	–2.24
	(.81)	(.78)
SLOPE Dummy 1985	–.48	–3.19
	(.72)	(.77)
SLOPE Dummy 1986	–.30	–4.06
	(.73)	(.77)
INTERCEPT	165.41	–15.18
R^2	0.39	0.51
Standard Error	152.9	157.6
DW	2.04	1.93
N	771	580

Note: Standard errors in parentheses.
Source: Authors' calculations using Consumers' Association data.

(*TIME*) has a positive sign but is statistically significant only in the case of sales. For these transactions every additional two-week period between receipt of instructions and exchange of contracts adds £8 to the average client's bill.

The changing structure of conveyancing fees between 1983–6 is given by the coefficients on the successive intercept and slope dummy variables. The first point to note is that for purchases the significant change lies in the downward shift of the intercept, whereas for sales there is a significant reduction in the slope, which implies a reduction in the degree of price discrimination. The nature of these changes may be seen most clearly by examining Figures 5.1 and 5.2 in which the relationship between fees and house prices in 1983 and 1986 is depicted for purchases and sales respectively. In the case of purchases, the straight line

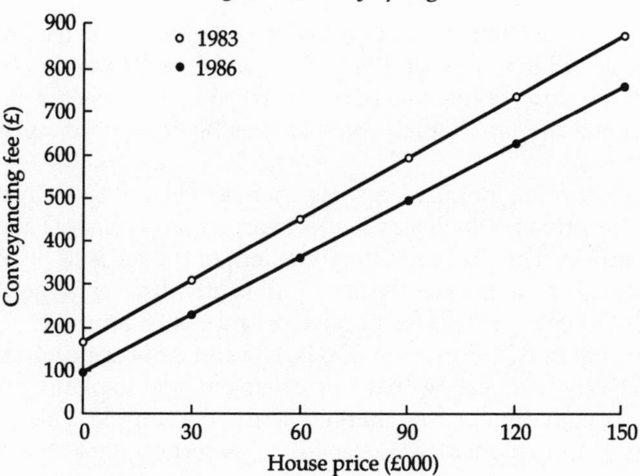

FIG. 5.1. Conveyancing fees for purchases
Source: Authors' calculations.

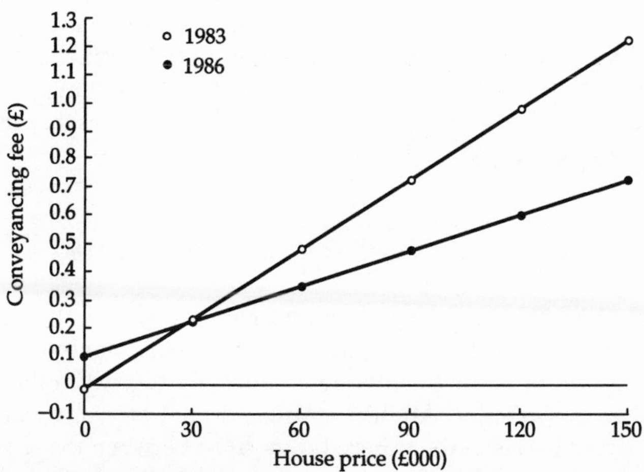

FIG. 5.2. Conveyancing fees for sales
Source: Authors' calculations.

shifts downwards between these two years—a parallel shift with the slope almost unchanged.[21] For sales, in contrast, the straight line pivots

[21] The 1986 intercept dummy coefficient has a 't' value of 1.84. This is statistically significant at the 5% level on a one-tail test. The intercept dummies will partly reflect the impact of cost inflation for all solicitors. In the absence of deregulation we would expect the coefficients to be positive. The fact that they turn out to be negative reinforces the downward impact of competition on conveyancing fees.

in such a way that in 1986 the discriminatory element of the fee is almost exactly half of what it was in 1983—£4 instead of £8 per £1,000. The reduction in the slope of this line is very marked and shows the extent to which the range of fees charged for sales has been reduced during the four year period.

Another interesting point to note is that between 1983–6 there is a realignment of pricing which leaves fees charged on purchases and sales virtually identical. The discriminatory element of the fee is £4.35 on purchases and £4.11 on sales—clearly not significantly different. The same is true of the intercepts—£94.43 for purchases and £94.88 for sales.

The coefficient of determination (R^2) is 0.39 and 0.51 for purchases and sales respectively, suggesting that our pricing model explains up to 50 per cent of the variation of fees charged across the sample. This is a reasonable degree of explanatory power for cross-section data of this kind, particularly as our model does not account for local market conditions which may vary considerably across the towns and regions in the United Kingdom. The Durbin–Watson (DW) statistic is essentially used as a specification test for which the observations were placed in ascending order of the explanatory variable (*PH*). Should any significant nonlinearities be present, these would be reflected in a systematic pattern of residuals which would be picked up as a low Durbin–Watson statistic. On the basis of the statistics reported in Table 5.2, the null hypothesis of zero autocorrelation could not be rejected and this suggests that the relationship is correctly specified.[22]

5. ANALYSIS OF VARIANCE: SERVICE QUALITY

The analysis of variance of satisfaction ratings associated with purchases is reported in Table 5.3. There is only one statistically significant result: clients' perception of value for money is inversely related to the size of the fee paid to the solicitor. All other ratings do not appear to vary systematically either between the transaction year or between the size of the fee paid. These results, therefore, support the view that high-fee clients do not appear to receive a superior service, or, if they do, they certainly do not perceive the service to be superior. One implication may be that, as far as conveyancing is concerned, there is little scope for differentiating the quality of service provided, but this conclusion does not appear to be supported by the evidence associated with sales.

Table 5.4 reveals that as far as value for money ratings are concerned,

[22] The OLS regression estimation and all diagnostic testing were carried out using version 9.1 of the SPSS batch system. We also experimented with a quadratic functional form but the results were inferior to the linear specification, in terms of both explanatory power and significance of the coefficients.

Table 5.3. **Analysis of variance: Satisfaction ratings with service provided (purchases)**

Satisfaction ratings	Source of variation	
	Year of transaction	Cost of transaction
	F	F
1. Satisfaction with information from the solicitor	1.29 (3,783)	0.62 (5,783)
2. Satisfaction with access to the solicitor	2.13 (3,782)	0.75 (5,782)
3. Value for money	1.12 (3,780)	6.08* (5,780)
4. Satisfaction with time the conveyancing took	1.80 (3,776)	1.68 (5,776)

Note: Degrees of freedom in parentheses. * indicates a statistically significant F statistic at the 5% level. F statistics associated with interaction effects were uniformly insignificant and are not reported.

Table 5.4. Analysis of variance: Satisfaction ratings with service provided (sales)

Satisfaction ratings	Source of variation	
	Year of transaction	Cost of transaction
	F	F
1. Satisfaction with information from the solicitor	2.87* (3,576)	1.48 (5,576)
2. Satisfaction with access to the solicitor	4.25* (3,575)	1.92 (5,575)
3. Value for money	1.76 (3,574)	2.59* (5,574)
4. Satisfaction with time the conveyancing took	2.52* (3,572)	0.86 (5,572)

Note: Degrees of freedom in parentheses. * indicates a statistically significant F statistic at the 5% level. F statistics associated with interaction effects were uniformly insignificant and are not reported.

the results for sales are the same as with purchases. However, there appear to be significant effects (at the 5% level) associated with the information provided by, and access to, the solicitor as well as with the time taken. The cell means (not reported) indicate that average satisfaction ratings rose between 1983 and 1986 from 3.33 to 3.54 with respect to access, from 2.99 to 3.25 in the case of information provided, and from 2.96 to 3.21 with respect to the time the conveyancing took. Although this is a clear indication of quality improvements in later years, the absence of any significant interaction effects suggests that they are essentially independent of the fee levels paid by the clients.[23]

The English system of property transfer typically involves a 'chain' of people buying and selling houses. Both the sale and the purchase of property can be a harrowing time for a client, especially if the lawyer does not keep the client fully informed of what is happening. It is therefore interesting to note that the significant increases in levels of satisfaction concern sales rather than purchases. The solicitor is much more in control of a sale rather than of a purchase, and, consequently, it is easier to provide more information, give greater access to the client, and speed up the transaction. Our results suggest a uniform improvement occurring at all fee levels in these quality characteristics. This emerges as a significant effect associated with deregulation and the growth of competition. Further research would be necessary in order to determine the potential for quality improvement in relation to purchases.

6. CONCLUSIONS

In this paper we considered the introduction of competition into a market for legal services which had been protected for almost two hundred years. The analysis showed that the legal profession was able to apply a simple and effective price discrimination scheme by charging a conveyancing fee which is positively related to the value of the property being transacted.

The emergence of a threat of new entry into the field was sufficient to set in motion strong competitive forces within the profession. Fees started to fall in 1984, following the policy announcement to liberalize conveyancing, and a full three years before licensed conveyancers entered the market. By 1986 the discriminatory element in the combined fees charged for sales and purchases of property had fallen by one third—from £6 to £4 per £1,000 of property value.

An intrinsic advantage of the solicitors' price discrimination scheme is that it is inflation-proof. Since house prices have risen ahead of inflation in recent years, conveyancing fees have generally kept up with the cost of living. Moreover, although our analysis shows that fees have fallen as a proportion of house prices following the policy initiatives, the rapid acceleration of house prices over the 1983–6 period has actually cushioned the profession from the worst effects of competition. Solicitors'

[23] A pilot study based on a smaller sample up to 1985 and reported in S. Domberger and A. Sherr (1987), 'Competition in Conveyancing', *Fiscal Studies*, 8: 17–28, revealed no significant changes in these satisfaction ratings between 1983 and 1985. This indicates that the impact of competition intensified in 1986.

real fee income fell slightly during this period because conveyancing fees have remained broadly constant in nominal terms. In the absence of the rapid increases in house prices, the economic impact of competition on the profession may have turned out differently.

Another finding that deserves mention is that the impact of competition has been far more pronounced in the conveyancing of property sales than of purchases. In particular, there has been a perceptible improvement in satisfaction ratings which suggests that the scope for improving the service is greater in the case of sales because the work involved is routine and subject to greater control by the solicitor than that associated with purchases.

A general conclusion to be drawn from this study is that the threat of competition has yielded significant welfare benefits. Price discrimination has been reduced, conveyancing costs have fallen in real terms, and there has been a measurable improvement in consumer satisfaction. Whether price discrimination, which remains substantial, will persist or eventually vanish altogether is a more difficult question to answer. The outcome will depend on the extent to which fixed-priced conveyancing, already being offered by some solicitors and licensed conveyancers, will take hold in the profession. However, uncertainty about the quality of service provided by fixed-price conveyancers and the associated costs of search could help the maintenance of price-discrimination. Clearly, the ultimate consequences of the breaking up of the solicitors' conveyancing monopoly are yet to be determined.

6

The Regulation of Financial Services: Lessons from the UK for 1992

COLIN MAYER*

1. INTRODUCTION

The 1986 Financial Service Act (FSA) introduced for the first time a comprehensive system of regulating financial services in the UK. With it came a plethora of rules relating to the activities of investment businesses that distinguishes financial services from most other sectors of the British economy.

One justification that may be sought for the regulation of this, but not other sectors of the economy, is that investors are at greater risk than consumers of other products. In fact, according to Franks and Mayer (1989), the losses that clients of investment management firms have suffered on account of financial failure appear to be small, probably well below those in other industries, such as the building industry where entry and exit of firms is commonplace. Why then has an extensive system of regulation been imposed on investment managers but not builders?

An obvious answer comes from comparing investment managers with banks, not builders. Banks are vulnerable to risks of runs and the concern exists that runs could spread through a banking system in a contagious manner. The regulation of banks is therefore justified by the systemic risks to which the banking system is liable.

It might be thought that the rationale for the FSA came from similar considerations. In fact, there are good reasons for believing that this was not the case. As Section 2 describes, the FSA emerged as a response to the Gower Report (1984) which in turn was prompted by the financial failure of a number of investment businesses. The concern of the Gower Report was investor protection not systemic risks and the objective of

* Professor of Economics and Finance at Warwick Business School.

This paper draws on research performed with Professor Julian Franks on the regulation of investment managers. I am very grateful to him for detailed comments on this paper. I have also received useful comments from John Kay and participants at the INSEAD conference on 'European Banking after 1992'. The paper was written while the author was Houblon-Norman Fellow at the Bank of England. The views expressed in this paper are those of the author, not those of the Bank or any other institution with which the author is associated. Any errors are the sole responsibility of the author.

the FSA was to correct deficiencies in existing legislation relating to investor protection.

While the justification for regulation of non-banks was different from that of banks, the form that it has taken is quite similar. Section 3 describes the regulation of financial services in the UK. This raises two questions. First, is the regulation of non-banks justified at all and, secondly, has the right system of regulation been enacted?

Section 4 sets out the principles of regulating financial institutions. It distinguishes between market failures created by problems of asymmetric information and systemic risks. It suggests that the appropriate response to these two types of risk are very different. Furthermore, since asymmetries in information afflict some investors and firms more than others, the level of protection offered against asymmetric information should be allowed to vary across institutions. This heterogeneity stands in marked contrast to the uniformity that is required of regulation for systemic risks. The principles described in Section 4 are used to evaluate the regulation of financial services in the UK in Section 5.

While these are important considerations for the British authorities, the issues raised are of much wider interest. The principle of 'home country authorization' which lies at the heart of EC proposals to complete the internal market by 1992 attributes the primary task of supervising financial institutions to the relevant authority of the Member State of origin. This requires that minimum standards of regulation be set. However, both levels and forms of regulation differ considerably across countries and in financial services, more than in banking, conflicts have emerged between the objectives of different regulators. Such is the degree of disagreement that as yet, as Section 6 describes, there remain many unresolved issues.

Section 7 concludes the paper.

2. THE HISTORY OF REGULATION OF FINANCIAL INSTITUTIONS IN THE UK

There have been significant developments in bank regulation in the UK over the past decade. Following the secondary banking crisis of 1973, and the 1977 EEC Banking Directive, the Banking Act was passed in 1979. Before the Act, any partnership, company, or individual could take money on deposit. No licence was needed and no undertaking had to be given about the assets of the business or the way in which the business was conducted. Whether a particular deposit-taking business was treated as a bank depended on the privileges granted to it by the Bank of England and its reputation among the established members of the banking community.

Following the Act, deposit-takers had to be classified as either 'recognized banks' or 'licensed institutions'. The minimum conditions that a bank had to fulfil[1] were that: (i) it enjoyed a 'high reputation and standing in the financial community'; (ii) it provided 'either a wide range of banking services or a highly specialized banking service'; (iii) the business was performed 'with integrity and prudence'; (iv) it was under the direction of at least two individuals; and (v) it met minimum net asset requirements that were stipulated in the Act but had to be also considered appropriate by the Bank of England. Licensed deposit-takers had to satisfy the equivalent of (iii) to (v) but instead of (i) merely had to demonstrate that all directors, controllers and managers were 'fit and proper' to carry out the business. Following the collapse of Johnson Matthey Bankers, an institution of supposedly high status, new legislation was introduced in 1987 that created a single category of authorization and required all institutions to be able to satisfy 'fit and proper' tests.[2]

The Act also introduced a Deposit Protection Fund under which 75 per cent of sterling deposits were protected up to a maximum deposit, excluding interest, of £10,000, raised to £20,000 by the 1987 Act.[3]

While the Act has clearly altered the process by which UK banks are regulated, legislation was designed to interfere as little as possible with the informal supervisory procedures that had previously existed. The broad criteria listed above leave the Bank of England with a wide measure of discretion in interpreting the law. While its authority derives from statute, the running of the system still depends to a large degree on moral suasion.[4]

In many ways the more significant regulatory changes that have occurred over the past decade have affected non-banks rather than banks. In part this reflects the composition of structural developments that have taken place in the City of London. While commercial banking has altered, it is the non-deposit taking financial services that have experienced fundamental changes. The ending of several restrictive practices amongst financial institutions in 1986, and the introduction of new financial instruments during the 1970s and 1980s, have combined to transform the way in which the financial-service sector is structured and operated. In particular, the entry of a large number of new, frequently foreign, institutions convinced the authorities that the regulation of financial services had to be tightened.

[1] Schedule 2 of the Banking Act 1979, amended in the Banking Act 1987.

[2] Rules were also changed regarding ownership of institutions, permissible exposures, the function of auditors, and the power of the Bank of England to obtain information.

[3] The maximum amount payable to any one depositor is therefore £15,000.

[4] Peter Cooke, the Head of Banking Supervision at the Bank of England, discusses recent developments in bank supervision at greater length in Gardener (1986). The failure of the Johnson Matthey Bankers in 1983 resulted in a tightening of the 1979 Act in 1987.

Following the collapse of several institutions at the end of the 1970s and in the early 1980s,[5] the UK government commissioned a broad review of the regulatory structure.[6] This led to the publication of a White Paper in 1985 that proposed a new framework for investor protection and which formed the basis of the 1986 Financial Services Act. Prior to the Act, the principle statute governing securities investment was the Prevention of Fraud (Investments) Act of 1958. This required dealers in securities (with some exceptions) to be licensed and to be subject to conduct of business rules. The scope of the Fraud Act was limited and, in particular, did not relate to a serious concern that existed at the time about the sale of life insurance policies. Furthermore, the Fraud Act was felt to emphasize honesty of investment business to the exclusion of broader questions of competence. Perhaps as a consequence, it failed to prevent the collapse of several small investment management firms.

The response was the enactment of a comprehensive system of regulating financial services. Save with a few exceptions, any person performing investment business comes under the terms of the Financial Services Act. The Act provides for rules regarding the 'conduct of business', 'fit and proper' tests, capital requirements, cold-calling, clients' monies, and disclosure of information. There is an elaborate system of authorization of firms, a compensation scheme, and a complaints and arbitration procedure. There are several regulating organizations that monitor the activities of firms and separate bodies that prosecute fraud. In all, according to one estimate,[7] the direct costs of the regulatory bodies is around £20 million per annum and the costs to financial institutions of complying with the Act is over £100 million. In contrast, Franks and Mayer (1989) report that over the whole of the period 1979 to 1987 investors lost approximately £15 million due to financial failure in the investment management business.[8] The UK regulatory system has been described as ill-considered (Veljanovski 1988), unduly costly (Lomax 1987), and stifling for competition and innovation (Goodhart 1988). Are the costs justified? Is regulation (beyond prevention of fraud and theft) warranted at all? Has the UK enacted an appropriate form of regulation?

3. REGULATION OF FINANCIAL SERVICES IN THE UK

The first thing that strikes the reader of the UK Financial Services Act (apart from its complexity and length) is the broad terms in which much

[5] The most significant was the investment management firm, Norton Warburg, in 1981.

[6] The Gower Report, 1984.

[7] Lomax 1987.

[8] However, Franks and Mayer are careful to emphasize that since malpractice tends only to be revealed when financial failure occurs, actual losses may be substantially in excess of reported losses.

of it is couched. For example if you look up capital requirements under the Act all that you find is the following:

The Secretary of State may make rules requiring persons authorised to carry on investment business by virtue of sections 25 or 31 above to have and maintain in respect of that business such financial resources as are required by the rules [and may] make provision as to assets, liabilities and other matters to be taken into account in determining a person's financial resources for the purposes of the rules and the extent to which and the manner in which they are to be taken into account for that purpose.[9]

This level of generality reflects the distinctive blend of statutory and self-regulation that characterizes the UK system. The regulatory powers conferred by the Act are transferred to a designated agency called the Securities and Investment Board (SIB). The agency was required by the Act to stipulate a set of rules and regulations regarding the conduct and operation of investment businesses. However, unlike most regulators, it is not the primary function of this agency to regulate businesses directly (save in a few exceptional cases). Instead, the primary function of the agency is to certify a number of clubs (called Self-Regulating Organizations (SROs)) whose membership derives from different parts of the investment business. Certification requires acceptance by the agency of the rules of the clubs and the way in which the rules operate. The primary relevance of the agencies' rules is therefore to act as a bench-mark, or more accurately a minimum to which the rules of the clubs have to conform. The clubs do not have any direct powers under the Act except to sanction members who do not comply with their rules and ultimately to expel them. The importance of this stems from the fact that any business that is designated as an investment business under the terms of the Act has to be a member of a club (or, in the exceptional circumstances mentioned above, directly authorized by the agency).[10] Therefore the operation of an investment business is inconsistent with rejection or expulsion from a club.

This blend of the statutory and self-regulation is by no means exceptional in the UK. Unqualified solicitors, patent agents, midwives, dentists, pharmacists, and veterinary surgeons are prohibited by statute from practising. Unqualified doctors are not debarred but must not parade as medical practitioners and are not allowed to practise within the National Health Service. The blend of the statutory and self-regulation is thought to be more flexible than a statutory system and more effective than self-regulation (which is, for example, used to regulate take-overs in the UK). It can respond to the needs of investors and firms without requiring the

[9] Sect. 49, Financial Services Act 1986.

[10] Alternatively a firm may be a member of a recognized professional body (such as one of the accountancy associates) or authorized under the Insurance Companies or Friendly Societies Acts.

ratification of Parliament but at the same time provides regulatory authorities with powers to force compliance and prosecute for fraud.

It is not clear how such a system balances risks of regulatory 'capture' by members of the club against the provision of excessive investor protection. The latter is likely to be a feature of systems where politicians and government officials, who are sensitive to the political consequences of fraud and financial failure, administer the regulatory process. This is an important issue and it raises questions about the organizations of regulatory bodies, hierarchical relations between governments and regulated industries, and the role of clubs. I will have little further to say on this, save to cite examples of where over-regulation may have resulted from statutory requirements.

Investment businesses are defined as those businesses involved in the dealing, managing, or advising on investments. There are five SROs and the broad allocation of businesses between SROs is shown in Table 6.1. A firm that performs more than one activity is frequently a member of more than one SRO. In that case it is assigned a lead regulator, who is usually responsible for the largest part of the firm's business.

In applying for membership to an SRO, a firm has to demonstrate that:

(a) It is *fit and proper* to carry on investment business. In its assessment, an SRO will take account of an applicant's proposed line of business, financial position, expertise and past record.

(b) It has *adequate capital* to run the business. Capital requirements are related to annual expenditures by firms, their volume of business,[11] and the position in investments that they take on their own account.

(c) It complies with certain rules regarding the *conduct of its business*. These relate to advertising, unsolicited approaches to individuals ('cold-calling'), published recommendations, written agreements with customers, investment advice offered, churning of clients' accounts, independence, and the disclosure of material interests. Firms are expected to 'know their customers' in the sense that they should have reasonable grounds for believing that recommendations made are suited to the circumstances of particular clients.

(d) It holds *clients' money* in separate bank accounts from those of the firm.

In addition to being screened when first applying for membership, firms are monitored regularly and on an *ad hoc* unannounced basis. The frequency of monitoring depends on the nature of the business: more complex and risky businesses are subject to more frequent monitoring. For example, while firms that are acting on a purely advisory basis are

[11] Proposals to introduce volume of business requirements have in some cases been shelved.

TABLE 6.1 The structure and membership of the self-regulating organizations

SECURITIES AND INVESTMENTS BOARD (SIB)

	Association of Futures Brokers and Dealers (AFBD)	Financial Intermediaries, Managers and Brokers Regulatory Association (FIMBRA)	Investment Management Regulatory Organization (IMRO)	Life Assurance and Unit Trust Regulatory Organization (LAUTRO)	The Trust Securities Association (TSA)
ORGANIZATIONS	Association of Futures Brokers and Dealers (AFBD)	Financial Intermediaries, Managers and Brokers Regulatory Association (FIMBRA)	Investment Management Regulatory Organization (IMRO)	Life Assurance and Unit Trust Regulatory Organization (LAUTRO)	The Trust Securities Association (TSA)
SECTORS	Options and Futures Brokers, Dealers, Managers and Advisers	Independent Investment Brokers, Managers and Advisers	Investment Managers who are part of larger companies	Companies selling life assurance and unit trust investments	Brokers and Dealers

generally only audited annually, those that are involved in dealing and clearing transactions may be subject to monthly monitoring.

In the event of a default, investors are eligible for compensation in respect of the defaulting firm's liabilities up to a maximum amount of £48,000 subject to the limitation that compensation payments in total should not exceed £100 million in any one year.[12]

4. THE PRINCIPLES OF REGULATING FINANCIAL INSTITUTIONS

The case for regulating banks rests on two propositions.[13] The first is that banks are central to the smooth functioning of an economy: widespread failures amongst banks could seriously disrupt other sectors of an economy. The second is that banks are vulnerable to runs. The shortfall of the net realizable value of bank assets (loans) below that of liabilities (deposits) creates a risk of default in the event of depositors choosing to withdraw their funds. If the risk of depositors withdrawing their funds from one bank is increased by the failure of another bank, then the banking system may be threatened by individual failures. An externality is therefore created by a combination of interrelationships between banks' solvency levels and the role of banks in an economy.

In the case of non-banks, it was noted above that one of the requirements of the Financial Services Act is that clients' money be held in separate bank accounts. Clients' funds are therefore threatened by failure of deposit-taking banks but not by those of investment businesses. The market failures that justify bank regulation do not in general apply to investment businesses. However, there are two that appear relevant to investment firms: systemic risks and imperfect (or strictly asymmetric) information.

Systemic Risks

By analogy with banks, a prima-facie case for regulation exists where the functioning of one part of the financial system is essential to the rest of the system or the economy as a whole, *and* where interlinkages exist between the performance of different financial institutions. Whether a particular class of financial institution and activity is central to economic activity is a subject on which opinions differ. However, few would deny that widespread failures amongst brokers and dealers could seriously

[12] Claims not exceeding £30,000 are paid in full; thereafter 90% of claims are paid up to £50,000.

[13] For a more extensive discussion of these issues see Bernanke and Gertler 1987; Bhattacharya and Gale 1987; Diamond and Dybvig 1986; and Jacklin and Bhattacharya 1988.

jeopardize the operation of a securities market. The liquidity of a market relies on efficient procedures for dealing in securities and settling and clearing transactions. Furthermore, significant interlinkages exist between brokers, dealers, and other financial institutions. The failure of one firm can have serious consequences for others. Respondents to a survey of 32 UK investment managers in 1988, reported in Franks and Mayer (1989), stated that the average loss that their firm would have suffered if one of their counterparties (brokers or dealers) had defaulted on 31 March 1988 was £3.9 million. If all their counterparties had defaulted they would on average have lost £35 million.

In view of their central role in a security market and the interlinkages that exist between firms, there is a prima-facie case for the regulation of brokers and dealers. The position of investment managers (mutual funds, pension funds, life-assurance firms, private-client firms) within an economic system is less certain. While they permit investors to diversify portfolios at low cost and possibly benefit from the expertise of others, investment managers can be by-passed by direct investment. Many security markets operate with rudimentary forms of investment management. Furthermore, interlinkages between investment managers and other firms are less pronounced than those between brokers and dealers. Provided that investment managers do not hold client funds, then, in the absence of fraud, costs to investors of financial failure are limited to interruption of business. These are probably small since the assets of failed firms that have not been subject to fraud are usually transferred at low cost to other firms. Other creditors may be affected but provided that investment managers do not borrow to take investment positions on their own account, the value of an investment manager's debts should be restricted to those that are required to run the business. As a consequence, extensive protection of investment managers against systemic risks is probably not justified. As the limitations on compensation schemes described above suggest, systemic considerations were not at the forefront in the design of the Financial Services Act in the UK.

Asymmetric Information

The second class of market failure results from asymmetric information. There are three types of risk to which the uninformed investor is exposed: uncompensated wealth transfers (in particular fraud and theft), incompetence, and negligence. Attempts to compensate for these risks by raising prices for finance and services provided create adverse selection and moral-hazard problems. The fraudulent, incompetent, and negligent drive out the honest and the competent (adverse selection), and encourage dishonesty and negligence (moral hazard).

Financial markets are likely to be particularly prone to information problems for two reasons. First, unlike the sale and purchase of goods, financial services involve ongoing relations between client and firm. Investment managers, for example, provide advisory and portfolio services over an extended period of time. Secondly, the quality of services supplied is frequently difficult to evaluate. It takes time to evaluate the quality of services provided and experience may be a poor guide to where dishonesty may occur. It is widely thought that much fraud and misappropriation remains undetected. In the absence of sensitive benchmarks against which to evaluate performance, detailed monitoring will be required to detect losses.

Market failure due to asymmetries in information is usually discussed in relation to bank lending (see, for example, Jaffee and Russell 1976; and Stiglitz and Weiss 1981). In fact, granted that the function of a bank is to screen and monitor borrowers, it is far from evident that this is the most relevant or pervasive example in financial markets. The area in which asymmetries in information are likely to be more pronounced is at the interface between private investors and institutions. The incentives on and abilities of institutions to evaluate quality of borrowers is likely to exceed those of individuals. Free-riding on information collection will be more prevalent amongst a large group of private investors than a small number of large institutions. Market failures due to asymmetric information are therefore more serious in institutions serving private clients, deposit-taking banks, and investment managers with a private clientele (retail markets), than those primarily transacting with other institutions and companies—broker-dealers and investment managers with an institutional clientele.

Drawing together the two classes of market failure, Table 6.2 summarizes the failures that are associated with banks, brokers, dealers, and investment managers with private and institutional clients. Systemic risks are a real concern in banks, brokers, and dealers. They are less seri-

TABLE 6.2. Market failures in financial services

		SYSTEMIC RISKS	
		YES	NO
ASYMMETRIC INFORMATION	YES	BANKS	PRIVATE CLIENT-INVESTMENT MANAGEMENT
	NO	BROKERS, DEALERS	INSTITUTIONAL CLIENT-INVESTMENT MANAGEMENT

ous in the investment-management business.[14] Asymmetric information creates market failures in banks and investment managers that service private clients but not in brokers, dealers, and investment managers that primarily transact with institutions.

Responses to Market Failures

What is the appropriate response to these market failures? In looking to regulation to correct these failures, economics warns us that regulators will be prone to capture (Stigler 1971) and self-regulatory professions will raise members' income by imposing barriers to entry (Shaked and Sutton 1981). The setting of minimum standards may worsen the welfare of those who wish to consume cheap, low quality service, and result in overinvestment in training and the provision of high quality services (Shapiro 1986). The scope of regulation should therefore be limited to areas where there is a clear case of market failure. Elsewhere, the proper functioning of markets should be encouraged.

In determining the scope and form of regulation, the first point to note is that the two classes of market failure described above are very different. Systemic risks are essentially financial in nature. Bank runs result from shortfalls of realizable asset values below those of liquid deposits; brokers and dealers face risks of insolvency from losses on own positions. A central component of the regulation of banks, brokers, and dealers is therefore the requirement that these institutions hold sufficient capital to reduce risks of financial failure to acceptably low levels.

In contrast, the risks arising from asymmetric information do not primarily relate to financial performance. Instead they reflect the nature and activities of a business and the type of individuals that it employs. Therefore, in correcting for failures arising from asymmetric information, financial requirements are unlikely to play a major role except in so far as they are indirectly related to the nature and activities of firms and the individuals within those firms. Instead, the correction of asymmetric information will primarily rely on the screening and monitoring of firms and individuals.[15] Adverse selection is diminished by imposing 'fit and proper' tests; and moral hazard is diminished by monitoring the 'conduct of business'.

Table 6.3 relates regulation to the three classes of institutions described in Table 6.2. Capital requirements should be required of banks, brokers, and dealers but not of investment managers. 'Fit and

[14] Note that in distinguishing between investment managers and other types of financial institutions, only pure investment managers that neither hold client balances nor take own positions are being assumed. Firms that hold client balances have some of the features of banks and firms that take own positions may create similar systemic risks to brokers and dealers. This is discussed further below.

[15] See Leland (1979) for the case for setting minimum standards.

TABLE 6.3. Investor protection in financial services

		CAPITAL REQUIREMENT	
		YES	NO
'FIT AND PROPER' CONDUCT OF BUSINESS TESTS	YES	BANKS	PRIVATE CLIENT-INVESTMENT MANAGEMENT
	NO	BROKERS, DEALERS	INSTITUTIONAL CLIENT-INVESTMENT MANAGEMENT

proper' tests and 'conduct of business' rules should be required of banks and investment managers that service private clients, but not brokers, dealers, and investment managers that primarily transact with institutions. The imposition of uniform regulation for different classes of financial institution is therefore inappropriate.[16]

Tables 6.2 and 6.3 and the above discussion deliberately exaggerate the distinction between different classes of firms. Some institutions will not be able to evaluate the quality of firms with which they transact any better than individuals. Some individuals may feel competent to screen and monitor firms themselves. Some forms of systemic risk are more serious than others. The consequences of a collapse of a banking system cannot be equated to those of a broker-dealer system in a bank-based financial system in which security markets are small and insignificant. There is therefore in practice a continuum of failures from financial collapse to minor disruption and from serious information deficiencies to minor asymmetries. This heterogeneity argues further against uniformity of regulation.

There are two forms that investor protection may take. It may be limited to information disclosure or provide explicit guarantees against financial failure in the form of insurance. The credit rating of corporate bonds and commercial paper is an example of pure information disclosure. Credit-rating agencies provide no guarantees against the financial failure of firms that they have rated highly. Similarly, financial institutions could be rated in terms of the quality of their organizational

[16] It might be thought that the default of a fraudulent or incompetent institution could have wider implications by threatening the solvency of others. However, this is no different from the normal risks of investment. The appropriate response is to require institutions to hold sufficient capital to be able to weather isolated defaults and to relate capital requirements to the riskiness of counterparties.

TABLE 6.4. Screening and monitoring of investment businesses

		'CONDUCT OF BUSINESS' RULES	
		YES	NO
'FIT AND PROPER' TESTS	YES	BANKS, LESS WELL-ESTABLISHED INVESTMENT BUSINESSES	LESS WELL-ESTABLISHED INVESTMENT ADVISERS
	NO	ESTABLISHED PRIVATE CLIENT-INVESTMENT BUSINESSES	ESTABLISHED INSTITUTIONAL CLIENT-INVESTMENT BUSINESSES

arrangements and the quality of personnel employed. These ratings could be provided by private-sector agencies. Rules regarding the criteria by which institutions are rated could be made explicit so that the performance of the monitoring agency could be evaluated. This form of protection may be quite adequate for institutions that are primarily transacting with professionals.

Other investors may prefer the higher degree of protection afforded by insurance. In the case of firm-specific risks, private-sector insurance may be available. In the case of systemic risks, losses are by definition correlated across firms and insurance will only be available to the extent that risks can be internationally diversified.[17] Systemic risks that cannot be diversified will require underwriting by the government as lender of last resort.

To summarize, regulation should range from requirements on information disclosure to insurance. Where market failures reflect risks that are correlated across firms then governments may have to intervene. But where market failures result from risks that are essentially firm-specific (fraud, negligence, and incompetence) then private provision of monitoring and insurance will frequently be adequate. The criteria by which private agencies monitor the performance of firms is a proper concern of public agencies, just as the government lays down disclosure rules for the auditing of company accounts. Beyond that the role of government is limited.

[17] However, there may be other reasons for the failure of insurance markets to develop. See, for example, Rothschild and Stiglitz 1976.

There is an important exception to this. Where wealth transfers, in particular fraud, occur then enforcement frequently requires the imposition of criminal penalties. These are appropriately prosecuted by a public agency, such as the police, not a private institution. The *ex post* imposition of criminal penalties should, however, be distinguished from *ex ante* monitoring of the quality of firms and institutions which can frequently be delegated to the private sector. The more severe are *ex post* penalties and the greater the incidence of detection, the lower are the *ex ante* requirements. The USA, for example, emphasizes *ex post* detection and deterrence more than the UK and as a consequence requires less *ex ante* screening and monitoring of certain classes of financial institutions.

One form of *ex post* penalty is the erosion of a firm's or individual's reputation. Established firms have more to lose from a revelation of malpractice than a new entrant and, prima facie, there is a case for more extensive *ex ante* screening ('fit and proper' tests) of new than established firms. However, as the Johnson Matthey case and the amendments to the 1979 Banking Act illustrate, reputation is not always a reliable defence against wealth transfers. In particular where client balances are held, not only are systemic risks increased but also fraud is easier to perpetrate.

If malpractice is not easily identified by (at least certain classes of) investors then *ex post* monitoring ('conduct of business' rules) will still be required, even of the most reputable firms, to ensure that investors are duly compensated for losses sustained. Where the quality of services is readily established but the quality of individuals or firms is not, then 'fit and proper' but not 'conduct of business' tests are warranted. The stringent testing of prospective new entrants to most non-financial professions (for example, medicine, the law and accountancy) but the lax evaluation of established practitioners suggests that this is frequently encountered outside of financial services.[18] It may also apply to investment businesses that do not handle client assets and merely perform advisory services.

This suggests a third set of considerations—the nature of firms—to be included with the type of investor and the scale of systemic risks in designing a regulatory framework. (Table 6.4 illustrates.) Banks that hold client balances and less well-established investment businesses (except those that merely provide advice) require 'fit and proper' and 'conduct of business' tests. Established private client-investment businesses need only comply with 'conduct of business' rules and established investment businesses that only transact with professional investors may escape regulation altogether.

Since asymmetries of information create a barrier to entry, some of the

[18] A less favourable interpretation would echo the warnings of the economic literature that self-regulating professions erect barriers to entry to preserve monopoly rents.

costs of conducting 'fit and proper' tests should be borne by established firms. Enhanced competition diminishes the costs of regulating excess profits of established firms.

These principles will be applied in the next section to an evaluation of the regulation of financial services in the UK.

5. AN EVALUATION OF THE REGULATION OF INVESTMENT MANAGERS IN THE UK

The first point to note about regulation in the UK, as it was described in Section 3, is that it satisfies many of the principles set out in Section 4. First, there is variety in the regulation of financial institutions as reflected in differences in the rules of the SROs. Secondly, self-regulation distances the execution of regulation from the government. There are, however, several respects in which it diverges. This will be illustrated in relation to the regulation of one class of financial institutions, investment managers.

As described in Table 6.1 in Section 3 there are two SROs that regulate the investment management business: FIMBRA and IMRO. The distinction between the two is that the former draws its membership from independent investment advisers and the latter from firms that are usually part of larger corporate entities. FIMBRA is primarily concerned with institutions that deal with private clients; IMRO's members often have institutional investors. However, the distinction between the two is not precise. Several members of IMRO have private clients. As a consequence, while there are significant differences in the way in which the two bodies operate, 'fit and proper' tests and 'conduct of business' rules are required of both memberships. Even institutions that just transact with other professionals are subject to an onerous system of regulation. Investors are therefore not offered the alternative of transacting at lower cost on mutually acceptable terms with unregulated firms.

Investment managers are required to satisfy the four sets of rules described in Section 3. These include a requirement that investment managers separate client balances from their own. Some investment managers are parts of licensed deposit-takers in which case, quite appropriately, they are subject to the Banking Acts, including quite onerous capital requirements. More surprisingly, investment managers that do not hold client balances are also required to hold capital.

Capital requirements are set in relation to the value of expenditures of investment managers over a particular period of time.[19] In the cases of

[19] Firms are subject to the maximum of an absolute minimum capital requirement of £5,000 and an expenditure based requirement which is either six-weeks or three-months' worth of expenditure depending on whether they act as principals in transactions or take counterparty risk.

large firms with high expenditures these requirements can be substantial. At one stage, there was also a proposal that requirements be related to the volume of business of firms, in which case even small firms that actively managed portfolios on behalf of clients would have been required to hold substantial amounts of capital.[20] In the event, volume of business has not been used as a criterion for determining capital requirements.

The objective of the capital requirements was to diminish the risks incurred by investors. Negligence or incompetence could cause an investment manager to execute transactions on behalf of clients incorrectly, in which case firms would require resources to compensate investors. In addition, perhaps through no fault of their own, investment managers might encounter delays in the settlement of transactions, or still worse a failure of a counterparty to settle at all, in which case the investment manager may be liable for losses sustained by investors.

These risks are very real. The survey of UK investment managers mentioned in Section 2 revealed that five firms reported errors amounting to 30 per cent of the value of transactions over the six months, October 1987 to March 1988.[21] One firm reported a loss of over £0.5 million. Section 2 recorded that counterparty default could be even more serious.

Although investors are clearly at risk from execution errors, settlement delays, and counterparty default, the appropriate response is not to require firms to hold capital. Large execution errors are very infrequent. Only nine of the thirty-two respondents reported significant execution errors. Very few firms have ever encountered counterparty default. The risks are small probabilities of large losses. As a consequence, large amounts of capital would be required to provide complete protection against these risks at substantial costs to firms. For example, the capital requirement on the thirty-two respondents to the survey would have had to have been on average five times higher than existing requirements to meet the losses sustained by one counterparty default and twenty-eight times higher to protect against a simultaneous collapse of all counterparties.

More effective protection can be provided at lower cost by pooling risks and insuring firms against the idiosyncratic losses of execution errors, settlement delays, and counterparty default.[22] Professional

[20] The proposal was that capital requirements be the maximum of the absolute minimum requirement and the expenditure requirement that were described in the previous paragraph, and either 0.1% or 0.3% of the previous quarter's value of purchases and sales, depending on whether firms were acting as principals or taking counterparty risk.

[21] While this includes the Stock Market Crash, execution errors are not restricted to such exceptional periods.

[22] Of course, counterparty default may be part of a systemic collapse. However, there is a serious danger of double counting if protection against systemic risk is provided at the level of brokers and dealers as well as investment managers.

indemnity insurance is widely used as a method of providing protection against execution errors. Firms arrange lines of credit with banks to secure short-term finance of settlement delays. Until recently, investment managers looked to the Stock Exchange Compensation Fund as a form of protection against counterparty default.[23] In the presence of uncorrelated risks, the total amount of capital that has to be held by insurers who pool risks is substantially below that which would be required of investment managers.

The other risk to which the investor is exposed is purely financial. Investment managers may become insolvent merely because they are unable to pay their fixed overheads or because they have sustained losses on investments made on their own account. Capital would appear to be more relevant to these. But again capital is only appropriate if serious losses can be sustained and these are correlated across the industry as a whole.

As mentioned in Section 3, the costs of investment managers becoming insolvent are probably small. Most investment managers (that have not been fraudulent) who encounter financial distress are readily taken over by other firms. This is not an infrequent occurrence and for the most part it does not impose costs on investors beyond the disruption and inconvenience of interruption of business. These on their own certainly do not justify onerous regulatory requirements.

Risks of financial collapse could be correlated across firms if they held significant own positions. That would give investment managers some of the features of brokers and dealers. However, Section 3 suggested that the consequences of systemic problems in investment management may be less severe than those in broking and dealing. Less onerous capital requirements should therefore be required of investment managers than brokers and dealers and those requirements should only be related to the own positions of investment managers. Alternatively, the imposition of capital requirements on investment managers could be avoided altogether by requiring separation of own positions.[24]

The distinction between broker-dealers and investment managers appears to be recognized in the USA. Brokers and dealers are subject to stringent capital requirements. Investment companies that issue securities to the public (for example mutual funds) are required to hold a fixed amount of capital ($100,000).[25] Investment advisers that do not issue securities and just invest in other firms' quoted and unquoted securities

[23] Compensation is now only available to private investors.

[24] Separation of own positions is in the spirit of structural regulation that is advocated by Kay and Vickers (1988). But for a critique of this, see Mayer (1988).

[25] Subject to certain stipulated minima, these are computed in relation to either a firm's aggregate indebtedness or its customer receivables after applying a 'haircut' (of 15 to 30%) to the market value of its equity positions.

are not required to hold capital under the Investment Advisers Act 1940.[26]

Investment managers should not be required to hold capital. Some types of investment managers should probably not be subject to onerous 'fit and proper' or 'conduct of business' tests. Some businesses should therefore be largely unregulated and others only regulated in limited ways. This stands in marked contrast to the onerous requirements that have been imposed on all investment managers in the UK.

Where has the UK gone wrong? The main deficiencies of UK regulation come from trying to impose too great a degree of uniformity across the financial system as a whole. The distinction between systemic risks and investor protection and the association of different classes of risk with different forms of protection has not been made sufficiently precise. It was noted in Section 2 that there is a presumption in the Financial Services Act that investment businesses should hold capital. That is appropriate for some but not all. There is the requirement that individuals be 'fit and proper' and businesses conducted appropriately. Some investors will welcome these requirements. Others will not, at least once they become aware of the costs that they are being indirectly forced to bear.

Elimination of capital requirements will not reduce the level of investor protection. Insurance can provide more protection than capital at lower cost. Furthermore, current investor compensation schemes are, as described above, very limited. Savings from reduced capital requirements could, at least in part, be used to augment existing levels of compensation.

6. AN EVALUATION OF PROPOSED HARMONIZATION OF REGULATION IN THE EUROPEAN COMMUNITY

Proposals for harmonizing regulation in the European Community in 1992 are still at a formative stage. A Directive on investment services was published in December 1988. This proposes that principles of home-country authorization that have been applied to banks in the second banking co-ordination directive should extend to investment businesses. Under this principle a firm that is authorized in one Member State should be able to establish branches or provide services elsewhere in the Community without requiring further authorization. Furthermore, access to host security markets and membership of Stock Exchanges should be available to overseas firms where appropriate.[27]

[26] California imposes a minimum capital requirement of $25,000.

[27] This does not apply to credit institutions in countries that do not accept credit institutions as members of their Stock Exchanges.

The Directive proposes that rules relating to prudential supervision ('fit and proper' tests), 'conduct of business', and financial soundness be within the exclusive jurisdiction of home Member States and that a compensation fund be administered by home countries. However, at present it is felt that harmonization of rules relating to 'conduct of business' and compensation schemes is not feasible. For the moment, it is suggested that 'conduct of business' rules continue to be enforced by the host country and that *host* compensation schemes apply to branches of investment businesses. In the longer term it is envisaged that a uniform system of rules will apply to 'fit and proper' tests, 'conduct of business' tests, and capital requirements and compensation schemes.

This uniformity across nations is as misconceived as uniformity across institutions in the UK. Like the UK authorities, the Commission is failing to distinguish adequately between the avoidance of systemic risks and investor protection. Where only investor protection is at issue then a diverse range of levels of protection can and should coexist. It is quite appropriate that some investors should be able to purchase investment management services with low levels of protection at relatively low cost from any country inside (or indeed outside) the Community. Other investors will seek higher levels of protection from firms, irrespective of their country of origin. Conversely, investment management firms should be able to supply services offering particular levels of protection anywhere within the Community. What is required is a system by which investors know the level of protection that they are being offered. To meet this end, there could be various categories of authorization corresponding to recognized levels of protection. This could be implemented through an extension of the club principle described above to an international setting: the authorization of investment management firms by different (self-) regulatory authorities. Alternatively, private agencies could be used to evaluate the degree of protection offered to investors.

Where there are systemic risks then the coexistence of several degrees of protection is not feasible. The public-good element of the financial system means that different levels of risk cannot in general be tolerated. In contrast to regulation of investment management, competition between national authorities threatens *under-regulation* of banks, brokers, and dealers. The response in banking has been international harmonization of regulatory rules, in particular those pertaining to capital adequacy. Likewise, if the principle of home country authorization is to apply, a uniform system of regulating brokers and dealers throughout the Community will be required.

However, it is questionable whether the principles set out in the second banking directive should be extended to investment businesses. The payments system is central to the operation of all countries' economies. In contrast, there is appreciable variation in the relevance of security markets to different members of the Community. Security markets (bond or equity) play a less central role in bank-based systems, such as in Germany, than market-based systems, such as in the UK. There is therefore little justification for applying the same level of protection to security markets in all countries in Europe.

Even if home-country principles of authorization are accepted then diversity in the regulation of investment managers should be tolerated. Furthermore, while capital should appropriately be required of brokers and dealers to protect against systemic risks, it should not be required of investment managers. As described in the previous section, the risks involved in investment management are primarily non-financial in nature and where there are financial risks the costs associated with them are comparatively small.

7. CONCLUSIONS

This paper has described regulation of investment businesses in the UK and considered current proposals to harmonize regulation of investment services in Europe.

It noted that there are several appealing features of the current regulatory system in the UK. The mixture of self- and statutory regulation offers considerable scope for effective and flexible regulation. The multiplicity of regulatory organizations is appropriate in view of the different risks involved in the provision of financial services. Unfortunately, the heterogeneous nature of investment businesses has not been fully recognized. The notions of 'fit-and-properness' and the requirement that businesses satisfy rules of conduct have been too readily accepted as requirements of all firms. Most seriously of all, capital requirements have been expected of firms where financial risks are small or absent.

The paper set out principles by which investor protection should be designed. The first consideration was whether investment businesses were prone to systemic risks in the sense that, first, there were significant interactions between the financial performances of firms and, secondly, their continued operation was essential to the functioning of an economy. On this basis, a distinction was drawn between banks, brokers, and dealers on the one hand and investment managers on the other. The systemic risks present in the former group justified the imposition of capital requirements. In contrast, the risks in investment management relate primarily to fraud and the conduct of business for which screening and monitoring are required.

The second consideration that was discussed above was the nature of the investor. Asymmetries of information give rise to market failures that undermine the operation of certain industries. Asymmetries are likely to be prevalent in the investment business because of the continuing nature of the relation between client and firm, and the difficulties involved in evaluating the performance of firms. Within the investment business, asymmetries in information will be pronounced where there are large numbers of small uninformed investors. Market failures will therefore be particularly serious in retail businesses. Professional investors may feel more competent to evaluate performance. Different regulatory rules, ranging from information disclosure to insurance, will be appropriate depending on the nature of the investor. In the absence of systemic risks, there will be considerable opportunities for delegating regulation to private-sector auditors and insurers.

The European Commission is proposing extending the principles of home-country authorization from banking to financial services. It is questionable whether this is appropriate. Unlike the payments system, the relevance of investment business to the functioning of economies differs appreciably between Member States. Thus the costs of sytemic collapse and the appropriate level of protection also differ.

Leaving this point of principle aside, the European Commission is following the UK authorities in trying to impose too great a degree of uniformity across financial institutions and investors. Capital requirements should not be required of all financial institutions. The same levels of protection should not necessarily be provided to all classes of investors.

As the internationalization of security markets progresses, the system-wide role of particular national markets will diminish. This is already in evidence in Europe with Eurobond markets operating alongside domestic markets and offering investors and firms choices between relatively regulated domestic and unregulated international markets. Likewise, international listing of shares has diminished the reliance of companies on domestic equity markets. Once internationalization is taken to the point at which companies can be quoted in several different markets then competition between markets in terms of the protection that they offer and the prices that they charge will be possible. There will then be more scope for a return to the decentralization of regulation to individual markets which currently prevails without the associated barriers to international trade.

References

Bernanke, B., and Gertler, M. (1987), 'Banking and macroeconomic equilibrium', in W. A. Barnett and K. J. Singleton (eds.), *New Approaches to Monetary Economics*, Cambridge: Cambridge University Press.

Bhattacharya, S., and Gale, D. (1987), 'Preference shocks, liquidity and central bank policy', in Barnett and Singleton (eds.), *New Approaches to Monetary Economics.*

Diamond, D., and Dybvig, D. (1983), 'Bank runs, deposit insurance, and liquidity', *Journal of Political Economy*, 91: 401–19.

Franks, J. R., and Mayer, C. P. (1989), *Risk, Regulation and Investor Protection: The Case of Investment Management*, Oxford: Oxford University Press.

Gardener, E. P. M. (1986), *UK Banking Supervision*, London: Allen & Unwin.

Goodhart, C. (1988), 'The costs of regulation', in A. Sheldon (ed.), *Financial Regulation—or Over-Regulation*, London: Institute of Economic Affairs.

Gower Report (1984), *Review of Investor Protection*, Cmnd 9125, London: HMSO.

Jacklin, C. J., and Bhattacharya, S. (1988), 'Distinguishing panic and information-based bank runs: Welfare and policy implications', *Journal of Political Economy*, 96: 568–97.

Jaffee, D. M., and Russell, T. (1976), 'Imperfect information, uncertainty and credit rationing', *Quarterly Journal of Economics*, 90: 651–66.

Leland, H. E. (1979), 'Quacks, lemons and licensing: A theory of minimum quality standards', *Journal of Political Economy*, 87: 1328–46.

Lomax, D. (1987), *London Markets After the Financial Services Act*, London: Butterworths.

Rothschild, M., and Stiglitz, J. E. (1976), 'Equilibrium in competitive insurance markets: An essay on the economics of imperfect information', *Quarterly Journal of Economics*, 90: 629–50.

Shaked, A., and Sutton, J. (1981), 'The self-regulating profession', *Review of Economic Studies*, 48: 217–34.

Shapiro, C. (1986), 'Investment, moral hazard and occupational licensing', *Review of Economic Studies*, 53: 843–62.

Stigler, G. J. (1971), 'The theory of economic regulation', *Bell Journal of Economic and Management Science*, 2/1: 3–21.

Stiglitz, J. E., and Weiss, A. (1981), 'Credit rationing in markets with imperfect information', *American Economic Review*, 71: 393–410.

Veljanovski, C. (1988), 'The introduction', in A. Sheldon (ed.), *Financial Regulation—or Over-Regulation*, London: Institute of Economic Affairs.

7

The Reregulation of British Broadcasting

MARTIN CAVE* AND PETER WILLIAMSON†

1. INTRODUCTION

Almost everywhere broadcasting is a highly regulated industry. Despite the growth of international, satellite-based broadcasting firms, in most countries the bulk of decisions determining the system of television and radio broadcasting are made by government. Control over the structure of broadcasting is usually exercised by the national government, although the implementation of regulatory functions, such as allocation of broadcasting licences, is often undertaken by an independent regulatory agency. Either the public sector provides broadcasting services directly, or it regulates the number, type, and conduct of companies in the industry. There is, however, no universal model for the structure, regulation, and operation of broadcasting. The degree to which television and radio broadcasting is centralized/decentralized, commercial/noncommercial, and regulated/unregulated differs among countries, the outcomes being a product of the historical, ideological, and political forces in each national setting.

Until recently, the broadcasting industry has not been widely viewed as a fit subject for economic analysis, except in the USA. But recent developments in broadcasting technology have promoted a liberalization of the industry in almost all countries, and it is becoming increasingly the practice to apply the tools of industrial economics and the economics of regulation to it. Economic analysis based on one system cannot usually be transposed without modification to the broadcasting environment of another country. Nevertheless, there has developed a body of literature on the economics of television regulation which has general application and which, together with the increasing number of UK studies, provides a framework for the economic analysis of broadcasting in this country.

* Dean, Faculty of Social Sciences, Brunel University.

† Professor at the Department of Strategic and International Management, London Business School.

We are grateful to Allan Brown for agreement to reproduce some parts of Brown and Cave (forthcoming) and to Matthew Bishop for helpful comments. This chapter covers events to 1992.

This survey sets out the basic issues relating to the economics of television regulation in the UK. For analytical convenience we distinguish five stages of production and distribution of television programmes namely:

(1) Programme production and acquisition.
(2) Networking—the wholesaling of programmes to local broadcasters.
(3) Local channel management—the selection of material for transmission by local stations.
(4) Programme delivery.
(5) Revenue collection.

There is some arbitrariness in the classification, but it does demonstrate the wide variety of ways in which broadcast programmes and other video material can be made and distributed. Table 7.1 shows how the five functions identified are discharged in a number of broadcasting (or video distribution) organizations. It can be seen that there exists a varying degree of vertical integration within television broadcasting in the UK.

Most of the discussion in this survey deals with stages 2 to 5. There is overwhelming evidence that many of the structural features described in the table are an intended or unintended product of regulation, in particular:

(a) the existence of public sector broadcasters;
(b) the control of entry into various stages of the industry;
(c) requirements to acquire programmes from independent producers;
(d) restrictions on ownership which place limitations on the number of stations any one company can own, and on cross-media and foreign ownership;
(e) restrictions on sources of finance;
(f) control over the composition of output, as evident, for instance, in the positive programming requirements set out for Channel 3 in the Broadcasting Act 1990.

These restrictions operate as well as those which apply to all branches of the economy, such as taxation, and those common to all media, such as obscenity laws.

The paper is organized as follows: Section 2 outlines some possible economic rationales for the regulation of broadcasting; Section 3 describes UK broadcasting regulatory institutions. Section 4 outlines the consequences of the 1990 Broadcasting Act while Section 5 examines the tendering process for Channel 3 in more detail. Section 6 considers some current and forthcoming issues.

TABLE 7.1. The distribution of functions in different television systems

System	The BBC	Commercial television		Satellite broadcasting (BSB)	Video-cassettes
Production	BBC and independent production (some programmes imported)	C3 (from 1993) Regional ITV contractors (especially five 'network' companies), independent production plus some imports	Channel 4 (from 1993) Independent producers or ITV companies (plus imports)	Produced by BSB or acquired	Usually film studios
Networking	BBC	Jointly by C3 companies through independent Network Director	Channel 4	BSB	Video distributors
Local programme selection	BBC	Regional contractors	Channel 4 (channel is programmed nationally)	BSB (national programming)	Local video-rental shop
Programme delivery	BBC	By a separate privatized transmission Company (NTC)	By a separate privatized transmission Company (NTC)	Leased satellite	Normally consumer
Revenue collection	Collection of licence fee through Post Office	Regional contractors (advertiser-financed)	National sales of advertising time	Some advertiser-financed and some pay channels	Local video-rental shop (pay-programming)

2. ECONOMIC JUSTIFICATIONS FOR BROADCASTING REGULATION

Although the broadcasting industry exhibits certain peculiar features arising from the 'public good' nature of broadcast programmes (discussed below), in other respects its regulation has much in common with that of other industries. Thus in broadcasting at elsewhere it is useful to distinguish between positive and normative theories of regulation. The former seek to explain how the differing interests of the participants in the industry—producers and consumers—interact to produce a set of regulations which benefits the parties in different ways. The government is seen as an actor which uses its regulatory capacity to pursue its own interests—usually the acquisition of votes or money—and which is influenced by other agents through a political and economic process.

In contrast, normative theories of regulation start from the proposition that the government is pursuing certain 'benign' objectives and intervening in the broadcasting system in order to pursue such goals as economic efficiency or equity. Normative motives for regulation can themselves be usefully divided into two groups. In the first case, the nature of the regulation is 'economic'; the government intervenes to avert the market failures or departures from efficiency to which an unregulated system would otherwise be prey. This can be distinguished from 'social' regulation, through which the government pursues certain social objectives in the 'public interest' such as the protection of the population from unsuitable broadcasting material, or the development of national culture. For some forms of regulation the distinction is not hard and fast. The Australian programme-content rules, for example, have both the economic function of protecting domestic industry and the social functions of promoting national pride and cultural values. Beneficial externalities are thus deliberately prescribed by this form of broadcast regulation. The provision of certain types of programmes considered to be 'merit goods' is a further motivation for government intervention in broadcasting (see Section 6).

This survey concentrates mainly upon normative approaches to regulation of the economic kind, but other approaches are considered at various stages. It is therefore useful to indicate at the outset what are the special features of broadcasting which can be seen as justifying regulation. (For a fuller account of television economics see Noll *et al.* 1973; Owen *et al.* 1974; and Hughes and Vines 1988.)

Most economic arguments for regulation arise from the public-good aspect of broadcast programmes. The expense involved in producing or purchasing a television programme is a fixed cost. Once the outlays have been incurred and the programme produced it can be recorded on video tape or on film, and its cost to the original producer is then independent of the number of stations which acquire the rights for its rebroadcast. That is, once made a programme can be broadcast on additional stations at virtually zero marginal cost. Equally, once transmitted a programme can be seen by an additional viewer in the reception area at the low marginal cost, normally borne by the viewer, of operating his or her reception equipment. The existence of high 'first copy' costs is characteristic of many media, but it is particularly acute in the case of broadcasting. The implications are profound: efficient consumption of programmes requires, in the absence of price discrimination, a charge to the viewer of zero. How can the financing of the industry ensure efficiency in these circumstances?

There are three conventional sources of finance for television broadcasters: out of general taxation; by advertisers; or by direct charges to broadcasting audiences. It is widely appreciated that there are problems in terms of economic efficiency with each of these approaches.

In the case of the first option, finance by taxation or licence fee (where it is assumed that penetration of television is such that a license fee is equivalent to a poll tax), the difficulty arises not in the marginal price of viewing—which is set optimally at zero—but in the incentives which face the broadcasting firm. Since viewers cannot convey their preferences in a detailed way or directly control the programming made available by broadcasting organizations, the latter may be tempted to substitute their own preferences for those of their viewers. This is a classic agency problem in which the principals (viewers) cannot convey information to, or control the agent (the broadcasting organization). As career advancement in public-sector broadcasting organizations may depend more on the judgement of peers than on audience size or appreciation, the welfare loss associated with the agency problem has the potential to be considerable.

The case of advertiser support in broadcasting seems at first sight to provide an efficient solution to the problem. Programmes are made available 'free' to audiences, while those audiences are then sold on a wholesale basis to advertisers, from whom stations derive revenue. The difficulty is that the whole process involves advertisers standing in an intermediate relationship between consumers and broadcasters (Spence and Owen 1977). The problem is that the broadcaster receives revenue from the advertiser which is broadly proportional to the audience size, but largely independent of the audience's preferences or willingness to pay for the programme. As a consequence, in the absence of close substitutes the profit-maximizing advertiser-financed broadcaster, rather than providing programmes which are greatly appreciated by smaller audiences, will always have an incentive to provide programmes which are watched with scant enjoyment by larger audiences. Rothenberg (1962) describes such strategies as 'lowest common denominator' programming.

A related problem with advertiser-supported television arises from the risk that popular programme types will be excessively duplicated. The argument here is a straightforward application by Steiner (1952, 1961) of Hotelling's principle of minimum product differentiation: a limited number of competitive channels will broadcast similar programmes designed to appeal to the same mass audience, and neglect minority tastes. When the number of channels is larger, the problem of programme types being excluded diminishes, but that of duplication of costs remains. The only way to remove the problem of duplication is to assign all channels to the same firm to broadcast complementary programmes. In a system of broadcasting financed by advertising, therefore, the problems of inappropriate incentives and programme duplication introduce a bias in the programme-selection process, and this militates particularly against programmes appealing to minority audiences which have, but cannot express, a high willingness to pay.

The obvious way to capture willingness to pay is to charge for the programmes. In a framework of multi-channel broadcasting, a useful way to visualize the industry's structure is one of monopolistic competition (Spence and Owen 1977). But if broadcasters are constrained to charging a uniform price, the effect of pay broadcasting is to drive a gap between the price and the marginal cost of viewing an additional programme, and hence to restrict consumption, because a positive price for programmes will exclude some potential viewers.

Thus both advertiser-financed broadcasting and pay broadcasting generate inefficiencies. In the former case the major problem is the bias in programme selection. In the latter case restricted consumption is the principal difficulty, although pay broadcasting too discriminates to some extent against programmes highly appreciated by a small minority, as the high prices necessarily charged to break even drive away potential viewers. As with all second-best problems, it is impossible to say a priori which of the two inefficiencies is the more severe. It is likely however that if the number of channels is low, the harmful effects of bias will be limited too, as minority programmes would not gain access to the air waves in any case because of channel scarcity. When the number of channels is greater, the harmful effects of bias in programme selection will be more considerable, as highly appreciated minority programmes, which might be broadcast profitably under charging, may fail under advertiser-finance to generate the audience necessary to break even. It has been shown that if the competitive broadcasters have the option of either advertiser-finance or pay broadcasting, they will find it more profitable to choose charges as against advertiser support, the more viewers dislike advertisements and the lower their value to advertisers. On certain assumptions—notably, that pounds paid by advertisers for audiences are equivalent in welfare terms to dollars paid directly by audiences to view programmes—the more profitable source of finance is also better in welfare terms (Wildman and Owen 1985). This result provides support for permitting competition between various forms of finance, and some ground for optimism about the outcome.

The normative 'economic' theory of broadcasting regulation identifies market failures arising from the public-good nature of the industry. These failures can be eliminated by public production (but which is subject to the difficult agency relation mentioned above), or by subsidization of particular programme types. Accordingly, the UK Peacock Report (Committee on Financing the BBC 1986, p. 148) recommended the provision of subsidies on the ground that they would secure availability of 'those programmes which the public recognise as being in their own interest to have produced but which cannot be delivered by the market'. However, subsidizing the production of any programme which costs less than the consumer surplus it generates, given the other programmes available, would require the collection of information which is not at present available. It would also be difficult to acquire such information, as asking households what value they place on viewing a hypothetical programme is likely to elicit ill-informed or opportunistic answers. Mistakes would also be costly. In any case, the number of such programmes may be small, especially in a multi-channel world. It is worth noting that the same argument can be applied to all cultural industries where there are substantial 'first copy' costs. Where entry barriers are low or non-existent, as in book publishing, arguments for public subsidy are relatively infrequent. As broadcasting becomes more competitive, they may be muted there too.

3. THE DEVELOPMENT OF BROADCASTING REGULATION IN THE UNITED KINGDOM

Broadcasting in the UK has always been highly regulated. From the outset, radio transmissions were restricted by the terms of the Wireless Telegraphy Act 1906, which required all operators to gain a licence. During the First World War, control was made even tighter for defence reasons, but thereafter the radio manufacturers promoted broadcasting as a commercial service. Even then consumer sovereignty was not given much prominence. Thus in 1922 John Reith, then General Manager of the privately owned British Broadcasting Company and later to become first Director-General of the public British Broadcasting Corporation, made the memorable remark that 'it is occasionally indicated to us that we are apparently setting out to give the public what we think they need, and not what they want, but few know what they want, and very few want what they need' (quoted in Coase 1950, 47).

It was thus natural that, following the report of a government committee, radio broadcasting was placed as a monopoly in the hands of the BBC, and controlled directly neither by government nor industry but by a regulatory body—the Board of Governors. Over the following years the BBC fought vigorously to maintain its monopoly against encroachments from continental broadcasters and even some fledgeling radio cable systems.

The Birth of Commercial Television

When television broadcasting began in 1936, it too was assigned to the BBC, despite a proposal from the General Electric Company (GEC), a major electrical company, that a consortium of 'responsible' private companies should provide the service. But after the Second World War, as television ownership became widespread, there occurred one of those sudden government-driven changes in policy that have occasionally disturbed the serenity of broadcasting regulation in Britain.

The background to this major decision illustrates the importance of control of the legislature in British regulatory policy. The BBC's Charter was renewed in 1946 until the end of 1952. A committee, chaired by Lord Beveridge, was appointed in 1946 to consider broadcasting policy, and its majority reported in 1951 in favour of maintaining the BBC's monopoly. The Labour government was not, however, able to realize its intention of re-chartering the BBC as a monopoly before it fell in October 1951. The issue thus passed to a Conservative government which had misgivings about the BBC's monopoly and was subject to pressure to allow commercial (i.e. advertiser-supported) programmes.

Among the various groups which combined in lobbying for commercial television were: advertising agencies seeking new outlets for promotional material; a number (initially small) of Conservative Members of Parliament opposed to the BBC's monopoly; and some former BBC employees. Opposition was bipartisan and intense (Lord Reith, for example, likened the introduction of commercial television to that of dog-racing or smallpox), but the Conservative party was finally won over. An Act establishing commercial broadcasting was passed in 1954.

The provisions of that Act failed to satisfy the most fervent proponents of free enterprise. An Independent Television Authority (ITA) was created which would own and operate transmitting stations, and would supervise (but not provide) the programmes. The programmes would be made by contracting companies appointed by the Authority. The Authority was required to ensure competition in the supply of programmes and 'a proper balance in their subject matter'.

In relation to advertising, the Act required the Authority to limit the duration of commercial messages and to produce and publish an advertising code. It specifically forbade sponsorship of programmes (the form of advertising then prevalent in the United States).

The 1954 Act imposed numerous obligations on the ITA but at the same time gave it wide discretion over how to satisfy them. The requirement to ensure competition was particularly onerous, as the spectrum allocation policy adopted by the government restricted each area of the country to a single channel. The plan the ITA chose involved making different contractors responsible for programmes on different days of the week. But it also intended to introduce further competition by allowing companies to sell programmes to one another on a competitive basis.

The ITV Cartel

This latter aim was not realized. Commercial television was initially unprofitable, and the companies responded by developing 'networking' arrangements with one another for the exchange of programmes. The ITA had initially envisaged programme exchanges on a competitive basis, but what emerged was a monopolistic 'network carve-up' in which the major companies divided the production of network programmes among themselves. This co-ordinated programme planning obviously had strong commercial logic, as each major company could save on production facilities, but the arrangement thwarted the Authority's aim of achieving competition between programmes.

The ITA sought advice on the legality of the companies' arrangements, and was told that it could be argued that the companies were putting themselves outside their contractual obligations. But in the event the ITA acquiesced in the arrangement, its tolerance surviving even into the age of enormous profits. Although television in Britain ceased to be a monopoly in 1955, commercial television itself effectively became a cartel.

The existence of the cartel, and of the excess profits it permitted, enabled the regulatory agency to impose public-service obligations on the commercial broadcasters. Specific requirements were imposed in respect of news, current affairs, religious, children's, and other programmes. And compliance was made more likely by a contract-renewal process in which holders of the monopoly franchises competed every ten years or so against potential entrants on the basis of their past record. However, the rules of the game were not explicit, and the decision-making process was anything but transparent.

The regulatory framework created in 1926 and in the early 1950s remained largely intact until the 1980s. New terrestrially transmitted radio and television channels (Independent Local Radio, BBC2, and Channel 4) were integrated within it. Significant authority rested with the regulators—the BBC Board of Governors and the Independent Broadcasting Authority (IBA) which took over from the ITA in 1972.

The 1980s saw significant developments in regulatory structure. A Broadcasting Complaints Commission had been established. The Cable and Broadcasting Act 1984 established a separate Cable Authority to regulate cable television. By its dissolution in 1990, it had issued licences for cable systems passing up to 65 per cent of UK television homes. A further body, the Broadcasting Standards Council, was established in 1988 on a non-statutory basis to exercise control over matters of taste and decency.

The Broadcasting Act 1990 produced an important rearrangement of regulatory functions. A new body, the Independent Television Commission, was established and responsibility to regulate cable television was transferred to it. At the same time, a separate organization, the Radio Authority, was set up to regulate independent national and local radio. The Office of Fair Trading was also assigned the task of reporting on the BBC's fulfilment of its independent production quota and of verifying that the networking arrangements proposed by Channel 3 satisfied the competition test. The Broadcasting Complaints Commission continued to operate as before, while the Broadcasting Standards Council was placed on a statutory basis. Thus television was subject to regulation by four national statutory organizations and radio by three.

The 1980s also saw the beginning of attempts to introduce and regulate satellite broadcasting. The Independent Broadcasting Authority allocated the high-powered direct broadcasting by satellite (DBS) channels assigned to the United Kingdom, to British Satellite Broadcasting in 1986. Its programmes came on the air for the first time in 1990. However, the first satellite television service available in the UK was provided by Sky Television, which was broadcast on Astra, a medium-powered satellite based in Luxemburg and not subject to British regulation (though if supplied on cable the channels are subject to normal regulation). In 1990, the two companies merged to form British Sky Broadcasting using the Astra satellite. The UK's DBS assignments have not yet been reallocated. While relatively few homes have opted for broadband cable television (269,000 at the start of 1992, out of 1.3 million homes passed), satellite broadcasting has been more successful. It was being received in 2.4 million UK homes by the end of that period.

4. THE BROADCASTING ACT 1990

The origins of the Broadcasting Act 1990 can be found in a decision taken by the government in 1985 to set up a Committee of Inquiry into financing the BBC, chaired by Professor (now Sir) Alan Peacock. It was expected that the Committee would concentrate on the principal issue laid before it—whether the BBC should be financed by advertising rather than by a licence fee. On that question it came down against advertising on the BBC. But in addition it came up with a range of proposals affecting other parts of the broadcasting system, especially ITV, and a new approach to analysing broadcasting policy.

The Committee's starting point was that the era of scarcity of TV channels arising from spectrum limitations was soon to come to an end. The growth of cable and other delivery systems created the possibility for freedom of entry and the application of consumer sovereignty to broadcasting, subject to rules for consumer protection made necessary by the intrusive nature of the medium, and mechanisms to ensure subsidies for the provision of certain types of minority or experimental programmes. The Committee was thus the first to apply economic concepts in a systematic way to the broadcasting industry.

Following the publication of the Report, in 1988 the government issued a White Paper on Broadcasting Policy which was subsequently the basis for the Broadcasting Act 1990. The main provisions of the Broadcasting Act can be summarized as follows:

(i) New Entry

The Act provided for a new terrestrial channel (Channel 5) to be allocated by competitive tender. The frequencies available allow coverage of about 70 per cent of television homes. The licensee will be required to supply proportions of originally produced and commissioned programmes which will increase over time. It will also be required to undertake the necessary retuning of household videos in order to avoid interference.

(ii) Competition for Advertising

The Act allows Channel 4 (now established as an independent corporation) to sell its own advertising time, in place of the previous system whereby ITV companies sell advertising on both channels, and pay an annual subscription to Channel 4. The Act thus introduces competition for C3 in the air-time market from Channel 4, as well as from the growing audiences of advertiser-supported cable and satellite services.

(iii) Independent Production

The Act imposes quotas of independently produced material on all channels. The 25 per cent target for qualifying programmes is to be satisfied from the start of 1993. The ITC will monitor Channel 3's performance, while the Office of Fair Trading will report on BBC's performance of its targets.

(iv) Allocation of Licences

Channel 3 licences, the new Channel 5 licence, and cable licences after the expiry of their present terms are awarded by competitive tendering.

The same procedure is to be used by the radio authority in allocating national radio licences. An account of the operation of the Channel 3 tendering system is provided in the next section.

(v) Content Regulation

Different positive programming requirements apply to Channel 3 and Channel 5. All broadcast programmes are subject to the Obscenity Act and to scrutiny by the Broadcasting Standards Council which the Act endowed with statutory powers.

Thus the Broadcasting Act 1990 sets out a new framework for greater competition in both broadcast and advertising markets and, particularly, it introduces new competitive methods for the allocation of licences. Although these procedures were first applied in allocating a national radio licence, the event which attracted most attention was the allocation in 1991 of Channel 3 licences from 1993 by competitive tendering. This and alternative means of allocating licences are discussed in the next section.

5. THE ALLOCATION OF BROADCASTING LICENCES

All systems of broadcasting regulation face the problem of allocating scarce—and often highly profitable—broadcasting frequencies. The allocation can be done by a variety of means: through comparative hearings (in which the regulatory body determines the worthiest applicant on the basis of programming and other criteria); through a lottery; or through an auction or tendering process. The adoption of the last method for allocating Channel 3 and other broadcasting licences was one of the most controversial aspects of the 1990 Act.

Tendering Criteria

Before the passage of the Broadcasting Act 1990, franchises for advertiser-supported radio and television had been allocated by the ITA or IBA. After a comparative process in which applicants outlined their programming plans, staffing proposals, financial intentions and other aspects of their projected activities, the regulator decided which competitor would be awarded the franchise without giving detailed reasons for the decisions adopted.

This system led to considerable disquiet. This was due partly to the rather unedifying spectacle of a public body deliberating in secret over the allocation of highly profitable rights to a public asset—the airwaves. Over certain periods, franchises in some regions had been highly profitable—in Lord Thompson of Fleet's memorable words, a 'licence to print money'. But apart from the unsatisfactory nature of a public body distributing large profits streams in an unaccountable way, criticism was also directed at the circumstance that franchises were sometimes taken away on no other basis than subjective preference for a rival's programming plans which sometimes turned out to be unrealizable (Briggs and Spicer 1986). The anxieties were well captured by the last Chairman of the IBA, Lord Thompson of Monifieth, who at the last franchise round in 1980 made the often-quoted observation: 'there must be a better way'.

The 'better way' adopted in the Broadcasting Act of 1990 was a system of competitive tendering for the licences with an entry qualification for bidders. Competitive tendering was seen as being a means of squeezing out of the system the substantial inefficiencies and rents which the Prime Minister and others had detected in the industry. The licences would run for ten years in the first instance, with the possibility of renewal after six years, subject to satisfactory conduct. There is thus likely to be one round of bidding entry.

The mechanics of competitive tendering went through several variations before the Act was passed. The idea originally surfaced in a majority recommendation of the Peacock Committee (1986) that ITV licences should be allocated by competitive tendering, with the licence normally going to the highest bidder; but if the IBA decided to award it to a contractor other than the one making the highest bid, it should be required to make a full, public, and detailed statement of its reasons.

The logic of the Peacock majority was that the regulator would be expected to lay down minimum criteria relating to the quality and range of programmes which bidders would have to satisfy. But the IBA could decide that a company offering a lower price was giving more 'value for money' in terms of public service than the highest bidder and award the franchise to it. However, when the proposal reappeared in the Government White Paper on broadcasting (Home Office 1988), licences were to be allocated by competitive tendering to the highest qualified bidder, where to qualify a bidder had to pass a threshold defined in terms of consumer protection and specified positive programming requirements.

These provisions were largely embodied in the Broadcasting Bill, but during its passage through Parliament the quality requirements were strengthened, with the result that the final system which emerged gave the newly created regulatory authority (the Independent Television Commission or ITC) considerable discretion to determine whether a bidder did meet the requirements. The Act contained requirements that a sufficient amount of time be given to high quality news and current affairs programmes, that a sufficient amount of time be given to other programmes of high quality, and that a sufficient amount of time be given to regional programmes, religious, and children's programmes. In addition, programmes had to be calculated to appeal to a wide variety of tastes and interests. No more detailed definitions of the meaning of terms such as 'sufficient' and 'wide' were supplied in the Act. The Act also entitled the regulator to reject a bid on the ground that the company's business plan seemed unlikely to provide the finance necessary to sustain the promised programming.

A further change from the White Paper was the restoration of an 'exceptional circumstances' provision, which entitled the ITC to award the licence to an applicant other than the highest bidder under certain conditions. The Commission could grant the licence to an applicant who had not submitted the highest bid where it appeared to the Commission that the quality of the service proposed by the applicant was exceptionally high and substantially higher than the quality of service proposed by the highest bidder. Interestingly, there was no provision in this clause for balancing differences in quality and differences in bid—though applicants may have expected that this would happen in any case.

The final system was thus the outcome of compromises between those seeking an open and competitive tendering system which would attract a large number of bidders and a less-open system which confined the contest to a smaller number of qualified applicants. One of the key factors likely to discourage applicants was the need to pass a necessarily subjective quality threshold. This raises the immediate question of whether such a requirement was necessary, and whether it was appropriately specified. One possible objective index of quality is a programme's cost or 'production values'—the lavishness of the sets, the size of the cast, etc. But a cost-based measure would have poor incentive properties. A more satisfactory alternative would be to use Audience Appreciation Indices, collected regularly by broadcasters to monitor the degree to which programmes are enjoyed. Such measures would provide an *ex post* proxy for quality based upon viewers' own experience. But they were not to play a role in the new regulatory system, which relied instead upon a subjective evaluation of programming intentions.

Risk Sharing

An interesting feature of the tendering system which emerged was the way in which it split risks between the government and the licensee. Bidding for a broadcast licence over a ten-year period is a risky business. It requires projections of costs and revenues over an extended period, in circumstances where both are uncertain. Past evidence suggests that overall television advertising revenues are strongly sensitive to the rate of growth of GDP or consumers' expenditure: typical estimates of the expenditure elasticity are well in excess of one. This makes the revenue stream dependent upon developments in the economy, with consequences which are developed elsewhere in this article. However, the period over which the Channel 3 licences were advertised (1993 to 2002) was also to be a period in which new advertiser-supported and pay-television services would become available. These could eat into Channel 3's audiences.

Not only was there uncertainty about demand for the new services, but estimates had to be made of their likely source of funding. To the extent that the revenues were from advertising, the new channels would compete directly with Channel 3. To the extent that they were financed by monthly subscriptions, Channel 3's dominant position in the television advertising market would remain undiminished. But Channel 3 ran the risk of losing some of the most valuable components of its audience to the pay channels.

Bidders thus had to make revenue forecasts in conditions of great uncertainty about revenues. Projections of costs were also uncertain. The bulk of ITV viewing had always been of nationally networked programmes broadcast in the evening peak-hours. The companies had come together to agree a budget for and the composition of such programmes, and the regulatory body—the IBA—had always had to approve the schedule. The Broadcasting Act relieved the companies of this direct supervision, but required them to enter into a networking agreement, in the absence of which one would be imposed by the Independent Television Commission. The Act did not, however, lay down the extent of networking; that would have to be resolved by the successful licensees. Nor did it lay down the budget, which would also have to be agreed once the licences had been awarded. These provisions left bidders in something of a quandary as they had to formulate their tenders in ignorance of the institutional arrangements for networking, the extent of the network and the network budget. Added to this was uncertainty about how the network budget would be allocated amongst licensees. In its Invitation to Tender for Channel 3 licences, the ITC (1991) had set out an illustrative proposal which shared network costs amongst licensees in proportion to their net advertising revenue, with special arrangements being made for the smallest companies. These proposals were only illustrative, however, and it would be up to the licensees to agree a cost-sharing arrangement once the licensing process had run its course.

Since the tenders were based upon the difference between an uncertain-revenue stream and an uncertain-cost stream, the range of possible profits and loss associated with each licence was enormous. However, the procedure adopted sought directly to mitigate these risks in two ways.

The first involved an arrangement whereby each licensee's payments to the Treasury consisted of two components: a percentage of annual qualifying revenue (likely to consist predominantly of advertising revenue) and a cash bid. The percentage of qualifying revenue varied from 0 per cent for small regions on the borders of profitability to 15 per cent for the national breakfast-time licence. In the case of the five largest licences (Central, London Weekday, London Weekend, North-West England and South-East England) it was 11 per cent. The effect of this arrangement was to share some of the risks of fluctuations in advertising revenue between the government and the licensee. The system was calibrated in a way intended to ensure that the majority of payments to the government came through the proportionate payment as a percentage of qualifying revenues.

A second risk-reducing factor for the company was the decision to index the annual cash payments. Without indexation, companies would be required to bet upon a particular rate of inflation, and there was risk that licences would go to those bidders with the highest inflationary expectations. The bids could have been indexed to a number of variables, including advertising revenue and the nominal value of gross national product; or they could have been indexed inversely to broadcast costs. However, for simplicity the decision was taken to index the payments to the Retail Price Index. The decision affects the time profile of real annual payments. Indexation keeps them constant in real terms, while its absence would require the companies to make their largest payments at the outset, assuming positive rates of inflation. On those two scores, greater certainty and the different time profile of payments, one would expect indexation to increase the willingness of bidders to pay for the licence. For these reasons, the Treasury, normally hostile to indexation, exceptionally agreed to it for the annual payments.

Compliance

These two factors reduced uncertainty to some degree, but a third and potentially more powerful issue remained in the background: how rigorously would the regulatory body enforce the contract, especially in hard times? Under the Act, the formal position is that when a Channel 3 licence is awarded to an applicant, that applicant must first satisfy the ITC that it has access to the necessary funding, and then enter into a detailed licence agreement with the regulatory body. The Annex to the licence will specify conditions relating to the provision and content of the broadcast service, reflecting proposals submitted by the licensee at the time of application. Thus the ITC intended to build into the licence the programme commitments brought forward by the applicant in the bidding process.

The purpose of this was to allay anxieties arising from the previous failure of the IBA—the ITC's predecessor—to enforce in all circumstances programming promises made at the competitive phase of the franchise process. The two best-documented examples of this are the events at London Weekend Television following the initial grant of its franchise in 1968 and the circumstances surrounding the granting of the national breakfast-time television licence to TV AM in 1980 (Potter 1989; Leapman 1984). In both cases, the successful applicant for the franchise committed itself to ambitious programming plans which proved in the event to be commercially disastrous. (Ironically, the same broadcaster, David Frost, was involved in both applications.) The outcome in each case was a change in management and ownership of the stations and acquiescence by the regulator in a substantial reversal of the original programming commitments. As well as greatly irritating unsuccessful applicants for the franchises, the IBA's failure to enforce compliance, following its demonstrated ignorance of the commercial realities of broadcasting, made a nonsense of the quasi-competitive process for franchise allocation.

The introduction of tendering for Channel 3 licences under the Broadcasting Act 1990 put the question of compliance and sanctions into even sharper relief. The programming restrictions imposed by the Broadcasting Act would clearly reduce the revenue potential of Channel 3. The value of the licence would thus depend upon the interpretation of what are, by any standards, rather vague requirements. If the ITC were to be elastic in its interpretation of the requirements, or even formally to relax them, this would alter the value of the bids. This introduced a new dimension to overbidding: licences might go to those applicants who perceived the Commission's future conduct to be the most accommodating to the broadcasters' interests.

A number of remedies were considered for dealing with this problem. The Peacock Committee proposed a system of graduated penalties (a 'yellow card' and a 'red card') beginning with fines and leading to withdrawal of the licence. Another possibility was to introduce a performance bond, which would be forfeited if a licensee continued to breach conditions. This was abandoned as impracticable.

Thus the Broadcasting Act 1990 relies upon financial penalties leading ultimately to revocation of the licence. If the Commission is satisfied that a licensee has failed to comply with any condition of the licence and has given the licensee a reasonable opportunity to make representations to it about the matters complained of, it may require the licensee to pay a financial penalty which in the first instance may not exceed 3 per cent of the licensee's annual qualifying revenue. Subsequent penalties may not exceed 5 per cent of qualifying revenue. The next weapon available to the Commission is to reduce the licence period by up to two years. Finally, the Commission may revoke the licence.

As well as imposing these penalties, the Commission may also deny the licensee the benefit of renewal of licence if it is not satisfied with its conduct. The Broadcasting Act provides that the licensee may apply to the Commission for renewal of the licence at the start of the seventh year—i.e. four years from its expiry. The Commission is required to refuse an application if it is not satisfied that the licensee would provide the licence service over the extended period, or on certain other grounds relating to changes in franchise area or hours or days of broadcast. If the Commission does grant a renewal, it determines the amount of the renewal payment on the basis of what it judges would be payable if it were granting a fresh licence to provide the service. Clearly if the Commission has reservations about some aspect of the service provided by a licensee, it may choose not to renew the licence.

Thus the Act provides the Commission with a carrot and a number of sticks to secure compliance with the licence conditions. But there still remain doubts about the interpretation of some of the conditions, especially those relating to the requirement to produce specified amounts of programming of various kinds, such as religious programming (where questions of classification can sometimes be problematic) and the interpretation of the phrase 'reasonable proportion' in relation to provision of high-quality programmes of all types. The ITC's rulings on these matters might make the difference between the solvency or insolvency of a licensee. Nor would they be subject to appeal, except through the expensive and usually unsuccessful process of judicial review.

How credible are the ITC's threats to impose financial penalties or to revoke the licence? Seen from the standpoint of the bidder, this is likely to depend upon the source of the broadcaster's difficulties in meeting the licence conditions. If all the successful applicants were to bid equally high, so that they were all subject to financial difficulties in the event of an unexpected recession or loss of market share of the channel as a whole, then a licensee might argue that it would be difficult for the ITC to enforce the licence conditions across the board if to do so would put the whole system into bankruptcy. On the other hand, if the bidding process yielded—as it was to—different outcomes from different licensees, with some retaining a comfortable margin while others were on the limits of profitability, then it would be more credible that the ITC would impose penalties on one or two companies. If that led to a revocation of the licence or withdrawal from it by the company, then another licensee might take over broadcasting in the relevant region for the period until the licence could be readvertised subject to a new competitive tender. This could be done almost immediately, and in circumstances which caused relatively little disruption to the viewers in the area of the defaulting licensee.

The likelihood of even this eventuality depended upon a judgement of the objectives of the regulatory body. Several observers have detected a tendency for the IBA to be subject to 'regulatory capture', demonstrated by the use of its powers to protect the firms in the industry which it regulated. The ITC, although staffed by virtually the same officials and comprising several former members of the IBA, is now subject to much more detailed legislative obligations; it will also enter into more explicit and public licence arrangements with the successful applicant. The effect of this will be to make threats of sanctions more credible, provided that all licensees do not fall into difficulties at once.

The Form of Bidding

An important provision in the legislation affected the number of bids which a single company could make. Several parties, including the regulatory authority and many of the incumbents, favoured a limitation on the number of licences which any company could apply for. The incumbent's motive for this preference is obvious; the regulatory body was concerned that multiple bidding, including bidding by incumbents for other licences than their own, would disrupt the unity of the ITV system. In the event, however, no such restriction was introduced. Companies could bid for as many licences as they liked, but they would be debarred from holding a licence (or a stake of 20 per cent or more in a licence) in more than one 'large' and one 'small' franchise area. Multiple bidders were asked to specify an order of preference over licences which the ITC would take into account in the event that they were successful in more than the permitted number of areas.

No doubt in expectation that most licences would be contested, the tendering system contained no provision for a reserve price, apart from what was implicit in the first (proportionate) part of the tender. This was to prove one of its most notable, and for the government, expensive features.

Some discussion was also devoted to the form of the auction or tender (see Cave 1989). Tendering has attracted a large amount of attention from theoretical economists in recent years, especially in the case of so-called 'common value' assets, which—unlike objects of personal or sentimental value—have broadly the same value for all bidders. Despite possible differences in costs among potential applicants the common value—or, more generally, the 'correlated value'—model is the appropriate one for tenders for broadcast licences, at least in the case of profit-maximizing bidders. Tenders or auctions can be conducted in various ways. The main alternatives are public or oral auctions in which the auctioneer successively announces prices and a buyer is found, and 'sealed-bids' tenders. Public auctions may be either English—in which prices are successively raised until only one bidder remains, or Dutch—in which the price is successively lowered until the object is bought by the first bidder. Sealed-bid tenders award the object to the highest bidder either at the price offered by that bidder (a first-price tender) or—more rarely—at the price offered by the second-highest bidder (a second-price tender). One of the main theoretical results of auction theory for the common-value case is that, provided bidders are risk-neutral, the various forms of auction produce different average levels of revenue. The reason for this is that in a common-value auction, bids are not determined exclusively by the bidder's tastes but depend upon (possibly different) judgements about potential revenues and costs. This may lead to the phenomenon known as the 'winner's curse' whereby the highest bidder realizes at once that he or she has placed a higher value on the franchise than anyone else, and may thus have overestimated its value. Logically, however, a sophisticated bidder should realize this danger and bid less aggressively. The seller can reduce anxieties about the winner's curse by publicizing any information available about the licence. This reduces bidders' uncertainty and encourages them to bid closer to their true expected value than would be the case if they had poor information and were more anxious about over-bidding.

The reason that different forms of auction yield different expected values in the common-value case is that they provide different levels of information about other bidders' valuations. The English auction yields the most information, and hence the highest expected revenue, because any bidder can observe all other bidders' behaviour. Next is the second-price tender, which exploits the valuation of at least one other bidder. Finally, the first-price tender and Dutch auction furnish no information, and thus leave bidders most fearful of the winner's curse. When bidders are risk-averse however, the ranking is less clear-cut. The English auction still yields more revenue than a second-price tender, and the equivalence of Dutch and first-price tenders is preserved. But the first-price tender may now yield higher revenue than an English auction. But even these provisional rankings are slightly misleading, as they assume a given number of bidders, known to one another. It is more realistic that the number of bidders depends upon the form of the auction. Even more importantly, when bidders do not know how many other bidders are involved—as may occur in a sealed-bid tender but not at an oral auction—risk aversion may encourage them to bid more for fear of losing the licence to an undisclosed bidder. This last consideration proved to be particularly important to some bidders for Channel 3 licences, who—discovering that they were the only candidates—were able to bid derisorily small amounts.

A further consideration, largely neglected by auction theory, is risk-aversion on the part of the seller. It would clearly be embarrassing to the government either to elicit no bids for a licence or to allow one to be acquired at a low price. Choosing a pathway between these dangers no doubt became a major consideration. As grounds for disqualification mounted, the choice of a sealed-bid tender, the most discreet method and that commonly used for auctioning common-value idiosyncratic licences such as government contracts or rights to exploit natural resources, seemed quite defensible.

Seen from the standpoint of the government, then, the arrangements for allocating Channel 3 licences introduced by the Broadcasting Act were intended to provide a careful balance between the objectives of extracting rent from the industry and ensuring that the interests of the viewers were fully satisfied. The regulatory authority was given some discretion both to reject bids which in its opinion did not satisfy the programme quality or 'quality-of-money' tests and to invoke an exceptional circumstances clause. The arrangements for the tender, which included a percentage of qualifying revenue and indexed annual cash sum, were designed to protect the companies from some risks associated with bidding. At the same time, it was undeniable that bidding for a licence was a risky business involving difficult strategic decisions. How the competitors faced these decisions soon became clear.

Bidding Strategy

Applicants for Channel 3 licences thus faced a difficult and uncertain environment. To add to the difficulties, bidding was costly. The ITC's Invitation to Apply required applicants to submit detailed programme plans and financial projections. These were to be accompanied by general statements of broadcasting philosophy and the identification of key personnel. The effect of this was to make bidding a fairly costly exercise: it is estimated that many bids cost in excess of £1 million, much of it spent upon management, economic, and programming consultancy. (Thames Television's unsuccessful bid cost £1.75 million.) The system also gave incumbents a built-in advantage, as they had teams already assembled—although this was in some cases counterbalanced by their inheritance of excessive labour-forces and inefficient working practices. Current presence in a region also gave incumbents access to information about other potential bidders. In order to prepare a bid, it was necessary to recruit local personnel and to undertake research into the region. Such activity was almost invariably picked up by the incumbent, and the absence of such activity gave the incumbent a clear indication as to how to bid. At least one incumbent set up a special unit to scour the area for potential rivals. (A more direct 'information strategy' is to discover a rival's bid and top it. This is rumoured to have occurred in at least one case.)

As we have seen, a potential bidder also had to choose the kind of operation which it favoured. There were two broad alternatives: to establish substantial production capacity within the region to make either regional or—in this case of the larger licensees—network programmes, in the style of the existing ITV companies, or to set up as a 'programme-publisher', buying-in most programmes from independent producers or other organizations, possibly confining its own programme-making activities to local news and current affairs. Both variants were countenanced under the Act and in the ITC's Invitation to Apply, but those taking the programme-publishing route saw themselves as obliged to show co-operative arrangements with one or more independent producers, in order to guarantee programme availability, and credible cost control.

This was the background against which bidding strategy had to be formulated. Here the uncertainties multiplied. First, the exceptional circumstances clause offered two routes to success in a contest among qualified bidders. One was to stake everything upon high programme quality and make a very low bid in the expectation that the exceptional quality clause would be invoked. The other and more conventional route was to bid high. In principle the former route might lead to success, but it was fraught with perils. The exceptional quality clause only applied when the quality offered by another bidder exceeded that offered by the highest bidder by an exceptional amount. Without knowing the quality offered by the highest bidder, it was impossible to forecast the quality difference, even before the inevitably subjective nature of such judgements was allowed for. In any case, since most viewing would be of networked programmes, quality remained largely outside the direct control of an individual licensee. Finally, in the event of the ITC awarding a licence upon exceptional quality grounds, it would have to give reasons for its choice. It was recognized that this might make the regulator more liable to judicial review, and thus more reluctant to invoke the procedure.

A second major uncertainty was whether one's rivals would succeed in passing the ITC's quality tests. As noted, these fell into two categories—a programme quality test and a 'quality-of-money' test, passed by demonstrating a capacity to sustain the programming proposed in the bid over the lifetime of the licence. If you thought your rivals were likely to fail one or both of these tests, then there was no reason to bid high. However, making that judgement was highly complex. Bidders did not, of course, have access to one another's plans and projections, and there was also considerable uncertainty about the rigour of the tests. The Chairman of the ITC went out of his way to indicate that they would be quite stiff, but no one outside the ITC was in a position to know exactly how stiff.

This left bidders in an unusually difficult position. The decision to be taken was a life-and-death one. Various strategies were available for bidding high or bidding low, and they all depended upon the conduct of rival bidders. On top of this was considerable uncertainty about the standards to be adopted by the regulatory body. Thus each bidder may have seen the problem in a different light. But despite this, it is possible *ex post facto* to identify a number of distinct strategies in the bids, especially those of incumbents. This variation in strategies contributed to the surprise value of the outcome.

The Outcome

Of a total of forty applications made for the sixteen licences, thirty-seven were for the regional Channel 3 licences and three for the national breakfast-time licence. The bids are set out in Table 7.2. Astonishingly, of the thirteen licences contested, only six were allocated to the company making the highest bid (in three further cases there was only one bidder). The aggregate cash bids of the successful applicants amounted to £231.60 million. Had the ITC chosen in each instance the highest bidder, the aggregate would have amounted to £323.49 million—an additional £91.89 million per year.

Of the seven highest bids rejected, five were rejected on the grounds that they failed to satisfy the programme-quality test and two were rejected on the grounds that the highest bidding company would not be able to maintain its proposed service throughout the period for which the licence would be in force. On no occasion was the exceptional circumstances clause invoked. As discussed in Section 2 above, the regulatory authority is not obliged to offer a detailed explanation of why a particular application failed the quality test, and none has been published. At the same time, the ITC has been prepared to explain to certain unsuccessful applicants which aspects of the programme quality hurdle they failed to pass.

Examination of the bids suggests that companies, especially incumbents, pursued a variety of strategies in trying to gain the licences. In the case of two substantial licence areas, Central Scotland, and East, South, and West Midlands, there was only one application and the cash bid in each case was £2,000. Evidently the incumbent became aware that there was no competition for the licence and bid almost the smallest amount possible. A similar event may have occurred in Borders, where Border TV, the sole applicant, bid £52,000.

Another group if incumbents appears to have submitted high bids. These include Anglia in the east of England, Tyne Tees in north-east England, TVS in south and south-east England, TSW in south-west England, HTV in Wales and the west of England, and Yorkshire television. In two of these cases, however, those of TVS and TSW, the Commission took the view that the cash bid was so high that it would be impossible for a company to sustain its programme service over the period of the licence. Thus in these two cases the highest bid was rejected and the second-highest bid (£23 million lower in the case of south and south-east England and £8 million lower in the case of south-west England) was accepted. These decisions proved in many ways the most controversial.

Two other major incumbents, Granada in north-west England and LWT in the case of the London Weekend licence, appear to have decided to submit relatively low bids (£7.6 million and £9 million respectively) for potentially valuable regions. These bids could have been based on pessimistic expectations of how far they could go, but they were more probably hoping that their higher-bidding rivals would either fail the quality hurdle or be denied the licence by the exceptional circumstances clause. Their hunch was right, and although the highest bid for the London Weekend licence was £28 million greater than that submitted by LWT, and the highest bid for north-west England was £26 million higher than that submitted by Granada, both LWT and Granada retained their licences. Why did Granada and LWT not bid the minimum amount against their sole rivals? Presumably because they thought that to do so might antagonize the regulator.

There remain three further small regional licences covering the Channel Islands, the north of Scotland, and Northern Ireland where in each case the incumbent was awarded the licence even though it was the lowest bidder. It is possible that here too the incumbent was expecting this outcome and tailoring its bid accordingly, but the disparities could equally be due to differences in assumptions about revenues and costs, or to strategic bidding.

This leaves a relatively small number of cases where the licence has been allocated to the highest non-incumbent bidder. The two cases in question were the London Weekday licence, where Carlton was successful, bidding £7.5 million more than the incumbent Thames, and the national breakfast-time licence where Sunrise Television was successful, bidding £20.5 million more than the incumbent TV-AM. The disparities between the winning bid and that made by the incumbent suggest that in these two cases the companies were seeking to emulate the successful policy of Granada and LWT. The ITC was evidently satisfied that the two winning bids were consistent with sustaining the programmes promised over the lifetime of the licence.

The aftermath of the bids was a period of some turmoil. Several companies sought judicial review of the ITC's decision, and one of them, TSW—which was excluded because its bid was too high—took its case to the House of Lords. Although TSW's case was finally unsuccessful, the process elicited a number of documents from the ITC outlining why its bid was rejected on financial grounds. These included doubts about the high level of growth of advertising revenue implicit in the bid and

TABLE 7.2. The bidders

Region	Homes with TV (millions)	Company	Bid (£m.)	Quality threshold		Financial viability		
				Yes	No	Yes	No	Not disclosed
Breakfast TV	21.4	*Sunrise*	34.61	•		•		
		TV-AM*	14.13	•				
		Daybreak	33.30	•				
London Weekday	5.0	*Carlton TV*	43.17	•		•		
		Thames*	32.70	•				•
		CPV-TV	45.32		•			•
London Weekend	5.0	*London Weekend**	7.58	•		•		
		London Independent Broadcasting	35.41		•			•
Midlands	4.0	*Central**	£2,000	•		•		
North-West	2.8	*Granada**	9.00	•		•		
		North West TV	35.30		•			
Yorkshire	2.5	*Yorkshire TV**	37.70	•		•		
		White Rose TV	17.40	•				•
		Viking TV	30.12		•			•
South & South-East	2.3	*Meridian Broadcasting*	36.52	•		•		
		TVS*	59.76	•			•	
		Carlton TV	18.08	•				
		CPV-TV	22.11		•			

Wales & West	2.0	*HTV**	20.53	•		•		•
		Merlin Channel 3	19.37		•			
		Wales & West	18.29		•			•
		C3W	17.76	•				•
East	1.9	*Anglia**	17.80	•		•		
		Three East	14.08	•				•
		CPV-TV	10.13		•			•
North-East	1.2	*Tyne Tees**	15.06	•		•		
		North East TV	5.01	•				•
Central Scotland	1.4	*Scottish TV**	£2,000	•		•		
South-West	0.7	*Westcountry TV**	7.82	•		•		
		TSW*	16.12	•				•
		Telewest	7.27		•		•	
Northern Ireland	0.49	*Ulster**	1.03	•		•		
		Lagan TV	2.71		•			
		TVNi	3.10	•				•
North of Scotland	0.49	*Grampian**	0.72	•		•		
		C3 Caledonia	1.13		•		•	
		North of Scotland TV	2.71		•		•	
Borders	0.28	*Border TV**	£52,000	•		•		
Channel Islands	0.04	*Channel TV**	£1,000	•		•		
		C13	£102,000		•		•	

* Incumbent successful bidders.

scepticism about the company's ability to borrow from the bank to cover early losses.

The identification of successful licensees was by no means the end of the licence round. Under the provision of the Broadcasting Act, licensees are required to make an agreement for the networking of programmes. In the absence of an agreement being reached by January 1992, the ITC had the opportunity to impose one. Any agreement, whether reached voluntarily by the licensees or imposed by the ITC, was subject to scrutiny by the Office of Fair Trading, which had to apply the 'competition' test to ensure that the arrangement provides proper conditions for competing suppliers of programmes to get them on the air. The successful licensees found it difficult to agree on networking arrangements when there were such substantial differences in their financial situations, arising from different levels of bid. The scrutiny of the networking agreement fell finally to the Monopolies and Mergers Commission.

Conclusions

The history for tendering for Channel 3 licences has many interesting lessons both for companies involved in the process and for the government and its regulatory agencies. For the government, it was a mixed success. The absence of a reserve price (in addition to the reserve price set through the first component of the tender) enabled two successful companies to carry away valuable licences by making minimum bids. It is reasonable to presume that higher reserve prices were not set because the government either expected that there would be substantial numbers of bidders for each licence and that uncontested bids would be confined to low-value regions, or was worried that no bid would materialize. In this they were of course mistaken, and the tax payers will pay for the mistake for the ten years from 1993, although viewers may conceivably benefit from higher programme spending.

Another awkward aspect of the process was that what emerged was at best a quasi-competitive process. The regulatory body had the capacity to eliminate many applicants, and used that power copiously. The evidence of the bidding suggests that at least some companies anticipated that their rivals would be eliminated and made significant bids, but at a level much lower than would be suggested by observing other companies' behaviour in broadly equivalent regions.

It must be remembered however, that TV licences hedged around with the qualifications and subject to the enforcement system set out in the Broadcasting Act 1990 are anything but straightforward commodities. The complexity of bidding for such licences is bound to deter many potential bidders.

Thus it would be misleading to suppose that the same difficulties would inevitably occur in the allocation by tender of more easily definable licences requiring less subsequent regulatory enforcement. For example, there is little reason to suppose that the difficulties attending the C3 licence auction, which arose from an uneasy combination of competitive bidding and regulatory disqualification, would arise in the case of airport take-off slots or the radio spectrum. Although the Channel 3 licence race showed up weaknesses in the tendering system, it was a fairly exacting test of the principle.

6. THE FUTURE

The past ten years have seen a major reregulation of British broadcasting. The Peacock Committee described the arrangements then existing between the BBC and the advertiser-financed sector as a 'cosy duopoly'. This referred not only to the prohibitions on entry of new stations or channels, but also to the deliberate attempt to restrict competition for finance. Thus advertising time available on ITV and C4 was sold together by the ITV companies, rather than on a competitive basis, and the BBC was excluded from selling advertising. Even the arrangements for allocating ITV and other licences (described in the previous section) lacked the transparency necessary to ensure cost competition.

The cosy duopoly has now largely been swept away by the Broadcasting Act 1990 and other measures. The introduction to this chapter identified five stages in broadcasting. Change has come to each of them. Thus mandatory independent production quotas and the success of several 'programme publishers' such as Carlton and Meridian in the competition for Channel 3 licences have created, and will create, further opportunities for expansion of the independent production sector, initially brought to birth by the development of C4. New networks have come into existence, based on new delivery technologies. Local Channel 3 companies, now chosen on a new basis, are subject to quite different cost pressures than of old. New programme delivery methods have emerged, and Channels 3 and 4 are now delivered by a separate and privatized transmission company (NTC) rather than as before by the regulator. Finally, new technologies permit the collection of revenues by 'smart' cards which give access to encrypted programmes, conditional upon the viewer having paid a subscription. Thus the new technologies have been combined with competition at each stage and deliberate disintegration of the previously vertically integrated production processes. Although the new channels have so far captured a relatively small proportion of total viewing time, it is likely in the future that BBC 1 and 2 and Channels 3 and 4 will find their audiences substantially eroded over the next decade. In the USA, the three major networks' share of viewing fell from 90 to 62 per cent from 1980 to 1990. A similar outcome may be observed in the UK.

There remain, however, two significant pieces of unfinished business in the regulatory reforms in broadcasting. The first concerns concentration of ownership. The Broadcasting Act prohibits or restricts ownership of licences by various categories of company, including non-EC nationals. National newspaper companies are also precluded from owning more than a 20 per cent stake in any licensee. The Act restricts any company holding Channel 3 licences to a maximum of two, one large and one small, subject to an additional proviso that their service areas may not be contiguous. Take-overs of companies owning the Channel 3 licences were prohibited until the beginning of 1994.

The necessity of such heavy restrictions on concentration of ownership within broadcasting and on cross-media ownership, has been questioned. Limited overseas evidence suggests that such constraints may not be necessary on economic grounds, to restrict monopoly power (Besen and Johnson 1985). There are, however, arguments for restricting concentration of media ownership on political grounds, to promote a plurality of opinions.

It has been argued that the current rules may be difficult to enforce in cases where a company has over-bid for a licence and is unable to sustain its terms. Unless the government is prepared to remit part of the annual payment, then the only possible arrangement by which it can continue in operation may be for it to be taken-over by an adjacent company, thus permitting economies of scale in the operation of the two stations. (The alternative would be for the company in difficulties to lose the licence and for it to be readvertised by the ITC.) In addition, it has been suggested that the arrangements place UK commercial broadcasters at a disadvantage compared with their rivals in Europe, which are subject to no size restrictions at home but which—if they are from countries in the European Community—can hold British licences.

These matters may well be put to the test over the next few years. More generally, the whole question of concentration of ownership within a single medium such as television broadcasting or across several media—for example joint ownership of both newspapers and television stations—is likely to rise higher up the political agenda.

The second major piece of unfinished regulatory business is caused by the expiry of the BBC's Charter at the end of 1996. The existing Charter has already protected the BBC from some degree of dismemberment as it effectively prevented the Conservative government from hiving off and privatizing the BBC's transmission system. But its expiry created an opportunity for the government to redefine the role of the BBC in the new regulatory framework.

That new role hinges critically upon the definition of public service broadcasting, which the BBC has claimed as its mission since the days of John Reith. The Corporation's own interpretation of the term has tended to be broad, embracing a range of information and entertainment programmes intended to appeal to all tastes. In practice, it has been essential for the BBC to provide services appealing to all sections of the viewing and listening public in order to justify its finance by a licence fee paid by all television households, irrespective of their viewing of BBC programmes.

But there is an alternative definition of public service broadcasting based upon the potential market failures in the broadcasting industry described in Section 2 above. According to this view, the role of the public sector is to provide a framework for the broadcasting of programmes which are socially desirable but privately unprofitable: as Peacock put it: 'those programmes which the public recognise as being in their own interest to have produced but which cannot be delivered by the market'. If such a set of programmes exists, this is likely to be a different range of programmes from those currently broadcast on the BBC, and to be concentrated on minority or experimental programme types. Moreover, even though the public sector may have to finance or subsidize such programmes, there is no necessity for them to be made by a public-sector organization. The funds could be allocated on a competitive basis to private programme makers.

If this second conception of the role of the public sector gains currency, then it would imply a different role for the BBC. Much of its output would be financed by charges or by advertising, rather than as at present by the licence fee. Indeed, if the remaining category of 'public-service broadcasting' ceased to appeal to a wide enough range of viewers and listeners, the whole system of licence fee finance might become politically unsustainable and the BBC might cease to be a major broadcaster.

How things turn out for the BBC depends not only on the government, but also upon changes in the broadcasting market-place in the next few years. The reforms of the 1980s have created a springboard for new services to enter and to compete on more equal terms with Channel 3 licensees, which from 1993 have to make annual payments for the benefit of their privileged position within the system. If they spread quickly throughout the economy, and if moreover the new commercial pressures applying to Channels 3 and 4 erode the BBC's audience share, then the pressures for a significant change in the BBC's role will be the stronger. If this occurs, the 1990s will not only see the effects in the market of the regulatory changes of the 1980s, but will also see major new regulatory changes as well.

References

Besen, S. M., and Johnson, L. L. (1985), 'Regulation of broadcast station ownership: Evidence and theory', in E. M. Noam (ed.), *Video Media Competition*, New York: Columbia University Press.

Briggs, A., and Spicer, J. (1986), *The Franchise Affair*, London: Century.

Brown, A., and Cave, M. (forthcoming), 'The economics of television regulation: A survey with application to Australia', *Economic Record*, 68 (Dec. 1992), 377–94.

Cave, M. (1989a), 'An Introduction to television economics', in G. Hughes, and D. Vines (eds.), *Deregulation and the Future of Commercial Television*.

—— (1989b), 'The conduct of auctions for broadcast franchises', Fiscal Stúdies, 10: 17–31.

—— and Williamson, P. (1991), '"Make or Break Strategy": The great Channel 3 licence race', *Business Strategy Review*, 2/3: 53–90.

Coase, R. (1950), *British Broadcasting: A Study in Monopoly*, London: Longman, Green.

Home Office (1988), *Broadcasting in the Nineties: Competition, Choice and Quality*, Cm 517, London: HMSO.

Hughes, G., and Vines, D. (eds.) (1989), *Deregulation and the Future of Commercial Television*, Aberdeen: Aberdeen University Press.

ITC (1991), *Invitation to Apply for Regional Channel 3 Licences*, London.

Leapham, M. (1984), *Treachery? The Power Struggle at TV-AM*, London: Allen & Unwin.

Noll, R. G., Peck, M. J., and McGowan, J. J. (1973), *Economic Aspects of Television Regulation*, Washington, DC: Brookings Institute.

Owen, B. M., Beebe, J. H., and Manning, W. G. (1974), *Television Economics*, Lexington, Mass.: Heath.

Peacock, Alan (1986), *Report of the Committee on Financing the BBC*, Cmnd 9824, London: HMSO.

Paulu, B. (1981), *Television and Radio in the UK*, London: Macmillan.

Potter, J. (1989), *Independent Television in Britain, Vol. 3, Politics and Control 1968–1980*, London: Macmillan.

Rothenberg, J. (1972), 'Consumer sovereignty and the economics of TV programming', *Studies in Public Communications*, 4: 45–54.

Setzer, F., and Levy, J. (1991), *Broadcast Television in a Multi-Channel Market Place*, OPP Working Paper Series, Washington, DC: Federal Communications Commission.

Spence, M., and Owen, B. (1977), 'Television programming, monopolistic competition and welfare', *Quarterly Journal of Economics*, 91: 103–26.

Steiner, P. O. (1952), 'Program patterns and preference and the workability of competition in radio broadcasting', *Quarterly Journal of Economics*, 66: 194–223.

—— (1961), 'Monopoly and competition in television: Some policy issues', *The Manchester School of Economics and Political Science*, 29: 107–31.

Wildman, S. S., and Owen, B. M. (1985), 'Program competition, diversity and multi-channel bundling in the new video age', in E. Noam (ed.), *Video Media Competition*, New York: Columbia University Press.

8

Information Asymmetries and Product-Quality Regulation

NORMAN IRELAND*

1. INTRODUCTION

In this chapter our concern will be for the consumer buying goods and services in the private sector. The focus will be on the case where the consumer has to complete the transaction (or at least contract to complete the transaction) before finding out the exact quality of what he is buying. Such goods or services are usually referred to as experience goods, and the typical case of interest is when the seller knows the true quality of the product while the buyer only observes this after purchase. Thus the seller has more information than the buyer at the moment of contract: there is asymmetric information. The extent of asymmetric information varies across markets. At one extreme the market for, say, sugar has reasonably full information: the product is fairly homogeneous (although even here in a highly monopolized market there are a number of different brands and varieties, for example, of brown sugar), and is bought regularly. At the other extreme there are markets for second-hand cars, package holidays, financial services, and home improvements. In these latter cases each transaction is of a product which can be of a very different quality from others which are available at the same time. They are essentially 'one-off' transactions. Also the consumer may have little experience to guide him in assessing the quality offered. In the large middle ground between these extremes, are all the products available in your local shops, which can be examined, but not usually used, prior to purchase. We will find it helpful to distinguish between 'repeated-market' products and 'one-off' products. In the former the seller needs to sell the product regularly to the same or different consumers. Institutions such as the Consumers' Association, via its publications, will increase buyers' information, and reputations will be developed. In a pure 'one-off' sale no dynamic effects are involved.

The asymmetric information which is present in so many transactions leads to a number of problems of economic efficiency and simple justice.

* Professor of Economics, Department of Economics, University of Warwick.

In terms of economic efficiency, the key questions are whether markets can function at the right level and lead by exchange to the best reallocation of goods and services. That is, first, whether potential sellers and buyers can meet and agree a price which makes the transaction welcome to both. For example, if there were some forged £5 notes in existence you may be reluctant to give five one pound coins in exchange for a £5 note. (You may be even more reluctant to give four one pound coins in exchange for a £5 note!) Second, the forged £5 notes would lead to the partial withdrawal from use of £5 notes and the inconvenience of using other denominations of notes and coins as substitutes. Thus the 'bad' notes drive out the 'good' from the market, and no one wants to hold £5 notes. This is an example of 'Gresham's Law' and is an extreme case of the well-known 'lemons model' of Akerlof (1970), to which we will return below. The efficiency loss is separate from the problem of justice. If you pay £5 to a counterfeiter for a bad note then you expect your loss to outweigh his gain in the view of a just society, and you also expect that appropriate action is taken to avoid this happening or to redress the injustice if it does occur. It follows more generally that institutions should be developed to check product qualities and product descriptions and to enforce appropriate standards of quality, advertising, and other promotional activities.

In a repeated rather than a one-off market, consumers have the opportunity to punish sellers of bad products, not just by withdrawing future custom, but also by linking good or bad reputations to particular sellers. For their part, sellers may seek to signal their trustworthiness by offering warranties or similar devices to reassure buyers and to promote a good reputation with consumers. The credibility of current warranties is enhanced if past warranties have been honoured. Note that in these terms a new firm is at a disadvantage. In essence, the incumbent's (good) reputation acts as an entry barrier to competition. Then market-wide quality regulation can reduce the entry barrier by validating the new product, and thereby increase competition.

Our survey of UK quality regulation will be concerned with quality standards, codes of conduct, warranties and dispute procedures, advertising standards, and market efficiency. Some of the regulatory mechanisms are voluntary and some reflect legal obligations. We will divide the chapter into three main parts. First the key theoretical issues will be summarized in Section 2. In Section 3 the legal minimum trading standards, certified quality standards, and advertising standards are discussed, together with procedures which exist for adjudicating complaints. These form the basis for consumer protection from bad products. In many areas of market transactions, however, action has been sponsored or assisted by the Office of Fair Trading (OFT) in order to reduce consumer dissatisfaction. In Section 4 we briefly outline the recent history of some of these moves and relate them to the theoretical issues that we have discussed. We take three examples: second-hand cars, home improvements, and package holidays. A final section presents conclusions.

2. KEY THEORETICAL ISSUES

Information Asymmetry and Adverse Selection

If sellers know the quality of their products but buyers do not, then the market suffers from an information asymmetry. If buyers will only pay a price reflecting the average quality of product on offer, then sellers of high quality products may withdraw from the market since their products are not realizing their real value. This decreases the average quality of offered products and thus the market price, implying a further round of withdrawal, decline in average quality and market price. Asymmetric information thus leads to partial or complete market failure. The market fails since the price which seeks to average out or 'pool' the stock attracts the bad product and not the good. This is the case of adverse selection. Its importance is that markets fail to take place: that Pareto-improving trades are not implemented.

There are a number of markets where such failures occur: most obviously in markets for second-hand goods. The setting of Akerlof's 1970 model is indeed in the second-hand car market. Here, if the quality of cars offered for sale cannot be determined by buyers then buyers will not be willing to meet prices higher than the average value of cars in the pool available to buy. Then people with bad cars will wish to enter them into this pool while those with good cars will tend to keep then, rather than sell at a lower price than their value. The result is that the second-hand cars available to buy become more dominated by bad cars; this then reinforces the adverse selection as the average value, and thus price of cars in the pool decreases, until all good cars are driven out of the market. Of course, there will always be some good cars supplied since some owners will die, emigrate, receive company cars, or decide they want a bigger or smaller car sufficiently strongly to suffer the low selling price. Thus there is a limit to the extent of market collapse since there is always a chance of picking up such a bargain. Also a bad car may have some value and this also supports market activity. Analyses of used-car markets have sought to weigh up the efficiency loss of many trades, that could take place but don't, against the possible cost of removing the informational asymmetry. The argument is that people keep their good cars longer than they ideally would want to in order to avoid the loss of only obtaining the pool price rather than the true value of their cars. The inefficiency is that some cars are not traded when they would be traded under full information when the good car is separated from the pool and its proper value obtained. The conclusion is that full information has value to society, not just to reduce feelings of injustice when a purchase turns out badly, but also to permit markets to operate fully and allow individuals to carry out Pareto-improving exchanges. Consumer policy thus has to address the issue of improving consumer information and allowing products to trade at their correct values.

Advertising: Will the good product win in competition?

A product where the quality can be checked prior to purchase is termed a search good, and advertising can only inform consumers of existence and price. However, with 'experience goods' advertising may provoke trial purchases by consumers wishing to test the quality. Even though repeat purchases may not be forthcoming from disappointed consumers, if bad goods are advertised with exaggerated claims they may still be profitable. Basically provided the population of consumers is large, new market segments can be targeted in turn. Even the product brand name can be changed, or indeed the firm wound up and the enterprise relaunched in a new firm. The question then arises as to the profitability of selling bad products by intensive promotion, rather than incurring greater cost to design and produce a good product. Although advertising which prompts both immediate and repeat purchases has a greater return than advertising that only yields immediate purchases, this has to be weighed against the greater profit margins of bad (too cheaply produced) products. If the market is characterized by infrequent purchases and frequent changes in product brands then the bad product supplier may make more profit and obtain more sales than the suppliers of good products. Examples of such markets that come to mind include 'time-share' property, builders' services, and many direct-sales goods advertised in magazines. A formal model of how advertising may allow bad products to fare better than good products is given in Schmalensee (1978).

Conditions for when advertising and sales promotion intensity do signal quality are discussed by Milgrom and Roberts (1986). In their model of Nelson's (1970, 1974) original insight, they portray the firm with a high-quality product having to prove its superiority, relative to low-quality suppliers, by setting an initial price and visible advertising level such that buyers could not sustain a belief that the firm has only a low-quality product. This implies behaviour by the high-quality supplier which, when imitated by a low-quality supplier, would lead to overall losses for the low-quality supplier. The point is that the high-quality supplier can withstand initial period losses in return for establishing the quality of its product and obtaining the resulting profits in later periods. Thus any visible way of 'burning money', such as saturation advertising, signals the product's quality. No direct information content of advertising is necessary. A full discussion of the Milgrom and Roberts model is in Belloc (1991). The efficiency problem for this method of signalling is first that the signals are expensive, and secondly they may be so expensive as to make separation from the pool of suppliers unprofitable, as in Schmalensee's (1978) example. To improve signalling, firms will attempt to inform the buying public directly through advertising messages. These messages will then involve claims as to the product's quality, and such claims require monitoring since otherwise they are just 'cheap talk'.

The problem for consumer protection is then to improve the reliability of claims made in advertising and other promotional activities. Again there are two motives. First, there is the injustice for the consumer of being sold a product which has less quality than has been claimed. Secondly there is the inefficiency of suppliers of good products being unable to signal (or having to incur high costs to signal) their quality to consumers and perhaps having to exit the market, or of many potential consumers being put off by the general reputation of the market (how would you go about buying a time-share property?). Regulation of advertising is thus likely to spring from two directions. First, of course, consumers will be keen to avoid being duped, and will also desire to have confidence in sellers they deal with. Second, there will be pressure from those sellers who wish to preclude the bad products, partly because they wish to hold a large market share and would like to remove what they consider as unfair competition, and partly because they wish consumers to enter the market and this requires consumer confidence. In particular, regulation may make signalling higher quality easier or cheaper, and thus informing the market becomes more feasible. Note that advertising practitioners as a whole also have an incentive to ensure reasonable advertising standards, since otherwise heavy advertising would become associated in the minds of consumers with poor products rather than good products. This would destroy the basic argument that firms create good reputation by advertising and remove much of the demand for the advertising industry.

Warranties: The Double Moral Hazard Compromise

Warranties must not reduce the legal rights of the consumer concerning minimum quality standards, but may be seen as offering more extensive protection and also protection that is more certain and more easily accessible. Cooper and Ross (1985, 103) point out three important characteristics of warranties. These are:

- A warranty typically provides less than full insurance: the consumer is disappointed if he has to make a claim on the warranty.
- Warranties are often supplied by the seller rather than by third parties, although there are some exceptions to this.
- The extent of warranty protection is not clearly related to the reliability of the product: a better product may for example have a shorter warranty. More generally there is often a standard level of warranty—perhaps a one-year guarantee against failure—irrespective of the actual failure rate.

Obviously these characteristics do not hold in complete generality. For example 'extended' warranties on consumer durables, including cars, are sometimes available in the UK from third-party insurers at an extra cost. Also, the price or coverage of such insurance may vary with the product's objective and observable characteristics. Nevertheless the extra cost is often such as to render the insurance extremely expensive, at least for full cover. It is often linked to service contracts which are priced separately, for instance a new car may have to be serviced at expensive nominated main agents of the manufacturer. There is certainly considerable validity in the Cooper and Ross characterization.

The explanations for the existence of product warranties include signalling quality and insuring against risk. The first two characteristics above indicate that insurance is not the full story. Similarly, there is little evidence that to find the best quality all you need to do is look for the best warranty. Thus signalling is also an insufficient explanation for the extent and pattern of warranty protection. Cooper and Ross rather focus on the moral hazard faced by both producers and consumers. Their result is that the extent of warranty protection is limited by the moral hazard that producers face if there is little warranty protection, and that which the consumer faces if there is very high protection. If the producer spends money or effort the product quality can be improved. The incentive to make such expenditures increases as the level of warranty protection for the consumer increases. On the other hand the consumer can exert care in his use of the product. The greater the warranty protection of the consumer, the less is his incentive to use the product carefully. At the extremes either the producer or the consumer does not take account of the social costs or benefits of his actions. Since neither the producer's nor the consumer's actions are directly observable, they cannot contract to produce or use the product with a given level of care (although hard-to-verify clauses concerning 'fair wear and tear' and 'product misuse' are often included). The second-best outcome that can be achieved through a warranty cannot reach the first-best outcome that could be obtained if the producer's and consumer's actions were observable. Under reasonably general conditions the second-best outcome will involve a partial warranty, so that each party has some incentive to prevent the product from failing. Provided the supplier's and consumer's efforts are complementary in reducing the risk of failure both their effort levels will fall short of what would be optimal if they were directly observable and hence enforceable by contract.

An example of where only a very limited warranty is likely is in the case of a car. Here, a five-year warranty would promote harsh driving since the driver would not be liable for the cost of repairs (although this might be mitigated by conditions requiring regular servicing). On the other hand a very short warranty would lead to the seller not taking care that the car was of real quality. Similarly the warranty on electrical goods can only be set for a given period rather than the unobservable amount of use. If the period of warranty of a particular brand was fairly long relative to other similar goods, then those consumers who were heavy users of the product would favour that brand. This brand would then suffer from such adverse selection of buyers, both in terms of the cost of servicing the warranty and in terms of relative performance. Hence the difficulty of using warranties to signal quality.

An additional problem in the operation of warranties of all kinds, including commitments made by product descriptions in advertisements, is the question of how quality levels can be verified. This may require an appeal of third parties in the event of a dispute. The criteria adopted by such third parties may be difficult to predict and the process may involve costs for both buyer and seller. This problem is that of redress, and will form a prominent part of our discussion of the UK experience in developing institutional responses to the problems of asymmetric information of product quality.

3. UK EXPERIENCE

Trading Standards

The regulation of product quality in the UK rests partly on the enforcement of minimum quality standards by means of a legal basis summarized by the 1979 Sale of Goods Act and the 1982 Supply of Goods and Services Act. To this should be added detailed statutory requirements for specific goods and services: examples are food standards and safety regulations for furniture and electrical installations. The second main pillar of quality regulation is the operation of self-regulatory trade associations. Also, the 1982 White Paper 'Standards: Quality and International Competitiveness' led to various programmes of support within the Department of Trade and Industry for adopting, extending, and reviewing quality standards. Broadly speaking, the legal definition of minimum quality is that a product should be fit for its normal purpose and should be fit for any particular purpose that the customer has made known to the supplier. It should also be as described by the supplier. Similarly any service supplied should be performed with reasonable care and skill and in a reasonable time. Quality standards are technical specifications of products which have been approved by a recognized body. Thus a 'Kitemark' signifies both that the product has been manufactured to a specific British Standard and that the manufacture took place under a consistent quality-management system (satisfying BS5750).

The concept of a standard (BS5750) for a certified quality-management system has received strong emphasis, and is likely to be applied to a growing range of activities. For example, certification schemes could be designed for higher education, fruit and vegetable supply, and transport. The National Audit Office (NAO 1990) commissioned a study of a sample of certified companies compared to one of uncertified companies which found some evidence of higher increase in turnover for certified companies. However, the evidence for a profit effect was not conclusive. Also, the usual question of the direction of causality arises: those firms which are growing faster might be in a better position to revitalize their management systems.

Since British Standards can be considered above minimum merchantable quality, they do offer a way to prove a product is of good and above-average quality. They have also been adopted in various safety legislation as required standards. Nevertheless, the number of standards does not cover all products. Also the quality premium within the standard (the amount by which the quality exceeds the minimum merchantable quality) is likely to be quite variable. These factors may explain why major retail chains make little use of kitemarks. As the DTI informed the National Audit Office: 'existing marks had not achieved in this sector sufficient recognition and status to provide a major selling advantage to users' (NAO 1990, 17). A new 'quality mark' was therefore planned but has been delayed in order to launch it across a wide range of products. In general, a key problem with all such quality standards is that the necessary accreditation can be both expensive and time-consuming for the producer. Also, there are many goods and services where certification is often impractical owing to the nature of the product (a kitchen extension, for example). Even if a product has some quality certificate problems may occur. The complexity of merging UK and other EC standards as the single European market evolves is yet another difficulty in yielding a simple set of quality marks which are understood and accepted by the consumer.

What happens if the product or service falls short of the consumer's expectations? If the product is not fit for its purpose then it can be returned to the supplier—which is the shop selling the product rather than the manufacturer. Most consumers achieve a satisfactory outcome (see OFT 1990, and 1991). If the shop disputes the consumer's view and the consumer remains aggrieved, there is a choice of actions. An advice centre or local Trading Standards Officer may take action on the consumer's behalf; the consumer can seek compensation through a small-claims court; or the consumer can complain to a trade association for conciliation or arbitration.

Since the first move is always to seek satisfaction from the supplier, many complaints are resolved immediately. Nevertheless, over 600,000 consumer complaints are received by local authorities and advice centres per year (OFT 1988) while only some 12,500 are handled by the small-claims court system. These figures are mirrored in a survey conducted by the OFT (OFT 1986) where 5,000 respondents provided evidence that most complaints related to items such as furniture, household appliances, cars, car servicing, building work, and holidays. Not one of the respondents actually took court action, and less than 2 per cent threatened court action. Although many complaints may have been unjustified, and many may be resolved fairly painlessly, it does appear that the small-claims system is very much a last resort for the consumer: the inconvenience of attending the court, as well as the trauma of any court appearance, act as a strong disincentive. One must bear in mind however that the implicit rather than explicit threat of taking court action may play a role in achieving customer satisfaction and may not be observable. This however does rely on such action being credible and in this respect it should be noted that claims higher than £500 could not be heard in the small-claims court at the time of this survey. Although a number of proposals of the Report of the Review Body on Civil Justice (Lord Chancellor's Department 1988) are aimed at extending the role of the small-claims court (see Thomas 1991), there remains a need for less formal and more clearly defined dispute procedures.

One alternative consists of the codes of practice of trade associations. These associations will attempt to conciliate between a consumer and one of their members, and may also be prepared to bring in independent arbitration. The consumer usually pays a fee, which is returnable if his claim is upheld, but has no further risk. The vast majority of cases referred to trade associations have been related to package holidays (Association of British Travel Agents); also very active have been cases concerning motor cars (Motor Agents Association) and furniture (National Association of Retail Furnishing). Thomas (1991) gives some data on the frequency of use of these conciliation schemes and also contrasts the proportion of cases referred to arbitration rather than directly conciliated. For example: whereas ABTA and MAA referred about 5 per cent of cases to arbitration, NARF referred virtually none.

Our discussion of some of the theoretical issues in the last section pointed to some of the problems in regulating quality. The law can only attempt to enforce accuracy in product description and fairly basic quality levels. In complex products it may be that only some aspects can be assured: for example some safety aspects of cars may be regulated, but not many elements of performance. Even though the consumer believes he has a case he may be in error or he may believe that an adjudicator will take a contrary view. The small-claims court continues to be a daunting prospect for most consumers, who are often more prepared to return to the seller and accept the seller's opinion as the outcome of the claim. Of course they might then remove their future custom if they are not satisfied. For expensive products where quality is very variable, such as package holidays or cars, the consumer prefers to use the claims procedures of the trade association if they do not obtain a settlement from the seller. Their reasons for taking this route may well reflect the realization that the trade associations do wish to maintain public confidence and also have specialist knowledge in considering the particular cases.

All dispute procedures, whether legal redress or appeal to trade associations, can be interpreted as the enforcement or interpretation of the consumer's rights. If the consumer was promised a three star hotel but was allocated to a two star hotel the package holiday was not as described and the consumer has an obvious claim. On the other hand, if the consumer was allocated to a three star hotel which was still being built, the consumer has to establish the state of the hotel when he stayed there. The consumer has an incentive to exaggerate the problem; the seller of the holiday has an incentive to understate the problem. The trade association acting in the best interests of its membership will wish to uphold the reputation of package holidays and avoid bad publicity. The balance of incentives that it faces may well be reasonably just. Nevertheless some problems remain as we will see in Section 4. The furniture retail industry does not have a reputation problem as an industry. Reputations relate to particular stores. A product which causes consumer dissatisfaction can be dropped and replaced by another. A customer complaint is of an observable defect and can be dealt with by conciliation more cheaply than by arbitration. Of course, some retailers will specialize in the shoddy end of the market. Here however the retailer may not be a member of the National Association. Membership of the trade association acts as a signal of product reliability.

Advertising Standards

The Advertising Standards Authority is a self-regulatory organization which controls the content of advertisements in all non-broadcast media.

Television and radio advertising have similar regulatory bodies (the Independent Television Commission and the Radio Authority), as do telephone-message services. The control takes the form of applying the British Codes of Advertising and Sales Promotion Practice. These Codes 'provide that all advertisements should be legal, decent, honest, and truthful, that they should be prepared with a sense of responsibility both to consumers and society, and that they should conform to the principles of fair competition generally accepted in business'. An industry body, the Committee of Advertising Practice collaborates in the supervision of advertising standards. This regulation is thus directed at the information content of advertising, rather than the 'as advertised on TV' signal of dissipative advertising expenditure discussed by Milgrom and Roberts.

There are three main ways in which advertising standards are enforced. First, the Committee of Advertising Practice gives pre-publication advice as to the legitimacy of advertisements in so far as compliance with the code is concerned (it does not advise on points of law). Second, the Advertising Standards Authority operates continuous monitoring of published advertisements. This takes the form of a rolling sample from all newspapers and magazines. 50–60 titles a week are seen, and every twenty-fifth advertisement checked to identify breaches of the Codes. In addition more detailed surveys are undertaken from time to time. Lastly, the Advertising Standards Authority receives complaints from the general public and firms. These complaints are investigated first at a preliminary level to see if the issue falls under the Codes of Practice and is pursuable, and then, in the event that it is deemed pursuable, a more thorough investigation ends with the complaint being reported as upheld or not, or with a statement indicating that no such judgement is possible. The latter occurs when verification of statements is not possible or when the issue is a matter where the line between acceptability and unacceptability is not clear. If complaints are upheld, the offending advertisements are withdrawn or amended. It is not however the case that punishments such as fines are levied on either the product suppliers or the advertising practitioners: the ASA seeks to control advertising standards by publishing its findings and requiring corrective measures. However, it is possible for the Director General of Fair Trading to seek a High Court Injunction against advertisers considered to be in contravention of the Control of Misleading Advertisements Regulations 1988, although this would only occur after other means of advertising control had been exhausted.

The extent of advertisements which fail to satisfy the Codes of Practice can be seen from detailed surveys. A survey of national newspapers for a two-week period in May 1991 considered 35,000 display and semi-display adverts. It found that between 0.2 and 9.6 per cent of the total could be criticized, with eighteen of the thirty-one titles scoring less than 3 per cent. Many of the adverts causing concern were picked up only for minor technical problems. Significant errors included (ASA 1991):

- Unacceptable health and slimming claims.
- Important conditions on special offers and promotions which were totally absent or not clear.
- Over-emphasis on speed and power in car advertisements.
- Improbable earnings claims in advertisements for jobs or business opportunities.
- Unqualified 'environment friendly' claims for products.

Most months, nearly a thousand complaints are received from the public, although some may relate to a case already under investigation. Of the 715 complaints received in May 1991, 134 were deemed to require investigation, 281 required further information or action, and the rest were referred to other regulatory bodies, or were related to advertisements already under investigation, or were judged not to warrant consideration. The majority of complaints upheld each month are because the advertisement was not truthful, either in a matter of fact or in the way the facts were presented to give a false understanding.

Although there is no doubt that mechanisms exist which lead to misinformative advertising being withdrawn, there must be some doubt as to the existence of significant deterrents to such advertising. Both major and minor companies figure in the list of firms for which complaints are upheld. On occasion transgression may be unintentional, but even this implies insufficient quality control by firms of their own advertising copy and reflects the rather soft action taken by the regulatory body. Of course, reputations for making advertisements which frequently appear in the 'complaints upheld' list may be costly to the firms involved. However, the ASA reports are not within the normal reading material of the general public and their market effect is largely dependent on the attention given to them by more general media. In terms of the question posed in Section 2 (whether or not bad products can drive out good by heavy advertising) the answer seems to be far from clear. The ASA appears efficient in investigating breaches of the Codes of Practice. It also has the advantage over a purely legislative system of operating quickly, and being able to interpret the Codes of Practice in terms of the general principles involved and to reflect changing business conduct and public attitudes. For example, moves are currently being taken to form a 'European Advertising Standards Alliance', to promote similar self-regulated Codes of Practice throughout the EC. The ASA can thus be considered as a flexible regulatory body. To some extent the frequency of complaints may indicate the success of the ASA in educating the public about the Codes of Practice and the ASA's willingness and fairness in investigating complaints. On the other hand, the frequency of complaints, particularly in some areas of business, seem to point to the need for more emphasis on a policy of deterrence. Certainly the problem of any system of advertising regulation is that the benefits of misleading advertising have often been gained by the advertiser before regulatory action can occur. It would also be interesting to assess how often leading advertising agencies (presumably well-versed in the Codes of Conduct), acting for large corporations, figure in upheld complaints. One possible way forward would be to shift the system of funding the ASA away from the current levy of 0.1 per cent of advertising bills towards funding from a levy which relates to the frequency of recent upheld complaints.

4. THREE STORIES OF QUALITY REGULATION

Odometer Readings in Second-hand Cars

The quality of a second-hand car is in part a function of the quantity of use it has received. The odometer in a car supposedly gives this information. However the mileage reading can be falsified. Although this is a criminal offence, it is widespread: surveys conducted by local authorities suggest that 20 per cent of cars monitored have had their mileage altered. This problem is particularly important within the UK for two reasons. First, a large proportion of new cars are bought by fleet owners and many of these cars enter the second-hand market as nearly new, well-maintained, but high-mileage cars. The profit from falsifying the mileage of such a car can be well in excess of £1,000. The extent of this fraud prompted the setting up in 1988 of a working party chaired by the OFT to consider schemes for recording the history of a car so that tampering with the odometer would be obvious. The report of the working party was supported by the Associations of County and District Councils, the Association of Metropolitan Authorities, the AA and RAC, the Consumers' Association and National Consumer Council, the National Association of Citizens' Advice Bureaux, the OFT, and motor trade associations, including the Motor Agents' Association, the Society of Motor Manufacturers and Traders, and the Society of Motor Auctions. The proposals were that a vehicle's mileage should be recorded by the DVLC (Driver and Vehicle Licensing Centre) when the vehicle is relicensed and when it changed hands. This information would be available to potential buyers and thus significantly changing the mileage would be very risky. Hopefully the fraud perpetrators would then be deterred; certainly, trapping them would become more straightforward.

The proposal of the working party was based on their view of the cost of 'clocking' to the community. This was described as consisting of the costs of trying to combat clocking under the current system, by tracing car histories and prosecuting alleged offenders, the loss of profits of reputable garages from trade taken away from them, and the loss to buyers who pay more than they should do for a 'clocked' car. These represent the arguments of the costs of limiting injustice and the injustice itself. In our Introduction we stressed the adverse selection problem leading to market failure. Here the cost is the lost transactions due to sellers of good (low-mileage) cars being unable to separate themselves from the pool of doubtful cars on offer, and thus being unable to realize the correct value of their product. This kind of cost seems missing from the arguments in the report, and an explanation could be that the motor trade attempts to circumvent the 'lemons problem' by backing its sales of second-hand cars with the reputation of long-established traders and heavy promotion of warranties. This removes or at least reduces the market failure as far as buyers are concerned, but only at the cost of buying from a limited number of traders and paying a premium which may be high. Also, consumers' organizations may be reacting to complaints from buyers of clocked vehicles. In neither case is the private seller represented, and his failure to secure the right price for his car is largely ignored. Although this point should not be taken out of proportion, it is worth bearing it in mind when focusing on the history of the proposal.

The government stated some sympathy for the proposal: its response was to query whether the cost of collecting and processing the data could be met by the users of the service. Thus a buyer would pay a fee to obtain the mileage record of a candidate car, whether the car was being offered for sale by a private individual or by a trader. In the event the DVLC appeared to favour contracting the service to a private firm already engaged in providing information concerning stolen, debt-attached, and rebuilt cars to the motor trade. Two problems then arose. One was the fee to be charged Trading Standards Officers when pursuing their enquiries: the TSOs claimed this would be too much for their budgets. The second problem was that the firm decided it would ask the current mileage of the car before releasing its information. Thus the (until now unsuspecting) owner of a 'lemon' would be unable to pass on the car without perpetrating a fraud which would be observed by the firm. At the time of writing this chapter, the outcome looks as if the mileage data will not be collected by the DVLC, but that one or more private firms may operate a business of checking mileages for motor traders, enabling guarantees of mileage to be given. Note that this does nothing to help the private-sale market, since there is no easily available source of checking mileages for the private buyer; on the other hand the reputable motor trader will be able to differentiate his product better, and thus charge a higher premium. (It is already noted that in the USA motor traders with new car franchises can obtain higher prices for their second-hand cars than other traders, presumably reflecting the fact that they pick the best trade-ins to sell themselves and put the rest to auction, see Genesove 1990.) Also note that the enforcement activities of the TSOs have not been assisted. Finally, one of the ways in which information can be provided to the motor trade is from fleet owners when they dispose of their stocks—usually at auctions. There is no incentive for fleet owners to provide this information (indeed if the possibility of clocking increases the price their vehicles obtain at auction, the incentive is to remain silent!).

Home Improvements

The problems arising from building work such as household repairs and extensions appear to be widespread. There are of course the 'cowboys' who take a deposit and disappear or who botch the job in ways immediately undetectable. On the other hand there is the conflict which can occur if the customer has an expectation of the result which is simply unreasonable, at least given the budget agreed. One problem here is that, in order to obtain the business, the builder needs to marry a low price with an assurance of an agreeable result. The customer may be led to have incorrect expectations even from an honest and skilled builder operating at minimal profit levels. The answer to defeat the cowboys and ensure consumer satisfaction with the responsible builder must involve a form of guarantee which signals the reliability of the work but does not lead the builder offering the guarantee into difficulties with unreasonable customers.

The problem is essentially that of 'double moral hazard', which we have already discussed. Thus it is of no surprise that a key initiative proposed by a Working Party in 1988 was the development of an assessment and approval system for builders' guarantee schemes. Such a scheme would make it easier to identify a reputable builder. A 'fair deal' contract was also to be developed. If a standard contract could be found to be acceptable, this would have a number of obvious advantages. The fine print of a builder's guarantee would not need to be studied. Further, such a contract would act as an easily recognizable signal of reputation, and arbitration or conciliation resting on the terms of the contract would be relatively easy since expertise would be gathered about the interpretation of the terms of the contract. However, there are difficulties in bringing such a reform into operation. Principal among these is the prospect that just a few firms will adopt the new contract. Then there may be an adverse selection of consumers for these firms: they may particularly attract either those consumers who will press for the most advantageous interpretation of the contract, or consumers may more likely look for the protection of the contract when the job they wish done is of an awkward nature—perhaps where the bad characteristics of the job are known to them but not to prospective builders. The difficulty of getting builders to accept such a contract would be much less if it was clear that it would be publicized widely and heavily so that it would soon become standard practice. Again however the cost of such publicity is high, and it is not clear who would provide the funds. At the current time the 'fair deal' contract is still under discussion. It is not clear whether it will end up as the industry standard or a rare event, used only by some firms for some jobs. In order to instil confidence in the market, and to clearly distinguish the 'cowboys', a clear standard contract between firm and customer is essential.

Package Tours

A third case where the OFT has recently urged reform is the market for package holidays. There were two prime sources of complaint. One was the use of surcharges. These effectively meant that the consumer could be faced with a large unanticipated price rise just before commencing the holiday. Of course, it could be argued that flexible prices which could respond to variations in fuel cost and currency fluctuations were efficient in that they allowed the risk to be shared between customers and firm. The problem however is that the customer has little way of checking the validity of the surcharge. Indeed in a report (July 1988) the OFT stated that fuel surcharges were being used to inflate profit. As a result the Association of British Travel Agents (ABTA) announced proposals in June 1989 to avoid the need for 90 per cent of surcharges from that summer onwards.

On another front, progress was less speedy and some concerns remain. These relate to the question of who is responsible (who can be asked for compensation) if the holiday is not according to specification or fails to meet minimum criteria. The package holiday companies claimed that they purchased services from airlines, hotels, etc. and could not be responsible if these suppliers did not fulfil their commitments. The OFT recommended that the tour companies adopted a code of conduct that essentially admitted responsibility for the whole set of services. The argument was that the tour company should make sure of the quality of what is sold through its brochures, and that, for example, the individual holiday-maker is in no position to sue an overseas hotel owner. The EC Directive on Package Holidays has now made the operator liable and the ABTA code of conduct for its members now reflects this approach. A number of problems may remain. If the tour company disputes the complaint made by a customer about hotel accommodation, there is little that can be done without good documentary proof such as photographs etc. When the complaint is investigated, the faults may have been corrected.

5. CONCLUSIONS

In this conclusion it would be nice to be able to report success in UK regulatory policy in the field of product quality. Indeed there do seem to be a number of reasons for optimism. Among these is the development, for an increasing range of products, of British Standard quality standards which signify, not only that the design is able to deliver the performance, but also that quality-control mechanisms are in force in their manufacture to ensure that faults are reasonably rare. Secondly, the worst excesses of advertising and promotion are controlled by the application of a code of practice, although it does seem likely that considerable profits can still be made out of 'bad' advertisements before action is taken. Thirdly, complaints from consumers about the product they purchase are often rectified by the seller, and trade associations apply codes of practice which permit conciliation or arbitration of disputes. There seems no reason to doubt that the balance of incentives, for these associations, are such as to yield a reasonably fair result both for the consumer and for the seller.

Nevertheless, there seems to be a number of remaining causes for concern. First, the legal framework for obtaining redress seems to remain a rarely used last resort and could be repackaged and publicized more effectively. One would think that the Small Claims Court would be thought more accessible if it were renamed the Small Claims Arbitrator, burying the notions of guilt and innocence. Also the trade associations (apart from obvious examples such as ABTA) do not always appear to publicize their activities and the method of access is sometimes obscure. Second, the major causes for concern lie in particular markets where facts are difficult to verify and asymmetric information is very significant. In these markets attempts have been made to reduce the imperfections, but progress has been slow. The two cases where this has been most apparent is that of the setting up of a mileage history of a second-hand car and putting building work on a clear contractual footing. In both these cases the incentives of traders within the industry were ambiguous. The apparent outcome in the case of 'clocking' is that the market will become increasingly segmented between those traders who sell mileage-guaranteed cars (at high prices) and the remainder of the market. Individuals will not be able to check quickly the mileage record of a prospective car. The government's failure to underwrite the required finance of the proposed scheme was particularly disappointing since it gave no weight to the social importance of the private market for cars. It was also surprising because it represented a possible missed opportunity to tackle the problem of the estimated 580,000 unlicensed cars on the road: a record of mileages when licensed could be designed to reveal periods when cars were unlicensed and this would have to be accompanied by clocking in order for unlicensed use to be hidden. It would soon become accepted that an unlicensed period in a car's history was a signal of doubt, leading to lower valuations, and a real cost of evading the licence fee. Such indirect effects appear not to have been considered. One reason might be that the current beneficiaries of being able to keep a car which is off the road unlicensed are in fact motor traders.

The setting up of a standard formal contract for building work might have a similar spin-off provided the contract could reasonably balance the double moral hazard problem that we discussed in Section 2, and thus prove acceptable to the reputable trade. Such contracts would obviously include the agreed price for the work to be done. Thus these contracts could not be used by builders who intended to evade tax on the job since the builders' accounts could be required to show copies of these contracts. To the extent that protection would be more readily available to consumers using firms adopting the standard contract the balance of forces would be altered in favour of the reputable company and tend to discredit the tax-evaders. Again, the effect of quality regulation on tax evasion (and particularly the possible gains in tax-take from regulation) does not seem to be part of the calculus determining the extent of government support for establishing and promoting such key elements of consumer protection.

Thus our conclusion has to be that, despite a number of real advances, recent history of consumer protection by quality regulation has included a number of missed opportunities. In the next decade, the regulatory focus may well shift towards being EC-wide. Indeed, nothing else would be logical or acceptable. It will be interesting to see whether or not progress in developing efficient markets, where the consumer can buy in confidence, is accelerated.

References

Advertising Standards Authority (1991), *Monthly Reports*.

Akerlof, G. A. (1970), 'The market for lemons', *Quarterly Journal of Economics*, 84: 488–500.

Belloc, B. (1991), 'Advertising and quality', in J.-J. Laffont and M. Moreaux (eds.), *Dynamics, Incomplete Information and Industrial Economics*, Oxford: Blackwell, 212–28.

Cooper, R. and Ross, T. W. (1985), 'Product warranties and double moral hazard', *Rand Journal*, 16: 103–13.

Genesove, D. (1990), 'Adverse selection in the wholesale used car market', mimeo, Princeton, NJ: Princeton University.

Milgrom, P. and Roberts, J. (1986), 'Price and advertising signals of product quality', *Journal of Political Economy*, 94: 796–821.

National Audit Office (1990), *Department of Trade and Industry: Promotion of Quality and Standards*, HC 157, HMSO.

Nelson, P. (1970), 'Information and consumer behaviour', *Journal of Political Economy*, 78: 311–29.

—— (1974), 'Advertising as information', *Journal of Political Economy*, 81: 729–54.

Office of Fair Trading (1986–90), *Annual Reports*.

—— (1990), *Consumer Loyalty*.

—— (1991), *Consumer Strategy*.

Schmalensee, R. (1978), 'A model of advertising and product quality', *Journal of Political Economy*, 86: 485–503.

Thomas, R. (1991), 'Consumer protection: Strategies for dispute resolution', in K. J. Mackie (ed.), *A Handbook of Dispute Resolution*, London: Routledge, 157–73.

White Paper (1982), 'Standards: Quality and International Competitiveness', Cmnd 8621, London: HMSO.

9

Regulation and Standards Policy: Setting Standards by Committees and Markets

PETER GRINDLEY*

1. INTRODUCTION

A major problem for the regulator is how to set standards. Compatibility standards are vital for telecommunications, where equipment must match the network, for television services, where receivers need broadcasts, and for mobile phones, where handsets need base stations. They are equally important in more mundane areas such as plugs and sockets, electric supply voltages, railway gauges and even which side of the road we drive on. It may seem that the advantages of everyone using the same standard should be clear and it would be a simple matter to agree a standard. Yet the recent history of some spectacular failures to establish standards, for high-definition television, cordless telephone, and satellite broadcasting, show that standards are hard to set, and that results when a regulating authority is involved are often worse than when the market is left alone.

The difficulty is co-ordinating the decisions of the various firms and users involved in deciding standards for a new product. Standards for private goods such as video cassette recorders or computers, which need compatible pre-recorded tapes or computer software, are usually determined efficiently by market competition. In other areas, where the public interest is seen as more pressing or where the standard overlaps with other regulation, such as the allocation of radio spectrum, it is often believed that the regulating authority should co-ordinate if not decide standards.

The problem for the policy-maker is how to find a balance between the use of official standards bodies and market forces to set standards, called *de jure* and *de facto* standards. The worry with market determined standards is that there are often costly standards wars and these may result in fragmented standards, with some stranded users of a losing

* Center for Research in Management, University of California, Berkeley, Calif.

standard. Owners of Betamax VCRs discover that there are few pre-recorded tapes for rent, and owners of non-DOS compatible personal computers have difficulty finding software and pay high prices for it. Though these costs are usually manageable and can be dealt with within the market, the costs of confusion in other areas may be more severe and call for public intervention. Social costs are high if each television station uses a different transmission method or a group of drivers tries to drive on the wrong side of the road. Official standards committees try to avoid these problems by deciding standards before firms and users make irreversible decisions. However, official standards may bring more problems than they solve. Vested interests and other organizational problems may block the committees. With crucial commercial interests involved it is often impossible to reach agreement purely by committee, and the time scales involved may be too long in areas of rapid technological change. Also the authority is tempted to add other policy aims which can ruin the standard. As a result either agreement is not reached or the official standard may fail in the market-place.

For these reasons it may be better to make more use of markets for standards setting, despite the risks, even in regulated industries. Where total reliance on markets is not appropriate, hybrid mechanisms for greater involvement of market forces may be possible to reduce the problems of co-ordination by committees. In either case the role of the authority becomes more one of facilitating rather than selecting standards.

The standards of most concern here are compatibility standards for the interface between two products. These differ from the perhaps more familiar type of standards for minimum quality, such as health and safety regulations, or weights and measures. European Single Market legislation, for example, more often refers to quality standards than compatibility standards. Minimum-quality standards regulate the market and protect the consumer. As such they benefit the market as a whole and do not have the same strategic importance for the firms and users as compatibility standards. They may be dealt with effectively over longer time horizons by the standards bodies.

In this paper we first outline three major recent cases, for high-definition television, cordless telephone and satellite broadcasting, where official standards have been to some degree unsuccessful, to illustrate the potential problems involved. We then summarize the policy problems for both official and market standards. We analyse the causes of these problems and suggest some remedies. Finally we summarize the implications for standards policy.

2. SETTING REGULATED STANDARDS

High-Definition Television

The original High Definition Television (HDTV) system was developed by the Japanese broadcasting service, NHK, in the 1980s. It provides greatly improved picture definition over colour television and a larger, wider screen. To be adopted a television standard needs agreement between programme producers, broadcasters, and equipment manufacturers, as well as being acceptable to viewers. The official forum for deciding the standard is within the national and international broadcasting authorities. With no other systems in sight either in Europe or the USA, the Japanese proposal at first seemed well on the way to being adopted as a world-wide standard. It had gained the endorsement of the US national standards committee and no opposition had surfaced from Europe. However, this was not to be. At the crucial meeting of the International Radio Consultative Committee (CCIR) in Dubrovnik in 1986, the Europeans refused to accept the standard. Led by the French, they quickly put together proposals for their own HDTV system, called MAC. With the prospect of a single global standard gone, the USA reopened their national standard to fresh proposals and began developing more advanced systems. It now looks as though there will be three incompatible systems world-wide. This repeats the fragmentation of current colour TV standards into three regional groups (NTSC, PAL, and SECAM) which occurred thirty years ago (Pelmans and Beuter 1987). Serving the smaller regional markets none of these is likely to have the great success once predicted for HDTV and at best the introduction of the service has been delayed by several years.

This outcome is unsatisfactory for several reasons. The benefits of having one world-wide standard for programme production, transmission, and manufacture have been lost, with few compensations. The aim of the Europeans was to protect the remnants of their consumer electronics industry. It is unlikely to do this. MAC development is many years behind the Japanese, who are bound to provide most of the studio equipment and also much of the transmission equipment and receivers whatever standard is used. Moreover, major private satellite broadcasters, such as Sky Television in the UK, are rejecting MAC in favour of the existing PAL colour system, and the prospects for MAC are highly uncertain. The USA has also been concerned to protect its national manufacturers, but as most of these are foreign-owned, a more powerful influence has been the terrestrial broadcasters. These are threatened by HDTV, which is best delivered by satellite or cable, and they have persuaded the US Federal Communications Commission that the standard should be transmittable from land-based stations. This will restrict performance, while the delays in the screening process will delay HDTV in the USA by at least five years. Either of these may ruin its chances of success. An unplanned benefit of the delay is that more advanced all-digital proposals have been developed, though this may not significantly add to HDTV's chances. As with MAC, even if a system is developed, most of the equipment will be Japanese made (for further discussion see Grindley 1991; Farrell and Shapiro 1992).

In a case such as this is it not easy to compare what might have happened had the choice of HDTV system been left to market forces, as regulators are involved to some extent even if only in allocating radio bandwidth. However, compared with the delays and fragmented standards following the official route, it is likely that left to themselves satellite and cable services would have introduced the NHK system when and if they felt there was a market for it. They have been restrained from doing this in Europe by licensing conditions and in the USA by the prospect of an FCC-backed terrestrial standard. Market introduction would probably have been gradual, as it has been in Japan, where even with official support the manufacturers are now using an intermediate stage with Extended Definition TV. Given this gradualism, HDTV is probably not as great a threat to western industry as it has been portrayed.

This case shows the ineffectiveness of standards bodies in obtaining agreement when faced with major clashes of commercial interests, here from the manufacturers and broadcasters. Also industrial and political aims have crowded out those of finding efficient standards. The official standards process has actually made fragmented standards more likely than would giving the market a freer hand, with ultimately few visible benefits.

Cordless Telephone

Cordless telephone provides a useful contrast between an attempt to involve markets in the standards-setting process in the UK and the more traditional committee approach to standards used for the European Community as a whole. The UK experiment failed dismally, due partly to operator errors but mainly to product restrictions and low commitment inherent in the policy, which did not give the market process a chance to work. The European standard should eventually provide a workable standard, but this is taking a long time and it is unlikely that any public cordless services will be promoted enthusiastically there.

Telepoint is a UK public cordless-telephone system, launched in 1989 as the 'poor man's mobile phone', which uses radio base-stations to access the public network. Objectively there should have been a market for a low-cost system but it was handicapped by product limitations, which allowed only outgoing calls and restricted use to within a hundred metres of a base-point, and by slow installation rates. It attracted almost no users and services were withdrawn within just two years. The policy setting up Telepoint aimed to mix market and official mechanisms for setting standards. The problem was that the policy left technical details to the operators to decide after issuing the licences, but still laid out the main rules for the system. Two-way calling was barred as the licensing authority did not want this to compete with its plans for the more sophisticated Personal Communications Network (PCN) to follow. It insisted on four operators to ensure a high level of competition, leaving little incentive for investment, especially as it was clear that market shares would have to remain roughly balanced. Finally the means of determining a common standard were never made clear and it was eventually set a year after the start of operations not by market competition but by the authority. In fact each service remained incompatible to the end, which guaranteed fragmented standards and made it even harder for users to find a base-station. Not surprisingly the operators lacked commitment and the public were confused, killing the services (Grindley and Toker 1992).

Behind this, the main policy aim of the regulator was to use Telepoint to develop a standard for cordless telephone which, being proven in the market-place, would be well-placed for adoption as the European standard. The Telepoint standard was developed very quickly, within two years, but the failure of the services was a poor recommendation and left it with little chance of adoption.

In contrast the European Commission has used a traditional committee approach to setting cordless standards. This is the opposite to the market by selecting between standards submitted for approval. The process has been under way for about five years and is expected to be complete in another five. The main standard being studied is from a consortium of major European manufacturers. Once a standard is set any public services would probably be the responsibility of the national Public Telecommunications Operators who, with the exception of France, have shown little interest in them. There has been some flexibility here in that Telepoint was allowed as an interim standard and had it been more successful this could have led to its adoption.

Telepoint shows the problems caused by trying to bring external policy aims into the standards process. These may distort the standard to such an extent as to make it unworkable. The apparently more successful European procedure still shows major problems with committee standards in the time taken to approve a technology which has essentially been available for years and with no assurance that services will be provided. The process is vulnerable to being bypassed by more quickly developed standards from outside. Rather than disproving the value of market standards Telepoint indicates that if markets are to be used they should be given broad freedom to determine the standard by competition and not just used for technical design. Getting the balance right in hybrid policies of this kind is clearly difficult.

Satellite Broadcasting

Satellite television in the UK has seen a contest between two systems, one licensed by the broadcasting authority and the other operating independently. The official service, British Satellite Broadcasting (BSB), was licensed in 1986 but only began broadcasting in 1990. This crucial delay was caused by the long approval process and waiting for the development of MAC, the first stage of the European HDTV standard, which BSB was required to use. The other service, Rupert Murdoch's Sky Television, took advantage of the delay and pre-empted BSB. It started broadcasts over a year earlier in 1989. Sky avoided the licensing requirements by transmitting from Luxemburg on non-restricted channels. It used the existing PAL standard so did not need to wait for MAC. By the time BSB services were launched, Sky had an audience of two million homes. BSB could not attract new users quickly enough and within six months it collapsed into merger with Sky.

Standards are crucial because of the MAC requirement and because users would only be prepared to invest in one or other system, which needed separate receiver dishes. Given Sky's lead there could only be one standards winner. Its installed base of viewers already made Sky look like a winner and was beginning to attract significant advertising. BSB tried to differentiate its service with high-quality programming but this was ineffective and expensive. Being tied to MAC was a further disadvantage as there were no MAC television sets and an additional decoding stage was needed. When they merged, BSB services were transferred to Sky and the stranded BSB viewers were given help switching their equipment.

In this case the official standard was clearly bypassed by a market-generated one. Adoption by the standards authority was a hindrance as it delayed the service and restricted it to a technology which was not fully developed. The UK government had thought that it had a controlled policy experiment on its hands and wanted to use this to promote high-definition television. If UK plans for HDTV have suffered, this is partly the result of viewers electing against it in this way. Sky's victory shows how effective a flexible and fast-moving market standard may be against an official one. The contest was not cheap. BSB spent £700 million and Sky £550 million in its first two years, but it was resolved rapidly. As for other policy concerns, at least some viewers and UK manufacturers of receiving equipment have benefited from Sky's success.

3. REGULATED AND MARKET STANDARDS

Market Standards

For many standards government intervention is not needed or appropriate, and standards setting may safely be left to market competition. A large part of the success of products such as video cassette recorders and personal computers has been due to the efficiency and speed with which product design converged to a single main standard. Once the common standard became clear in these products, complementary software markets in pre-recorded tapes or computer programs grew up to support them and the main markets then grew rapidly. The availability of tape rentals and PC software packages were the keys to the growth of these markets (for these and other cases see Grindley 1992).

Market standards work by competition between alternative designs. This is the reason for their effectiveness but is also a source of problems. While it is extremely valuable to have a range of alternatives generated by the market, the ensuing standards wars are costly and to some extent unpredictable. The dynamics are that a small advantage early on may be the signal to the market that this will be the winning standard. Complementary support snowballs and although it may not be technically the most advanced standard it is very hard for another one to dislodge it. For example, the arrangement of the typewriter keyboard was already obsolete when it was introduced a hundred years ago, but has lasted to this day (David 1985). Alternatively, if a leader does not emerge until later, there may be several standards each with a small installed base, large enough to survive but not to attract adequate support. Fragmented standards divide the market so that no one standard is truly successful. The expansion of railway traffic in nineteenth-century England was retarded by the different railway gauges which had evolved for regional services, and one of these, Brunel's Great Western Railway, resisted conformity for over fifty years. Similar compatibility problems have reappeared recently on a European-wide scale with the introduction of high-speed train services. Also, users who have invested in a losing, minority standard are 'stranded' with little software and service, as owners of Betamax VCRs discovered. Finally, if the standard is proprietary the design owner may restrict access and use its monopoly power to charge high prices (Farrell and Saloner 1986; David 1986; Grindley 1990*b*, 1992).

These problems of stranding, fragmentation, technical obsolescence, duplication of effort, and monopoly power often occur with market standards but it is possible to overstate the risks and in most cases the market itself finds ways to minimize them. Many historical cases of fragmented standards occurred because they grew up under a different set of conditions when, say, international transport and communications were less important than today. If the issues are understood from the beginning markets usually converge to a single standard. If the costs of fragmentation and stranding are high then all the more reason for users to support a single standard, so the numbers involved may be small. Thus only about 2 per cent of the VCR machines in existence are now on the losing Betamax standard. In any case technical change may soon give an opportunity to switch to the leading standard with the next upgrade. Converters may be developed to help stranded users, as happened with BSB subscribers in UK satellite broadcasting where the merged Sky service was anxious to build up its audience and subsidized the conversion of receiver dishes. An 'obsolete' standard may have outlived its technical shelf-life but still give great value to users through their investment in software and training, as MS-DOS continues to do in personal computers. Competition and duplicated development effort may be necessary to generate new technology, while proprietary standards are becoming more of a rarity in a world where open standards are more effective in attracting broad support and winning contests, as seen in VCR and PC. A sense of proportion is needed in assessing the costs.

Even so there are areas where the costs of the standards chaos possible under the market are more serious. Markets can be harsh on the losers. The costs of being stranded may be more than an individual can bear, or may fall not on the firms making the decisions but on society as a whole. For example, the costs of replacing expensive medical equipment which no longer has maintenance support or of retraining specialized skills in a technology made obsolete by a standards war, may be beyond what individuals can afford. Confusion in the use of the radio spectrum with several transmission standards makes broadcasting difficult for everyone, not just the maverick broadcasters. There are also some standards which may be beneficial but need to be co-ordinated centrally by an authority which sees the whole picture, particularly for changes to a standard. A change in the side of the road a nation drives on clearly has to be arranged by government ruling, individuals cannot change it themselves. In cases such as these there may be a need for government intervention to co-ordinate and regulate the standards process. The government may already be involved as a regulator of the industry, as in telecommunications and broadcasting.

The questions are how best to achieve standards co-ordination and where to draw the line between using market and official or committee standards. Some of the factors in this decision are given in Figure 9.1. Before we are ready to make an evaluation, however, we need to explore some of the difficulties of using regulation and the committee process.

	Market	Committee
Favouring markets	+ Clear decision Fast Commercial goals Acceptable to market Open process Product focus Design variety Global	– Agreement difficult Slow Technical bias Remote from market Covert lobbying External policy agenda Monolithic Local/national
Favouring committees	– Standard wars Duplicate devel. costs Fragmented standards Stranding Locked in obsolescence	+ Orderly process Single launch Unified standard Provision for losers Technically superior

FIG. 9.1. Comparison factors for market and committee standards

Problems with regulated standards

An official standards authority aims to set standards outside the market, if possible before products are developed and launched. This is achieved by a process of negotiation and selection using committees representing manufacturers, complementary producers, users, and government. Standards bodies are of various types, from voluntary industry associations with no direct legal powers to regulatory authorities with strong enforcement capability. However, they all co-ordinate standards by some form of consultative, consensus process and most have some policy overtones, otherwise we have a market standard. They may also perform many other functions in addition to defining standards, including information exchange, providing a discussion forum, drafting standards, testing and documentation. We are concerned with their role setting new standards and take the supporting functions as given.

The intent is that if a standard can be set first, before substantial development takes place, then this avoids duplicated R&D costs, standards wars, and stranding. It reduces the uncertainty about the new standard, so that manufacturers and complementary producers can then develop products in a stable environment. On this reading the only problem is whether deciding a standard too early reduces variety and cuts off potential technologies before they have a chance to develop.

Unfortunately the process does not work as well as this. It may introduce as many problems as it solves and the net results are often worse than leaving things to the market, with all its risks. Some prominent failures are described above. These are not unconnected cases but stem from the inherent difficulties of using committees to make decisions for new technology. The variables are numerous and fast changing and the outcomes are crucial to the firms' commercial interests, so that it is hardly surprising that consensus is less effective than market competition.

The problems are in four areas. First, it is very hard to get agreement in committee. Even if reached it may not be upheld in practice. Vital commercial interests are involved and these are too important to the firms' futures to be decided purely by committee. Firms are bound to compete in product development and possibly to try to pre-empt the decision by launching products on the market. If a decision goes against them they may attempt to bypass the official standard in the market. We have seen Sky do this to British Satellite Broadcasting. Also, in HDTV the Japanese system has become the *de facto* studio standard if not the broadcasting standard. Thus the agreement itself may be of little value unless it is backed up by market forces.

Second, the official standards bodies tend to concentrate on technical rather than commercial aspects and so use too narrow criteria. They are often surprised when the most advanced standard is not adopted by the market. This bias is partly a response to the difficulties of obtaining commercial information and partly historical. Standards contests show us that the most advanced standard often does not win, and that it takes other aspects such as obtaining broad support, complementary investment, and distribution to establish a standard. Yet technical excellence may be relatively unimportant once a basic level of user-acceptability is reached. VHS was technically inferior to Betamax VCR, an the IBM PC was less-advanced than other systems, yet both were huge successes.

Third, the official process changes the focus of competition from the product itself to influencing the standards authority. It introduces an additional player in the game, the authority itself. Firms' efforts are diverted into finding out what the regulator is thinking and trying to influence it in their favour. The merits of the product may get overlooked. Also the authority is usually poorly equipped to make the commercial judgements needed for success in the market-place. As a government body it has different objectives than the firms and cannot have all the information, especially business information. It must rely on the firms to supply this information, which apart from being at second hand will also be selective regarding the merits and costs of alternatives. The only way to fully understand the product is intimate involvement at the firm level. The game for the firms becomes to lobby rather than win users. Yet relying on adoption by the standards authority is often a bad strategy for the firms. It may be no guarantee of success, as was the case for Telepoint and BSB, and looks set to be for MAC, and possibly the US HDTV standard.

Most important is that the authority may bring in its own policy agenda beyond setting an efficient standard. It is hard to resist the temptation to use standards to promote national industry. Such policy looks costless, as the standard is sensitive to small nudges one way or another in the early stages. However this is not costless. For the same reasons of sensitivity, distorting the standard to fit other policy aims easily makes it unacceptable to the market. Telepoint is a case where the standard was restricted to fit other policy aims to promote UK manufacturers and orchestrate mobile telephone competition, and this led to an unworkable standard.

Finally, the committee process takes a very long time, and one of the crucial elements in setting a new standard is speed. There is a narrow window of opportunity to establish a standard. An official standard may find it hard to meet the pace. This gives a chance for a faster moving market solution to pre-empt the official standard and establish itself as the *de facto* standard before the official standard appears. The process is also inflexible, so that needed modifications to the standard which become apparent as the product is being introduced either cannot be made or take too long. For Telepoint, vital changes to correct basic product errors by adding pagers and two-way calling took over a year to be approved and were still not introduced when the services failed.

This combination of problems may mean that the standard is unattractive or, worse, that the process is so confused and delayed that the product fails when launched. Telepoint and BSB standards both failed. HDTV has been damaged, possibly terminally, by fragmentation and delay. The committee may also fail to avoid the costs of market solutions. There is little saving of duplicated development costs as firms still compete. The competition is distorted as the object is adoption by the authority not what is most attractive to the market. The chances of fragmentation still exist as firms may launch products ahead of time or try to bypass the official standard. Where different authorities are involved, as they are for international standards, the chances of fragmentation are actually increased by official standards, as they have been with HDTV, colour TV, and most national telecommunications standards. Finally an official standard may be just as likely as the market to confer monopoly power on the winner.

These are not only problems for regulated standards. Many of the difficulties using committees apply equally to voluntary industry standards bodies. Committees became a focus for disagreement between manufacturers and music companies for Digital Audio Tape (DAT) standards, and also made little progress on agreeing Unix open computer software standards until commercial pressures became strong (Grindley and McBryde 1992; Grindley 1990a). Markets do not always work. In digital audio the DAT standard has been squeezed out by Compact Disc, though in many ways it is the more useful product. However many of the failures to establish a standard (video disc, mini-CD) may be attributed to unwanted products rather than the standards process.

4. COMBINING MARKETS AND REGULATION

Why committees fail

Setting standards is a co-ordination exercise, to get manufacturers, complementary producers, and users to adopt a common interface design. The larger the installed base of a standard, the more complementary products are supplied, and the greater the demand for it by users. The standard benefits each group and the more widespread the adoption the greater its value. Though there may be some reduction in variety and possible monopoly effects associated with the standard, the network benefits usually far outweigh these costs. The problem is that the benefits are not evenly distributed. If the winning standard is proprietary then the owner may restrict use or charge high licence fees to other producers. Even if, as is more likely, the standard is open and made available to all producers, so there are no net losers, some firms may gain more than others. The developer of the standard has a first mover advantage on the market and the others can only follow after a delay. The leader may be able to hold on to its position by making further technical improvements. With this uneven distribution of gains firms will compete to have their standard adopted by the committee. It is a negotiation game in which players may never agree on a standard as each wants to lead and will continue to argue the merits of his own standard. This is why the standard may need to be taken to the market to decide, either with or without the involvement of the committee.

The contest is a 'battle of the sexes' game, well-known in game theory, in which two players both gain by agreeing to do the same thing but one gains more than the other. The players vie with one another to be first to choose and unless the game is expanded to include other factors there may be no resolution to an endless argument. Most of the usual ways out of this impasse do not work for compatibility standards (see Kay, 1993, for the application of game theory to business strategy). The regulator tries to adjudicate the decision, and this is one reason for the technical bias of committees, but it cannot evaluate the conflicting claims effectively for the reasons we have given above. If it makes a selection it is almost bound to please nobody. Similarly this cannot be a repeated game (in which case players could take turns to lead) as once the standard is set it is locked in for the duration. Deciding the outcome by hierarchy, such as following the largest firm, is also unsuitable with new technology where the market is new and leadership often changes, though it may be used after the fact once standards exist to decide which of several incompatible standards should become the common standard.

The only way out of the dilemma is for one or more of the players to make a commitment to a standard. This means making a sunk-cost investment in the market-place. The other players must then decide whether to compete with the standard in the market or follow the committed standard. This clears the impasse. It may be combined with continued negotiations in committee to help smooth competition by exchanging information, but once the players have decided to compete in the market the game has changed and must be followed to its conclusion. The effectiveness of market competition is that it cannot continue endlessly. Costly investments (decisions) are made and these are tested against the market. Because of the costs involved the process must be finite and the results decisive. It is very clear whether the market has adopted or rejected the standard and this point is reached after a short time. Market competition allows great flexibility so the standard can be quickly modified if it is not meeting any demand. In Japan, with no regulatory obstacles, HDTV strategy was soon changed in response to slow consumer adoption to introduce it via Extended Definition TV. For Telepoint the UK market rejected the system decisively. If the licensing terms had not been so restrictive the system could have been revised in time and perhaps been successful.

Using markets

This helps explain the effectiveness of markets in setting standards and the value of bringing them into the process in some way. This includes the option of using fully market determined standards, which years of regulation should not make as 'unthinkable' as we may imagine. Often we do not want to go this far and we should first consider hybrid policies for cases where some public control over standardization is necessary, as when the risks of stranding and fragmentation are too high. It has been shown that under some conditions a hybrid policy combining committee negotiations with market commitments may be better than either the committee or the market on their own (Farrell and Saloner 1988). The question is finding the right balance. At this point we can only suggest some possible approaches and more experience is needed before we can make any clear recommendations.

At one level, market mechanisms may be used to improve the selection process, while still leaving the authority to make the final decision.

Firms are likely to withhold some information to improve their standard's chances of selection. This is especially so for cost information, which is harder to verify than technical. As a result the regulator often chooses a technically excellent but expensive standard. One way to induce firms to reveal their true costs is by auctioning the rights to set the standard (Farrell and Shapiro 1991). This motivates firms to optimize the costs and features of the product. To avoid monopoly problems this should also include the condition that the final standard be licensed at 'reasonable' (low) royalties to other producers. Unfortunately a problem with this approach is that there are usually few suppliers for large systems, and there is unlikely to be an effective market bidding for the standard. The recent experience of the UK in auctioning television programme franchises have not been encouraging for this kind of auction, with widely varied bids and threats of lawsuits to follow.

Having clear rules for selection may also help avoid strategic game-playing. Options are to decide a winner by a date deadline, by the first to establish a clear lead, or by the first to surpass a performance threshold. All have problems but the first, deadline, has the best chance of cutting short the to-and-fro tournament between the firms.

Although we may improve the committee process in these ways the basic problems of evaluation, lobbying, and external agendas remain. It may be necessary to go to the next level and turn over the standards decision more completely to market competition, on the basis that the committee can never resolve the differences. The questions are where to draw the boundary and how much influence the authority retains. On the basis of our experience so far the boundary probably needs to move a long way towards the market. If market competition is used for the main decisions then it needs a minimum of interference. This does not mean that the authority takes no part in the standard but it lays out only broad rules within which the market develops and establishes the standard on its own. It retains its traditional roles of facilitating standards and providing channels for information exchange and negotiation within market competition. This has always been a major part of what standard bodies do (Sanders 1972; Verman 1973). If there is a change it is to encourage firms to make more use of this facility. The authority also still needs to try to correct possible market problems. It should almost undoubtedly require that the standard is openly licensed, with reasonable royalties, to avoid giving monopoly power to the winner and discourage standards wars. It may include incentives or provisions for taking care of stranded users.

Beyond this the authority should not treat standards as an opportunity to pursue an external agenda for other industrial policy. Standards setting is a delicate business and is easily disturbed, and should as far as possible be kept separate. Competition policy may be pursued by an open licensing requirement to avoid monopoly rather than by forcing the number of competitors or other powerful restrictions. Market structure, including the number of competitors, may remain the concern of existing anti-monopoly rules. Trade and infant industry arguments may also best be dealt with aside from standards. The market cases show that strong standards flow from well-managed firms, not the other way round. Standards are not robust enough to be general policy tools. At an international level, policies to support national champions are probably the main reason for globally fragmented standards, rather than any market mechanism. Changing this may have to wait for some basic realignment of international thinking.

Market standards for AM Stereo

One of the few examples of what can happen in turning over regulated standards to the market is AM stereo radio in the USA, described in Berg 1987. The FCC had evaluated proposals through committees for over twenty years from 1961 to 1982 without coming to a decision. Possibly because external pressure for a decision for this non-vital product was weak, the committees went round in circles trying to decide between a number of standards. This was brought to a halt in 1982, when in a surprise policy change the FCC announced that stations would be allowed to choose what standard they wished provided it fitted within their bandwidth allocations. The first system (Kahn) was launched within two months and began recruiting local radio stations. Others followed quickly. The main competitor (Motorola C-QUAM) was introduced about six months later. This had superior technology, support and financial backing and overtook Kahn. AM stereo became an established service within a three year period. Standards converged on the C-QUAM standard but left a sizeable minority stranded with Kahn, which held on to the installed base it had built up before C-QUAM entered.

The market was able to establish a standard quickly, in three years compared with the previous twenty years of fruitless negotiation, but the case also shows the problems of fragmentation. Markets are harsh on the losers and lawsuits against the FCC are a possibility. However, the fragmentation was in part a hold-over from the previous delay. When this was unexpectedly lifted it did not give all the alternatives an equal start. Those who had been counting on FCC adoption were ready to being broadcasting immediately and knew their only chance against better funded rivals was to try to get in first. As the geographic coverage does not overlap very much the costs of fragmentation from the user side may not have been excessive.

5. CONCLUSION

The roles of official standards bodies have evolved for historical reasons. Their traditional concern has been with the technical functioning of a network or the maintenance of quality and service standards across an industry. The technical approach, working through layers of committees towards consensus, is well-suited to this kind of regulation. It does not work well for the fast decision-making needed with interface standards and new technology. Co-ordinating the various interests involved may need market competition. The outcomes of several recent officially mediated standards have compared poorly with the successes of some private standards set in the market-place. Indeed standards bodies may be better equipped to deal with negotiations after standards have evolved, to move towards a common standard as painlessly as possible, than to set them in the first place.

We need to re-evaluate how market forces may be brought into the standardization process. So far attempts to combine markets and regulation have not always been successful. In some cases this has been because attempts have not gone far enough. In Telepoint, details were left to the market but the main decisions remained with the regulator. Where the market has been allowed enough freedom, as in satellite television (inadvertently) and AM stereo, a standard has been set efficiently if not perfectly. Left to themselves markets have shown that they will set *some* standard very efficiently, and whatever may be said about its technical merits the standard has passed an important test of user acceptability. The role of the authority then becomes to provide the conditions for the market to work and if necessary correct potential excesses. If it tries to do more, to orchestrate the standard, it is as likely to hinder as help.

Finally, standards should not be seen as a simple way to implement industrial policy. It is too easy to ruin a standard's chance of success. Providing information and alternatives via standards bodies is beneficial to all parties, but once this becomes direct manipulation the risk is that the standard becomes unworkable. Policy to support national industry should be kept separate from the actual standards setting. Market standards cases have shown that a successful standard depends on the committed backing of strong firms, rather than the other way round. Concerns such as trade protectionism or industrial development should be dealt with directly, if possible, and not made part of the standards. After all, good standards benefit support industrial and users as much as manufacturing, and these are also at risk with poor standards.

References

Berg, S. (1987), 'Public policy and corporate strategies in the AM stereo market', in L. Gabel (ed.), *Product Standardization.*

David, P. (1985), 'CLIO and the economics of QWERTY', American Economic Review, 75/2: 332–7.

—— (1986), 'Narrow windows, blind giants and angry orphans: The dynamics of system rivalries and dilemmas of technology policy', in F. Arcangel, *et al.* (eds.), *Innovation Diffusion*, iii, New York: Oxford University Press.

Farrell, J. and Saloner, G. (1986), 'Economic issues in standardization', in J. Miller (ed.), *Telecommunications and Equity*, New York: North Holland.

—— (1988), 'Coordination through committees and markets', *Rand Journal of Economics*, 19/2: 235–52.

—— and Shapiro, C. (1991), 'Standard setting in high definition television', mimeo, University of California, Berkeley, Calif.

Gabel, L. (ed.) (1987), *Product Standardization as a Tool of Competitive Strategy: INSEAD Symposium*, Paris: North-Holland.

Grindley, P. (1990a), 'Standards and the open systems revolution in the computer industry', in J. Berg and H. Schumny (eds.), *An Analysis of the Information Technology Standardization Process*, Amsterdam: Elsevier.

—— (1990b), 'Winning standards contests: Using product standards in business strategy', *Business Strategy Review*, 1: 71–84.

—— (1991), 'Replacing a product standard: The case of high definition television', Working Paper No. 100, Centre for Business Strategy, London Business School.

—— (1992), *Standards, Business Strategy and Policy: A Casebook*, Centre for Business Strategy Report, London Business School.

—— and McBryde, R. (1992), 'The standards contest for digital audio: Compact disc and digital audio tape', Working Paper No. 114, Centre for Business Strategy, London Business School.

—— and Toker, S. (1992), 'Regulators, markets and standards co-ordination: Policy lessons from Telepoint', Working Paper No. 112, Centre for Business Strategy, London Business School.

Kay, J. (1993), *The Foundations of Corporate Success*, Oxford: Oxford University Press.

Pelkmans, J. and Beuter, R. (1987), 'Standardization and competitiveness: Private and public strategies in the EC colour TV industry', in L. Gabel (ed.), *Product Standardization.*

Sanders, T. (1972), *The Aims and Principles of Standardization*, Geneva: International Organization for Standardization.

Verman, L. (1973), *Standardization: A New Discipline*, Hamden, Conn.: Arden Books.

10

Regulation in the European Community and its Impact on the UK

FRANCIS MCGOWAN* AND PAUL SEABRIGHT†

1. INTRODUCTION

The 1980s (and the second half of that decade in particular) saw a striking increase in the extent to which regulatory activity in the European Community impinged upon the United Kingdom. This is ironic in view of the deregulatory philosophy widely espoused during the decade (and particularly so as this philosophy was embraced by the UK and the European Commission much more strongly then elsewhere in the Community). Such a development has raised in a stark form the question what the respective spheres of competence of the UK's and the EC's regulatory institutions should be, and whether the evolving division of powers is likely to make economic sense. Regulatory sovereignty can admit of many degrees, and considerable regulatory powers have been effectively transferred from the UK to the EC while in no way leaving the UK itself powerless in regulatory matters.

An important economic principle underlying the distribution of powers is the inelegantly titled principle of 'subsidiarity' (see 'Editorial comments', *Common Market Law Review*, 1990). This states that the power to make regulatory decisions affecting economic activity should be exercised at the most local jurisdiction unless there is a compelling reason for it to be exercised by a more central authority. So decisions should be taken by village or town councils, otherwise by county or metropolitan councils, otherwise by regional authorities, otherwise by national authorities, and only then if these prove unsatisfactory should they be taken by supranational authorities such as those of the European Community. This principle raises two major questions: first, why is subsidiarity an appealing principle at all, and secondly, what are the 'compelling reasons' that could justify centralization? This paper tackles these two questions in turn. It does so by focusing on the nature of the market failures that regulation is designed to redress, pointing to some

* School of European Studies, University of Sussex.
† Churchill College, University of Cambridge.

of the regulatory failures that may in turn characterize policies to meet these market failures, and suggesting that both subsidiarity and centralization are best understood as means of minimizing the costs of regulatory failure. In particular, it considers the phenomenon of regulatory 'capture', in which the implementation of a regulatory policy is characterized by the pursuit of interests other than those of the community in its widest sense. Subsidiarity has its rationale, we suggest, in making regulation responsive to the interests that are actually affected by it, and the justification of centralization lies in its ability sometimes to overcome regulatory capture at a local level.

First, Table 10.1 summarizes some of the major developments since the late 1960s. It lists in separate columns judgments of the European Court, treaties, decisions of the Council of Ministers, and actions of the European Commission that have changed the general regulatory relationship between the EC and its Member States (besides, in some cases, substantively regulating particular activities or sectors). It will be noted that the speed of events has significantly increased since the 1985 White Paper on the Single Market and the adoption of the Single European Act in 1986; the decision to implement the Single Market has been the prelude not only to accelerated developments in the regulation of specific industries but also to a series of radical changes in the relationship between the EC and Member States (many of which were not envisaged at all in 1985). The pace of change is in marked contrast to that of the 1970s and early 1980s, when Commission proposals were repeatedly bogged down by the need for unanimous agreement in the Council. The Single Act revived the principle of majority voting, dormant since the 1965 'Luxembourg compromise' which effectively granted each Member State a veto.

The table is necessarily indicative and sets out to show not only the development of regulatory responsibilities but also the gradual extension of regulatory scope. Most notable has been the growth of activities in the areas of competition and environmental regulation; for reasons of space we focus primarily on the former, though many of the issues raised in the paper have broader application. It is worth noting how the emergence of competence in one area (e.g. telecoms regulation or water quality) has been steadily extended to other utilities in the first case and to other environmental problems in the other. It is also worth noting the interaction between the different activities. Commission initiatives have been generally followed up by Council actions, with the Court reinforcing the Commission's competence by overturning Member State objections or clarifying the applicability of Community Law, while major legislative actions (such as new Treaties or amendments) establish new areas of activity and powers. The overall trend over the period has been for an accretion of responsibilities at the Community level.

TABLE 10.1. The development of community regulation

Year	Court judgment	Treaty	Commission action	Council decision
1969			First Vehicle Emissions Directive proposed	
1970				Vehicle Emissions Directive adopted
1973			Mergers Regulation proposed	
1974			Surface Water Directive proposed	
1975				Surface Water Directive adopted
1979	'Cassis de Dijon'[a]			
1980				Transparency of State Funds to Public Enterprises Directive adopted
1983			Proposal for Combating Pollution from industrial plant Proposal for Limiting Emissions from Large Combustion Plant	
1984			'Memorandum Two' (on airline liberalization)	Pollution from Industrial Plant Directive adopted
1985			Single Market White Paper New approach to product standards	
1986	'Nouvelles Frontieres'[b]	Single European Act[d]		
1987			'Green Paper' on Telecoms liberalization	First Airline Package adopted
1988			'Terminals' Directive (using Article 90.3) Internal Energy Market proposed	Large Combustion Plant Directive adopted
1990			Rail Transport initiative	Merger Regulation First Energy Package adopted
1991	'Terminals'[c]	Maastricht Treaty[e]		

[a] Developed mutual-recognition principle with regard to product standards regulation.
[b] Established applicability of Competition rules to Air Transport.
[c] Established the application of Article 90.3 to liberalize market structure.
[d] Revived majority voting, developed environmental responsibilities, enshrined Single Market objective.
[e] Extended Community regulatory role.

2. SUBSIDIARITY

Why should this be otherwise? Why should the onus of proof lie on any proposal to undertake regulation by a central rather than a local authority? There are two main kinds of reason. One is that, on many questions, local authorities will be better informed than central authorities about the needs and preferences of those citizens who are affected by the market failure the regulatory intervention is designed to redress. This need not be so in all cases (for instance, central authorities may have access to more sophisticated opinion-polling techniques, or certain regulatory tasks may benefit from scale economies in the expertise required). But as a general rule the quality of such information is likely to be diminished by distance of the regulators from the locality regulated. The second reason is that local authorities should also be more directly accountable to their citizens, and therefore under greater pressure to ensure that regulatory decisions are shaped by those needs and preferences rather than the whims or interests of the regulators themselves. This accountability may be a feature of the political system, which gives local citizens a voice in their own affairs: the presumption in favour of local regulation arises because national regulators are accountable to many other citizens than the ones directly implicated in a particular decision, and the influence of the preferences of the affected citizens on them may well be swamped by national trends. Alternatively, accountability may be enforced by the ability of citizens to leave a local jurisdiction whose regulatory policy does not meet their needs, and move to an alternative local jurisdiction that does (to exercise their right of 'exit', in Hirschman's (1970) phrase). Here local regulation is preferable because it increases the number of alternative regulatory jurisdictions between which footloose citizens may choose; it enhances the scope for 'competition between regulators' to offer solutions to the failure of competition between firms.

Tiebout's (1956) theory of local public goods provides some insight into the circumstances in which competition between regulators could be expected to lead to efficient decision-making, and therefore also to the many ways in which such competition may be inefficient.[1] A system of regulating market failure (consisting not just of laws but also institutions to enforce those laws) can be considered a special case of a local public good. The most important (and restrictive) conditions under which competition between local jurisdictions for the supply of local public goods would be efficient were shown by Tiebout to be the following:

[1] Since writing this paper in 1992, the authors have done further work on issues relating to the optimal level of regulation, some of which modifies the emphasis they would place on the Tiebout model as a framework of analysis. See Begg (ed.) 1993 and Seabright 1994.

1. Costless mobility of citizens between jurisdictions.
2. A large number of jurisdictions.
3. No external effects between jurisdictions.

These were in addition to technical assumptions such as that each public good has an optimal number of consumers (to ensure a determinate number of communities), and complete information about alternative possibilities. The absence of external effects meant that the costs of each good would be borne by the residents of the jurisdiction supplying it, and the excludability problem would be solved by the dependence of consumption upon location. Effectively, local jurisdictions would act rather like firms, supplying differentiated products to consumers, with a larger number of products required the greater the variety in consumers' tastes.

If these conditions were all met, the Tiebout model implies that competition between local jurisdictions would lead to an efficient provision of regulatory activity. Centralization of regulation could not improve on local regulation, and would suffer from the same disadvantages in providing regulatory services as those faced by the command economy in providing goods and ordinary services. However, it is evident that in reality the Tiebout conditions are very far from being met.[2] This is particularly true where the issue is whether regulation should be carried out at a national or an EC level; here there are very major costs (including linguistic and cultural costs) to the mobility of citizens between Member States, and twelve is a small number of competing jurisdictions given the large number of regulatory questions on which each pronounces. In addition there are many aspects of regulation in which the external effects between Member States are quite significant.

The failure of the Tiebout conditions to be met in practice suggests ways to think about the circumstances in which the presumption of subsidiarity might be overridden. Gatsios and Seabright (1989) discuss the main reasons why it might sometimes be desirable to undertake regulation at an EC rather than a national level. They focus mainly on the presence of externalities between Member States. These can arise in many areas: when regulating competition, for instance, consumers may be more widely dispersed across Member States than workers and shareholders, leading national authorities to place inadequate weight on the costs to consumers of market power. When regulating environmental externalities, national authorities may be insufficiently concerned about transfrontier pollution (this is a particular problem in the case of acid rain—see Newbery 1990). When regulating for consumer protection, national authorities will often erect barriers whose major purpose is to

[2] Hughes and Smith (1991) document how local government activity in Europe has a vastly different character from what one would expect if the Tiebout conditions were met.

keep out foreign firms. These external effects can lead to a form of regulatory prisoners' dilemma, in which all are made worse off by the pursuit of the self-interest of each.

Nevertheless, Gatsios and Seabright point out that the diagnosis of an international regulatory prisoners' dilemma is not sufficient to make the case for delegating national regulatory powers to the European Community. If Member States could simply agree to modify their domestic regulatory policies to achieve a co-operative outcome, such an outcome could be implemented by national governments without any need for delegation of the relevant powers. But in fact there are two main reasons why co-operative outcomes, even if desirable in principle, may not be feasible in the absence of delegation. One is the problem of co-ordination; the other is the problem of credibility. Both depend essentially on the fact that there is incomplete information on the part of firms, Member States, and the European Community itself, about the characteristics and motivations of the other players in the regulation game.

3. CO-ORDINATION AND CREDIBILITY BENEFITS OF CENTRALIZATION

Any co-operative European solution to regulatory failure at the national level will be the outcome of a process of negotiation between Member States. Since Member States have less than full information about each other's aims and negotiating strategies, and since they will each tend to be better informed about conditions in their own industries than in those of other Member States, there may be very significant costs and delays in the process of reaching agreement. This will be particularly true where there is no single optimal solution to the market failure involved, but several that differ only in the distributions of benefits and costs between Member States. In such cases each Member State has an interest in holding out for the alternative solution or solutions most favourable to itself.

The best example of this problem is in the field of product-standard regulation. In the domestic economy, optimal-standards regulation depends on striking a balance between the desirability of consumer choice, the need to remove asymmetries of information between consumers and producers, and the reaping of economies of scale in production. The desirability of consumer choice suggests there should be more alternative products available; the presence of asymmetries of information usually requires a limitation on the available alternatives so that consumers can effectively discriminate between them; and economies of scale tend to require restriction in the number of alternatives so that efficient scale can be reached in the production of each. Even if it is possible to determine the optimal number of product specifications that strikes the appropriate balance between these considerations, it will often be quite arbitrary which particular specifications are chosen. For instance, it may be best to have n different combinations of price and alcohol content among the available specifications of blackcurrant liqueur on the market. But there may be a large number of alternative sets of n combinations, any of which would be as good as any of the others. If countries regulate these matters individually, then in the absence of international trade it will be possible for each one to choose (perhaps arbitrarily) one of the optimal combinations for its own domestic market. But if these countries subsequently seek to form a common market they face the possibility that their choices of standards have been different: m countries may, even if they are identical, have determined between them as many as $n \times m$ different specifications for blackcurrant liqueur. At the same time the optimal number of standards for the new enlarged market will not be the same as the optimum for each of the individual markets.[3] It will typically be greater than n, but less than $n \times m$, unless all economies of scale in production had already been exhausted at national market size, and consumers faced no greater difficulty in discriminating among $n \times m$ products than among n.

The simplest form of co-operative solution to the product standards problem in a common market would be 'mutual recognition' of standards, whereby all $n \times m$ nationally permissible specifications would be permissible in the enlarged common market. Since 1985, this has been central to the European Community's 'new approach'—largely because of difficulties in achieving more ambitious co-operative solutions. In the case of certain relatively undifferentiated products, such as blackcurrant liqueur, such a solution may be fairly close to the best achievable. It increases the range of choice available to consumers while not diminishing, on average, the size of market available for any one of the specified products. Unfortunately, there are many products for which mutual recognition may be a long way from the optimal solution. This may be so for two reasons, one static, one dynamic. Statically, the optimal number of standards in the enlarged market may be much less than $n \times m$. This may be because there remain significant unexploited economies of scale in national markets, either in production or in consumption. This has the consequence that the Community's 'new approach' to standards will be least satisfactory in precisely those areas in which the potential gains from the Single Market are highest.[4] Alternatively, the complexity

[3] For more details of product diversity in monopolistic competition, see Dixit and Stiglitz 1977; Lancaster 1980; and Lawrence and Spiller 1983.

[4] In a world of differentiated products, it is quite difficult to know the extent of unexploited scale economies in national markets, because even highly disaggregated data tell us market sizes for groups of products rather than single products.

of product differentiation may make it hard for consumers to discriminate between a large number of products (as in certain financial services). This matters if the cost of making wrong decisions is high. It is particularly important in health and safety matters, which were specifically exempted by the European Court from the mutual recognition implications of the Cassis de Dijon judgment.

The dynamic reason why mutual recognition may be far from optimal lies in the distorting incentives it creates for national standards authorities. Even if mutual recognition of existing product standards is nearly optimal, national authorities may bias their decisions on future standards towards low cost, low quality combinations. This is because, knowing that approved products may be sold throughout the Community, national authorities know that much of the harm due to low standards will fall on consumers in other Member States, while the cost savings will accrue to their own national firms. Although over time certain national authorities may acquire reputations for high quality (as the Deutsche Institut fur Normung has undoubtedly done), these reputations may be insufficient to remove the risks to consumers that required product standard regulation in the first place.

In these circumstances there are good reasons for attempting to reach more restrictive co-operative solutions than mutual recognition—some degree of standard harmonization is required. Harmonization in this strong sense will always imply that certain products which were previously permitted in some Member State will no longer be permitted, at least in the remainder of the common market.[5] Given the expense of altering product specifications, this will impose costs on the firms of Member States, to an extent that differs according to which of the alternative sets of harmonized standards is adopted.[6] In the process of negotiation, Member States have incentives to block some agreements in order to reach others that involve them in less transitional expense. This is not just a desire to avoid transitional costs as such, but may also be a form of 'rent-snatching', since these costs constitute a barrier to entry and may thus be used to keep out foreign firms.

Harmonization of standards may therefore be considerably easier when co-ordination on one of several alternative co-operative solutions is delegated to a supranational agency such as the European Commission. This is so not just because the costs of collecting the relevant information are pooled, but because incentives to block or distort the negotiation process are thereby diminished. The European

[5] Even if they continue to be permitted in the Member State that originally approved them, competition from products with alternative specifications will reduce the expected size of their market.

[6] This applies to existing products as well as to new products that are developments of existing ones. But it will not matter for completely new products, where international agreement without transfer of powers may well be straightforward.

Commission, though itself vulnerable to lobbying, has less incentive than Member States to misrepresent the cost of regulation to particular firms in order to influence the regulatory outcome in their favour. Naturally the Council of Ministers has to approve proposed co-operative solutions—but the overall cost of reaching them may be considerably lower if the basic solution has been proposed by the Commission first.

'Mutual recognition' in a slightly different sense has been an important element in the Community's approach to the regulation of financial and professional services. The Second Banking Directive and the Non-Life Insurances Directive have both attempted to ensure that financial institutions licensed in one Member State can operate in another, though this must be done under local rules (this principle is known as the 'passport rule'; see Servais 1988; Davis and Smales 1989). There has been some attempt to make sure that local rules are not devised so as to discriminate *de facto* against new entrants. But as in the product market, there are significant ambiguities in what mutual recognition requires, breeding opportunities for strategic regulation by national authorities. Regulation of financial services may impose conditions either on the service products that may be offered or on the institutions offering them. The imposition of conditions on institutions is hard to utilize for strategic purposes, since these must in future apply without discrimination to firms of all Member States, both incumbents and potential entrants to a national market. But restrictions on permissible products are easy to manipulate strategically, for it is in the nature of competition in services that entry to a market is often best achieved by differentiating the product from that of incumbent firms. Any restriction on product differentiation is therefore potentially a barrier to entry. And this suggests that while a policy of mutual recognition may be satisfactory in regard to the conditions imposed on institutions supplying services, there may be significant gains from centralizing regulatory decisions that restrict product differentiation.

Of even greater importance than the difficulty of reaching co-operative regulatory outcomes is the problem of enforcing them. A well-known feature of prisoners' dilemmas is that, even though the parties have an incentive to agree to co-operate, they also have an incentive to break agreements they have made. Each Member State, for example, would like other Member States to police atmospheric pollution vigorously while it regulates with a comparatively light hand. In many circumstances where the parties interact repeatedly, co-operative agreements can be made self-enforcing through the threat of future retaliation for present breaches. But these conditions are only imperfectly fulfilled when the agreements are international agreements concerning regulation, for two main reasons. The first is that all self-enforcing co-operation depends upon the parties' discount rate being sufficiently small. But democratic governments often have short time horizons and therefore strong incentives to breach agreements for short-term advantage. Secondly, the complexity of regulation and the multiplicity of alternative instruments for achieving a country's economic objectives can make it difficult to observe whether agreements are being kept or not; and without reliable monitoring of compliance the retaliation that sustains co-operation cannot be invoked. These reasons both suggest that for many kinds of international regulatory agreement, more than tacit co-operation is needed to ensure credibility. Some form of international delegation of powers may be required.

The clearest case of international delegation of powers with such a rationale is the passage of the Merger Regulation of 1990, that has given the European Commission the power to investigate directly all mergers between parties with a combined annual world-wide turnover exceeding 5 billion ECUs. In principle Articles 85 and 86 of the Treaty of Rome already give the Community's institutions competence in the control of mergers—an interpretation upheld by the European Court in a series of judgments during the 1970s and 1980s.[7] But the merger regulation has both clarified the precise nature of that competence (thereby diminishing the risk of double jeopardy from EC and national regulation, and also stating more clearly than before the criteria according to which mergers are to be approved), and entrusted the power to implement an agreed policy to an institution with fewer incentives than Member States to breach the agreement in favour of national special interests.

One reason why the control of mergers is such a natural area for the exercise of supranational competence is that its implementation is bound to be highly discretionary. The distinction between discretionary and non-discretionary regulation is not sharp, but broadly captures the difference between systems in which general rules are set and compliance monitored, and one in which terms of reference are set for an agency that decides rules in particular cases. Non-discretionary systems comprise the kind of regulation that could in principle be enforced by a legal system (certain kinds of pollution regulation are the best example).[8] Merger control is a central case of discretionary legislation. They key difference between these two kinds lies in the nature of the information problems to which they give rise, and therefore in their vulnerability to capture by national or other special interests. Under non-discretionary regulation it is clear what the rules are. The remaining uncertainty for regulators concerns which firms are complying with them; the uncertainty for firms concerns their risk of detection if they are in breach. Under discretionary regulation, by contrast, there is uncertainty not only

[7] See for example the Court's judgments in the *Continental Can* (1974) and *Philip Morris* (1987) cases, discussed in Korah 1987.

[8] These differences between the United States and the United Kingdom are well documented by Vogel (1986).

about the facts relating to particular firms but also about the precise aims that the regulatory agency is pursuing. Credibility problems of co-operative solutions are often worse in the case of discretionary regulation, because it is harder (both for firms and for other Member States) to observe whether the actual aims and intentions of regulatory agencies are consistent with what governments claim them to be. In the case of non-discretionary regulation, the rules are known, and whether or not firms are abiding by them can be established by relatively simple investigation (as for the presence of nitrates in drinking-water). Furthermore, there are often incentives for third parties to discover and publish the information—either affected individuals, organizations or pressure groups (as in the case of pollution), or the press (who can make a story more readily out of a clear breach of regulations than out of a complex case of regulatory capture). But non-discretionary regulation is certainly not sufficient to ensure credibility, for sometimes member states can abide by the general terms of agreements on non-discretionary regulation, while cheating on the side of enforcement (see House of Lords 1989).[9]

Broadly speaking, where there is a strong need for regulation to be responsive to the circumstances of an individual case, its implementation will tend to be discretionary, and therefore co-operative regulatory agreements between Member States will be harder to monitor, reinforcing the prima facie case for centralization. But the strength of this argument depends upon the availability of institutional mechanisms that make capture by special interests less likely at a supranational than a national level; to know how likely this is, it is necessary to explore more fully the general phenomenon of regulatory capture.

4. REGULATORY CAPTURE

One of the well-known hazards of economic regulation is that regulatory agencies may be 'captured' by the firms whose activities they oversee (see Stigler 1971; Peacock *et al.* 1984; Vickers and Yarrow 1988; Laffont and Tirole 1991). This happens usually because asymmetries of information between government and firms require the regulatory agency to be closely involved with firms on a day-to-day basis, with a resulting tendency to identify with the aims of the firms themselves. This diminishes the credibility of government's professed aim to alleviate the market failures arising from unregulated activity.[10] However,

[9] The varying records of Member States in complying with the Single Market programme is detailed in Commission of the European Communities (1990).

[10] Peacock, *et al.* (1984) found clear evidence in the UK and West Germany that since 'regulators ... wish to avoid taking legal proceedings at every failure to comply with

'firm capture' is only one way in which the aims of regulatory agencies may come to diverge from those that they are ostensibly established to pursue. Another way is by 'government capture', in which the agency comes to be too closely identified with the aims of government itself (such as the desire to protect employment in marginal constituencies). The regulation of particular firms may be more effective if government can commit itself in some way not to intervene subsequently for political purposes in day-to-day regulatory activity: indeed part of the rationale for the UK government's privatization programme consists in the inability of previous governments to make such commitments of non-interference in the running of nationalized industries.[11]

At first sight, there is some reason to expect supranational agencies to be relatively less vulnerable both to firm capture and to government capture; at the cost of being less likely to share the overall aims of the Member State taking the decision to delegate. Indeed, supranational agencies may be correspondingly more vulnerable to capture of a third kind, which may be called 'bureaucratic capture', where the aims of a regulatory agency come increasingly to reflect the individual aims of their staff (for an account of utility regulation that incorporates the individual claims of regulators, see Evans and Garber 1988). Bureaucratic capture may be an important hazard for national agencies too; but we consider its particular implications for the EC below.

Regulatory capture, therefore, consists of two linked phenomena. First, the interests reflected in the activity of regulators do not adequately represent all those affected by the activity concerned. Secondly, this inadequacy is not accidental, due merely to oversight on the part of the political authorities, but is due to a difficulty on the part of those authorities in committing themselves to reflecting the interests in question. So far we have written as though the main issue at the EC level is whether regulation will reflect individual national or more broadly European interests, with the latter being more desirable in the presence of significant external effects between Member States. But it is evident that regulation will frequently fail to reflect even national interests adequately because of capture at the national level. The failure of the EC to

regulatory requests, and given the costs to regulators of improving their information about compliance . . . firms will behave tactically and fail to implement all requested changes'. If international agreement raises the expected rigour of enforcement, this may be expected to improve the compliance records of firms. However, a study by Vogel (1986) compares the relatively voluntarist approach to environmental regulation in the UK with that of the USA, and concludes that in spite of their different styles these have produced remarkably similar compliance records.

[11] However, the *process* of privatization may itself have adverse consequences for commitment. For example, when it privatized British Airways, the government accepted a less competitive structure for the airline industry than earlier policy statements suggested it wanted, by effectively abandoning its goal of fostering a strong rival ('second force') to BA in order to get a good price for the state-owned carrier.

satisfy the stringent conditions of the Tiebout model of local public goods means that mobility of citizens between Member States cannot provide a remedy for the inadequacy of national regulation, so we must consider the consequences of the capture of European regulatory agencies by industry, political and bureaucratic special interest groups, as well as national ones.

Two important conclusions follow. First, it is not always true that the quality of regulation is improved by increasing the influence of under-represented interests in the regulatory process. For instance, Laffont and Tirole (1991) show that, where a regulatory agency is captured by producer interests, increasing the influence of hitherto excluded environmental pressure groups may worsen the quality of regulation: environmentalists share with producers an interest in restricting output below the optimum (this is a compelling example of the problem of the Second Best; partial responses to regulatory capture may be worse than no responses at all). By extension, international agreements may be harmful if they result in co-operation on some but not all of the policies relevant to a particular activity (Gatsios and Seabright 1989, sect. 3). Winters (1988) has drawn attention to the potentially damaging consequences of a competition between Member States for control of markets by subsidy wars. It is certainly possible that co-operation on other aspects of the Single Market without effective co-operation on state aids could be worse than no co-operation at all. It is only if consumer interests are enfranchised, both in the process of regulation and in the issues to be addressed by that process, that an efficient solution is likely.

The second important conclusion is that the degree of centralization of regulation is only one dimension of the question how the credibility of regulatory policy may be enhanced by appropriate design of regulatory institutions. Just as important are two other dimensions: how far should regulatory agencies be answerable to the political process in a day-to-day sense? And should they be sectorally specific or specialize in particular issues (such as competition or the environment)? It tends to be believed (by both theorists and practitioners) that agencies are more immune to capture if they are free from day-to-day political interference while being subject to periodic review according to pre-established criteria,[12] and if they specialize in issues rather than the regulation of particular sectors.

While the evidence on balance supports this interpretation, it will be seen that there are many significant exceptions. And these other dimensions of institution design are an important reminder that international

[12] The Director General of Fair Trading, Sir Gordon Borrie, called recently for the establishment of a competition agency to administer the European Merger Regulation, one that would be distinct from the European Commission. 'Politicians', he wrote, 'should be excluded from sitting on such an agency' (*Financial Times*, 11 Nov. 1991).

transfer of regulatory powers as such may be of little help in solving a problem of regulatory capture if the special interests involved are not specifically national ones. Many of the problems of regulation have arisen simply because of the under-representation of the interests of consumers, irrespective of their nationality.

We still know very little about the factors that determine the weight which different economic interests will have in the determination of policy. Some of the earliest 'economic theories of the state' (Downs 1957) assumed that political influence was wielded by voting, and that the interests of the (actual or potential) median voter therefore had a disproportionate influence on policy-making. Such theories have some difficulty in explaining why producer interest groups usually appear to wield more power than consumers, since corporations as such have no votes (though employees of certain corporations in marginal constituencies may have very vital votes). Later theories of 'rent-seeking' activity (Krueger 1974) have emphasized that producer groups do have money, and can spend it on more or less dubious means of influencing policy in their favour. It is evident now that lobbying can make many other forms intermediate between the promise of votes and the direct payment of bribes; the effectiveness of spending resources (including time) on lobbying is likely to be highly non-linear, a fact that may account for the weakness of many consumer organizations[13] (since on any one regulatory question consumers are likely to have less at stake than producers). The implications of this for international transfers of regulatory powers are highly ambiguous, and suggest that to conclude supranational agencies are always less prone to industry capture than national ones is naïve. It may be that producer groups will be able to dominate regulatory policy even more effectively at EC than at national levels; alternatively, the economies of scale in lobbying may make consumer organizations more effective at European levels than they have so far been in any Member State.

5. SECTORAL AND GENERIC REGULATION: THE EUROPEAN EXPERIENCE

To what extent does the experience of the 1980s support the view that generic regulatory bodies (those charged with environmental protection or the policing of competition, for instance) are less immune to capture then sectoral regulators? The European Commission is divided into a

[13] It is striking that the most vigorous and influential protests against abuse of the EC's anti-dumping mechanisms have occurred when duties have been imposed on intermediate goods (such as silicon chips) rather than final goods (such as denim jeans); in the former case there is a producer group whose interests are harmed by the protectionist policy.

number of Directorates (broadly equivalent to departments or ministries), some of which have narrowly defined, sectoral responsibilities. As in many national governments, there is a widespread perception that these sectoral directorates have been captured by the industries they were responsible for. The nature of the relationship is not surprising given that the role of bureaucracies dealing with such industries as transport, energy, and telecommunications has for most of the history of the Community been primarily promotional, attempting to develop Community policies or co-ordinate the actions of government departments and industries. Explicit regulatory responsibilities have been a relatively small part of their activities until recently, and as a result the nature of the relationship between these sectors and the Commission was rather different.

The development of regulatory responsibilities at a Community level has raised the issue of capture much more explicitly. The application of Community law, particularly in the area of competition policy, has obliged sectoral directorates to develop policies which have fundamental consequences for the organization of the industries in question: previously legitimate conduct (for example a utility's exclusive right to market telecommunications equipment or to import electricity) has been challenged as contrary to the Treaty of Rome. However, although these sectoral directorates have responsibility for developing the policies, they often continue to identify with industry concerns. As a result the role of the horizontal regulatory authorities has become more important.

The development of Community policy in two areas (competition and the environment) demonstrates the extent to which horizontal regulation can act as a counterweight both to sectorally organized (and arguably captured) Directorates in the Commission and nationally based (and arguably captured) authorities. In these cases, it is possible to identify a more rounded perspective, based perhaps on a set of principles and supported by a strong legal basis. In the case of competition policy, the overarching principle is that of an open and integrated Community market. Any collusive or anti-competitive behaviour which prevents such a market from developing is contrary to the principles of the Treaty. In the case of environment, the overarching principle is that of environmental protection. This was not recognized as of fundamental importance by the governments when the Treaty of Rome was signed, and accordingly there is no direct mention of the issue in that Treaty. As environmental concerns developed over the 1970s and 1980s and Member States sought to address them, so the Community competence developed, eventually in the incorporation of environmental regulation into the Single European Act, and the more recent plans for a European Environmental Agency. (Haigh 1989)

The growing influence of directorates with generic responsibilities does not make the problem of capture unimportant. Competition and environmental protection, while important and general principles, are not synonymous with the general interest. Indeed, as the arguments of Laffont and Tirole (1991) remind us, in a second-best world it can be possible to have too much of a good thing, and the pursuit of competition or environmental protection, if enshrined in Directorates with a momentum of their own, may override other legitimate considerations. However, these considerations suggest that it is not enough to see regulatory capture in terms of a simple struggle between industry special interests and the general interest: regulation is the outcome of a process of negotiation between bodies representing different interests, none of which operate purely altruistically. Whether or not the process is judged to have been captured is a feature of the outcome as a whole, and not of any particular agency that contributes to that outcome.

This can be illustrated by a recent example of Community policy. There are a number of sectors such as the utility industries which are structured monopolistically and operate collusively. Whereas their 'special status' has traditionally been accepted, or subject to benign neglect by the Commission, increasingly the structure of such industries has been questioned by the Competition Directorate.

In recent years, the Commission has developed its powers under Article 90 of the Treaty of Rome. Article 90 deals with publicly owned industries and sectors which enjoy special or exclusive rights, forbidding any action contrary to the Treaty (particularly the Competition provisions). The Article also makes clear that the Treaty rules apply to undertakings providing services 'of general economic interest or having the character of a revenue-producing monopoly' though it does provide scope for exemption (if the performance of specific tasks would be affected by this provision). Of most importance is the fact that the Article provides for the Commission to act on its own initiative. Article 90(3) states that 'The Commission shall ensure the application of the provisions of this Article and shall, where necessary, address appropriate directives or decisions to Member States.'

In the electricity industry, for example, the Commission has proposed organizational changes to the industry as a prerequisite for introducing competition (and in particular the effective dismantling of the tight vertical integration which characterizes most national systems). In principle, Article 90 could be applied to the sector as it has in the telecommunications sector (de Cockborne 1990). It could be argued that the exclusive rights or monopolistic practices permitted by the Treaty in the electricity industry only cover some aspects of electricity supply. Consequently, where there was scope for competition then the incumbent industries should not retain their present monopolies. The use of Article 90 would allow the Commission to introduce a directive restricting those rights to where a natural monopoly existed, opening up the rest of the industry to Community competition.

The Competition Directorate intended to pursue this approach in tandem with other measures designed to open up the electricity and gas markets in the Community. However the use of Article 90 to impose a liberalization of trade in the EC electricity and gas industries has been suspended at least for the time being (*Agence Europe*, 23 January 1992). Instead the Commission will pursue these objectives through the less controversial avenue of Article 100a. Under this provision, directives which remove barriers to the completion of an Internal Market, can be passed by a qualified majority in the Council, but cannot be imposed directly. The experience of reforming the electricity industry highlights another important feature of the reforms in this sector, shared by other sectors, namely the reliance on a gradualist approach. Such has been the opposition of most governments and industries in the Community that a rapid transformation of industrial structures and the regulations governing them has been rejected in favour of a phased procedure.

Both the decision to suspend the use of specific legal mechanisms and the phasing-in of reforms illustrate the dynamics of developing regulatory responsibilities at the Community level. The presence of horizontal or generic regulators does not mean that the regulatory solutions they propose always prevail. In practice, such solutions are inevitably diluted in the negotiations. Furthermore, the perceived need for consensus building means that there is often a striking lack of consistency between successive decisions, as outcome viewed as 'victories' for one Directorate are balanced by subsequent concessions by the victor. The recent decision by the Commission to forbid the take-over of Canadian aircraft manufacturer de Havilland by a Franco-Italian consortium is a case in point. The Competition Directorate overrode the opposition of firms and their governments involved in the merger, thereby enhancing the credibility both of the mergers regulation and of its own position as a Community regulator. Subsequently, it was also able to resist pressures from within the Commission to dilute its authority on the application of the directive (by involving a wider range of Commission interests). But the strong protests registered by a number of parties at the Directorate's ruling in the de Havilland case suggest that it may wish to proceed more cautiously in a number of future cases.

In such cases, the regulatory task has to be perceived as a highly politicized struggle amongst officials. It is appropriate in these circumstances to ask what are the aims of the officials involved: in particular, to what extent are they concerned to bring about particular outcomes, as opposed to building up more long-term influence? The answer becomes especially important in cases where the regulator is essentially imposing an apparently 'deregulatory' regime. Traditional models of regulatory capture tend to suggest that deregulation reduces the scope for rent-seeking behaviour, and consequently the rents appropriated by regulators. Why, in such circumstances, would the pressure for deregulation ever come from a bureaucratic body such as the Commission? A more realistic view would suggest that generic regulatory authorities may be as susceptible to lobbying and rent-seeking as their more narrowly based national and sectoral counterparts—but the interests they represent are nevertheless different ones, and may favour outcomes that involve less rent-seeking in aggregate.

In fact, it seems evident that pro-competitive initiatives by the Competition Directorate have significantly increased the power and status of that Directorate at the expense of others, particularly since the application of general rules of competitive conduct (and the granting of derogations from those rules) remains very much a discretionary matter. Even if these developments have resulted in lower levels of rent appropriation overall (an outcome which is far from certain), the interests of the Competition Directorate will influence future regulation in ways that cannot always be assumed to be unambiguously in the public interest. None the less, to the extent that its interventions have so far involved representing more effectively the interests of consumers, they are to be welcomed. Important questions remain about the extent to which it might be desirable for the future implementation of competition policy at a European level to be undertaken by a body with greater formal independence from the rest of the Commission. What is at issue is not whether competition considerations are the only ones that matter—they are clearly not—but whether a clearer appraisal of the trade-offs between all the relevant considerations can be achieved by ensuring that the competition considerations are evaluated by a separate body. A system for separating these considerations exists in Germany, where the *Bundeskartellamt* must address only competition questions; this has not prevented it from being overruled on numerous occasions by the minister concerned, but such overrulings at least make visible the tension between the principles at stake.

6. SUBSTANTIVE POWERS AND LEGAL FORMULATIONS

Our theoretical discussion suggested that the main reason why Member States might accede to the assumption of regulatory powers by EC institutions was the benefits of a delegated co-operative solution to regulatory prisoners' dilemmas. While this has undoubtedly been a significant motive, the experience of recent years suggests the transfer of power has often had a more mundane explanation: the full implications of the legal powers vested in Community institutions have only belatedly been realized. One of the most interesting developments of the last few years has been the assertion of powers granted in the Treaty of Rome, but which had remained dormant for several years or were not applied to specific sectors.

For example, recent applications of Article 90 mark a new departure since its application lapsed after a vigorous debate in the early years of the EEC. The lack of precision in the powers granted, and its relative unimportance by comparison with other aspects of competition policy may have been partly responsible for this lapse, but political sensitivity may also have been a factor (Pappalardo 1991). Certainly, the use of the Article over the 1980s has proved to be one of the most sensitive issues for governments in terms of regulatory sovereignty. We have already noted that it has been the focus for a number of Court judgments, which have clarified the potential of the provision, generally supporting the Commission's interpretation. Governments may well have hoped originally that future Court assessments of the provision would have taken a more limited view of the scope of the legislation.[14]

The role of the Court in defining the scope of regulation has been of considerable importance in advancing the Commission's (and particularly the Competition Directorate's) regulatory role, underlining our initial argument that the strength of horizontal or generic regulation lay in its legal basis. Indeed the extent to which the Commission's actions are supported by the Court's interpretation of Treaty provisions has been recognized by opponents of many Community regulatory actions.[15]

Nevertheless, there remains considerable force in the observation that, in practice, the extent to which the powers of the Commission are asserted over particular industries depends considerably on the presence or absence of credible national regulatory authorities that can implement regulation in line with the interests of the Community at large. There have already been a number of cases where implementation of regulations and directives by national authorities has been criticized by the Commission: in its progress reports on completing the Single Market, the Commission has noted the slow pace of some Member States in putting agreements into action. This problem is likely to be more difficult in the case of specific regulatory tasks where national regulators will be expected to comply with the spirit of decisions made by

[14] This is of course one instance of a gamble which Member States have taken with the Community: that the Court would set the frontiers of Community regulatory scope differently, presumably more narrowly than has turned out to be the case. And it illustrates the way in which the legal framework of regulation can take on a momentum of its own.

[15] An instance of this came at the end of 1991. In line with Community directives on fare-setting in the air transport industry, the UK regulator the CAA reported a number of fares originating in the UK to the Commission on the grounds that they contravened Community rules. So far, the CAA is the only national regulatory authority to take this action.

the Community, but will have greater scope both for interpreting those decisions, and for determining whether or not actions should be taken to pursue them.[16]

7. THE INTERACTION BETWEEN UK AND EC REGULATION IN THE 1980s

In a number of industries, the regulatory process in the Community (principally in the area of utility regulation) has been an informal one. The formal mechanisms and institutions of control have been rather weak and the 'behind the scenes' bargaining between governments and companies have been correspondingly more significant. In these areas the coincidence of the interests of publicly owned or publicly guaranteed firms and the governments of the Member States has smoothed the process of such self regulation (though often there are elements of a regulatory relationship within the public-ownership framework). In most cases, regulation of market conduct beyond price levels has been non-existent or has not been able to impose much control over the sectors, these being dependent upon the commitment and support of governments.

The development of Community policies in these areas has to some extent had the effect of codifying and formalizing the procedure of regulation, bringing conduct in such sectors under the purview of the Commission. In so doing—subject to the requirements noted above—the choices and pressures of national or subnational governments/authorities become open to scrutiny, criticism, and reform in so far as they contradict or fail to implement policies agreed by the Member States.

The thrust of many of the policies proposed by the Commission has parallels with the process of regulatory reform which accompanied privatization in the UK. Since privatization, the UK has become the principal exception to the pattern of informal regulation characteristic of most other Member States. Here, the privatization programme has involved the creation of formal regulatory systems for all the major utility industries (in the case of airports and air transport the Civil Aviation Authority has played such a role since its establishment in the 1970s). Moreover, the thrust of policies has been towards increasing the scope for competition within the sectors where the privatized industries operate. While there have been shortcomings in the ways the industries were privatized (particularly the extent to which many firms retained their

[16] In the negotiations on the Treaty on Political Union, British opposition to the incorporation of a chapter on social policy was based on the (correct) perception that the very presence of such a chapter, irrespective of its precise content, would transfer some of the power to make future policy from Member States to the Court of Justice.

market dominance in the transfer from public to private ownership), the regulatory structures established with privatization have in a number of cases proved to have significant leverage in easing the way to greater competition.

In each case, the privatized industries have been brought into the remit of national competition law (and the supervision of the Office of Fair Trading and the Monopolies and Mergers Commission) and a specific sectoral regime, supervised by an industry regulator. These sectoral agencies have operated usually as a complement to and occasionally as a substitute for the exercise of competition policy. The most significant component of their bargaining power consists in the power to make a reference to the competition authorities (MMC/OFT). These bodies can in turn recommend changes in the powers of the regulator.[17]

The UK Offices are the principal example of a coherent regulatory policy in the EC.[18] Moreover, the UK offices of regulation appear to have avoided some of the problems of regulatory capture which have been described above. Arguably, this is because of the primacy placed upon competition in the regulatory task; while the agencies have been organized sectorally, they have been created to pursue this objective and can utilize the competition-policy framework in the UK towards that end.

In this respect, the UK experience might be regarded as revealing important lessons for the rest of the Community. The weakness of national structures elsewhere in the Community can be attributed to the fact that many of the problems addressed in the new UK system are not yet important in other EC countries. But as the EC develops its policies, such problems are likely to emerge; how far, then, are similar institutions required in other Member States?

In the area of utility reform, it is not the intention of reforms at a Community level to create new agencies for regulation (in contrast to the areas of merger control—where a permanent 'task force' has been established to decide on relevant cases, and environmental policy—where an Environmental Agency is to be set up to formulate proposals for future action and to ensure existing measures are being enforced by

[17] The system was conceived as a relatively light form of regulation, avoiding the excessively interventionist character of US regulatory systems (where state-level Public Utility Commissions engage in a highly detailed process of regulating utilities pricing policy and are staffed by several hundreds or even thousands of employees). While the UK sectoral agencies have indeed been kept small, they have been unable to stand back from day-to-day operation of the industries as much as was originally envisaged. For example, the issue of price scrutiny has involved the regulators in the wider issues of regulation, either in the form of revising the price formula or examining performance or investigating price discrimination between different classes of customer.

[18] Even in countries with private utilities, there is little formal regulation; decisions on electricity pricing in Belgium are made by a committee of industry, consumer, and other representatives, while the German *Länder* provide limited resources for the scrutiny of utility pricing proposals as part of a wider price scrutiny role.

national authorities). The Commission in its proposals appears to believe that a mixture of 'unbundling' industries (creating separate accounting systems for different activities), greater transparency in their relations with national governments, and the scrutiny of policy by the Commission will suffice. Is this reasonable? Can the commission monitor its reforms across so many industries without national authorities? The UK experience suggests that the visibility of specific sectoral agencies has probably reinforced the commitment to regulation (even if many of the relevant powers rest with national competition authorities).

One of the interesting dimensions of the UK experience is the extent to which it has for the most part worked in tandem with the Community. This seems to imply that at least in the regulation of the conduct of companies there may be complementarities to be exploited, though they may depend on a prior commitment towards a more openly competitive framework. While the Commission cannot take a view on the issue of ownership *per se* under Article 222 (which states that the treaty 'shall in no way prejudice the rules in Member States governing the system of property ownership') it has—as we have seen—developed policies designed to introduce greater competition. In these cases, the UK has played a dual role as both a supporter of Commission proposals (against the opposition of most other governments) and as a model for the Commission to point to in proposing changes (demonstrating that alternatives to existing models are possible).

It is ironic, then, that the very fact that the UK has engaged in substantial structural change has frequently brought it under adverse scrutiny by the Commission and into conflict with EC regulators. The area where the Commission has made its most visible interventions has been that of competition policy, where a number of powers have been invoked. The most notorious cases have been those where the terms relating to a privatization were regarded as constituting state aid: the government's arrangement with British Aerospace for the take-over of Rover (where a variety of incentives involving tax allowances and property undervaluations were included involving effective subsidies to British Aerospace) was effectively disallowed by the Commission which sought to remove the subsidy (though this is still under review following the rejection by the Court of Justice of the Commission's investigation on procedural grounds).

In other cases, the structural change entailed by privatization has permitted the Commission to intervene in a sector where traditionally it has been unable to act. The best example of this was in the case of the British privatization of the electricity industry. Here the government sought simultaneously to privatize and partially to restructure the industry (see Vickers and Yarrow 1991). Both the government's organizational changes and the special arrangements made for protecting the nuclear component of electricity supply were scrutinized by the Commission. The structural changes, which involved the agreement of contracts between different parts of the industry comprising various restrictions on market access (such as the extent to which industrial consumers could be 'poached' within distribution regions) were approved by the Commission. The case of nuclear power, where a system of quotas and levies were introduced to protect the market share of British nuclear power-stations, was subject to a number of conditions: the level of subsidy was limited and was constrained to end by 1998 (Commission of the European Communities 1991).

These cases only underline the need for a regulatory mechanism to counter actions sanctioned or supported by national governments which are contrary to Community law. It is worth noting that these cases have pitched the Commission against the firms and governments, not the national regulatory authorities. Outside of the one-off conditions of privatization, most actions have been conducted by such agencies.

The development of regulatory competences at the UK level is probably sufficiently developed to permit the conduct of most Community-based regulation at a national level. It is less clear whether subsidiarity can be applied to the same extent in the rest of the Community; would national regulation in most other Member States be credible? The cases where privatization created regulatory problems which were then addressed by the Commission might imply that a balance of subsidiarity has been found between broad regulatory principles established at a Community level, implemented (or not) at a national level and scrutinized and (if found wanting) enforced at the Community level. However, for this division of regulatory labour to be effective, the Commission's willingness and capacity to follow up national implementation must also be credible.

CONCLUSIONS

This paper has discussed the assignment of regulatory responsibilities in the European Community between the Community's own institutions and those of its Member States. It has done so both normatively, using theoretical arguments about subsidiarity and its shortcomings, and positively, looking to see the extent to which actual assignments conform to what is theoretically desirable. There is a striking discrepancy between these two perspectives, with the actual assignment of responsibilities being determined much more by fashion, historical accident, the discovery of dormant legal powers, and the outcome of bureaucratic power struggles, than by an objective consideration of the normative criteria. It would be naïve to be surprised by this discrepancy, but only natural to ask what are the implications of this discrepancy for the future evolution of the Community.

In some respects, the developments of the 1980s have been very positive. In particular, the growing strength of certain generic agencies like the Competition Directorate have served on balance to enfranchise a set of interests that the regulatory process has for too long ignored. The passing of the merger regulation transferring certain powers from national to EC institutions is a transfer of sovereignty that makes sense in spite of the principle of subsidiarity. It would be unwise, however, to think that its implementation (which must by its very nature remain substantially discretionary) will necessarily escape in the future the problems of regulatory capture; in particular, it still remains unclear whether industrial or consumer interests will benefit most from economies of scale in lobbying at a Community level.

In other respects (including environmental regulation) a proper respect for subsidiarity does not seem to have been influential in determining the extent of the Community's powers. In particular, there has been inadequate distinction between those environmental issues that have genuine cross-border implications (such as sulphur dioxide emissions) from those whose effects are confined to individual Member States (such as the cleanliness of drinking-water). This has partly been because, with the growing strength of environmental lobbying in the political process of Member States, initiatives by the EC have been welcomed as a spur to the sluggardliness of governments, even if the initiatives might more properly have originated in the Member States themselves. There has also been a perception that some of the benefits of closer political links between Member States are most likely to be achieved if the EC's institutions gain more power and influence in the aggregate; such concerns have sometimes dominated questions about the proper province of the Community's powers. It would be most unfortunate if the evolution of Europe were to be unduly influenced by the belief that stability is possible only under centralization; the example of Switzerland is enough to indicate the falsity of that belief.

In certain areas, the development of Community regulatory responsibility has been properly respectful of the existing regulatory capacities of Member States, but has faced the difficulty that Member States differ in their capacities. The UK's developed system of sectoral regulatory agencies is a case in point. These agencies have been surprisingly effective in meeting their stated objectives (and have sometimes acted to undo a number of the more unattractive features of the original form of the privatization); by and large they have also avoided the more obvious manifestations of regulatory capture. It is of course possible that the mix of political circumstances, the developments of markets, and the personalities and priorities of regulators have contributed to this outcome;

changes over time might lead to a different regulatory result.[19] But so far their record has been encouraging. However, partly because these agencies were the natural consequence of a privatization programme, they have few counterparts in other member states. The EC's policy in this area has consequently been beset by uncertainty, with periods of activism (such as over the application of Article 90) alternating with a greater emphasis on regulatory co-ordination without the actual transfer of regulatory power.

The discrepancy we have highlighted between the normative and the positive analyses of the assignment of regulatory powers in the Community does not imply, then, that actual developments have necessarily been adverse. It does suggest that an uncritical enthusiasm for and an uncritical aversion to centralization for its own sake are both dangerous attitudes, not least because both attitudes have enough adherents to influence to political process substantially. And it also suggests that the rewards to a more sophisticated understanding of the process by which the actual assignment of regulatory powers comes to be determined over time is an extremely important focus for future research, and might even contribute to a less simplistic normative theory than the one we have outlined here.

References

Begg, D., *et al.* (1993), *Making Sense of Subsidiarity*, London: Centre for Economic Policy Research.

Bradburd, R. and Ross, D. R. (1991), *Regulation and Deregulation in Industrial Countries: Some Lessons for LDCs*, Washington, DC: World Bank.

Civil Aviation Authority (1984), *Airline Competition Policy*, London: CAA.

Commission of the European Communities (1990), *Completing the Internal Market: An Area without Internal Frontiers*, Brussels: Commission of the European Community.

—— (1991), *Twentieth Annual Report on Competition Policy*, Luxembourg: Office for Official Publications of the European Community.

Common Market Law Review (1990), 'Editorial comments: The subsidiarity principle', 27/2.

Davis, E., et al. (1989), *Myths and Realities*, Centre for Business Strategy, London Business School.

—— and Smales, C. (1989), 'The Integration of European Financial Services', in Davis, *et al.*

de Cockborne, J. E. (1990), 'Liberalising the Community's electricity market: Should telecom show the way?', *International Business Law Journal*, 7.

[19] See Bradburd and Ross (1991) on the idea of 'life cycles' whereby a regulator's objectives shift over time.

Department of Transport (1984), *Airline Competition Policy*, London: HMSO.
Dixit, A. and Stiglitz, J. (1977), 'Monopolistic competition and optimum product diversity', *American Economic Review*, 67: 297–308.
Downs, A. (1957), *An Economic Theory of Democracy*, New York: Harper & Row.
European Commission (1985), *Completing the Internal Market*, Luxembourg: Office for Official Publications of the European Communities.
Evans, L. and Garber, S. (1988), 'Public utility regulators are only human: A positive theory of rational constraints', *American Economic Review*, 78.
Gatsios, K. and Seabright, P. (1989), 'Regulation in the European Community', *Oxford Review of Economic Policy*, 5.
Hirschman, A. (1970), *Exit Voice and Loyalty*, Harvard, Cambridge, Mass.: Harvard University Press.
House of Lords (1989), *Fraud Against the Community*, 5th report, Select Committee on the European Communities, Session, 1988–9, London: HMSO.
Haigh, N. (1989), *EEC Environmental Policy and Britain*, Harlow: Longmans.
Hughes, G. and Smith, S. (1971), 'The economic theory of regulation', *Bell Journal of Economics*, 2.
Joskow, P. L., and Rose, N. L. (1989), 'The effects of economic regulation', in R. Schmalensee and R. D. Willig.
Kay, J., and Vickers, J. (1988), 'Regulatory reform in Britain', *Economic Policy*, 8: 285–351.
Keep, E., and Sisson, K. (1992), 'Owning the problem: Personnel issues in higher education policy-making in the 1990s', *Oxrep*, 8/2: 67–78.
Korah, V. (1987), 'The control of mergers under the EEC Competition Law', *European Competition Law Review*, 8/3.
Krueger, A. O. (1974), 'The political economy of the rent seeking society', *American Economic Review*, 64.
Laffont, J. J. and Tirole, J. (1991), 'The politics of government decision-making: A theory of regulatory capture', *Quarterly Journal of Economics*, 106 (Nov.).
Lancaster, K. (1980), 'Intra-industry trade under perfect monopolistic competition', *Journal of International Economics*, 10.
Lawrence, C. and Spiller, P. (1983), 'Product diversity, economies of scale and international trade', *Quarterly Journal of Economics*, 98.
Newbery, D. M. (1990), 'Acid rain', *Economic Policy*, 10 (Apr.).
Pappalardo (1991), 'State measures and public undertakings: Article 90 of the EEC Treaty revised', *European Competition Law Review*, 12.
Peacock, A. et al. (1984), *The Regulation Game*, Oxford: Blackwell.
Seabright, P. (1994), 'Accountability and decentralization in government: An incomplete contracts model', Discussion paper no. 889, London: Centre for Economic Policy Research.
Servais, D. (1988), *The Single Financial Market*, Luxembourg: Office for Official Publications of the European Communities.
Stigler, G. (1971), 'The economic theory of regulation', *Bell Journal of Economics*, 2/1: 3–21.
Tiebout, C. M. (1956), 'A pure theory of local expenditure', *Journal of Political Economy*, 64/5: 416–24.
Vickers, J. and Yarrow, G. (1988), *Privatization: An Economic Analysis*, Cambridge, Mass.: MIT Press.

——(1991), 'The British electricity experiment', *Economic Policy*, 12: 187–232.

Vogel, D. (1986), *National Styles of Regulation*, Ithaca, NY and London: Cornell University Press.

Winters, L. A. (1988), 'Completing the European internal market: Some notes on trade policy', *European Economic Review*, 32: 1477–99.

11

Modified Regulation of Telecommunications and the Public-interest Standard

WILLIAM J. BAUMOL*

The costs of regulation are well known and are an unavoidable part of the process. Its most obvious burdens are, of course, the record-keeping, reporting, and other social administrative tasks that it must impose upon the regulated firm. In addition, regulation brings with it the heavy costs of the delays to which it subjects the decision process, preventing the rapid responses to evolving market developments that efficiency and competitiveness require. Probably equally serious are the artificial prices imposed and the resulting distortion of the incentives for efficiency.

In view of these social burdens of regulation, it is widely agreed that the public-interest standard entails two broad conclusions for regulatory policy:

1. In those areas in which competition or potential competition is sufficiently pervasive and powerful, continued regulation imposes an inefficiency burden upon the general public that is unjustifiable and should therefore be eliminated, leaving the tasks of control of pricing and production to market forces.

2. Even in those limited arenas in which continued regulation is justified by the unavailability of adequate competitive constraints, the task of regulation should merely be to seek replication of the behaviour patterns which would have emerged if competition had been effective. In other words, regulation should never be more constraining than market forces and should impose no rules inconsistent with the normal workings of free markets.

In this paper it will be shown that the public-interest standard can serve as the foundation for a workable process of regulation in those situations where regulation remains appropriate, one which provides suitable safeguards against the exercise of market power in non-competitive arenas and is firmly founded on economic analysis. The conclusion that such a procedure is feasible and practical is not mere conjecture or a conclusion

* Professor at the C. V. Starr Centre for Applied Economics, New York University.

derived from theory alone. The success of (partial) deregulation processes such as the one that the American railroad industry has recently undergone demonstrates that it can be done and done most effectively.

THE PURPOSE OF ECONOMIC REGULATION

Economic regulation of industry has had one central and legitimate purpose: protection of the public from the detrimental consequences of inadequacies of competition, wherever there is good reason to believe that this is actually so. Two particular objectives encompassed in this general goal are: (i) the preclusion of prices that significantly exceed those that would prevail in an industry that was effectively competitive; and (ii) the prevention of excessively low prices that constitute cross-subsidy (particularly when the firm faces competition in one or more of its markets). Cross-subsidy which can subvert the competitive process, benefits one customer class at the expense of another and can, incidentally, weaken or even undermine the regulatory mechanism itself.

No economist, to my knowledge, denies the laudability of these goals and any public interest standard confirms the desirability of their pursuit. What the public-interest standard leads one to question, rather, is the suitability of the means that have sometimes been used to achieve these goals. This paper seeks to describe the means suggested by economic analysis for regulation of prices as a measure that most effectively serves the public interest.

WHAT IS THE PUBLIC-INTEREST STANDARD?

Just how can one provide an operational definition of 'the public interest', the concept on which my analysis is based? Economists make no pretence at expertise that entitles them to make pronouncements on the moral, sociological, psychological, or many of the myriad other elements that constitute the social welfare. However, the discipline has adopted the concept of economic efficiency as a necessary element of any policy which serves the general welfare. Economic efficiency is defined as a state of affairs in which, given the value of the resources utilized, one has taken advantage of every available opportunity to increase the economic welfare of consumers through the provision of larger quantities of outputs, better products, or a mixture of outputs better adapted to consumer preferences. In other words, economic efficiency entails the elimination of any economic inefficiencies—failures to achieve more for the public without any increase in resources used, or failures to reduce the quantities of resources used up in giving the public whatever benefits the economy provides to it. It should be obvious that whenever such economic inefficiencies occur one is wasting an opportunity to make the members of society better off.

Thus, the public-interest standard for economic regulation calls for it to adopt only rules and procedures that are consistent with economic efficiency, not because economic efficiency is the only goal of society, but because such efficiency is a necessary condition for maximization of the general welfare.

It is generally recognized that the most effective means to ensure economic efficiency is the competitive-market mechanism. Competition prevents sheer waste of resources because any firm that indulges in such inefficiency will soon enough find itself displaced by more efficient rivals. Similarly, it precludes the production of commodity mixes ill-adapted to consumer desires by inviting the entry of firms ready to serve consumer preferences more effectively. Thus, competition ensures that consumers are served with the combination of products they want, given the costs dictated by technological circumstances, and that consumers are provided with those products at minimal cost.

Competition, incidentally, also prevents the institution of cross-subsidies as well as the adoption of monopoly prices. It prevents cross-subsidy because, by definition, such an arrangement entails the over-pricing of the products that are the sources of the cross-subsidies and that, in turn, is an invitation to entrants to take over the supply of the overpriced products. In terms of economic efficiency the elimination of cross-subsidy and monopoly pricing by competition is important not just because of their inequity, but also because such undesirable pricing practices will distort patterns of both demands and outputs. Consumers will be deterred from purchasing items whose high prices bear little relation to their true economic costs and producers will be induced to turn out the items whose profitability has been artificially enhanced by interference with the market mechanism. Thus, rates wrongly chosen can become irresistible inducements for economic inefficiency, but free competitive markets prevent the adoption of such inefficient rates.

In short, to the economist the free competitive market becomes the embodiment of the public-interest standard. Such a market where it is present, should be left alone, without regulatory interference, because there is no more effective means known for the promotion of economic efficiency. And where the market is not competitive, a hypothetical competitive market's behaviour and performance should be used to provide the rules promulgated by the regulator who should seek to elicit from the regulated firm those patterns of behaviour that would emerge in the presence of competition. Regulation, in the view of economists, should avoid departures from these guidelines, and should certainly never deviate from them casually and without explicit justification.

Let us turn, then, to an examination of the sort of policies that follow from the public-interest standard—policies that other regulatory agencies and the courts in the United States have found to be operational and to provide full protection to consumers.

THE PUBLIC-INTEREST APPROACH TO REGULATION

The public-interest approach to regulatory policy proceeds from three fundamental principles, two of which have already been noted:

1. In those markets in which competition, actual and potential, is sufficiently strong to prevent any exercise of monopoly power by the regulated firm, substantial lessening or elimination of regulation will best serve the general welfare.
2. Where competitive forces are inadequate to constrain market power effectively the public interest calls for the regulator to act as a proxy or substitute for the market forces. Thus, only in the most exceptional cases, and only for clear and explicit reasons, should the regulatory rules seek to elicit behaviour by the firm different from what would emerge in a comparable competitive market.
3. Any rate charged for a service whose continued regulation is appropriate should be subjected by the regulator to a suitable floor and a suitable ceiling, that floor and ceiling being selected to approximate as closely as possible those that would have emerged if the market had been effectively competitive. The firm should be left free within these bounds to adjust its rates without delay or impediment to changing market and cost conditions.

The nature of the bounds dictated by the free-market standard will be explained below. First, however, I must digress to explain the meaning of the competitive market standard in an industry whose technology is characterized by the presence of some economies of scale and scope that make operation by a very large multiplicity of very small enterprises both undesirable and impractical.

THE ROLE OF SCALE ECONOMIES

Where an industry's operations are characterized by some scale economies important consequences follow for the nature of the pertinent competitive standard and the appropriate rules of price regulation. For one thing, scale economies preclude the financial viability of a rule requiring equality between prices and marginal costs, which is called for by the economists' standard model of perfect competition.[1] Prices which cover only marginal costs do not in general contribute to the covering of fixed costs, and this suggests why, when economies of scale are present, prices equal to marginal costs will not be viable financially.

Thus, perfect competition, with its well known requirement that prices equal marginal costs, can no longer serve as the sole guideline where phenomena such as scale economies are present. In such circumstances, perfect competition is not possible and, even if it were possible, it would not be desirable.[2] But this fact does not deprive the regulator of all recourse to a competitive market guideline. On the contrary, scale economies merely mean that a theoretical form of competition other than perfect competition becomes pertinent and serves as the benchmark for public-interest regulation of rates. That is, where economies of scale are present in markets in which regulation happens to be desirable, then the regulator is forced to look for guidance to an alternative competitive model to that of perfect competition.

Where scale economies are present effective competitive pressure can nevertheless derive from the existence of easy entry and exit, which leave incumbent firms constantly vulnerable to the threat of entry if they waste resources, charge excessive prices, earn excessive profits, or misbehave in other anti-competitive ways. Successful anti-competitive behaviour always constitutes a profit opportunity for entrants who are willing to be just a bit less greedy than the incumbents.

CONTESTABLE MARKETS

The threat of potential competition to an incumbent firm can come from many sources, foreign as well as domestic. Entrants need not be newly established firms that appear, as it were, from nowhere. They may enter from activities in closely related industries and markets, or even from firms already in the industry that have not yet achieved a substantial presence in the market at issue, entry then being effected via a small modification in the entrant's product line. In such a market perfect freedom of entry and potential competition preclude monopolistic behav-

[1] Perfect competition is the economists' model of the ideally functioning market (i.e. of maximal efficiency) when there are numerous participants (none of whom has any effect on the market price), a homogeneous product, freedom of entry and exit, and perfect information.

[2] Policy prescriptions that attempt to steer an industry toward perfect competition are undesirable where economies of scale occur because scale economies mean that large firms can produce outputs at a lower unit cost than can small firms: perfect competition, which requires a large number of small firms, would miss out on these cost advantages. It would not maximize welfare. Besides, perfect competition will not persist for long in an industry with scale economies, as bigger firms will be able to undercut smaller ones, causing them to exit the market.

iour and economic inefficiency. A market of that sort has been referred to as 'contestable'.

Regulation is, of course, important only for arenas in which actual competition is severely limited and in which technological and other considerations preclude the sort of perfect freedom of exit and entry just described and hence undermine the prospects of true competitiveness of the market. In such cases, it is essential from the viewpoint of the public interest for the regulatory agency to serve as a substitute for the market forces that are here impotent.

But what precisely should the regulator do here? Where returns to scale are not perfectly constant or where for some other reason prices equal to marginal costs are not acceptable, as we have seen, perfect competition is no longer usable as the bench-mark for regulation. In such circumstances it is only contestability that can serve as an operational bench-mark—as an ideal state of affairs whose consequences regulation can and should hope to reproduce in those markets that clearly approximate neither perfect competition nor perfect contestability.

The analysis of contestable markets confirms that optimality requires prices to be guided both by costs and by demand conditions. In a market with perfect freedom of entry, pursuit of profit will induce any incumbent firm to adjust its outputs and, hence, the prices of its products both to costs and to demand conditions. The demand for a particular product will determine whether or not expansion of the output of that product will yield additional revenues that exceed marginal costs and the firm will adjust its output and price accordingly, so long as the price and the attendant overall profits do not exceed the competitive levels—the levels that will make entry profitable.

OPTIMAL-PRICING RULES FOR FINAL PRODUCTS

The optimal-pricing policy that follows for the case where prices equal to marginal costs are not viable, necessarily precludes any simple, mechanistic rate-setting rule.

First, the principles in question call for differential pricing, that is, prices which vary in their ratio to marginal costs, from one product line to another and from one customer group to another. These variations should depend ideally on comparative demand conditions among product lines and customer groups.

Second, and equally important, the principles just enunciated indicate that customer interests will often be served better by flexible price arrangements such as two-part tariffs in which the customer's bill is composed of two portions—a flat fee and a payment proportionate to usage or, usually even better, by multi-part tariffs, that is, by flexible pricing packages. Of course, in such an arrangement the values of the component-price parameters, such as the flat fee and the charge per unit of usage, will themselves be based, optimally, on the pertinent cost and the demand for that item.

Third, as we will see, the contestable market standard shows that prices should not be permitted to lie below the incremental cost or to exceed the stand-alone cost[3] of the product in question. In a contestable market, price will never be set below incremental cost because that always (by definition) constitutes a loss of profit for the firm unless that price can be used successfully as a predatory instrument. But the absolute freedom of entry that defines contestability guarantees that no firm will ever be able to gather the excessive later profits that are the intended fruits of predation. Thus, in a contestable market prices below incremental cost will not occur (except through temporary error) because such a price represents a pointless and self-destructive give-away programme for the supplier.

In addition, in a contestable market no price will ever exceed stand-alone cost because such a price, by definition, is sufficiently high to make new entry profitable. A price of a service that is higher than stand-alone cost is defined as: (a) either a price that exceeds the costs (net of any entry-barrier costs) of an efficient entrant producing that service by itself (including the cost of, for example, the normal return on capital); or (b) a price that yields revenues for that service together with any other combination of services that exceed the cost of an efficient entrant would incur, in the absence of entry barriers, in supplying just that sub-set of the company's services. If there are no costs to entry or exit *per se* (as the concept of perfect contestability requires), any such price will rapidly attract enough new rivals to wipe out any excess of price over stand-alone cost. Thus, the contestable market standard calls for an incremental cost floor and a stand-alone cost ceiling on prices, with the firm left free to set price anywhere between these limits in accord with demand conditions.

Fourth, the demonstrable behaviour of prices in the contestable-markets model indicates that the firm in a regulated incontestable market must be left free to change prices without delays when market conditions vary. Rigidified prices can only lead to inefficiencies and mismatches between demands and supplies.

Finally, the contestable-market guidelines indicate that in the long run the regulated firm should be free to earn a full competitive rate of return, though for limited periods it may earn more or less than this, depending on market conditions.

[3] A definition of stand-alone cost is provided below.

RULES FOR REGULATION OF FINAL-PRODUCT PRICES

We have simply listed the rules that have emerged from the experience of regulatory agencies and from economic analysis to guide regulation in those arenas in which its continuation is judged to be appropriate. To get at their logic, we can learn much from a remarkable 1985 decision of the Interstate Commerce Commission,[4] a decision that encompasses the foundations of its current policies toward those elements of railroad activities in which competitive pressures are judged to be inadequate (that is, in regulatory terminology, in areas in which a railroad possesses 'market dominance' or its shippers are 'captive').

Early in the discussion of its economic framework the decision provides a section headed 'contestable markets'. While, as we will see presently, the decision relies heavily and explicitly on the logic of contestability, it asserts flatly and quite appropriately that the markets to be subject to continued regulation are those that are, in fact, *not* contestable: 'the railroad industry is recognized to have barriers to entry and exit and thus is not considered contestable *for captive traffic*'.

The question, then, is what is best done to control the pricing terms on which such 'captive traffic' is served. First, for this purpose, the Commission adopted a set of rules which is called 'constrained market pricing'.

Second, the Commission adopted for this purpose most of the criteria called for by economic analysis, for example, determining that 'adequate' returns are those that provide a rate of return on net investment equal to the current cost of capital (i.e. the level of return available on alternative investments). In formulating these rules, the Commission recognized, first, that because of scale economies (and related phenomena), solvency of the railroads is likely to require differential pricing. The Commission points out that where unattributable costs cannot be covered by prices set equal to marginal costs, then demand considerations as well as cost data must enter into decision-making, both in order to permit adequacy of revenues and in order to achieve efficiency. It proposes 'Ramsey pricing'[5] as the appropriate theoretical guideline for achieving this.

None the less, it recognizes that even the Ramsey pricing results would need to be adjusted or modified for practical reasons (e.g. measurement difficulties).[6]

[4] Interstate Commerce Commission, 'Coal Rate Guidelines, Nationwide', ex parte no. 347 (sub-no. 1), Washington, DC, decided 3 Aug. 1985.

[5] Ramsey pricing, a concept named after its discoverer, Frank Ramsey, is a pricing rule that produces an optimal compromise between the requirement that the regulated firm be able to earn a fair rate of return in the presence of fixed and common costs (and other sources of scale economies) and the requirement that the prices be those that most effectively promote economic efficiency.

[6] From Interstate Commerce Commission, 'Coal Rate Guidelines, Nationwide', ex parte no. 347 (Sub-No. 1), Washington, DC, decided 3 Aug. 1985.

PROPER FLOORS FOR PRICES OF FINAL PRODUCTS: INCREMENTAL COSTS

Regulators have long sought a test which enables them to determine whether some price of the regulated firm is too low, entailing cross subsidies or threatening predation, thereby damaging the legitimate interests of competitors. Today, it is widely recognized that the competitive market standard for regulation identifies the incremental cost of a service as the proper floor for the pricing of a product. It is a floor that precludes both cross-subsidy and predation, it stems directly from the competitive market standard for regulations, and is a necessary condition for the attainment of economic efficiency.

The *incremental cost* of a product, the quantity of whose output is some amount X, is the reduction in the outlays of a firm that would occur if it were to cease production of that item. In other words, it is the cost *caused* by the decision to introduce that commodity and to supply quantity X of the item; that cost, incidentally, is defined to include the cost of the required incremental capital, that is the current competitive rate of return on the incremental capital required by production of the item in question.

This definition immediately tells us why, if a commodity's price is such that its total revenue at least covers its incremental cost, then it cannot legitimately be said that the price is predatory in that the product is the recipient of any loss subsidy. For if the product's revenue covers completely the cost that its production causes the firm then its production is imposing no financial burden on any customers of the firm's other services and its supply entails no sacrifice of profits by the enterprise. Indeed, any excess of incremental revenue over incremental cost must obviously constitute a contribution to coverage of the fixed and common costs of both the service in question and of other company services.

We have already seen that under the competitive (perfectly contestable) market model of regulation the same guideline applies. No firm in such a market will more than very temporarily and inadvertently price below incremental cost, because that would simply constitute a pointless giveaway of profit—an act which has no purpose for a profit-seeking firm. On the other hand, if demand permits no higher price, a firm in such a market will nevertheless always find it profitable to supply any product so long as the price yields *any* margin of incremental revenue over incremental cost. For any such price, by definition, offers the normal return on the required incremental capital, and some contribution to coverage of fixed and common costs besides. Thus *no* price above incremental cost is precluded by the competitive market standard for regulation.

Finally, it is easy to see why violation of the incremental-cost floor is incompatible with economic efficiency and, hence, with provision of the item in question at lowest cost to consumers, for suppose that the product can be supplied by either of two competing firms, A and B, suppose, also, that while the incremental cost of the product when supplied by A is £5 per unit, the corresponding figure for B is £4, so that the latter is, clearly, the more efficient supplier. If, nevertheless, A sells the product at a price below incremental cost, say at £3.50 per unit, B may be unable to compete, and a moment's thought confirms that the same inefficiency can arise *whenever* A charges less than incremental cost. In short, an incremental-cost floor is required by competitive standard for regulation, by economic efficiency, for the prevention of predation and for the preclusion of cross-subsidy. But none of these rules out *any* price that does not violate an incremental-cost floor.

We shall return presently to the full implications of the incremental-cost standard and the practical issues that arise in the course of its administration.

THE PROPER CEILINGS ON PRICES OF FINAL PRODUCTS: STAND-ALONE COSTS

A second key issue faced by those who use the competitive model as the prime guide for regulation of pricing is the formulation of a criterion to be used in setting a ceiling over the price to be charged for a final product whose supplier is not effectively constrained by competition.

When the US Interstate Commerce Commission began its search, in about 1980, for a rate-ceiling formula, it turned first to fully allocated cost. However, in response to careful arguments by economists, by the railroads, and by others, it withdrew this approach and, early in 1983, offered what it called 'constrained market pricing' as its alternative.

Here, the ceiling proposed by the Commission was *stand-alone cost*,[7] a concept it acknowledged to have derived from the economists' writings on contestable markets.

> ... stand-alone cost (SAC) test ... is used to compute the rate a competitor in the market-place would need to charge in serving a captive shipper or a group of shippers who benefit from sharing joint and common costs. A rate level calculated by the SAC methodology represents the theoretical maximum rate that a railroad can levy on shippers without substantial diversion of traffic to a

[7] If a firm provides three products, A, B, and C, the stand-alone cost of products A and B is defined as the total cost that would be incurred by an efficient independent producer that faced no entry-barrier costs and produced the same quantities of A and B, *and no other products*. Thus, if and only if the revenues contributed by A and B together exceed their stand-alone cost will entry by a firm producing just those two items be induced.

hypothetical competing service. It is, in other words, a simulated competitive price. (The competing service could be a shipper providing service for itself or a third party competing with the incumbent railroad for traffic. In either case, the SAC represents the minimum cost of an alternative to the service provided by the incumbent railroad.)

The theory behind SAC is best explained by the concept of 'contestable markets'. This recently developed economic theory augments the classical economic model of 'pure competition' with a model which focuses on the entry and exit from an industry as a measure of economic efficiency. The theory of contestable markets is more general than that of 'pure competition' because it does not require a large number of firms. In fact, even a monopoly can be contestable. The underlying premiss is that a monopolist or oligopolist will behave efficiently and competitively where there is a threat of losing some or all of its markets to a new entrant. In other words, contestable markets have competitive characteristics which preclude monopoly pricing.

It is worth reviewing the logic of the stand-alone cost ceilings a bit more closely. The stand-alone cost of a service or group of services is defined as the minimum price at which an *efficient* entrant, using the best available techniques, could afford to supply the service or group of services in question, when supplying no other services. In this calculation the hypothetical entrant is required not to need to spend any funds in overcoming entry barriers. Such a disallowable entry-barrier cost is defined as any cost that an entrant must incur simply as a result of the fact that it was not the first firm in the arena. Such entry-barrier costs are excluded from the stand-alone cost ceiling because otherwise that ceiling would permit the incumbent to earn profits that would be denied to it in a contestable market—profit above the competitive level.

Examples of entry-barrier costs are easy to provide. If the second firm to enter a regulated arena faces higher costs than its predecessor in inducing the regulator to permit it to operate, that higher outlay is an entry-barrier cost that must be excluded from the ceiling. Similarly, if a second entrant must pay 2 percentage points in higher borrowing costs for its funds above those that would be paid by an earlier entrant as a result of the latter's lower competitive risks, that higher interest cost, also, is an excludable entry-barrier cost. However, scale economies neither constitute nor give rise to entry-barrier costs in the pertinent sense. If the first firm in the arena happened to be small and the second one large it is the latter that would benefit from its size; it is not simply a matter of which opened for business first. And scale economies effects on costs are surely beneficial to consumers who should not be kept from enjoying those benefits by the acts of the regulator.

In contestable markets, unimpeded entry will, virtually by definition, force the price of a product to lie somewhere below its stand-alone cost. For any higher price will make entry profitable and will enable the entrant to lure the incumbent's customers away. Just where price falls below that level depends on the state of demand. Thus, so long as prices do not exceed stand-alone costs they cannot legitimately be taken to be the product of an exercise of monopoly power. In sum, stand-alone costs constitute the proper cost-based ceilings upon prices, preventing both cross-subsidization and the exercise of monopoly power.

A simple example will show why this is so. First, suppose that a firm supplies two services, A and B, *which share no costs* and that each costs 10 units a year to supply. The availability of effective potential competition would force revenues from each service to equal 10 units a year. For higher earnings would attract (profitable) entry, and lower revenues would drive the supplier out of business. In this case, in which common costs are absent, incremental and stand-alone costs are equal to each other and to revenues, and the perfect competition and contestability bench-marks yield the same results.

Next, suppose instead that of the 20-unit total cost four are fixed and common to A and B, while 16 are variable; 8 of the 16 being attributable to A and 8 to B. If, because of demand conditions, at most only a bit more than 8 can be garnered from consumers of A, then a firm operating and surviving in contestable markets will earn a bit less than 12 from B. These prices lie between incremental costs (8) and stand-alone costs (12), are mutually advantageous to consumers of both services, and will attract no entrants, even in the absence of any entry barriers. In contrast, should the firm attempt to raise the revenues obtained from B above the 12 unit stand-alone cost, it would lose its business to competitors willing to charge less. Similarly, the same fate would befall it in contestable markets if it priced B in a way that earned more than 8 plus the four-unit common cost, less the contribution toward that common cost from service A. In sum, potential competition will, in the absence of entry barriers, prevent prices from exceeding stand-alone costs, but it cannot force those prices any lower.

The preceding discussion of the analysis and the regulatory principles that have accompanied the partial deregulation of the railroads and, later, that of telecommunications in the US shows that the process can follow a coherent logic consistent with economic reasoning, that it can be carried out in practice, and that it can stand up to legal challenge. The public-interest standard has shown itself capable of yielding a rational regulatory structure. That standard has also proved to be persuasive to regulatory commissions. While it has brought increased freedom of decision-making to the regulated firms, it has also imposed some obligations upon them, obligations designed to promote that public interest.

THE COMBINATORIAL CHARACTER OF THE FLOOR AND THE CEILING

A complication that has so far been evaded in this discussion is the role of joint costs or of the fixed element of common costs. By definition, neither of these is part of the incremental cost of any one service because it cannot be eliminated by cessation of the supply of that service alone. Yet joint costs and costs that are fixed and common clearly cannot be neglected in the process of public interest regulation.

The competitive-market model indicates unambiguously how these should be taken into account. Figure 11.1 will make the process clear.

	Services		
	A	B	C
Individual service incremental costs	£3	£4	£5
Incremental cost fixed and common to A and B	£7 (A and B)		
Incremental cost common to A, B, and C	£2 (A, B, and C)		

FIG. 11.1. Costs of telecoms supply

Figure 11.1 depicts the costs of a telecommunications supplier that offers three services A, B, and C. A and B are switched services, and we assume that economical switching equipment has so much capacity that it can meet the foreseeable needs of either service A or B, or of both together. The incremental cost of service A alone is £3, cost of B is £4, etc., as shown in the top row of boxes. The second row contains a longer box, indicating that the switching cost common to A and B is £7. Finally, the third row shows the costs common to all three services. The salary of the company chairman, the cost of advertisement of the company trade mark, etc.

Now the full combinatorial criterion for the floor on pricing requires that *all* of the following relationships be satisfied:

$PaA \geq IC_A = 3$
(incremental revenue of A must cover its incremental cost)
$PbB \geq IC_B = 4$
$PcC \geq IC_C = 5$
$PaA+P\,bB \geq IC_A + IC_B + IC_{A+B} = 3+4+7 = 14$
(incremental revenues of A and B together must cover their combined incremental costs including common and joint costs)

$PaA+PbB+PcC \geq IC_A + IC_B + IC_C + IC_CIC_{A+B} + IC_{A+B+C}$
$= 14+5+2 = 21.$

Reconsideration of the analysis underlying the incremental-cost floor will readily confirm why violation of any one of these requirements will constitute a cross-subsidy to the service or set of services at issue, and that it will violate the rules of competitive (contestable) market behaviour, as well as the requirements of economic efficiency. It should be noted also that this combination of tests entails absolutely no arbitrary allocation of any joint costs or any fixed component of any common cost. It employs only numbers that, at least in principle, are unique and observable, and are in no way arbitrary. Further consideration will confirm that the proper stand-alone cost ceiling is combinatorial in precisely the same way and for precisely corresponding reasons.

ADMINISTRATION OF THE COMBINATORIAL TESTS

Practical administration of the pricing standards that have just been enunciated, is, clearly, not a trivial affair, and its cost and complexities should not be concealed or denied. In particular, it should be recognized that it would constitute an intolerable burden upon the regulated firm if it were to be required to produce a full set of incremental cost and stand-alone cost figures for each of its services and each combination of its services every time some modification of some of its prices was proposed.

Before turning to practical means for administering such floors and ceilings it should be noted that at least incremental cost figures are not so difficult to obtain. For all practical purposes, the process is the same as that entailed in the calculation of fully-allocated costs but with the omission of the last step, the allocation of joint or common fixed costs by arbitrary convention. Undoubtedly, the calculation of stand-alone costs is at least somewhat more difficult.

We may then note that three avenues have been employed in practice in the administration of the floors and ceilings.

1. *Administration by complaining parties*

Under the terms of the first of these arrangements any prices proposed by the regulated firm are presumed to be legitimate unless a competitor or a customer or the staff of the regulatory agency complains about some price or combination of prices. The complaining party is first required to establish some presumption that the prices complained of are illegitimate. This is done in order to prevent harassment of the regulated firm by means of what the US Courts call 'sham litigation'. Once such a presumptive case is established to the satisfaction of the regulator the regulated firm is required to provide incremental cost or stand-alone cost data corresponding to the suspect prices *alone*. This can be done on a confidential basis to avoid revelation of information valuable to a competitor. The regulator can then judge whether the prices at issue do or do not violate the floor or the ceiling. Note that in making its case the complaining party can legitimately select *any* combination of services that it believes a priori to be most favourable to its case. This clearly enhances the degree of protection provided by the process.

2. *Conventional pseudo-ceilings*

In some cases in the US it has been agreed that stand-alone cost ceilings are too difficult to calculate. Instead, the regulator and the regulated firm have agreed upon some initial prices and if, after some period, it was found that they elicited no complaints, it was agreed that these numbers almost certainly did not exceed the stand-alone cost ceilings and so could serve as proxies for these costs. Allowing those numbers, thereafter, to be adjusted by the price-cap mechanism. The affected parties have treated them as very demanding underestimates of the stand-alone cost ceiling.

3. *The one-sided test*

A final administrative approach makes use of a theorem which asserts the following:

> suppose that, as the price-cap mechanism is designed to ensure, the regulated firm earns no long-term excess profits (i.e. it just covers cost, including the cost of capital). Then if *none* of its prices fails the test of the incremental-cost floor, no price can possibly fail the test of the stand-alone cost ceiling. That is, it is then redundant to submit prices both to the floor test and to the ceiling test. Either by itself will do the entire job because if the prices all satisfy the floors they must all automatically satisfy the ceilings.

Intuitively, the reason is clear. If the three-service company of our earlier illustration were to lose no money on service A or B, or their combination, and it were to make excess profits on C, it *must* make excess profits overall. Thus, if it earns no excess profits overall, it cannot possibly be overpricing C, when neither A nor B is underpriced. Zero excess profits overall can only occur if excess profits on C are offset by losses on A or B.

The formal proof of the proposition is simple, with the aid of a bit of notation. This time, for simplicity, let the firm produce two products, X and Y, whose respective output quantities are X and Y. Let C(X,Y) be total company expenditure and let $C(0,y)$ be the total cost if output of X is reduced to zero. Then, by definition:

$C(x,y) - C(0,y)$ is the incremental cost of X,
PxX is the total revenue from the sale of X,
$C(0,y)$ is the stand-alone cost of Y.

Hence, the incremental cost floor for X requires:

$$(1)\ P_xX \geq C(x,y) - C(0,y),$$

and the condition that profits not be excessive is:

$$(2)\ P_xX + P_yY \leq C(x,y).$$

Subtracting (1) from (2) immediately yields:

$$(3)\ P_yY \leq C(0,y),$$

which is the stand-alone cost criterion for Y. This completes the proof.

In sum, a number of practical procedures are available for employment of the incremental-cost floor and the stand-alone cost ceiling to test prices and these are now in use in the USA. Indeed, specialized firms have arisen in the arena and have accumulated substantial experience and skills in providing the data needed to carry out the tests.

FLOORS AND CEILINGS FOR PRICE PACKAGES

Price packages such as two-part or multi-part tariffs have already been mentioned. The multiplicity of price elements of such a package must, on the competitive-market standard, satisfy price-floor and price-ceiling tests of precisely the same sorts as just described, and for precisely the same reason. They raise absolutely no new issues of principle here.[8] We need only note that if customers are offered a suitable menu of packages among which they are permitted to choose, they must always benefit, because the range of options open to them is thereby increased. Thus, the offering of packages will generally be beneficial to customers and not only to the supplying firm that offers these price packages. This is a standard and generally recognized proposition in the economic literature.

THE PRICING OF FINAL PRODUCTS AND PRODUCT COMPONENTS

This completes the discussion of the competitive-market standard for the regulation of the prices of final products. In sum, it has been shown that:

1. If prices are not allowed to exceed the stand-alone cost ceiling consumers will thereby receive all the protection against overcharging that competitive market forces can give them.
2. If prices are not allowed to fall short of the incremental-cost floor, competitors will be accorded analogous protection of their legitimate interests.

[8] It is suggestive, on this matter to note that each such price element has an optional Ramsey value, also calculated via the usual formula, with no required modification.

3. In between this floor and this ceiling prices must be tailored to evolving market conditions, something that, it is to be presumed, management can do more effectively than a regulatory agency. Thus, under deregulation management's freedom of action and its ability to respond quickly and effectively to changing demand should not be curtailed, within the limits described.

4. Where competition is deemed sufficiently powerful regulation should, for obvious reasons, avoid interference with the market altogether.

This, then, is what one concludes about the regulation of the prices of final products. But in addition, there are intermediate goods and services, such as interconnection, whose prices must be decided upon. Here one supplier provides one component of the final product to another supplier which in turn takes this component and other components of its own to make up the final product.

We will see next that regulatory rules for the optimal pricing of such a component. The prices called for by the competitive-market guidelines for regulation are very different from those just enunciated for final products. We will see that the public interest requires *both* standards to be met simultaneously. That is, final-product prices must pass the tests already enunciated, and product-component prices must, at the same time satisfy the rule about to be described. Otherwise if either rule is violated, inefficiencies will arise in the system, whose costs consumers will have to bear.

THE OPTIMAL COMPONENT-PRICING RULE

Let us then examine the economic principles that govern efficient pricing of component service and seek to explain the logic of those principles. It will then be shown that the efficient pricing rules apply when the following two circumstances hold:

1. when the service in question is not an end-product in itself but is, rather, just a component of the final product, and
2. when the supplier of the component of the final product whose price is at issue, is also a supplier of the remaining components of the final product, but it is not the only provider of these other components.

The relevant pricing principle (which will be referred to as 'efficient component pricing') is that the supplier of such a product component is entitled to receive for it a price that makes that supplier indifferent as to whether the other components of the final product are provided by itself (that is, the traffic is carried entirely over its own lines, from origin to destination), or whether, instead, those remaining components are supplied by others (the traffic is carried over a joint route operated in whole or in part by competitors). This rule follows the well known economic principle that efficiency requires the price of a product to cover its full incremental cost, *including its opportunity cost*. This is so because, if the supplier of the component in question receives for it a price that covers its full opportunity cost, that means by definition that it will be just as well off whether the rest of the product is supplied by itself or by others: it will be indifferent between the two arrangements. It will be shown that this pricing rule is required by economic efficiency. Moreover, it will be shown that the principle of efficient component pricing will be followed automatically in unregulated and competitive markets.

There are many other cases in reality in which: (a) the supplier of a critical component of a final product also supplies the final product in which that component is used, but (b) where that firm is only one of a number of enterprises that supplies or is prepared to supply the other component(s) of that final product. A clear example is a pharmaceutical manufacturer, Firm A, which is the sole supplier of medical ingredient X on which it holds a patent. The final product may require other medical ingredients, capsule cases, packaging, and marketing services, all of which Firm A can also provide, though it is by no means the only enterprise that is in a position to do so. Another example is the manufacturer of a product which acts as its own wholesaler, but which also owns a retail outlet that can sell the product to final customers in competition with other retailers.

Efficiency clearly requires that provision of capsule cases, packaging, or of retail marketing services, etc., each be left in the hands of those firms that can do it most efficiently (cheaply), i.e. those who can provide these components by means that reduce to a minimum the cost of the labour, fuel, raw material, and other inputs used in producing the components. Looked at in this way, the choice is often interpreted as a 'make-or-buy decision' on the part of Firm A, the supplier of patent-protected component X. Firm A should make the capsule cases, the packaging, etc. if and only if it is the more efficient supplier of these items. Otherwise, the public interest dictates that Firm A should buy those components from a rival supplier who can provide them more efficiently than Firm A can do so for itself. The same considerations apply to the choice between retailing by the manufacturer-wholesaler and leaving of the task of retailing to others.

Whether Firm A will, in fact, make the efficient choice voluntarily is, clearly, a matter of the relevant price of the competing services of a component Y. If the price of Y when offered by a rival supplier is lower than the cost that Firm A will incur when making the item for itself, it will pay Firm A to buy component Y, rather than making it. Efficiency in

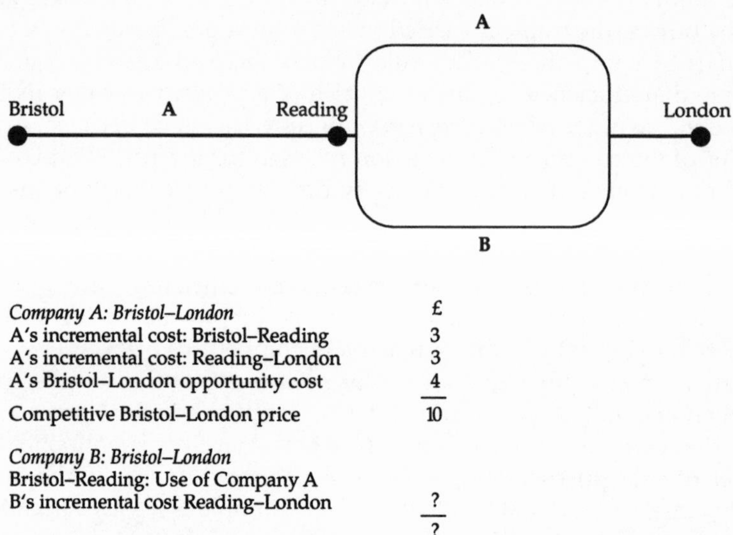

FIG. 11.2. The railwayman's problem

pricing, then, requires component Y to be priced below Firm A's pertinent costs if the rival firm is the most efficient supplier of Y, and it requires that price to be above Firm A's cost if Firm A is the more efficient provider of Y.

A third example, one involving two railway companies, A and B, will bring out the nature of the rule and its logic more clearly. Here, (Figure 11.2) railway A is taken to offer transportation from Bristol to Reading (route BR) and then on to London (Route RAL). Competitor railway B also serves Reading–London (Route RBL) and wishes to serve Bristol shippers as well by renting 'trackage rights' along A's Bristol–Reading route. The competitive price to shippers for the Bristol–London transport (the final product) is £10 per ton, and A's incremental cost along each of its two route segments is £3 per ton, as shown in the figure. Thus, A earns a net contribution toward its fixed and common costs equal to final product price minus its two incremental costs i.e.:

£10 – £3 – £3 = £4 for every ton of freight it carries.

In a competitive market, what will A charge B for hauling a ton of freight over its Bristol–Reading route? Let us assume that each ton of freight carried the rest of the way to London by B means that one less ton is transported by A. Then, even if there are other railroads in a position similar to A, none of them will rent B any space on its tracks unless

B pays them enough to make up for the cost of the loss in profit this imposes upon them. This clearly includes direct incremental cost—wear and tear of A's tracks, fuel, if A is required to supply the engine, etc. But, in addition, it requires that B pay for the incremental *opportunity cost* its traffic imposes upon A: the loss of £4 of contribution that A incurs for every ton of business that B is enabled to take away from A by its use of A's tracks.

Thus, the competitive market model tells us that the price of trackage rights (or of interconnection) must satisfy the rule:

component price = direct per unit incremental cost of the component supplier + its per unit opportunity cost
= £3 + £4 = £7 in our example.

We will see next, why this price is a requirement of economic efficiency, and why any other price for the component (interconnection) must invite inefficiency.

THE COMPONENT-PRICING RULE AND ECONOMIC EFFICIENCY

Thus, we come now to the critical efficiency role of the efficient component-pricing rule. We will show next that if the price of the component provided by Railway A, which can be described as 'the landlord's' is set in accord with this pricing rule, then the suppliers of the remaining ('tenant's') component (Railway B) will be offered the incentive that automatically assigns the business to the supplier who can provide it with the least use of fuel, labour, and other valuable inputs. On the other hand, pricing of the 'landlord's' competitive component—in this case A's Bristol–Reading service—at a price below that called for by the rule will be shown to violate the requirements of economic efficiency.

Economic efficiency requires that the competitive segment of the service be performed only by efficient suppliers, that is by those suppliers whose real costs incurred to supply the service—their incremental costs—are the lowest available. For this to be true, it must be possible for the more efficient suppliers to make a net gain when they offer the final product for a price that yields no such gain to a less-efficient supplier. This must be true whether the more efficient supplier happens to be the landlord or the tenant.

I first will demonstrate the basic efficiency result using our hypothetical numerical example, and then I will show how to generalize it, indicating that it is always true, not just if the pertinent numbers of reality happen to match those in my illustration. To avoid confusion I must, as a preliminary matter, also recall several standard propositions about profitability.

Proposition 1.
Incremental cost ('IC') includes the required profit on any required incremental investment, that is, the cost of the required capital. Therefore, if any service is sold at a price that covers the IC of that item, then that service is providing at least the minimum profit required for it to be viable for the supplier.
Proposition 2.
Nevertheless, if each and every one of a firm's services is sold at a price equal to its incremental cost, the firm's total revenues may not cover its total costs.
Proposition 3.
Consequently, it is normal and not anti-competitive for a firm to price some or all of its products so that they provide not only the (required) profit component of incremental cost but also some contribution to cover items such as common fixed costs which do not enter the IC's of the individual products. The appropriate and viable size of the contribution of any particular product depends, among other things, upon demand conditions for that product, and does not follow any standard mark-up rule or any arbitrary cost-allocation procedure.
Proposition 4.
Any service whose price exceeds its (per unit) IC provides a contribution in addition to the profit required on the incremental investment contained in the IC.

With all this in mind, let us proceed with our numerical example. Suppose, again that the final product in question (Bristol to London service) is sold at a price of £10; a price which is deemed competitive because it is above the incremental cost floor and below the stand-alone cost ceiling. Suppose the landlord, A, incurs an incremental cost for Bristol to Reading (which we will call ICBR) that equals £3, and an incremental cost for Reading to London service, ICRAL = £3. This leaves a contribution of £10 – £6 = £4 from each unit of final product sold, as we have seen.

The tenant, B, is a more-efficient supplier of transportation if its incremental cost, ICRBL, of Reading to London service is less than the landlord's. Similarly, they are equally efficient if the two incremental costs for the competitive portion of the route are equal while the tenant is the less-efficient supplier (it causes higher costs) if ICRBL greater than £3 = ICRAL.

Let us now see what the tenant earns if it is sold Bristol to Reading service at a price that satisfies the efficient component-pricing rule. That price, it will be recalled, is the incremental cost of that service plus the opportunity cost to the wholesaler of letting the retailer provide the final product, i.e. the £4 contribution. Thus, the rule requires Bristol to Reading service to be offered at a price equal to ICBR + opportunity cost

= £3 + £4 = £7. At that price, the tenant's gross earning per unit of final product is the £10 final price minus the £7 Bristol to Reading service price which is equal to £3, the landlord's incremental cost of Bristol to Reading transportation. There are now three possibilities.

CASE A.
If the tenant is the less-efficient supplier of Reading to London service so that its incremental cost exceeds its £3 gross earnings, it will lose money if it enters the business. So, in this case, it will be kept out, not by an improper price, but as a result of its own inefficiency. In this case, that is clearly the outcome required by the public interest.

CASE B.
If ICRBL = ICRAL = £3, the two firms are equally efficient suppliers of Reading to London services. In that case, it does not matter to society which of them provides it. Moreover, in this case the retailer will incur no loss by providing the service (its £3 gross revenue will just cover its £3 IC, including the required payment for incremental capital) so that it will be indifferent between entering and staying out.

CASE C.
The obvious third case, is that where the tenant is the more efficient supplier. In that case, the tenant will earn a contribution by providing the competitive service. In this case, the landlord will have no incentive to retain that transportation business for itself, because it will be able to do so only by accepting a reduced contribution that is lower than the contribution it obtains via the efficient component prices it obtains for its provision of the Bristol to Reading service.

In this third case, the landlord is said to have chosen 'to buy' the Reading to London transportation component of the final product, rather than 'making its own'. By following the principle of indifference—by setting its rental price so that it is indifferent to the landlord whether that transportation service is provided by itself or by a rival—it has been ensured that the task is carried out by the firm that can do it more efficiently.

Matters work out in a very different manner if the landlord is forced to offer its Bristol to Reading service at a rental price below the efficient component price. If, for example, the wholesaler is permitted to charge only £5 for Bristol to Reading service, because that is the price dictated by an arbitrary regulatory decision, the tenant's gross earning, that is, its final product price minus the rental price, would be £10 – £5 = £5 or £2 above the landlord's incremental cost for Reading to London service. If so, even if the tenant's incremental Reading to London service cost was £4, meaning that it is the *less*-efficient supplier of the competitive transportation service, it could enter the arena and earn a contribution from its inefficient activity. A moment's consideration indicates that this result is made possible because the imposition of the £5 price offers the tenant a subsidy from the landlord—a subsidy of £2 for every unit of service that the tenant elects to provide, and which is, in effect, obtainable by the tenant on demand.

The connection between the efficient component-pricing rule and efficiency should now be clear. It remains only to be shown that the result is of general validity and does not hold only for the numbers that happen to have been selected for my illustration. This can now readily be done by substituting algebraic symbols for the preceding numbers, showing directly that if Bristol–Reading service is priced in accordance with the efficient component-pricing rule, the tenant's net return per unit of final product it supplies must be equal to ICRBL – ICRAL, the difference between the landlord's and its own incremental cost of providing the Reading to London service. In short, the tenant will receive a contribution exactly equal to the saving made possible by the superiority (if any) of its efficiency. If the tenant is the more efficient firm, the landlord will have no incentive to do the job itself—it can readily be induced to 'buy' rather than 'make' the Reading to London transportation component. On the other hand, if the tenant is the less-efficient supplier, the efficient component price will indeed exclude it from the market, but that is precisely what the public interest requires.

This completes the analysis of the efficiency role of the component-pricing rule. We have now seen that its working is perfectly general. It *always* assigns the supplier's task to the firm that can do it most efficiently, and a lower price than that set in accordance with the rule—as can result if prices are set on an arbitrary basis—is always an invitation to an inter-firm cross-subsidy and the assumption of the supplier's role by a firm that is not the most efficient provider. This result should really not come as a surprise. It is well known that this is how economic forces set component prices in competitive markets, and we also know that competitive market prices are generally those necessary for the achievement of economic efficiency. Thus, our efficiency result also follows immediately via this indirect route—the competitive market model as the guide to efficient pricing.

We come, then, to the bottom line of the efficiency analysis, which yields a double-pricing rule:

1. final product prices must never exceed stand-alone cost but never lie below incremental cost;
2. if a component of a product is offered by a single supplier who also competes with others in offering the remaining product component, the single-supplier component's price should cover its incremental cost plus the opportunity cost incurred when a rival supplies the final product.

ON THE ATTRIBUTABILITY OF COSTS TO PARTICULAR SERVICES OR SERVICE COMBINATIONS

It has already been noted that the calculation of incremental cost entails no cost allocations. Any cost such as a fixed component of a cost common to several services (call them 'A' and 'B'), jointly incurred by them, is simply considered to be used incrementally by A and B together, but no part of such a cost is attributable incrementally to either service individually.

Nevertheless, it is to be emphasized that a large proportion of total common cost *is* normally attributable to individual services, and that seems to be true of telecommunications in particular. Some portion of common cost, C(A,B), incurred on behalf of services A and B, will nevertheless be attributable to A *alone* if that portion of C(A,B) was imposed by an increment in the volume of service A supplied. Thus, suppose there are operators, all of whom serve both domestic and international users of credit cards, and suppose that the elimination of international service by BT would permit it to reduce the total operator staff of 9,000 by 3,000 persons. In that case, even though every operator in the 9,000-person staff currently spends some time on each of the two services, it is clear that the cost of 3,000 of the operators is *exclusively* attributable to international service. The fact that operator cost is common to the two services is here irrelevant. It should be clear then that much, and sometimes even all, of a firm's total common cost is causally divisible and attributable in a unique and completely non-arbitrary manner to the individual services at issue. As already noted, this seems clearly to be true of telecommunications costs. The preponderant portion of common telecommunications costs can be traced to the services that cause them and there appear to be no significant examples of truly joint costs. Thus, even if arbitrary accounting conventions are utilized to allocate the unattributable residue of common cost, the resulting scope for distortion in any calculation of imbalances between prices and costs is very limited.

Because lines and calls are utilized together this may appear to change matters, and may suggest that the two are joint products consumed in fixed proportions, meaning that it is impossible to attribute any part of their combined cost exclusively to one or the other. But a moment's consideration confirms that this is not so. While no one can make calls without access to at least one line, households and particularly firms *often* make use of a multiplicity of lines, their number is chosen partly under the influence of price, and that is obviously also true of the number of calls. Because it is possible to vary the number of calls without varying the number of lines and vice versa, both lines and calls (and different types of call) have clearly identifiable and separable incremental costs.

Thus, there seems to be every reason to presume that a substantial proportion of BT costs (something in the order of 80 to 85 per cent has been suggested) seems to be separable and causally attributable incrementally to the individual services responsible for those outlays. It is only the remaining portion of total cost that can at all reasonably be suspected of having been allocated arbitrarily among those services.

IMPERFECTIONS IN RAMSEY CALCULATIONS IN PRACTICE

Something rather similar can be said about the Ramsey calculations of optimal prices. But, in practice, while it will often be possible to determine the order of magnitude of such a price with a considerable degree of confidence, some margin of error is likely to remain, particularly when change affects demand and cost conditions.

The regulator's public-interest goals make it necessary for him or her to seek to elicit prices that maximize economic welfare subject to the requirement that the revenues of the regulated firm cover its costs, including the cost of capital. These prices, generally referred to as 'Ramsey prices' will, in the most straightforward circumstances be those whose deviations from marginal costs are inversely proportionate to the corresponding elasticities of demand. This rule requires amendment in a number of circumstances, for example when demands for the services are not independent, so that the cross-elasticities of their demands are not zero, or when the services generate beneficial or detrimental externalities. In each case, the required modification of the Ramsey formula is well understood, and if the requisite data are available the amended calculations can be carried out readily.

The problem then is that some of the required data are not generally available, though it is usually possible to infer the orders of magnitude of the pertinent parameters from informal observation or by other means. For example, externalities are often believed to arise in the process of rental of telephone lines. When a new customer joins the network this also benefits the others who are for the first time enabled to reach this person directly by telephone. Where those other parties are friends or relatives this benefit will no doubt be taken into account by the prospective subscriber in deciding whether to subscribe, and thereby, the external benefits will effectively be 'internalized'. However, this will not, for example, be true of the calls prospectively received by the new subscriber from those business firms that will use the telephone as a marketing instrument to sell their wares to the subscriber.

Such uninternalized externalities, to the extent that they are present, are likely to call for some reduction in the Ramsey price for exchange-line rentals. It is, however, quite implausible that these uninternalized externalities are large in magnitude. Business firms undoubtedly internalize the benefits to customers of the company's line rentals, recognizing them as contributions to goodwill and as other, more-direct benefits to themselves. We have already noted that household customers take into account in their rental decisions, at least part of the benefit to friends and relatives.

In any event, even if this view of the matter is not entirely correct, the effect on the Ramsey prices is likely to be small. This has been confirmed by a set of explicit sensitivity tests, in which Ramsey prices were re-estimated, using rather high assumed values of the externalities, with little resulting effect on the calculated Ramsey values.

IMPLICATION FOR THE EVIDENCE ON REBALANCING

All of this is of considerable significance for BT's contention that the relative prices of lines and calls are badly in need of rebalancing, calling for a considerable fall in the latter and an offsetting increase in the former. Both the Ramsey calculation and the accounting estimates of fully allocated costs emphatically call for a substantial revision in this direction. Nothing in this paper is intended to imply that either the calculated Ramsey numbers or the fully allocated cost figures are to be considered representations of the underlying reality accurate to several decimal places. They are only to be considered as reasonable approximations to the pertinent facts, along the lines just described. This means that if their evidence favouring rebalancing were only marginal and lacked robustness, that evidence would merit little credence.

However, the opposite is clearly true. Even assuming a substantial margin of error, the disparities in both the Ramsey and fully allocated cost figures for lines and calls are so pronounced and robust as to call *unambiguously* for rebalancing, and for a rebalancing substantial in magnitude, even allowing for a considerable margin of error.

ON THE CONSEQUENCES OF REBALANCING

It should be emphasized that in the long run rebalancing can be expected to benefit all affected groups—British Telecom most obviously; the consumer of telephone services for reasons that are widely understood and accepted. Perhaps more surprisingly, it can also be expected to benefit Mercury and other prospective competitors of BT.

British Telecom will benefit by being permitted to compete effectively for the relatively profitable business of the high-volume customers, and by not being driven by artificial and indefensible regulatory constraints into specialization in serving low-volume customers, many of whom currently appear not even to cover their own incremental costs.

Mercury and prospective competitors will benefit by being offered entry into the low-user market on terms that will be attractive because they are profitable. The energetic entry of MCI and Sprint into this arena in the US proves that such a scenario is practical. Put the other way, under rebalancing competitors or prospective competitors will be rescued from the danger that regulatory defence of their protected niche will some day soon become untenable, because its irrationality and its high cost to consumers will become painfully obvious. This may well require rapid withdrawal of the protective regulatory umbrella at short notice, leaving the newer firms naked to the world, to battle unaided in arenas into which they were drawn not by any specialized efficiencies but by the fortuitous price distortions imposed by regulations.

Finally, consumers will benefit from rebalancing not only via superior resource allocation contributed by better approximation to free-market prices. They will gain by the opening of the small-volume market to true competition which, unbelievably, regulation currently prevents. Thereby regulation effectively imposes monopoly on that sector of the market which any dispassionate evaluation would surely deem to be in most urgent need of regulatory stimulation of competition. Even more than that, by ensuring that the services will not necessarily be provided by those suppliers who can supply them at lowest cost, consumers are in effect, forced to pay protection money in the form of prices that are sufficiently high to cover the costs of the inefficient suppliers. The irony is that they pay this money to protect themselves from the danger that, after rebalancing, true competition will arise and prosper in the consumer markets.

PRICING PACKAGES AND REGULATION

It would be equally irrational to extend regulatory 'protection' to customers against the advent of volume-related pricing packages. Packages, as already noted, are widely recognized to benefit customers by permitting them to choose among a greater variety of pricing options, thereby offering lower unit costs to a broad range of buyers. It even provides some degree of protection to low-volume users by permitting them to select packages with comparatively low rental charges and higher call charges. In that way packages promise to cushion the effects of rebalancing even upon low-volume customers.

THE TRANSITION PROCESS

Though the pricing principles described in this paper are designed to offer benefits to everyone and, certainly, to contribute to the social welfare, there is some reason to resist too abrupt a transition to the new regulatory regime. There are at least two reasons to allow some time for the transition. This does not, of course, mean mere postponement. On the contrary, the virtues of *gradual* change call for a beginning of the process with all deliberate speed, in order to avoid the need for sharp and consequently costly changes at some future date.

The disruptive effect of abrupt price change is probably the main reason that favours a gradual process of price rebalancing, and of adoption of uncushioned incremental cost floors, stand-alone cost ceilings, and the interconnection prices that follow the optimal component-pricing rule. It is clear that if customers know that prices are going to change and are notified about the pace and direction of that change they can, for example, make sensible adjustments in their planning for equipment purchases and installation. They can adapt their degree of reliance on different telecommunications arrangements, and business subscribers can provide early notification of prospective resultant changes in their own mode of operation to their own customers thereby, in turn, facilitating the planning process of the latter. Competitors, too, will benefit from adjustment time. Foreknowledge that the small-volume customer market is about to become more profitable, and that competition in the high-volume market is about to become more effective, is information that can be of inestimable value to Mercury and to other prospective competitors. It is well known that abrupt and substantial price changes cause large and unnecessary adjustment costs to consumers and firms alike. Even optimal prices, if instituted extremely rapidly and without advance notice, can lead to a transition process that is damaging and costly and hence really far from optimal.

The second argument for adoption of a gradual transition process is the infant-firm argument of ancient lineage. The notion is that particularly where scale economies are present, an entering firm must attain substantial size if it is to be able to survive the competitive process on its own. But, so the argument goes, it takes time for the entrant to build its customer base, to expand its financing, and to increase its productive capacity to the point of viability. Only governmental protection, it is held by those who espouse this view, can provide the entrant the time and circumstances that can permit it to attain full maturity.

There is some validity to this position, though it has its perils. Its premisses are not quite as self-evident as they seem. Small entrants can entrench themselves in easily defensible niches without government protection and from there expand to powerful market positions. Xerox and Polaroid were both new entrants not so long ago, and neither of them had to rely on a regulatory umbrella to ease their way.

The cost of protection of the entrant can be significant and constitute a heavy burden for customers who may never have it made up to them fully nor is there any guarantee that protection will stimulate the entrant to exercise ingenuity, expend effort, and struggle to enhance its efficiency in order to become a more effective competitor in the future. Above all, there is the risk, which has materialized all too often, that the infant will never grow out of its swaddling clothes. In such cases it becomes all but irresistible to the regulator to protract the infant-protection rules. The consequence is apt to be a cartel imposed upon society by the regulator, in the guise of competition. In that case the ageing infant will be guarded for the indefinite future against any need to compete, and can continue to overcharge customers at will in its protected arena.

Despite all these reservations, it must nevertheless be conceded that in some circumstances a persuasive case can be made for a limited period of protection of the infant. The arguments for it need no reiteration here. However, in such circumstances it is inexcusable to expand the period of infancy beyond very limited bounds, or to evade the obligation of stating clearly and firmly when and how the period of protection will come to an end. It is equally hard to justify any delay in the introduction of a gradual process toward reduction in the degree of protection. It is hard to see how any entrant can justify a protection period extending well beyond, say, half a decade, and there is surely no reason to avoid inauguration of the weaning process in say, the infant's second year.

Above all, just as everyone stands to gain from clear and firmly articulated regulatory rules, everyone will surely gain if the rules of the transition are spelled out early and explicitly as firm and dependable commitments. Vagueness in the rules is the ultimate embodiment of unnecessary and purposeless regulatory risk. It harms the entrant no less than it damages the incumbent. It weakens the effective regulatory protection of the interests of consumers—the arena where regulatory protection most clearly belongs. It is only an indecisive regulator who can fail to heed the urgency of precommitment and advance notice in the transition process.

12

Competition and Regulation in Telecommunications

MARK ARMSTRONG* AND JOHN VICKERS†

1. INTRODUCTION

Telecommunications was the first network-utility industry in Britain to be privatized. Policy decisions in the UK about the appropriate competitive and regulatory framework for a private firm with monopoly power therefore first arose in the industry, and a pattern was set that has been followed to varying degrees with gas, airports, water, and electricity supply. The industry has the longest and richest history of regulation, and controversy about policy towards the industry shows no sign of abating.

We begin our review of competition and regulation in the telecommunications industry in Britain by outlining the structure of the industry, its chief economic characteristics, and their evolution over time. Market failures—such as natural monopoly cost conditions in parts of the industry, a history of actual monopoly over nearly all of the industry, and network externalities between users—provide the rationale for policy intervention, and in Section 3 we set out some of the broad policy options. These are grouped under the headings of structure, entry conditions, pricing, and investment and quality, but the interrelationships between those issues will also be clear.

The policy choices made before and after the privatization of BT in 1984 are then described, in Sections 4 and 5 respectively. The decade began with some steps towards liberalization, but after deciding to privatize BT the government chose to limit competition, notably by its Mercury/BT duopoly policy. New regulatory institutions, including

* Gonville and Caius College, University of Cambridge.
† Professor at the Institute of Economics and Statistics, University of Oxford.

The paper is part of the project on 'The Regulation of Firms with Market Power', and financial support from the ESRC and from the Office of Fair Trading is gratefully acknowledged. We thank Michael Beesley, David Salant, and David Thompson for their comments on an earlier draft. The views expressed are entirely our own, and we are responsible for any errors. This chapter was completed in mid-1992. For a more recent account, see chapter 7 of C. M. Armstrong, S. Cowan, and J. S. Vickers (1994), *Regulatory Reform: Economic analysis and British Experience*, MIT Press.

OFTEL and RPI–*X* price control, came into being. We shall describe how OFTEL has acted in a reasonably pro-competitive manner subject to the limits set by government, and how RPI–*X* regulation, contrary to initial aspirations, has had to become tighter and more involved over time, and supplemented by a considerable amount of additional implicit regulation. At the turn of the decade, as earlier limitations on competition expired, telecommunications competition policy was reviewed, and a more liberal regime is proposed for the future. BT nevertheless remains dominant throughout most of the industry. Finally, in Section 6, there is a brief assessment of policy to date.

2. THE TELECOMMUNICATIONS INDUSTRY AND ITS ECONOMIC CHARACTERISTICS

Components of a telecommunications system

In thinking about the economics of the industry it is useful, though not always easy, to distinguish between (i) the public network and its operation; (ii) customers' apparatus attached to the network; and (iii) services provided over the network.[1] The network connects users by a combination of exchanges and transmission links. Networks are typically configured hierarchically with users connected to local exchanges, which in turn are linked by trunk or long-distance lines to regional exchanges, and ultimately to the international network.[2] Although radio technology is used in the traditional 'fixed-link' network—for instance in satellite transmission—the distinctive feature of mobile networks is that the final link from users to the local exchange is a radio link. Both wire and radio methods of transmission are increasingly able to transmit digital rather than analogue signals, and convergence with computing technology is becoming ever more important. Moreover, as fibre-optic and forms of satellite communication become more prevalent there is increasing convergence with parts of the broadcasting and entertainment industries. As well as the public network(s) the national telecommunications system contains numerous private networks, for example university internal networks.

In addition to the traditional telephone, the apparatus attached to the public network by users now includes mobile phones, radio-pagers, telex and fax machines, TV sets, and computing equipment. Moreover,

[1] In this paper we do not discuss the industry that supplies the equipment (exchanges, cables, etc.) that comprises the public network.

[2] This is efficient given the trade-offs in network design between switching and transmission. For example, it saves on transmission costs to send calls between two towns via two local exchanges and a single high-capacity long-distance link, rather than via a single central exchange.

many private networks are attached to the public network. The services provided over the network are the basic voice-telephony service, together with the 'value added' network services (VANS)—such as electronic mail, recorded messages, data services and, potentially, TV services—though the distinction between basic services and VANS is sometimes unclear.

Economic characteristics of the industry

For the purposes of policy analysis important economic features of the industry include its multi-product nature, the non-storability of its output, together with time-varying and stochastic demands, sunk costs and capacity constraints, externalities between users, and elements of natural monopoly. The last two factors deserve particular discussion because they are the main market failures that are the rationale for policy intervention, and they involve the other factors anyway.

A positive 'network externality' between users arises because existing subscribers benefit when new subscribers join. This may have policy implications for pricing structure, possibly justifying a subsidy to rental charges to encourage new users to join the network, and it is fundamental for policy on interconnection between rival networks, for without interconnection a small network would be severely disadvantaged relative to a large one. The wider social benefits of telecommunications—for example provision to sparsely populated areas and emergency services—are another kind of positive externality in the broad sense. These activities could be financed by direct subsidy out of public funds or by cross-subsidy from more profitable activities. Negative externalities may arise from network congestion, i.e. the inability of some users to make calls due to capacity constraints on links and exchanges. This is an important aspect of quality and a key influence upon time-of-day pricing.

An activity is said to be a *natural monopoly* if supply by a single firm is the most cost-efficient form of supply.[3] There is no strong reason to expect natural monopoly in the supply of apparatus or of network services, but aspects of network operation and construction may be naturally monopolistic to some degree. At the most local level there would be wasteful duplication if houses had telephone wires from several

[3] See Sharkey (1982) for an excellent account of the theory of natural monopoly and some applications to telecommunications. The empirical evidence on natural monopoly in telecommunications is mixed. For instance, Evans and Heckman (1983), and Hunt and Lynk (1991) find evidence to support the hypothesis that, prior to divestiture, the Bell network in the US as a whole was not a natural monopoly, whereas Röller (1990) reaches the opposite conclusion. Shin and Ying (1992) argue that local networks in the US are not naturally monopolistic.

suppliers, or if a local area had competing exchanges. But if additional wiring is occurring anyway—to provide cable TV for example—then it might be efficient to allow these cable TV companies also to provide a competing local telecommunications service. Mobile telephony is another and growing source of local competition. However, it is fair to say that most fixed-link network operations remain naturally monopolistic at the most local level for the foreseeable future. Note, however, that monopoly in each local area does not imply that there need be a single nation-wide monopolist of local services.

Traffic on trunk and international routes is much heavier, and this means that, because economies of scale in building capacity are exhausted, competition along such routes is more likely to be efficient. Anyhow, given that new capacity needs to be built along a route, it is not clear why the fact of having existing capacity should result in economies in building this additional capacity, especially if a second firm such as a railway or electricity distribution company already possesses land-rights by virtue of its other business. This suggests that there is little reason to expect severe natural monopoly conditions in trunk and international networks, and this conclusion is reinforced if rivalry provides a competitive stimulus both for cost reduction and the introduction of new products and services over time.

Telecommunications technology is changing fast, and it is hard to predict how the network will evolve in the years ahead. For example, the appropriate balance between mobile and cable links at local level is very uncertain, and so is the extent of future integration between telecommunications and entertainment and data services. The influence of competition and regulatory policies upon incentives for dynamic efficiency is of particular importance in the telecommunications industry.

The industry in Britain

What is naturally monopolistic in the cost sense and what is actually monopolized need not coincide. British Telecom (BT) dominates virtually all aspects of fixed-link network operation and basic voice-telephony in Britain, and in addition has strong positions in mobile telephony, apparatus supply, and VANS.

Network operation is a growth industry, with BT's call volumes increasing by up to 10 per cent per year, though this has been slowing down recently, while VANS and mobile services have been growing even faster. About 87 per cent of British households in 1989 had a telephone, compared to 42 per cent in 1972.

At present, the only national fixed-link competitor to BT is Mercury, a subsidiary of the international telecommunications company, Cable & Wireless. By the end of 1990 Mercury had a tiny share of local calls and exchange lines, about a 3 per cent share of switched long-distance traffic and a 5 per cent share of leased lines.[4] By contrast to fixed-link telephony, the mobile sector has been characterized by vigorous duopolistic competition between Cellnet, in which BT has a majority stake, and Vodafone. The latter company has succeeded in gaining slightly over half the market, which currently has a total of about 1.25 million customers. Apparatus supply has become much more competitive over the past decade: whereas BT had a statutory monopoly in the supply of telephones before 1981, in 1990 its share was about 53 per cent. Over the same period its supply of private branch exchanges fell from 83 to 40 per cent.[5] Cable television companies are now permitted independently, to offer local telephone services; at present this sector is very small, but growing fast. The VANS sector has been quite competitive.

In the year ending March 1992 BT's revenue (not including subsidiaries such as Cellnet and Mitel) was £13.3 billion, which was divided in the following manner:[6] inland calls 39 per cent, exchange line rentals 16 per cent, international calls 13 per cent, apparatus supply 9 per cent, and other sales and services (leased lines, VANS, telexes, etc.) 22 per cent. The company employed around 210,000 people, and made an operating profit before interest and tax of £3.4 billion, which is 25.5 per cent of total turnover and represents a return on capital employed of 21 per cent on a historic cost basis.[7] Table 12.1 gives information on BT's sales, profits, employment and investment over the past decade. OFTEL (1992*a*, 8–10) reports a breakdown by service of BT's financial results, on the basis of fully allocated historic costs. According to these figures BT faces a substantial deficit on the provision of access (connections and line rentals) but makes very high rates of return on calls, especially long-distance and international calls.

3. POLICY ISSUES

The aim of this section is to offer a general perspective on policy issues, which we have grouped under the four headings of structure, entry, pricing, and quality and investment.

Structure

A fundamental policy issue concerning structure is whether naturally monopolistic activities such as local network operation should be

[4] See DTI (1990, 51). [5] See OFTEL Annual Report for 1991.
[6] See BT's Annual Report for the year ending 31 March 1992.
[7] Pre-tax profit (after interest) in the year to 31 March 1992 was £3,073 million, which is 19.3% of capital employed.

TABLE 12.1. The performance of British Telecom

	1980	1981	1982	1983	1984	1985	1986	1987	1988	1989	1990	1991	1992
Turnover (£m)	3,559	4,554	5,708	6,377	6,830	7,585	8,317	9,339	10,185	11,071	12,315	13,154	13,337
Profit before interest and taxation (£m)	663	719	1,007	905	1,531	1,856	2,118	2,349	2,609	2,807	3,210	3,531	3,415
Return on capital employed (%)[a]	9.1	9.0	11.9	9.7	16.7	18.3	19.3	21.2	22.1	21.8	22.5	22.4	21.0
Return on sales (%)	18.6	16.5	17.6	14.2	22.4	24.5	25.5	25.2	25.6	25.5	26.0	26.8	25.6
Employees (000s)	240	247	252	249	245	238	234	236	236	243	248	227	210
Investment as percentage of turnover (%)[b]	30	29	25	24	22	24	24	22	23	26	25	22	19

[a] Capital employed is defined as total assets less current liabilities

[b] Investment is defined as the purchase of tangible fixed assets.

Source: BT Annual Reports (financial years end on 31 March).

'vertically' separated from potentially competitive activities such as long-distance network operation. Questions of this kind are pervasive in network utilities (e.g. transmission/generation in electricity).[8] There is the further issue of whether network operation as a whole should be separated from the supply and manufacture of apparatus, the supply of VANS and TV services, and the provision of mobile services. Vertical separation has the advantage that it removes the incentive for the firm in the natural monopoly activity to behave anti-competitively towards rivals in the potentially competitive activity. Ring-fencing the naturally monopoly activity might also ease the task of regulation by improving information flows, there being no need to allocate common costs, for example. But vertical separation can damage cost efficiency if there are significant economies of scope between the activities concerned. Another aspect of structure is regional. For example, having separate local network operators, each a monopolist in its own region, could enhance the effectiveness of regulation by facilitating cost comparisons and 'yardstick' competition.

As for the dynamics of policy towards structure, it is best to carry out any restructuring of a public enterprise *before* its privatization. Later restructuring leaves the government open to charges of breach of faith with shareholders and, in addition, may jeopardize government credibility generally in so far as *ex post* policy changes reveal *ex ante* policy errors. Thus the postponement of desirable restructuring may result in its never occurring. Moreover, persistent uncertainty about future restructuring is likely to inhibit efficient investment by the firm in question and also by its potential competitors. In the event, the government chose to privatize BT intact, but, as we shall discuss below, the appropriate structure for BT remains a live policy issue.

Entry conditions

A policy of free entry is appropriate for most industries because of the benefits of competition (actual and potential) in terms of low prices and incentives for cost reduction and innovation. The issue is less straightforward in parts of the telecommunications industry because of: (i) elements of natural monopoly; and (ii) the presence of a dominant and integrated incumbent firm. As regards point (i), arguments are sometime advanced for restricting entry. First, when there are economies of scale there is a trade-off between the benefits of more competition and higher unit costs as more firms enter. In particular, unrestricted entry might lead to excessive entry from the point of view of overall efficiency (see Mankiw and Whinston 1986). A second argument for limiting the

[8] On the theory of vertical integration see, for example, Tirole (1988, ch. 4).

number of firms allowed into an industry, which was used in support of the BT/Mercury duopoly policy, is that recent entrant(s) should be protected from further entrants while they establish themselves and recoup the sunk costs of entry. However, such a policy can also benefit the incumbent firm, and to a much greater extent. Third, there is the possibility that free entry could lead to undesirable 'cream-skimming'—entrants taking profitable market segments and leaving the incumbent firm unable to finance the rest of its operations. This may be a problem when there is policy-induced cross-subsidy.[9] For instance, if BT's rental charges were required to be set below cost as part of its social obligations, and if other services were potentially very competitive, then free entry might mean that BT became unprofitable overall unless entrants were also required to contribute towards the loss-making activity.

Turning now to point (ii), and assuming that some entry is desirable, the presence of a dominant and integrated incumbent firm like BT raises the issue of strategic entry deterrence. With vertical integration the danger is that the incumbent will deny rivals fair terms of access to monopolized activities such as local networks in order to extend its market power. Of course strategic entry deterrence can also occur without there being vertical integration. The literature on this important topic is vast, and this is not the place for an extended discussion, but see chapters 8 and 9 of Tirole (1988) for an account of the theory. The general policy implication of strategic entry deterrence is the need for regulation to curb its exercise in order to protect conditions of fair competition. Without regulation *for* competition, a policy of allowing entry is in danger of being rendered ineffective.

Unless the monitoring of anti-competitive behaviour is very effective, it may also be desirable to help new entrants into network operation while they build their sunk cost networks to develop an effective competitive challenge to a dominant incumbent. If the incumbent is vertically integrated, one way of doing this is to set favourable terms of interconnection into the incumbent's network. Another way to assist entrants is to allow them to enter selectively while placing universal service and other obligations only upon the incumbent—see the discussion of cream-skimming above. As we shall see below, the question of how to promote entry in the face of dominant incumbent advantages has been a very controversial topic in British telecommunications policy.

[9] There is a theoretical possibility that even without cross-subsidies being imposed by the regulator, free entry by similar firms could result in the incumbent being unable to make a profit. This is the problem of 'non-sustainability', usually examined in the context of the literature on the theory of contestable markets—see Baumol, *et al.* (1982). This theory has been controversial—see Vickers and Yarrow (1988, 53–61) for a summary of some of the criticisms of it.

Pricing

Since, in the medium term at least, competition cannot be relied upon to contain market power in all parts of the telecommunications industry, the control of pricing is central to regulatory policy. The general characteristics of RPI–X price-cap regulation, which was first introduced for BT, and its similarities and differences with traditional rate-of-return regulation are discussed elsewhere in this volume,[10] and the telecommunications industry provides excellent illustrations of policy choices regarding the scope of price control, setting X, regulatory lag, regulation of pricing structure (including quantity discounts), and so on. We shall discuss all these issues further in Section 5 below.

Quality and investment

Price control must be supplemented by quality control. Without such control the regulated firm would offset its price controls by reducing its standard of service. Some aspects of the quality of telecommunications services relate to current expenditures—for example the speed of installations and repairs, the responsiveness of directory enquiries, and the maintenance of public call-boxes. Others depend on investment—for example having adequate capacity to avoid congestion, and modern switching and transmission technology for new services. Policy options for promoting quality range from the incorporation of quality indices into the price control formula, liability for damages, and standard financial penalties for poor quality, to less formal methods such as warning the firm that low quality now will be reflected in lower prices at the next price review.

A related issue is whether investment activity should be an object of regulatory attention. If there is uncertainty about future regulatory policy and a fear that the firm might be denied a fair rate of return on sunk-cost investment, then a problem of underinvestment might arise, with adverse consequences for the rate of adoption of new technologies. The direction as well as the level of investment might be of concern. It is a matter for debate whether large infrastructure investments such as the possible extension of a fibre-optic network should be strongly influenced by public policy or determined in a regime of *laissez-faire*.[11]

In this section we have discussed telecommunications policy options in four important areas—structure, entry, pricing, and quality and investment. The interrelationships between those topics, for example

[10] See Chapter 15 by Rees and Vickers in this volume.

[11] The former approach was taken in France, where the government pursued an ambitious plan to cable a large number of households with optical fibre by 1992, and to use this network for a full range of interactive services.

between vertical relationships and the ease of entry, will have been evident. We now examine how policy-makers in Britain have chosen from those options.

4. THE REGULATORY FRAMEWORK AT PRIVATIZATION

This section describes the competitive and regulatory framework established for BT's privatization in 1984. Table 12.2 lists some of the main events in telecommunications policy over the past decade. The privatization of BT was not on the policy agenda at the beginning of the 1980s.

TABLE 12.2. Telecommunications policy: Some important events

1981	Beesley Report recommends liberalization of the resale of leased circuits (including simple resale).
	British Telecommunications Act splits BT from the Post Office and begins liberalization (without simple resale).
1982	White Paper announces the government's intention to privatize BT.
	Mercury is licensed as a national network operator in competition with BT.
1983	Littlechild Report on price regulation for BT recommends RPI–X price control.
	BT/Mercury duopoly policy announced.
1984	Telecommunications Act establishes new regulatory framework, OFTEL, and RPI–3 price control on inland calls.
	BT is privatized: 50.2 per cent of its shares are sold.
1985	OFTEL rules on the terms of interconnection between Mercury's and BT's networks.
	BT's first price changes after privatization involve major rebalancing of call charges.
	BT's bid for Mitel is referred to the MMC and cleared subject to conditions in 1986.
1986	BT continues with rebalancing of call charges.
1987	BT's quality of service comes under criticism.
1988	BT accepts contractual liability for some aspects of poor service and standard compensation terms are set.
	Review of BT's price controls raises X to 4.5 and extends the scope of regulation.
1989	The use of private networks is liberalized and BT's charges for leased lines are capped at RPI–0.
	More mobile operators (Telepoint, PCNs) are licensed.
1991	White Paper ends the duopoly policy.
	Price control is extended to international calls with X being correspondingly increased to 6.25.
	Controversy over interconnection terms with new entrants.
	Government sells second tranche of BT's shares.
1992	Several new fixed-link operators are licensed.
	Review of BT's price controls raises X from 6.25 to 7.5.

Rather, the focus was on tighter financial control and steps towards liberalization. The 1981 British Telecommunications Act split BT from the Post Office, and partly liberalized network operation—Mercury was licensed in 1982—together with apparatus supply and VANS, but did not allow simple resale.[12] (The Beesley Report (1981) had recommended that all forms of resale of leased capacity be permitted, and not just for value-added services.) These measures did little to threaten BT's dominance throughout the industry, but the 1981 Act nevertheless took important first steps towards competition.

Tighter financial controls over the nationalized industries, which were largely the result of macro-economic monetary policy commitments at the time, were preventing BT from investing in network modernization to the extent that was efficient on micro-economic grounds.[13] An attempt to overcome this problem of underinvestment by allowing BT to borrow from private capital markets (via 'Buzby bonds') did not get off the ground, partly because of the legal difficulty of distinguishing such borrowings from public-sector borrowings. Instead privatization—sales of equity rather than debt—was the favoured solution (see Department of Industry, 1982). Henceforth BT could borrow without increasing the so-called 'public-sector borrowing requirement'. Moreover, since privatization proceeds are treated curiously in the accounts as negative public expenditure, privatization had the advantage of reducing the PSBR yet further. Nominal macro-economic commitments had an important influence on privatization policy towards BT, though the real effect of that policy is principally micro-economic rather than macro-economic.

Having resolved to privatize BT, the government had to choose between the policy options discussed in Section 3 above. The main question concerning *structure* was whether BT should be broken up—for example whether its naturally monopolistic local network operations, long-distance services, and apparatus supply should be separated—in order to reduce the potential for anti-competitive behaviour. In the United States, following a lengthy anti-trust case, AT&T had just been ordered to divest itself of its regional operating companies.[14] By contrast, the British government decided to privatize BT intact as an

[12] Resale is a kind of wholesaling activity in telecommunications services. Resellers lease lines from BT or Mercury by the month say, and sell services by the minute after either adding value (e.g. supplying data to subscribers) or not (so-called 'simple resale').

[13] The extent of this problem (or at least whether privatization was a solution) is unclear—Table 12.1 shows the movement of investment (specifically, net expenditure on fixed tangible assets) as a fraction of revenue over the past decade, and there is little sign that this has been systematically higher since 1984.

[14] This was the result of an anti-trust case, which followed claims that AT&T was acting in a predatory manner against rivals in the long-distance market. In addition to divestiture, the judgment required that the regional Bell operating companies not to enter apparatus manufacture and long-distance network operation.

integrated dominant firm.[15] An important reason for this decision was the desire to privatize BT rapidly, and management was strongly opposed to a breakup. However, there were some structural constraints placed on BT. It was required to keep separate accounts for network operation, apparatus supply, supply of VANS, and mobile network operation.[16] This was to try to prevent predatory cross-subsidy from monopolistic network operation to more competitive activities. Any future apparatus manufacture was required to be done in a separate subsidiary. Finally, BT was forbidden from carrying TV services on its public network, though it was permitted to own stakes in cable TV companies.

Having decided against radical structural remedies, it was necessary to determine how best to regulate the conduct of the players in the industry. Regarding *entry*, the prohibition on unrestricted resale has already been mentioned, and a government statement in 1984 gave a commitment that this would continue to hold until 1989. In November 1983, a year before privatization, the government announced its 'duopoly policy'—that for the next seven years only BT and Mercury would be licensed to operate a nation-wide network with fixed links. This duopoly policy also prevented cable TV companies from providing telecommunications services except as agents of one of the duopolists. This policy severely limited competition in the main telecommunications service for the rest of the decade. Its stated rationale was to protect the infant Mercury, and induce it to enter, and to give BT time to adjust to the prospect of further competition. (The duopoly policy, like the policy of keeping BT intact, was also in the interests of BT and its management, whose co-operation was important for achieving the government's objective of speedy privatization.) The terms on which rivals—at that time just Mercury—could interconnect with BT's local and other networks were not settled in advance of privatization, and they have been a thorny issue ever since. Mobile services had their own duopoly policy, also lasting until 1989.

As for *price* regulation, the government was anxious to avoid the perceived problems of US rate-of-return regulation in terms of cost inefficiency, regulatory burden, and vulnerability to 'capture'. The Littlechild Report (1983) recommended RPI–X price-cap regulation. The chosen basket of regulated services included switched inland calls (except from

[15] British Gas was also privatized (in 1986) as a single entity, but a very different policy of restructuring occurred in the electricity supply industry in England and Wales before privatization.

[16] The mobile sector had a novel form of structure regulation whereby mobile network operators (Cellnet and Vodafone) were prohibited from retailing air time except via subsidiaries. The result has been very vigorous competition and low profits amongst the retailers (see Geroski *et al.* 1989).

call-boxes), and exchange line rentals.[17] This price-control formula was for the five years until July 1989 and X was set at 3. Charges for international calls, leased lines, connections, VANS, and apparatus supply were not brought under regulation, and except for an undertaking that exchange line rentals would not increase by more than RPI+2, BT had wide discretion to vary relative prices within the regulated basket. In addition, BT was not permitted to discriminate in its charges for calls along similar routes. Save for a general duty on the regulator to promote the interests of consumers and producers in respect of the price, quality, and variety of services, *quality* was not explicitly regulated at the time of privatization.

These policy decisions were taken by the government and appeared in the 1984 Act, licences granted by the Secretary of State for Trade and Industry under the Act, and in Parliamentary statements such as the duopoly policy statement. The Act also established the Director General of Telecommunications, the first DGT being Professor (now Sir) Bryan Carsberg, as head of the Office for Telecommunications (OFTEL), the regulatory body for the industry. Future regulatory policy would be shaped by OFTEL as well a the DTI. The DGT is required to ensure that all reasonable demands for telecommunications services are met and that their provision can be financed, and he has other duties including the promotion of competition. Licensing powers are with the Secretary of State, though some may be delegated to the DGT or exercised subject to his advice. OFTEL monitors and enforces licence conditions, and can change them either by agreement with the licensee or by making a successful reference to the Monopolies and Mergers Commission. Thus in effect there are three regulators—the DTI, OFTEL, and the MMC—and this pattern has been adopted in other industries such as gas and electricity.[18]

The regulatory authority of OFTEL goes beyond the rather limited powers and duties in the Act because it has always the threat of a reference to the MMC to seek regulatory change. The effects of the resulting implicit regulation—almost regulation by bargaining between OFTEL and BT—will be seen in the next Section.

5. REGULATORY DEVELOPMENTS SINCE PRIVATIZATION

In the six years up to November 1990, when the duopoly policy came up for review, the DTI itself was in the background as far as regulation was

[17] Littlechild proposed that regulation apply only to local tariffs. However, he envisaged a significantly more liberal policy towards competition than the duopoly policy that the Government adopted.

[18] It reflects the institutional structure for competition policy set up by the 1973 Fair Trading Act, which involves the Office of Fair Trading, the MMC, and government ministers.

concerned, and OFTEL held centre stage. One reference was made to the MMC by OFTEL in 1989 concerning the provision of 'chatline' and message services, and the Office of Fair Trading referred BT's acquisition of Mitel to the MMC in 1985 (see below). We shall discuss regulatory developments since privatization under the following headings, which became important roughly in chronological order: interconnection, apparatus manufacture and supply, service quality, the level and structure of prices, and the duopoly review of entry conditions. In terms of the broad policy issues in Section 3 above, these five topics might respectively appear to relate most naturally to entry, structure, quality, pricing, and entry, but the interrelations between those issues will be much in evidence.

Interconnection

Because of network externalities, the effectiveness of Mercury's competitive challenge to BT, and that of any subsequent entrant, would depend on the terms of interconnection to BT's network. No one would be able to use Mercury's long-distance links without using BT's local links at each end unless Mercury itself were to build a nation-wide local network. This would be grossly inefficient and unattractive to Mercury given natural monopoly in local network operations. In effect, therefore, BT had a monopoly on a necessary input for Mercury's operation, and any chance of effective competition along long-distance routes required that the price of this input be controlled.

Unfortunately, lengthy legal disputes delayed the resolution of the BT/Mercury interconnection question, and OFTEL made its ruling in October 1985. The policy dilemma was that if BT was forced (because of constraints on the level of its rental charges, say) to cover the fixed costs of network provision and operation and public service obligations partly out of call charges (i.e. if BT has an 'access deficit'), and if Mercury had access to BT's local network at marginal usage cost, then this could over time lead to inefficient cream-skimming with the result that BT would be unable to cover these fixed costs. On the other hand, in the face of BT's overwhelming dominance, competition was bound to be very limited at least initially, and in danger of being stifled altogether.[19]

In its 1985 ruling, OFTEL set Mercury's access payments to cover the costs (including required capacity expansion and a reasonable profit) of using BT's local network, and did not require Mercury to make a contribution to BT's deficit on exchange-line rentals and public-service obliga-

[19] Note that the interconnection decision, which is hard enough anyway, is made all the more difficult by BT's vertical integration. If local and long-distance networks were separately owned, the choice of interconnection terms would not bias competition for or against any particular long-distance operator.

tions. (The exact method by which these terms were arrived at was not made public.) However, what is known as 'equal access' was not required.[20] At the time this ruling was viewed as being broadly pro-competitive. Since 1985, however, there have been complaints from Mercury concerning the scope, speed, and quality of the interconnection provided by BT. Mercury had not made very great inroads into BT's market share, and the 1991 duopoly review again brought the issue of interconnection to the centre of attention (see below).

Apparatus manufacture and supply

At the time of privatization, BT dominated the supply of most types of customer apparatus, large private automatic branch exchanges (PABXs) being the only exception, but did not itself engage in their manufacture. Concern already existed that BT's dominance in network operation would give it unfair advantages over rivals in apparatus supply, and such worries were exacerbated when BT proposed to acquire a majority stake in Mitel, the Canadian PABX manufacturer, in 1985. The bid was referred to the MMC on competition grounds.

BT and Mitel argued that the merger would lead to synergies both between manufacturing and network operation, and between manufacturing and apparatus supply. The competition policy concerns were: (i) that BT's apparatus supply arm would unfairly favour Mitel's products over other manufacturers'; and (ii) that independent apparatus suppliers, for whom Mitel had been a major source, would be discriminated against by Mitel, with a consequent reduction of competition in apparatus supply.

The MMC (1986) adopted a compromise.[21] They recommended that the merger be permitted subject to conditions limiting, *inter alia*, cross-subsidy and the purchase by BT of Mitel apparatus for use or supply in the UK before 1990. The Secretary of State allowed the merger subject to weaker conditions. It was questionable whether the conditions could both safeguard effective competition and allow the claimed synergy gains.[22] In any event, Mitel's subsequent performance was poor, and in 1990 BT announced that it wished to sell the company.

[20] 'Equal access' would mean that all BT customers could gain access to Mercury's long-distance lines merely by dialling a short code, rather than having to become full Mercury subscribers. Hull, which for historical reasons has an independent local telephone company, has equal access to both the BT and Mercury national networks, with the result that Mercury has achieved a market share there of about a half, compared with a national share of around 5%.

[21] See Gist and Meadowcroft 1986.

[22] See the dissenting view of the Commission member D. P. Thomson in MMC 1986.

Quality of service

BT's quality of service was not explicitly regulated, and it became the subject of widespread public criticism especially in 1987, when there was also an engineer's strike and a severe storm that disrupted some services.[23] BT's position was not helped by the fact that it had stopped publishing its service-quality indicators after privatization. OFTEL intervened to improve quality (and information about quality). It found that, while dimensions of quality such as repair and installation delays and the proportion of call-boxes working had not worsened as much as some claimed, BT's quality was not as good as might have been expected given technological advance. The DGT concluded that BT should resume publication of its quality of service statistics on a six monthly basis, and should face financial penalties for poor quality, as would firms in more competitive markets. The broad alternatives were between the formal incorporation of quality components into the price-control formula, and a mixture of fixed penalties and contractual liability for poor performance. The latter approach was adopted for matters such as repair and installation delays, with standard compensation terms for residential users and larger compensation to businesses depending on the damage caused. Other aspects of quality and network modernization have been encouraged by moral suasion backed up by the threat of MMC referral or harsher price reviews in the future. Quality has improved considerably in recent years.[24]

Pricing

Apart from the issue of interconnection charges discussed above, there have been several important episodes of regulatory concern about pricing—the rebalancing of local and long-distance call charges in 1985 and 1986, the price review in 1988, the controversy over the balance between exchange-line rentals and call charges in the 1990 duopoly review, and, most recently, the 1992 price review.

Table 12.3 shows price movements of BT's regulated services and connection charges since privatization. Average prices have been required to fall annually in real terms by 3 per cent until 1989, then by 4.5 per cent, by 6.25 per cent from 1991, and by 7.5 per cent from 1993–7. Within this constraint, BT was free initially to change relative prices subject to a

[23] Partly in response to that criticism, BT did not increase the prices of regulated services in 1987, though it was entitled to an average increase of 1.3% under the RPI–3 formula.

[24] For instance, OFTEL (1992*a*, Table 7) reports that the percentage of national calls that fail has fallen from 4.2% in 1987 to 0.5% in 1991 and that the percentage of residential orders completed in 8 working days has jumped from 40% to 83% in the same period.

TABLE 12.3. Changes in selected real prices (%)

	1984	1985	1986	1987	1988	1989	1990	1991*	Cumulative change
Residential line rental	+1.9	+1.4	+1.2	–4.0	–4.4	+1.6	+1.6	+1.9	+2.6
Local calls:									
Peak	+1.6	–0.5	+16.0	–4.0	–4.4	–7.7	–13.0	–2.2	–14.0
Cheap	+1.6	–0.5	–5.9	–4.0	–4.4	–4.2	+0.2	–1.1	–15.8
National 'b' calls:									
Peak	–18.2	–12.3	–18.0	–4.0	–4.4	–7.7	–18.2	–5.5	–60.8
Cheap	+1.6	–0.5	–8.5	–4.0	–4.4	–7.7	–2.5	–0.8	–23.0
Weighted average of all regulated charges	–2.9	–3.1	–2.7	–4.0	–4.4	–4.4	–4.1	–3.5	–24.5
Residential connection charges	–4.9	+5.9	+9.1	+6.0	–4.4	+1.7	+1.6	+1.9	+19.4

* Quantity discounts were introduced and international calls were regulated in 1991.

Source: Based on Table 1 in OFTEL 1992.

ceiling on the real increase in rental charges of 2 per cent per annum. Perhaps the most striking aspect of Table 12.3 is the massive drop in the price of peak-time long-distance calls relative to other services. BT chose not to increase rental charges by as much as was permitted in the three years from 1986, something which is perhaps curious given its recent insistence on being freed to increase these further, but even so these charges have not fallen in real terms despite real average charges having fallen by more than a quarter overall. Recently, BT has sharply rebalanced call charges from peak to off-peak. Some rebalancing was called for because large cross-subsidies resulted from the old pricing structure of expensive long-distance calls and cheap local calls and rentals, which technological advances such as fibre-optics were exacerbating. Moreover, BT was especially keen to rebalance quickly because it feared competition from Mercury. Since Mercury's strategy was primarily aimed at business users, who make a high proportion of peak-time long-distance calls, there was an additional incentive for BT to choose to reduce charges in this area in particular.[25]

However, rebalancing was problematic in two respects. First, it

[25] Ideally, BT might have liked to reduce its prices only on those routes which faced competition from Mercury, but provisions against overt price discrimination would prohibit such behaviour.

tended to favour large users (especially of long-distance services) over smaller users—the existing pattern of cross-subsidy was from highly-priced long-distance calls to local services. Residential customers soon discovered to their surprise that an overall constraint of RPI–3 was entirely consistent with their bills rising in real terms. Second, BT's rebalancing involved price cuts in the areas where competition was stronger and increases where monopoly existed. If pushed too far, so-called 'rebalancing' could make a mockery of liberalization. Again, OFTEL investigated. It stated that rebalancing up to 1986 was justified by relative costs, but that there was no need for further rebalancing between local and long-distance call charges, and since then there has been no more of great significance.

The 1988 price review (OFTEL 1988) determined the regime of price control for the period from July 1989 until July 1993. The main conclusions, which were agreed with BT thus avoiding an MMC reference, were:

- a tightening of X in the main cap from 3 to 4.5, with BT not to raise its regulated prices before August 1989;
- an increase in the scope of control to include connection charges and operator-assisted calls;
- continuation and formalization of the RPI+2 cap on residential rental charges, and its extension to include connection charges;
- a requirement that BT introduce a Low User scheme; and
- a four-year duration of the new regime.

Additionally, prices for BT's previously unregulated domestic leased circuits were brought under a separate cap of RPI–7.

The Low User Scheme involved giving customers the option of cheaper rental charges together with 30 units of free calls, with calls in excess of the 30-unit limit being charged at a more expensive rate. The scheme encourages network membership, and so has advantages on network externality grounds, in a way that is targeted on users who might otherwise not join. It also promotes social objectives.

BT's rate of return in current-cost terms, which is not in the public domain, was a key determinant of the tightening of X. The DGT has since stated that X was set 'at a level which gives BT an expectation of covering the cost of capital employed for the services under control, and takes account of the risk for BT while providing demanding targets for improvements in customer service and increased efficiency'.[26] The role of rate-of-return considerations in RPI–X regulation is discussed in Chapter 15 in this volume by Rees and Vickers.

The duopoly review, though primarily concerned with liberalization, contained important proposals about pricing, and it is convenient to

[26] See BT Share Prospectus, Nov. 1991, 26.

describe these now.[27] First, the White Paper (DTI 1991) announced agreement between the DGT and BT that *X* in the main cap should increase from 4.5 to 6.25 and that international services should come under control, with an immediate 10 per cent reduction in international call charges (to be counted towards the overall RPI–6.25 reduction).[28] In addition, international private circuits were brought under the RPI–7 cap on domestic private circuits. As a result of these changes, regulated services now account for about 70 per cent of BT's turnover, compared with 50 per cent in 1989.[29] Second, the DGT indicated willingness to accept greater tariff flexibility subject to conditions. Thus BT is now able to offer optional schemes involving discounts to large users, i.e. low call charges combined with a high rental charge, provided that they are reasonable in relation to costs and not unduly discriminatory.[30] The effect of offering these quantity discounts will need to be monitored since they could otherwise provide BT with a means of selectively price-cutting in the market for large users, where its main competitive threat exists. Third, on rebalancing, the DGT decided against relaxing the RPI+2 cap on exchange line rentals and connection charges for residential and single-line business users, but agreed to an increase to RPI+5 for multi-line businesses. In addition, a new cap on the median customer's telephone bill of RPI–7 was introduced. Being thus constrained in rebalancing between call and rental charges, BT argued that liberalization without a requirement on competitors to make adequate payments towards its access deficit would lead to unfair and inefficient cream-skimming. We shall discuss this issue, which is the crux of recent disputes between BT and OFTEL, in the next subsection.

The 1992 price review (OFTEL 1992*b*) determined the regime of price control for the period from July 1993 until July 1997. Its main conclusions, which were again agreed with BT thus avoiding an MMC reference, were:

- a tightening of X in the main cap from 6.25 to 7.5;

[27] Needless to say, policies towards pricing and entry are intimately related, as the discussion of interconnection has already illustrated.

[28] The cost of providing international services is falling relatively quickly, and the figure of 6.25 was derived by keeping constant the estimated stream of profits under the RPI–4.5 regime after including international services.

[29] OFTEL (1992*a*, 9).

[30] BT has announced that from Sept. 1991 anyone spending more than £117.50 per quarter will receive a discount of up to 9% on their bill. In addition, for a fixed monthly fee users may opt for lower call charges, i.e. BT will be offering optional two-part tariffs. See Willig (1978) for the case that such schemes can benefit both the firm and all users under certain conditions. They enable large users to make a larger contribution to fixed costs at the same time as making them better off because of the lower marginal price. Other users could then benefit by lower fixed charges. However, if the firm faces competition—as BT does to some extent—quantity discount schemes can have undesirable anti-competitive consequences.

- a reduction in the maximum connection charge from £152.75 to £99 and a cap on future increases on this charge of RPI rather than RPI+2;
- a continuation of the RPI+2 cap on domestic and single-line business exchange line rentals;
- a stipulation that no individual prices (other than the above exchange-line rentals) increase by more than RPI in any year;
- any quantity discounts offered by BT will not count when assessing BT's compliance with the RPI–7.5 price cap (i.e. such discounts will fall 'outside the basket');
- BT's Low User Scheme should be strengthened; and
- investment targets, including digital services reaching 99 per cent of the population, should be attained by the end of the price control period.

Thus, this new regime constitutes a further strengthening of regulation compared to the result of the 1988 review.

The duopoly review of entry conditions[31]

Some measures of liberalization occurred in the year or so before the review of the fixed-link duopoly policy. The government's commitment not to allow simple resale expired in 1989, and some restrictions on the use of private networks were removed. Domestic, but not international, simple resale was permitted for private networks, and restrictions on connecting private networks were lifted. The duopoly policy in the area of mobile communications also expired in 1989. In that year, following the advice of OFTEL, the government licensed Telepoint and Personal Communications Network (PCN) operators to compete with Cellnet and Vodafone.[32]

The main duopoly review began in November 1990, when the government's commitment not to license fixed-link network operators to compete with BT and Mercury expired. The result was the White Paper, *Competition and Choice: Telecommunications Policy for the 1990s* (DTI 1991). Its central conclusion was that the duopoly policy should be ended, and that any application for a new licence to offer telecommunications services should be considered on its merits, although the duopoly policy in respect of international operators will be retained in the 'short term'. In

[31] For an analysis of policy and policy options towards entry in the UK telecommunications industry, see Beesley and Laidlaw 1989.

[32] Telepoint is a semi-mobile technology whereby users can make but not receive calls provided that they are within range of a suitable base-station. To date it has not been commercially successful, and all four of the original licensees have now ceased to offer the service. PCNs use a more sophisticated version of the traditional cellular technology with smaller cells, higher frequencies, and the ability to carry digital signals. They are not expected to come into operation until 1993.

addition, the review concluded that cable-TV companies should now be allowed to offer telecommunications services in their own right, not just with BT or Mercury, but that national public telecommunications operators should not carry entertainment services for a decade, though they can compete as before for local cable franchises through subsidiaries. In addition, mobile operators were permitted to provide fixed-link services, and the use of the assets of public-sector utilities such as British Rail for telecommunications was encouraged.

The most controversial issue arising from the duopoly review has been the question of interconnection of the potential new entrants to BT's network, and its relation to BT's tariff structure. BT claims that it incurs a large loss in providing network access—connections and line rentals—to consumers. (The breakdown of BT's financial performance reported above supports this claim, but it should be noted that any such breakdown may be sensitive to accounting and cost-allocation methods.) If this is a real problem, in the sense that a continuation of this policy would make BT unprofitable, then there are several alternative remedies,[33] including:

1. setting interconnection charges above marginal cost in order to finance the access deficit;
2. requiring rivals to make a fixed payment towards BT's access deficit;
3. financing unprofitable service obligations (including the deficit) by direct public subsidy;
4. placing public service obligations (e.g. a requirement to serve all reasonable demand) on rivals;
5. abandoning the policy-induced cross-subsidy by allowing BT to have higher line rental charges to remove the access deficit.

Moreover, it is not just a matter of access *pricing*: the extent and quality of interconnection are important too, and it has been argued that there was insufficient attention paid to this area in the original interconnection ruling in 1985. For instance, the ease with which a user can connect with a rival company may be vital. If, say, equal access was introduced then much of BT's incumbent advantage in the long-distance market might be removed.

On Option 5 the DGT decided against allowing a relaxation of the RPI+2 constraint on rental charges and this policy has been continued in the new price regime which lasts until 1997. In the White Paper the DGT acknowledged BT's concerns and proposed (para. 7.22) that 'BT should receive a contribution to its deficit on exchange lines through the interconnection agreement' with rival operators, i.e. that option 1. or 2.

[33] See pages 70–2 of the DGT's Statement in DTI (1991).

should be used. The DGT also said that equal access should be introduced as soon as possible (para. 7.12).

In the 1985 interconnect agreement Mercury did not pay an access deficit contribution, but in the White Paper the DGT suggested that Mercury should pay a contribution for increases in its business (but that it could receive a discount because of its public-service obligations) and that new entrants should pay from the start.[34] However, after vigorous protests from Mercury and nascent telecommunications operators, and the possibility that further entry simply would not occur under these terms, the DGT drew back from the idea of an unqualified access deficit contribution, and proposed that, until BT's market share had fallen below 85 per cent, the access deficit charge could be waived so that entrants would be required only to contribute towards BT's cost of carrying their calls.[35] In effect, the DGT took the view that the access deficit poses no serious problem to BT's profitability until competition becomes sufficiently strong. He was also influenced by the incumbent advantages that BT enjoys over entrants, notably those arising from the inability of customers to keep their phone number if they switch to a competitor, and scale-economy effects.

This outcome is in our opinion a reasonable compromise. In simplified form, and assuming that there is indeed a significant access deficit, the dilemma is essentially as follows. Regulatory policies are such that the incumbent makes a loss (the access deficit) in a more or less captive market (the provision of local telephone services). There is the prospect of more competition in the market for long-distance services. If the telecommunications industry were contestable, with the incumbent firm vulnerable to hit-and-run entry, then there would be the immediate problem that the incumbent could no longer finance the access deficit by super-normal profits on calls: another means of finance would have to be found. Higher access charges (option 5. above) is a natural answer, except that factors such as network externalities might make it desirable to have *some* degree of access deficit. That being so, and if a public subsidy is ruled out, then an implicit cross-subsidy from long-distance charges is the only solution. A guiding principle for such a cross-subsidy is that competitive distortions in the market for long-distance services should be minimized.

In fact, of course, the industry does not remotely resemble a contestable market, and the 'cream-skimming' problem is not an immediate one. On the contrary, as Mercury's own experience indicates, BT's domi-

[34] See DTI 1991, 73 for the DGT's remarks on the 'danger that the assistance of new entrants can be carried too far'.

[35] The definition of the 'market' has so far remained quite vague. It could mean the entire nation-wide long-distance market, as competitors would like, or something much narrower, as BT would like.

nance is not in jeopardy in the short term, and it is bolstered by substantial incumbent advantages. We conclude that there is no compelling case for requiring rivals to make an access deficit contribution in the short term, and that BT's apparent general level of profitability does not suggest any urgent need to relax the price controls that it faces. In the longer term, however, and especially if effective competition does indeed develop, then the access deficit should be diminished and/or financed differently.

ASSESSMENT AND CONCLUSIONS

Before the 1981 British Telecommunications Act, BT, which was still part of the Post Office, had a more or less complete monopoly of all aspects of network operation, apparatus supply, and supply of services over the network. In the areas of apparatus supply and VANS this picture has changed dramatically over the past decade. The new mobile services have also benefited from vigorous competition. In the primary business of fixed-link voice telephony, however, BT's dominance remains firmly established. This mixed picture is partly due to the fact that economic characteristics vary across sectors, for example the degree of natural monopoly, but is also related to differing policy approaches.

The 1981 Act began partial liberalization of the industry. Shortly afterwards the government decided to privatize BT, and major policy decisions had to be taken concerning structure, entry conditions, pricing, and quality and investment. The main structural decision was to privatize BT intact, rather than breaking it up vertically and regionally along the lines of AT&T. While this avoided delay in privatization and might have preserved any economies of scope in the supply of various services, it has made effective regulation and competition more problematic subsequently. Although the forced restructuring of private firms is not without precedent, as the cases of AT&T and the British beer industry illustrate, it is unlikely that BT will be broken up, at least not by a Conservative government. The time for restructuring was before privatization, as occurred in the electricity-supply industry. After privatization, issues of breach of faith with shareholders and policy credibility more generally make restructuring more difficult, though other political parties may be less influenced by these considerations. A structural measure short of divestiture would be to require BT to place its local network operations and/or its apparatus-supply business in separate subsidiaries, thus facilitating better information flows and a stronger check against cross-subsidy.[36] Government policy has, however, been to

[36] Such a step was mooted by the DGT during the duopoly review. The Office of Fair Trading (OFT 1991) has proposed a similar policy for British Gas.

rely on tighter regulation of conduct rather than any restructuring of BT.

The BT/Mercury duopoly policy announced in 1983 was the key decision on entry conditions. Its stated rationale was to induce Mercury to enter, and to give both firms time to adjust to the more competitive environment envisaged for the future. As with policy on structure, pressure from BT management and the urge to privatize speedily were also important political factors. In our view the duopoly policy has been detrimental to development of competition, and its main beneficiary has been BT itself. OFTEL made the important 1985 ruling on the terms of interconnection between the BT and Mercury networks, and it has monitored competition in areas such as apparatus supply and mobile networks. At the end of the 1980s, as previous commitments to restrict competition expired, further liberalization occurred in areas such as mobile services, private networks and resale. However, no major review of entry conditions in fixed-link telephony could occur until the seven year duopoly policy expired at the end of 1990. The relatively pro-competitive thrust of future policy that was decided in the duopoly review is a welcome development that stands in contrast to the decisions that were taken at the time of BT's privatization. The ensuing controversy over access terms and price rebalancing illustrates the point that regulation is often needed as a complement, rather than a substitute, to competition.

The centrepiece of conduct regulation since privatization has been the control of pricing. Contrary to original hopes for 'regulation with a light hand', it has proved necessary to strengthen it in several respects over time. The level of X has been tightened successively from 3 to 7.5 and the scope of regulation has increased so that 70 per cent, rather than about half, of BT's business is subject to price control. OFTEL has been proactive in this tightening of regulation, albeit within the constraints set by the earlier decisions made by government. Price rebalancing and quality levels were regulated informally before the 1988 price review. The duopoly review further tightened and broadened price control, and virtually all aspects of network operation are now regulated. After a difficult start, improvements in quality have been one of the successes of implicit regulation.

Against the background of a history of vertically integrated nationwide monopoly, modest progress towards a more competitive and better regulated telecommunications industry in Britain was made during the 1980s. In most respects, however, it was a decade of lost opportunities. The decision not to restructure BT, and especially the deliberate restrictions on competition contained in the duopoly policy, acted to preserve the essentially monopolistic character of the old system in the basic area of network operation. Neither did that policy enhance the prospects of competition in the longer term. A new and more liberal policy on competition in telecommunications is now in place. Pro-competitive regulatory policy will be needed to see it through.

References

Baumol, W. J., Panzar, J. and Willig, R. D. (1982), *Contestable Markets and the Theory of Industry Structure*, New York: Harcourt Brace Jovanovich.

Beesley, M. E. (1981), *Liberalization of the Use of the British Telecommunications Network*, London: Department of Trade and Industry.

Beesley, M. E. and Laidlaw, B. (1989), *The Future of Telecommunications*, London: Institute of Economic Affairs.

British Telecom, *Annual Reports*.

Department of Industry (1982), *The Future of Telecommunications in Britain*, Cm 8610, London: HMSO.

Department of Trade and Industry (1990), *Competition and Choice: Telecommunications Policy for the 1990s. A Consultative Document*, Cm 1303, London: HMSO.

—— (1991), *Competition and Choice: Telecommunications Policy for the 1990s*. Cm 1461, London: HMSO.

Evans, D. S. and Heckman, J. J. (1983), 'Multiproduct cost function estimates and natural monopoly tests for the Bell System'. In D. S. Evans (ed.), *Breaking up Bell*, Amsterdam: North-Holland.

Geroski, P., Thompson, D., and Toker, S. (1989), 'Vertical separation and price discrimination: Cellular phones in the UK', *Fiscal Studies*, 10/4: 83–103.

Gist, P. and Meadowcroft, S. A. (1986), 'Regulating for competition: The newly liberalized market for Private Branch Exchanges', *Fiscal Studies*, 7/3: 41–66.

Hunt, L. C. and Lynk, E. L. (1991), 'Industrial structure in US telecommunications: Some empirical evidence', *Applied Economics*, 23: 1655–64.

Littlechild, S. (1983), *Regulation of British Telecommunications' Profitability*, London: HMSO.

Mankiw, N. G. and Whinston, M. D. (1986), 'Free entry and social inefficiency', *RAND Journal of Economics*, 17: 48–58.

Monopolies and Mergers Commission (1986), *British Telecommunications PLC and Mitel Corporation: A Report on the Proposed Merger*, Cm 9715, London: HMSO.

Office of Fair Trading (1991), *The Gas Review*, London: OFT.

OFTEL (1988), *The Control of British Telecom's Prices*, London: OFTEL.

—— (1992a), *The Regulation of BT's Prices*, London: OFTEL.

—— (1992b), *Future controls on British Telecom's Prices*, London: OFTEL.

—— *Annual Reports*, London: HMSO.

Röller, L.-H. (1990), 'Proper quadratic cost functions with an application to the Bell System', *Review of Economics and Statistics*, 72: 202–10.

Sharkey, W. W. (1982), *The Theory of Natural Monopoly*, Cambridge: Cambridge University Press.

Shin, R. T. and Ying, J. S. (1992), 'Unnatural monopolies in local telephone', *Rand Journal of Economics*, 23: 171–83.

Tirole, J. (1988), *The Theory of Industrial Organization*, Cambridge, Mass.: MIT Press.

Vickers, J. S. and Yarrow, G. K. (1988), *Privatization: An Economic Analysis*. Cambridge, Mass.: MIT Press.

Willig, R. D. (1978), 'Pareto-superior nonlinear outlay schedules', *Bell Journal of Economics*, 9: 56–69.

13

The Development of Telecommunications Policy in the UK, 1981–1991

MICHAEL BEESLEY* AND BRUCE LAIDLAW†

1. INTRODUCTION

In this paper, we seek to show how the telecommunications market in the United Kingdom has been progressively opened over the ten years from 1981. By analysing the development of the regulatory framework over a decade we hope, first, to show that further substantial modification is still required and, more important, to indicate what kind of reforms are needed. During this period, a principal aim of the government's policy has been to promote effective competition in the provision of telecommunication services. We focus on competition in voice telephony, which accounts for over 80 per cent of the market, measured by revenues.

One innovation in applying policy over this period has been to set up a sector-specific regulatory body, OFTEL, with two main tasks:

- to regulate British Telecom's prices and profits; and
- to manage the development of competition.

To understand UK policy now, one must trace its formative influences at least from 1981, when the first substantial change occurred, the separation of the nationalized industry, BT, from the rest of postal services. External influences on UK policy have been very muted. At the start of the decade, US developments indicated what was possible but held few specific lessons. Subsequently, the EC developed and began to apply its own telecommunications policy; this drew from rather than influenced the British experience.

* Professor of Economics at the London Business School.
† Managing Director of BMP International, a telecommunications consultancy.

2. STATE OF THE TELECOMMUNICATIONS MARKET IN 1981

The opening of the telecommunications market was a response to the condition of the industry in the UK at the end of the 1970s. Three aspects in particular were the focus of concern:

1. the poor quality of the telephone service;
2. delays in the modernization of the national network;
3. the difficulty customers had in obtaining the most recent types of equipment.

We describe each of these briefly.

Poor service

Although the technical performance of the national telephone network had steadily improved in the years up to 1981, the volume of complaints from users about the service provided continued to rise. The explanation probably lies in the financial and institutional constraints on the adjustment of supply to increasing demand. Telecommunications was subject to Treasury rules on borrowing to finance investment. The severity of this constraint varied from year to year, with the overall effect of reducing the rate of investment.

As an institution, moreover, BT inherited from the Telecommunications Business of the Post Office deficient marketing and customer relations. The deficiency went beyond the arrogance towards customers to be expected of an assured monopoly. The organization was production-orientated and focused on the universal availability of a standard and basic service. Demand for non-standard services or equipment, even for items as simple as a telephone-answering machine, was neglected or suppressed.

System X

Up to 1981, the Telecommunications Business of the Post Office and the main British manufacturers co-ordinated the development and supply of equipment. The Post Office was the dominant partner in the cartel; it undertook or funded most of the development work, set the technical specifications and, most important, placed the orders that determined which products were made. Apart from the relatively small-scale production of handsets, the Post Office was not permitted to manufacture itself. The Post Office naturally gave priority to its own plans; its specifications and orders took little account of implications for exports. This organization had not produced a successful industrial policy; the export performance of the manufacturing industry had declined steadily for many years.

The development of digital switching technology crystallized several of the difficulties inherent in the relationship with the manufacturing sector. System X, the British design of digital telephone exchange sponsored by the Post Office, was heralded in the mid-1970s as a project of national importance that would produce a spectacular improvement in the performance of the national network and in the range of services it could provide to customers. However, installation of the new technology in the national telephone network was delayed for several years, partly because of delays in development and partly because of the financial and institutional constraints already referred to. In the meantime (indeed, up till 1987), BT invested heavily in an electronic, but non-digital exchange design, TXE4. This had a better performance and much lower operating costs than earlier designs, but could not be sold overseas.

In the event, System X has turned out to be a standard product, not noticeably better or worse than a dozen other designs produced overseas. The anticipated gains from digitalization on quality of service and overall productivity were, at best, postponed and have not been as dramatic as hoped for. The manufacturing cartel was reorganized after the withdrawal of BT's sponsorship in 1981–2 and the industry further concentrated. BT bought a second exchange design from overseas, subject only to requiring assembly in the UK. By so doing, BT secured much lower prices for its procurement of digital exchanges. For the manufacturers, therefore, the domestic market remains protected to some degree but has probably ceased to be significantly more profitable than exports.

Equipment standards

The clearest indication of poor service was the difficulty many customers found in obtaining permission to use new types of equipment, such as answering machines. As the variety of equipment available on the world market increased, and both manufacturers and retailers joined the criticism of BT's policies, it quickly became clear that piecemeal opening of the UK market would not suffice. A formal arrangement based on national technical standards was considered necessary.

The early involvement with the standards issue and the experience with System X were the main factors that lead to a shift of policy priority from sponsoring manufacturing to promoting new services in the UK telecommunications industry. For the government, promoting telecommunication services had many attractions:

- It enabled the sector to be linked to the computer revolution, even though the application of the same technical developments in telecommunications was bogged down.

- It enabled support to be given to small and new firms as well as the traditional recipients of sponsorship.
- Exhortation, awareness programmes, and pilot projects were relatively cheap forms of government activity.

This shift in policy led naturally to the narrowing in the scope of BT's monopoly and an espousal of liberalization.[1]

3. THE 1981 ACT

The primary purpose of the British Telecommunications Act 1981 was to complete the separation of telecommunications from postal services. BT came into existence as a public corporation independent of the Post Office in October 1981. It preserved in formal terms BT's 'exclusive privilege' as a provider of public telecommunication services and hence with the power to license others. Nevertheless, the government, acting through the Secretary of State for Industry (now Trade and Industry), was empowered to license competitive network operators and service providers. The Act also established the authority of the Secretary of State to approve the supply of apparatus. The Secretary of State was to be advised by the British Approvals Board for Telecommunications (BABT), whose committees provided an avenue for British manufacturers to influence the approvals process.

The regulatory framework was hybrid, therefore, with the government and BT having overlapping powers. While it was safe to assume that BT would not encourage competitive entry, it was not at first clear what use the Secretary of State might make of his licensing powers. The policy debate had crystallized around three distinct sectors:

1. Equipment owned and operated by users (subscribers' apparatus).
2. Value added network services (VANS).
3. Basic network services, both voice and data.

Value-added network services were defined as comprising the use of computer equipment to enhance messages in the course of transmission. It was thought that this characteristic would permit the liberalization of VANS to proceed without necessarily disturbing the monopoly of basic network services.

Network competition

What use could be made of the public telephone network first arose as a practical policy question in 1980, as the Bill was going through the

[1] The Carter Report (*Report of the Post Office Review Committee*, Cmnd 6850, July 1977) had first suggested the liberalization of equipment supply as part of a strategy to promote manufacturing but its recommendations had been largely ignored.

Commons. The issue was the terms on which commercial value-added services would be permitted to be provided by firms other than BT itself. The implicit assumption was that a technical distinction could be drawn between value-added services and voice telephony and used as the basis for regulation. The Secretary of State for Industry, Sir Keith Joseph, asked Professor Michael Beesley[2] to hold a public enquiry into the matter. Having his doubts about this distinction, he asked for his terms of reference to be widened to include consideration of the effects of any third party use of public networks, that is, of resale as a principle.

The Beesley Report's main findings were that a sustainable regulatory distinction between value-added services and telephone calls could not be found. As the USA in particular had shown, commercial developments in the UK could and should take place in the context of growing network competition. As part of that, there should be no restriction on the resale of capacity on BT's network; the effect on BT's net revenues would not be severe, largely because of the probability of rebalancing tariffs to reduce the profitability of long-distance services. Regulation should concentrate on ensuring that BT's conduct, in pricing as in other matters, did not discriminate against newcomers.

The government appeared to be surprised by the recommendations of the Beesley Report, which amounted to freedom to enter the voice-telephony markets on all fronts. Although the 1981 legislation (the Bill became an Act in July) gave the government the powers to follow the Beesley line, it was not prepared to go that far. The choice for network competition was seen as being between freeing resale and allowing entry by a new national network operator; the government opted for the latter. The decisive consideration was the expected effect of resale on the structure of the voice-telephony tariff. A rapid fall in long-distance charges offset by rising rental and local-call charges would benefit most business users, but adversely affect the average residential user. In July 1981, Mr Kenneth Baker, announcing the decision, welcomed the 'tone' of the Beesley Report but in effect deferred resale, while welcoming an initiative by Cable & Wireless, BP, and Barclays Merchant Bank to lay an optical fibre network along the railway lines linking major business centres in England (the Mercury Project).

BT as a nationalized industry

For the next year, policy concentrated on defining more precisely the scope of competition permitted on BT's network. BT's line of argument against permitting voice resale was in effect condoned. This argument had less to do with the absolute effect on its profits than with the effect

[2] M. E. Beesley (1981), *Liberalisation of the Use of British Telecommunications' Network*, London: HMSO.

on the pricing structure for voice telephony. It was assumed that competition would focus on long-distance services which were highly profitable (international services were even more profitable, but it was assumed that entry at that level was not practically possible). If BT reduced long-distance charges in response to entry, local charges and rental charges would rise. This 'tariff rebalancing' would undo the traditional subsidy of residential telephone services which was considered to be essential to the achievement of universal service.

Here, however, events conspired to undermine BT's defence of its monopoly. In October 1981, BT had managed to get permission for a significant increase in prices, above the rate of inflation. It had done so mainly because the government was determined to hold down public-sector borrowing, while acknowledging that BT had to be allowed to invest in network modernization. Higher prices would enable this investment to be largely self-financed; only £200 million needed to be borrowed (termed the external financing limit or EFL) in 1981–2 to meet BT's planned investments. By April 1982, it was clear that BT's management had failed to meet its targets for investment; the shortfall in spending was greater than the EFL agreed by the Treasury and cast doubt on the scale of the price increase agreed by the Department of Industry the previous autumn.

Thus, a direct consequence of BT's failure to spend the money was that it was obliged to reduce its prices immediately. In May 1982, BT introduced 50 per cent reductions in charges on 'low-cost' trunk routes. These were effectively the routes considered vulnerable to entry, whether by resellers or by Mercury. So, in the event, tariff rebalancing was begun without a storm of complaint from consumers. The same concerns, the funding of investment in network modernization and tariff rebalancing, accounted for the government's reluctance to permit resale. Resellers could probably have begun service faster than Mercury, inducing further tariff rebalancing than was achieved in 1982. If so, BT would have had to borrow more to maintain its rate of investment and consumer resistance to price changes might have grown.

In short, the policy debate about network competition and its implications for BT as a nationalized industry was neither intense nor long-lasting. The practical question was who would enter, what precisely would they do, and on what terms. The Mercury Project was the only proposition in front of ministers in 1981; naturally, it was accepted in principle, even though at this point it was unclear how important Mercury would become. The statement by Mr Kenneth Baker in July 1981 was encouraging but vague.

BT's failure to invest sums so painfully extracted from government had even more drastic implications. Throughout 1981, the government had sought a way out of the financing dilemma by permitting BT to raise funds in the City rather than borrowing from the government. The idea was somehow to divorce the government from underwriting the risks of investing in operations which it owned and controlled. Inevitably, the attempts failed. The financial instrument devised in 1981, termed the 'Buzby Bond' after a cartoon character featured in BT's advertisements of the time, was ultimately abandoned and privatization came into focus as a more fundamentally sound option for attracting private-sector funds into the expansion of BT's network.

4. PRIVATIZATION

Privatization of the large nationalized industries had not been part of the governing Conservative Party's manifesto at the last election in 1979. Rather, it now developed, with BT as the first example, as a result of the perceived failure of the government's first attempts to reshape and galvanize the nationalized industries. Part of these attempts was the Competition Act, 1980, Section 11 of which created powers for the detailed investigation of the efficiency of nationalized industries. Such investigations could not stray into questions of pricing and finance, which were effectively reserved to the Treasury. In effect, therefore, the 1980 vision of influencing nationalized industry conduct was to be strongly distinguished from that of industry in general. Privatization marked a sharp decline in the faith accorded that policy.

The decision to privatize BT had far-reaching consequences both for attitudes to network competition and for the regulatory framework for the sector. However, these aspects were not given much consideration at the time the decision was taken. As the announcement to Parliament on 19 July 1982 by the Secretary of State, Mr Patrick Jenkin, made clear, the decision to privatize was intended to resolve the problem of how to reconcile BT's investment programme with the government's tight limits on borrowing. He said, 'Unless something is done radically to change the capital structure and ownership of BT and to provide a direct spur to efficiency, higher investment could mean still higher charges for the customer.'

As has been noted, the price increases already granted had been more than sufficient to meet the level of investment achieved in the 1981–2 financial year. The privatization decision was not, therefore, simply a response to a short-term crisis. Rather it was the culmination of a two-year debate over the financing of investment. BT's modernization programme was expected to take at least ten years and cost some £20 billion.

The government accepted the rather exaggerated views of the strategic national importance of network modernization then prevalent.

Simply refusing BT permission to increase its investment programme (as had been done in the past) was therefore not an option. Increasing prices would not only be unpopular with customers, but inconsistent with counter-inflation policy and with promoting network competition.

A further factor in the decision, implicit in Mr Jenkin's remarks, was dissatisfaction with the quality of BT's management. Failing to spend an agreed annual budget is a cardinal sin in the public sector. Beyond that, BT appeared to be dithering over technical choices and failing to improve productivity as fast as was expected. The government were convinced that a transfer of ownership to the private sector would shake up internal decision-making and improve management quality in BT.

Privatization on such a scale was understood to require a long gestation period and anyway could not be successful if there was a risk of the government changing, so ministers could safely undertake not to execute their decision until after the next general election. Even so, parliamentary time for the enabling legislation was found in the 1982/3 session. The 1983 election was called a matter of weeks before the legislation would have been ready for Royal Assent; the Bill was reintroduced in the autumn of 1983 and finally became the Telecommunications Act in July 1984.

Divestiture

Although regulatory reform was not central to the privatization policy, it quickly became the focus of debate. A logical approach to the question of how to restrain the exercise of BT's monopoly power would have been to borrow from contemporary US developments; AT&T was divested of its local network operations as a result of the 1982 Modified Final Judgment, settling an anti-trust case brought by the Department of Justice. The issue was debated in relation to BT but BT's management was strongly opposed. Merchant bank advice was that trading records for component parts of BT would need to be established. As the internal accounts would have taken time to be developed, divestiture would therefore have meant postponing privatization for years, a delay ministers were unwilling to contemplate.

The issue of the divestiture is still implicit in policy debates. In the USA, it enabled competition in long-distance services to develop rapidly and produced seven financially strong regional companies. Several of these (termed 'Baby Bells' or 'RBOCs'[3]) have subsequently invested in the UK and other markets around the world. They are, however, increasingly irked at their exclusion from competitive voice-telephony markets in the USA, generating a long series of regulatory disputes for the US

[3] Regional Bell Operating Companies: the acronym is pronounced 'arbok'.

authorities. It seems inevitable that, in due course, some or all of the restrictions on the RBOCs will be removed. That is, divestiture appears to be a feasible long-term method of generating network competition as well as a short-term way of restraining the abuse of monopoly. Since privatization, BT has been careful not to organize its operations on a geographical basis, so that, although its internal accounting and management systems have greatly improved, divestiture would still be difficult in practice.

Mercury

Privatization also brought conflicting policy requirements, having very important implications for the development of competition in telecoms: success in the flotation of BT, in the sense of raising cash for the Treasury, and a credible defence against accusations of unleashing a powerful private monopoly. At first, concern was expressed that the sale of shares was on so great a scale that it would be difficult to obtain good value for BT's assets. It was realized, quite late in the day, that a second political objective could be secured by pricing the issue so as to attract a large number of private shareholders. Giving millions of BT's customers a stake in the company would then to a degree forestall criticism of rising profits. On competition, the way to stiffen the challenge to BT without putting BT's profitability at risk was to upgrade the existing network competitor.

The licence granted to Cable & Wireless in February 1982 to operate the Mercury network required it to build a digital network connecting thirty specified cities. Mercury's activities in voice telephony was limited in the licence to 3 per cent of BT's revenues. All of this was intended to reassure BT's management and customers that network competition would not endanger the modernization programme or mean higher prices, but was merely consistent with Mercury's business plans at that time. However, Mercury was not allowed to offer international services. This was a significant restriction but again, it had been dictated by concern not to reduce BT's ability to finance network modernization.

Henceforward, Mercury would not be merely a limited domestic rival to BT for business customers but a fully-fledged public service provider. Mercury's parents, particularly Cable & Wireless, would need to be persuaded to commit to a much larger investment. In return for this commitment, assurance was sought from ministers that other entrants would not be licensed. At this stage, Mercury was also against permitting resale. Out of the extended negotiation came the Fixed Links Duopoly policy, finally agreed between the government, BT, and Mercury in November 1983. Mr Baker's statement describing how BT and Mercury would operate and saying that there would be no further entry into public-network operation, at least until November 1990, settled the main lines of telecom policy until the Duopoly Review.

Cable television

The Fixed Links Duopoly cut across the government's previous promotion of cable-television networks as providing the basis for advanced telecommunication services at local level as well as delivering TV programmes to homes. Under the new policy, cable-TV networks were licensed as local telecommunication networks but were not allowed to connect to each other and were required to offer voice-telephony services in conjunction with BT or Mercury, effectively removing their competitive potential. The national total of telephone lines installed by the cable companies had at April 1992 barely reached 25,000.

Mobile radio

The licensing of cellular and other mobile radio services was exempt from the restrictions of the Duopoly policy. At this point, the potential of radio telephony to offer a competitive telephone service was considered no more than a remote possibility for the future. No provision was made in licensing the cellular networks to cover this possibility. In the event, cellular radio became a spectacular commercial success without having any wider implications for sector policy. Other mobile services to be licensed during the Duopoly, such as Band III and Telepoint,[4] have not repeated that success.

5. OFTEL

Part of the political solution to controlling private-monopoly power was to establish a separate body to take over BT's residual regulatory functions and be a quasi-independent player in the interchanges between industry and government. The Office of Fair Trading (OFT) was the model for the Office of Telecommunications (OFTEL). OFT had felt unable to take on the task of detailed sector regulation itself, but OFTEL was designed so that it could easily be merged with OFT at a future date.[5]

It was recognized that the problem of controlling single, large-firm

[4] Band III is a spectrum-efficient method of providing private mobile radio services; Telepoint is a dual service, operating at home as a digital cordless telephone and in public places as a mobile radio service.

[5] In the event, OFTEL's long-term future looks assured and its first Director General Professor Sir Bryan Carsberg has been appointed to head OFT.

power had only lately been tackled in the Competition Act 1980, which was an uncertain instrument for controlling BT. Hence BT's licence was furnished with intended guarantees of acceptable conduct. These were based on what might have arisen if BT had already been found to have acted against the public interest on a 1973 Act monopolies reference. Subsequently, these conditions were introduced into all PTO[6] licences; thereby, they became a general framework for competition in network operations rather than rules explicitly designed to constrain BT.

OFT can also evoke a general monopoly reference of BT if need be, though it is scarcely conceivable that it would not co-ordinate such action with OFTEL. The Monopolies and Mergers Commission (MMC) can enter as a referee in two ways: on appeal when changes in licence conditions are disputed between BT and OFTEL and as a consequence of a general referral on monopoly. This background is essential to an understanding of OFTEL's remit. Like OFT, OFTEL works in conjunction with the MMC and DTI; it has relatively little independent authority. Its primary tasks are to enforce the conditions in licences, to resolve commercial disputes and to advise the government. The Secretary of State retains the power to license new operators. If OFTEL is unable to resolve disputes with licensees, the issue can be referred to the MMC.

OFTEL's actual influence has exceeded its formal powers, partly because it alone among the regulatory agencies has the resources to deal with a wide range of detailed issues and partly because of the success of the first Director General of Telecommunications, Sir Bryan Carsberg, in carving out a pivotal role in policy debates.

Price control

Since 1984, the system of price control applied to BT has become widely recognized as a workable, and probably superior, alternative to US-style rate-of-return regulation. Its essence is a periodic settlement of a cap on the permitted rate of increase of prices[7] for voice-telephony services, based on a mix of financial projections and bargaining between OFTEL and BT. OFTEL must take a view on prospective profits, taking into account achievable productivity gains and the likely consequences of tariff rebalancing. The DG's duty to ensure BT's ability to finance its operations effectively sets the company's cost of capital as a lower limit to the impact that the price control could have on profits. While precise measurement of the cost of capital is difficult, in practice BT's reported profits appear to have remained well above that limit.

[6] Public-telecommunication operator is the UK term for a business licensed to run a public-telephone network.

[7] The price cap is termed RPI–*X*, indicating that controlled prices may rise by *X* per cent less than the rate of inflation as measured by the Retail Price Index.

The initial level of the price cap was set by the government taking into account the implications for the price of BT shares. In 1988, the value of *X* was determined by Professor Carsberg (the DG) projecting BT's financial performance and calculating the rate of reduction of prices that would bring profits down over four or five years to the cost of capital. If BT can do better than the DG believes, it can retain the extra profits until the next price review. The incentive to improve efficiency marks the most important difference from rate-of-return control applied year-by-year in response to applications by operators for price increases.[8]

The starting level of the price control was set at RPI–3 for five years in 1984 and tightened to RPI–4.5 in 1988 to apply for the four years from 1989. However, in 1990, the DG intervened to include international call charges in the basket of controlled prices. As it was expected that these would fall by 10 per cent a year, the control was redefined as RPI–6.25. The intervention was intended to be neutral in its effect on efficiency incentives, being a response to public concern about the high returns BT was earning on international calls (estimated by OFTEL as over 80 per cent on capital employed).

The inclusion of international call charges (and international private circuits from 1991) continued a trend to broaden the coverage of price controls to cover a higher proportion of BT's telephone services. The original control covered 55 per cent of BT's total revenues. By 1991, 73.5 per cent of total revenues and 90 per cent of telephone-service revenue were covered. The broadening scope of controls has been in response to concern that BT was increasing the profitability of unregulated services.

Additional constraints on prices are also in place, intended to curtail tariff rebalancing. At the outset, the annual rate of change of residential rental charges was limited to RPI+2; later a similar control on business rental charges was set at RPI+5. From 1989, a RPI–0 control on the median residential-consumer's bill has been applied.

Bargaining between OFTEL and BT on price controls intensified after 1988, partly as a preliminary skirmish in relation to the Duopoly Review, without leading to a breakdown. In the negotiations, the DG could threaten that he would recommend an acceleration of market entry; BT could exploit its information advantage. Both sides seem to have decided it was in their best interests to avoid a reference of the issues to the MMC.

Clearly, large-business customers have gained more than customers overall. The dictates of competitive developments, strongly focused on recruiting substantial customers, ensured that this would happen. But it is impossible to show that the price level of telephone service has fallen faster in real terms than it would have done in the absence of privatiza-

[8] See M. E. Beesley and S. C. Littlechild (1989), 'The regulation of privatised monopolies in the United Kingdom', *Rand Journal of Economics* (Autumn) for further comparisons.

tion, principally because a plausible model of the alternative pricing regime is absent. BT's management have given the impression that the financial targets implicitly given to them are demanding, while their efforts to contain costs have taken a long time to show results.

Network competition in the Duopoly era

In one sense, the period since 1984 represents a continuation of the pre-privatization policy of goading the nationalized industry to be more efficient, with different means being employed. More far reaching liberalization of network operation was put off until the outcome of the twin experiments with privatization and network competition was known.

By the start of the Duopoly era, the supply of telecommunication equipment had been liberalized and BT's operating monopoly had been moved behind the first point of connection of such equipment to the network. Having relieved BT of responsibility for shaping, or at least paying for, the UK's manufacturing strategy in telecommunications, reliance was now placed on the profit incentive within an increasingly open market. Liberalizing moves in VANS, mobile radio, etc., forced BT to concentrate more on its basic business of real-time voice telephony.

In this regard, OFTEL's first task was to ensure that Mercury could indeed survive and grow. Because any entrant required full access to customers, OFTEL's principal instrument was the interconnection agreement which it dictated in 1985. With this agreement, Mercury was enabled to invest sufficiently to meet its licence obligations. In 1987, when Mercury was able to show that the agreement did not enable it to make profits on many international calls handed over to BT for delivery overseas, OFTEL adjusted the charges to ensure that it could. With its interconnection agreement secured, Mercury was able to offer a discount of 15 to 25 per cent on calls compared to BT, depending on the precise mix of local, long-distance, and international calls made by each customer. Whether this was a sufficiently attractive saving to induce a customer to switch from BT depended on the cost and convenience of connection to Mercury. By charging more than BT for an equivalent connection, Mercury was able to focus its appeal on businesses with a high volume of telecommunication traffic. Even so, most potential customers and Mercury's own marketing staff appeared to find it difficult to evaluate whether their business would benefit from Mercury service and to solve the technical problems of connection.

Even with the protection of the Duopoly and the assistance of favourable interconnection terms, Mercury did not become the 'second national network' envisaged by the government's policy. Rather, it concentrated on serving customers in the City of London, particularly those making many international calls. At first, some 90 per cent of its business was accounted for by firms in City locations. Mercury found that, to meet the demands of its selected customer group, it had to offer good local, long-distance, and international services. It therefore built a local fibre-optic network in the City of London and five other business districts to complement the inter-city figure-of-eight optical fibre network laid along railway lines which had figured in its original proposal. Mercury also sought direct international transmission capacity, across the Atlantic in particular.

Mercury's interconnect business, that is calls conveyed for customers that remained directly connected to BT's local network, did not prosper. The number of single exchange-line customers with a 'blue button' telephone that could dial the codes to reach the Mercury network via a BT exchange-line grew very slowly; by 1991, less than 5 per cent of Mercury's revenues came from this customer group.

The only exception to the generalization that Mercury concentrated on directly connected customers in central business districts was Hull, where Kingston Communications, the independent, municipally owned, local telephone network, introduced a form of equal access[9] that enabled its customers to nominate BT or Mercury as their preferred long-distance and international operator. Under this arrangement, Mercury's share of outgoing calls from Hull quickly rose to more than 50 per cent.

As a result of these factors, although narrowly focused in terms of customers served, Mercury's network has turned out to be rather more diverse than had been anticipated. BT's initial response consisted mainly of concentrating investment on network modernization of services and areas where there appeared to be a challenge from Mercury and by a gradual rebalancing of tariffs. For example, BT decided to accelerate the conversion of its trunk network to digital working and to delay conversion of local networks. Tariff rebalancing lowered trunk tariffs and raised rental and connection charges. As it became clear that Mercury's challenge was having a significant impact on only a small percentage of BT's customers, albeit high-volume users, BT unsuccessfully sought permission to introduce volume discounts for calls.

The conclusion to be drawn from the competitive interchange between BT and Mercury during the Duopoly era is that BT was able to accommodate itself to the newcomer without difficulty. Mercury grew fast (sustaining a growth rate of about 40 per cent a year) but did not prevent the growth of BT's revenues or profits. BT was obliged to re-examine its commercial policies, but competition from Mercury has evi-

[9] Equal access is an arrangement whereby local network operators deal on equal terms with a number of competing long-distance operators. It exists in the USA, where equal access was stipulated as part of the grand settlement of industry structure known as the MFJ. In the USA, customers nominate (pre-select) a particular long-distance network that they wish to use.

dently not been the external shock that could induce BT's managers to make exceptional efforts to improve productivity. BT remains greatly overmanned by the best standards obtaining in overseas markets.[10]

International satellite services

Satellite communications have the technical characteristic of being able to bypass entirely complex public telephone networks, enabling transmissions to take place directly between users within the coverage area ('footprint') of a satellite. This characteristic permitted a gradual liberalization of satellite communications that form part of private networks and are not interconnected with public networks.

The 1983 Duopoly Policy expressly allowed for this exception. Even so, not until 1988 were licenses granted, and then only six were awarded to a diverse selection of applicants. The successful bids appeared to have been chosen on the basis that they intended to occupy non-competing niche markets within the UK (international links were prohibited). After much argument, a proposal from PanAmSat to offer a private network service by means of international satellite communications across the North Atlantic was also authorized in 1988 (PanAmSat did not require a UK licence, merely confirmation of the right to be connected to its customers by means of circuits leased from BT).

The surviving domestic satellite licensees, not presenting a challenge on voice telephony, were later given permission to operate internationally. So, during the Duopoly satellite communications were liberalized reluctantly and in a way that limited and deferred their competitive potential.

6. THE DUOPOLY REVIEW

Writing in early 1989 with the intention of opening debate about the scope for market entry when the Fixed Links Duopoly ended,[11] we set out a programme designed to address the central issue of increasing effective competition in voice telephony. It called for the following steps:

Immediately to:

1. Relax restrictions on the use of domestic bilateral private circuits.

[10] The standard measure favoured by the World Bank for comparing manning levels is the ratio of staff per thousand direct exchange-lines (DELs). The best telephone companies in the USA have reduced this ratio to about 4.6 (1990 figures); for BT, the ratio of staff per thousand DELs is about 8.9.

[11] M. E. Beesley and B. Laidlaw (1989), *The Future of Telecommunications*, London: IEA. We were afraid that the duration of the Fixed Links Duopoly would be extended by delays in decision-making; in the event, the duopoly has lasted at least eighteen months longer than originally intended.

At July 1989 to:

2. License public resale service providers.
3. Relax 200 metre rule to permit interconnection of privately constructed transmission facilities with public and other private networks within local call-charge areas.

Before April 1990 to:

4. Develop interconnection rules for public networks.
5. Accelerate implementation of new national numbering plan.

At November 1990 to:

6. Remove restrictions on provision of voice telephony by local broadband cable networks, including direct interconnection with other such networks.
7. License additional public networks.
8. Remove remaining restrictions on domestic own-account operations.

After November 1990 to:

9. Permit resale of international private circuits.

These steps would, we thought, encourage competition from large users acting on their own account, new public networks, cable networks, and resellers—in that order of relative policy significance. Our proposals on timing have proved optimistic, but all the steps were among the options considered between November 1990 and July 1991, when the Review was substantially completed.[12] Which steps have in the event been taken? What, so far as can be deduced, are the reasons for omissions or limitations? And how has competition between BT and Mercury been affected?

Private networks and resale

Steps 1, 3, and 8 were directed particularly at allowing large consumers of telephone services to develop their domestic private networks in any way they wish. In practice, such users would have to make a judicious selection among possible contracts for control and use of capacity, ranging from outright ownership and internal management to short-term leasing and devolution to network managers. The Review has produced movement on steps 1 and 3, but the most critical freedom—to mix leased and owned capacity for conveying calls in the UK on behalf of whomever wishes to pay for it—remains forbidden. Thus a potentially very effective form of resale entry is still inhibited. No explicit rationalization for this inhibition has appeared.

However, it is now possible for private network operators to make a rational choice between leasing transmission capacity from a public net-

[12] The main policy decisions were announced in the 1991 White Paper, *Competition and Choice: Telecommunications Policy for the 1990s*, Cm 1461, London: HMSO.

work or installing links for their own use. The economics of such choice have been clear for many years: own account operation pays if on a large scale and over long distances. The significance of this development is twofold. First, it provides a stronger constraint on prices of leased circuits, tending to hold them closer to costs. Second, it provides a stimulus to the relatively small number of large-scale private networks already in existence. These are almost entirely operated by current and former nationalized industries. These networks are to a large extent still dependent on microwave technologies; access to radio spectrum for this purpose has not been liberalized.

Steps 2 and 9 were directed at promoting resale entry. The July 1989 removal of restrictions on simple resale (that is, the use of leased circuits to bypass public switched-telephone networks) was foreshadowed in licences issued under the Duopoly regime; positive action to prevent it would have been required. The date passed without such action being taken. In this way, all domestic restrictions on resale were finally removed in 1989, but only a few entrants emerged in the UK, offering shared use of leased lines rather than competition with switched-voice services.

At first, potential resellers were caught by the application of apparatus approval regulations: no equipment that could operate a resale service was approved before the Duopoly Review began. Within the UK, margins for resellers have been squeezed by increases in price of leased lines (which none the less remain cheap by European standards) and local-call charges, and reductions in long-distance charges, as we anticipated in predicting little competitive effect from the 1989 liberalization. The main reason for the lack of commercial interest appears to be inaction on step 9. International restrictions on resale have largely remained in place and the strongest demand for resale came from businesses with widely dispersed international operations. A handful of American resellers have opened for business, offering cheaper international calls to North America; for most businesses, this represents too small a market to produce worthwhile savings. Regulatory authorities in other countries will not permit resale from their jurisdictions.

Steps 4 (developing interconnection rules), 6 (helping cable-based entry), 7 (licensing additional public networks), and 5 (formulating a new national numbering plan) were, we argued, necessary means to hold out prospects for profitable rival networks. We examine progress on each of these steps in turn.

Interconnection

Once the government and OFTEL had decided to encourage market entry, the question of its effect on BT's prospective profits and thus its capacity to finance its service obligations had to be dealt with. However, much to the surprise of other participants in the Review, OFTEL decided to settle this question before announcing which forms of market entry would be permitted. Its proposals could therefore only be discussed with BT and Mercury before being published with the White Paper in March 1991.

In the Review, BT's financing of its service obligations was largely identified with preserving cross-subsidies from call revenue to charges for 'access' to the network.[13] Arguments about the need to identify the specific costs of service obligations (that is, their impact on BT's net cash flow) and to consider alternative ways of funding them, which were current when the duopoly was being devised, dropped out of sight and still do not feature in OFTEL's strategy.

Early in the Review process, Mercury drew a considerable red herring across the path by advocating 'equal access', by which it appeared to mean reproducing in the rest of the country the situation in Hull, where the independent local telephone company has chosen to deal on equal terms with BT and Mercury as trunk operators while effectively excluding them from the Hull area. In the absence of divestiture by BT of its local operations, it is unrealistic to imagine equal access on Hull terms being projected nation-wide. Mercury had second thoughts once it became clear that equal access would be offered to all comers and so would remove its advantage as the main challenger to BT. The outcome of the debate was for OFTEL to propose a complex procedure for considering equal access which postponed a decision for at least two more years, during which the terms for competitive network interconnection could be sorted out.

As the Review proceeded, OFTEL at first gave great weight to BT's argument on the cross-subsidy of residential exchange lines. OFTEL responded by proposing two changes in the way interconnection charges are assessed:

- Charges for interconnected calls (the conveyance charge) to be based on BT's fully allocated costs plus a reasonable return on capital employed.
- An additional charge per call to share out the cross-subsidy among all interconnected networks (a Contribution).

BT would determine its own cost allocation, within the limits set by auditing of its accounts. The outcry by Mercury and potential entrants led OFTEL to change tack on the Contribution element and to give itself powers to check the cost allocations that underlay estimates of the cross-subsidy. There is now very little likelihood of Mercury or any entrant

[13] 'Access' is a term used to cover the installation and maintenance of a direct exchange-line.

being required to pay towards the alleged cross-subsidy, that is, to make a Contribution to BT's Access Deficit. In summary, this is because:

1. until 1997, the DG can exempt new entrants from paying such Contributions or rebate them;
2. thereafter, the DG can still rebate Contributions;
3. no Contribution payments will be required once the licence restriction on charging for residential rentals is lifted and this restriction may disappear as early as 1993.

Rebalancing and price controls

The Review also examined how BT's tariff structure had changed during the duopoly period (see Table 13.1). Broadly, the direction in which prices for voice-telephony service have moved has been determined by the initial margins between prices and costs, while the pace of rebalancing has been set by the competitive pressure from Mercury and the restraint exercised by price controls. There have been two waves of tariff rebalancing so far: the first under the RPI–3 regime showed a relatively faster rate of reduction on trunk prices, presumably in anticipation of the entry by Mercury, while the second under RPI–4.5 showed a relatively faster rate of increase in rental charges. In this second period, BT has taken full advantage of the headroom given by the RPI+2 limit on increases in residential rentals. DTI and OFTEL seem content to permit this trend to continue for some years.

The White Paper acknowledged the linkage between the pace of rebalancing and entry prospects. In particular, a faster rate of increase in

TABLE 13.1 BT's voice-telephony service: Price changes 1984–1991 (%)

	1984	1985	1986	1987	1988	1989	1990	1991
Rate of inflation	5.1	7.0	2.5	4.2	4.6	8.3	9.8	5.8
Permitted change	+2.1	+4.0	–0.5	+1.2	+1.6	+3.8	+5.3	–0.4
Actual change	+2.0	+3.7	–0.3	0	0	+3.5	+5.3	–1.0
Residential rental	+7.1	+8.5	+3.7	0	0	+10.0	+11.6	+7.8
Business rental	+6.8	+8.8	+3.9	0	0	+10.1	+11.8	+7.7
Calls:								
Local*	+6.8	+6.4	+6.4	0	0	+4.3	–4.5	+4.7
Trunk*	–10.2	–13.8	–12.0	0	0	0	–10.0	0

* Calls in standard period only; trunk calls 'b1' only.

Source: OFTEL, January 1992.

rental charges should enhance the profitability of entry at local level and diminish that of entry by trunk operators. OFTEL has frequently expressed concern that the pattern of market entry should not be distorted by incorrect price signals (meaning prices out of line with costs). In OFTEL's terms, 'inefficient entry'. This concern is largely misplaced. The distortion in BT's price structure is common to virtually all telephone companies world-wide. Since all are aware that, in the UK at least, rebalancing is expected to carry on apace, prospective entrants are most unlikely to be misled by it. In any event, in making the decision to enter companies are likely to be more concerned about how their own costs and their own perceptions of the market, differ from BT's.

Cable-based telephony

It has seemed for several years that cable-based telephony offered the best hope in the long run for effective competition with BT's local network. In turn, this is the area where competition offered the best hope of benefits to users once the restrictions of the Duopoly had ended. Cable TV interests appear to have got what they asked for out of the Duopoly Review, namely independence from Mercury, the prospect of standardized interconnection arrangements and the ability to combine operations. The question remains whether they have yet reached a position from which they can mount an effective challenge to BT in local telephone services. BT's desire for a faster rate of tariff rebalancing would suggest that it does not think this is imminent.

Additional licensees: trunk and international telephony

BT's arguments during the Review implied that it expected an intensification of competition in long-distance services. Several companies, in association with owners of rights of way, have submitted applications to enter the long-distance market. Licences have not yet been granted by the Secretary of State. It is not clear from the limited information in the public domain whether these proposals are for the kind of regional networks we advocated in 1989, which would combine limited trunk services with direct connections to customers, or would depend upon the introduction of equal access. We are inclined to doubt that extensive entry will occur in the long-distance market, for much the same reasons as resale has turned out to be a damp squib, and because of our scepticism about equal access, unless the entrants can identify and retain specific customer groups. The Duopoly Review has not significantly improved the prospects in the near term.

We predicted that proposals to offer international services only would not be welcomed by OFTEL and DTI. There seems no reason yet to amend this view.

Numbering

The planning of telephone numbers is significant for this discussion because of its potential to act as a barrier to entry.[14] Users will be less inclined to change from one PTO to another, or one type of service (fixed, cellular, etc.) to another, if to do so involves a change of number. OFTEL has been considering the issues for several years; its current plans are to extend the 'portability' of numbers as far as is technically possible and to introduce a separate prefix for each type of service, though no timetable has been set for these changes. Entrants would be assisted by early decisions, even if these are to do nothing.

BT/Mercury Competition

As we argued in 1989, the Duopoly Review was strongly conditioned by the need to ensure Mercury's continued growth as the principal instrument of increasing the competitive challenge in voice telephony. How has Mercury's position been affected by the Review? There are two principal aspects to consider:

- Mercury's position *vis-à-vis* new entrants, where the chief implication of the Review is that competitive entry would be adverse for Mercury but complementary entry favourable; and
- Mercury's direct competition with BT, where its costs are affected by the changes in the rules governing interconnection and its prospects are affected by BT's ability to counter its lower tariffs.

We have already concluded that entry to the voice telephony market will in general not develop swiftly following the Review. In so far as it does, we expect that it will tend to be complementary. The most important potential help to Mercury (as to the trunk entrants) would be entry into local network provision. The use of radio for this purpose awaits both technical developments and spectrum allocation decisions, so cable-based telephone operations remain Mercury's natural allies in offering users in general discounts to BT's prices.

So far as Mercury's interconnection charges are concerned, doubtless BT had hoped at the start of the Review to raise the amounts it received as well as to lay the basis for extracting more favourable interconnection terms from potential entrants. Its strategy of reallocating costs from local calls to access, and then calling for contributions from other PTOs to the access deficit thereby created, was only partially successful. Mercury's

[14] Revision of numbering plans also results in substantial costs for users and for PTOs. The costs have been estimated at about £200m. for the UK. For this reason, changes in numbering should be few and far between. It remains a matter of controversy whether another change is needed in the near future, or whether the initiative for change should be taken at national or European level.

access deficit payments, if they occur at all, will be considerably delayed; in the meantime, the reallocation of costs should mean that charges for the conveyance of local calls should be limited to be close to their present level. Standardization of interconnection payments, which could erode Mercury's position *vis-à-vis* trunk operators, has yet to emerge. Securing interconnection with BT is still an uncertain process, so Mercury retains much of its first-mover advantages; thereby, it has a useful base for alliances.

BT has at last obtained permission to use volume discounts targeted to the same set of large customers on which Mercury has concentrated its efforts. Since 1986, BT had been trying to produce an acceptable 'optional call plan';[15] in August 1991, the first to be accepted was introduced. Discounting can take either a weaker or a stronger form. The weaker is to grant all customers of a given size a quantity discount; this lessens the incentive to route traffic via Mercury because of the loss of volume going to BT (most Mercury customers retain at least some BT lines). The stronger form is to focus discounts as closely as possible on the particular set of customers Mercury now has, or is likely to acquire. BT is also now allowed to offer different call charges to groups of customers to whom it is providing other services.

We have yet to see how the new licence condition governing this will affect BT's trade-off—loss of revenue by giving discounts where Mercury is not involved versus gains by attracting specific Mercury customers. But the new rules, if difficult to interpret, do seem to be moving towards BT having to justify price discrimination between customers on the basis of avoidable, incremental cost differences. This, and the fact that the burden of proof to show such cost differences rests with BT, will continue to limit the tactical effectiveness to its weaker form and within stringent margins. In any case, Mercury can (and has) responded to BT's discount offers. The question now is how far it pays BT and Mercury to indulge in duopolistic rivalry and how far it pays to live and let live. Since Mercury's general position has been little, if at all, weakened relative to BT or other potential players, it seems most unlikely that war will break out. The growing market will make a continuing accommodation likely.

7. THE REGULATORY PROCESS

The Duopoly Review, by opening up many competitive options, should have a bigger impact on BT if these options are realized. But this is likely to take some time and, partly as a result, most of the options are likely not to be pursued to the point of producing a competitive challenge to BT.

[15] 'Optional call plan' is the term used to describe a tariff for voice-telephony services incorporating a volume discount.

The regulatory authorities themselves began the Review with a predisposition towards openness in the telecommunications market coupled with an aversion to unpicking the results of past decisions. The regulatory options were not clear at the outset: Cable & Wireless is now well established in the UK but the potential for network competition to improve BT's delivery of its services has not yet been realized. The experience of the BT/Mercury duopoly yielded clues as to the scope for future competitive entry but careful analysis was required to discern the likely future structure of the market. The authorities did not have much taste for quantitative analysis of the options.[16] Rather, the regulatory authorities largely relied on commercial interests to indicate which areas of the market they wished to enter.

The position after the Review is that entrants have, as before, to negotiate interconnection terms with BT, with OFTEL making a determination when they fail to agree. The discussions with BT must centre on conveyance charges, unaffected by the furore over Contributions. Views on OFTEL's likely determination will of course greatly influence negotiations and continued uncertainty on this point make reference to OFTEL inevitable, further delaying the arrival of effective competition. However, OFTEL did suggest that it might, at some point, make a standard determination covering a class of entrants. The DG has clearly recognized the impracticability of maintaining the 1984 approach in which interconnection was to be dealt with as a commercial negotiation within a loose framework of rules. While this remains the formal position, the reality is that OFTEL will manage the evolution of interconnection arrangements in future.

When the opportunity to enter the market is determined by the decision of the regulatory authorities, the regulatory process itself must be subject to scrutiny. The willingness of companies, particularly the North American interests, to invest in competitive opportunities depends on both policy priorities and the specifics of the regulatory framework. These still remain uncertain; in consequence the negotiations between the regulatory authorities and commercial interests have run on and look likely to continue for another year or so before producing a new settlement. We believe that the experience of the last ten years has revealed significant weaknesses that should be addressed.

Over the period, there has been a fundamental change in the regulatory process. In 1981, regulation was exercised informally by DTI and BT, with few other commercial interests that needed to be taken into account. This very informality allowed ministers to take radical decisions to change the structure of the sector. Now, there is a complex

[16] *The Infrastructure for Tomorrow* (1988), London: HMSO, was the only relevant official study published before the Review.

regulatory framework of rules and institutions and a multiplicity of interests. As the Duopoly Review has shown, the regulatory process can best be characterized as successive rounds of negotiation in which the regulatory authorities have sought to accommodate the expressed demands of incumbents, potential investors, and consumers. This inevitably constrains radicalism.

Encouraging local entry

The DG has signalled on a number of occasions his preference for encouraging competition at local level, as being most likely to produce the greatest benefits for users. This preference has not been carried through, probably because the DG has relatively little leverage on the licensing decisions which determine market structure. At the present time, there are two options for promoting local network entry: to release cable TV networks from present regulatory restraints and to encourage innovative applications of radio technologies. Neither has been dealt with very satisfactorily in the review.

Willingness to invest in local telephony, whether via cable TV or otherwise, is constrained by the residual regulatory requirement for universal service. The White Paper has little to say on this topic, but it is evident that universal service is still considered an appropriate principle for local entrants as well as incumbent PTOs. As applied to entrants, universal service entails an obligation to invest on a sufficient scale to serve all customers within a defined area. Thereby, flexibility in marketing is reduced and the risks of entry are significantly increased. As there is little practical benefit for users from imposing a universal requirement on entrants, it should be abolished.

The feasibility of local entry should gradually improve as BT's rebalancing of its tariff for voice telephony continues. However, the end result to be expected from rebalancing remains entirely obscure; OFTEL has given no sign of what the limit will be, nor has it published the data on which commercial interests could reach their own conclusions. The effect of this uncertainty will be to delay rather than to encourage entry.

Cable TV

Some basic constraints on cable-based telephony remain in place. First, there are simply far too many franchisees to mount an effective challenge to BT on the regulatory front. Second, franchise areas are too small to be run as independent local networks. Third, the television distribution business, to which the cable companies' local telephone business are tied, is making slow progress, even after a substantial inflow of North American investment.

The permission to interconnect freely with neighbouring franchises which has been secured may not be adequate compensation for the basic mistakes made in first tying franchise areas to local authority boundaries in urban areas and then arbitrarily limiting their linear extent to 50 km limit elsewhere. The result is inevitably a patchwork of franchises which make little commercial sense if considered as potential rivals to BT. Of course, the problem can be sorted out by the companies themselves; the rationalization of the industry is already underway. It seems likely that the number of participants will be reduced to between six and ten within a few years.

To be viable competitors, the surviving participants will certainly need to link their franchises in different parts of the country; that is, they will be long-distance as well as local operators. Given the option of trunk network operation, the North American telephone companies that now own the majority of franchises must await the final outcome of the interconnection debate before deciding whether the returns on investment in local telephony will be sufficiently attractive.

Radio applications

The Duopoly Review has also failed to shed much light on the future competitive balance between fixed and mobile voice-telephony services. With mobile radio, there are two distinct market-entry questions:

1. whether PCN services will appear on the market as cellular radio like services but without the capacity constraint on radio frequencies (and hence without the duopoly power that underpins cellular's high call-charges), or whether PCN and other radio applications will develop price/performance characteristics that enable it to rival fixed-link telephony services;
2. whether radio links can be generally mixed in with the fixed network or remain, like Telepoint to date, a specialist device.

Both of these are longer-term developments, but it is already evident that the regulatory process is unable to deal with them satisfactorily. The commercial failure of Telepoint to date has its origins in the mistaken regulatory requirement that network operators commit to nation-wide service while technical standards were still being debated. The Review has not resolved this problem which lies somewhere in between telecommunication and radiocommunication policies. The co-ordination between OFTEL, the agency for fixed-telephony services, and the Radiocommunications Agency, which handles spectrum management, is the responsibility of DTI; in reality, nobody is clearly in charge.

One arena in which this failure so far to deal with mobile radio satisfactorily is already important is interconnection. The logic of basing interconnection charges on BT's fully allocated costs is that all networks interconnecting with BT should pay the same, since BT's costs in handling a call from A to B are the same irrespective of which network handed it over for conveyance. However, the cellular radio networks have interconnection agreements with BT that are really quite different from that between BT and Mercury. The DG now has the scope for making standard determinations; he seems unlikely to use it for this purpose.

In summary, a competitive market structure may eventually emerge at local level, but as yet the regulatory process has not given a clear sign of the intention to assist such a development.

OFTEL and licensing powers

The imbalance in OFTEL's powers can also be seen in its dealings with BT. Regulatory pressure on BT to improve its performance could be applied either by tightening controls such as RPI–X or by intensifying the competitive threat. OFTEL can do the first, and has done so, but cannot exercise the second option. We suggested in 1989 that the DG should have the power to license entry, with the Secretary of State retaining the right to review refusals of licences on appeal. Reform along these lines has now become urgent.

The principal reason for concentrating licensing powers with the Secretary of State was concern to preserve universal service in the face of developing competition. As things have turned out, however, the issue of universal service has surfaced almost exclusively in the contexts of price controls on BT and the terms of interconnection with BT. These are matters that fall to be determined by OFTEL, not the Secretary of State. The regulatory process would be improved and simplified if OFTEL were to be given powers to issue PTO licences. As radio applications multiply, OFTEL should also be given powers to issue wireless telegraphy licences, with the Radiocommunications Agency providing technical advice.

OFTEL could not take on extra responsibilities without an overhaul of its internal organization; it is unable to carry out its present functions without repeated delays in decision-making. OFTEL's effectiveness as a regulatory body could be further strengthened if it was able to recruit more staff from outside the Civil Service. The present arrangements appear to have been dictated by the desire to align OFTEL and the agencies in other sectors closely with OFT and MMC. In the event, co-ordination with these more senior bodies has proved to be a relatively minor issue. OFTEL's major problem has been how to manage its relations with BT, Cable & Wireless, and other commercial interests. Civil Servants need to recruit external expertise to make the kind of technical and commercial assessments that are now OFTEL's stock in trade.

In summary, since 1981 telecommunications policy in the UK has moved from a position of merely experimenting with competition in voice telephony to regarding it as the principal method of ensuring continued improvements in the service provided to users and of implementing innovation in services. Competitive developments have been closely allied to the evolution of the regulatory process. We have concluded that this evolution should continue, in particular directions, to produce arrangements capable of managing the growth of competition.

14

The Regulation of Product Quality in the Public Utilities

LAURA ROVIZZI* AND DAVID THOMPSON†

1. INTRODUCTION

The privatization of publicly owned utilities in the UK—in telecoms, gas, electricity, water, and airports—has prompted extensive analysis and debate on the appropriate methods for regulating residual market power (see, for example, Vickers and Yarrow 1988). Whilst it is a familiar proposition of economic theory that an unregulated monopolist can usually be expected to distort both prices and product quality from efficient levels, the methods of regulation adopted in the UK were initially focused upon pricing decisions. The now familiar RPI–*X* control (see Littlechild 1983) placed a regulatory ceiling on the amount by which the enterprise could increase its prices over a specified period of time, typically five years, providing profit incentives for the enterprise to reduce relative costs (see Beesley and Littlechild 1989 for a discussion). However, in the case of the first two UK utilities to be privatized—telecoms and gas—no direct provision was made for the regulation of quality. Subsequent concerns with quality performance have led both to the introduction of quality regulation for these enterprises and to the inclusion of provisions relating to quality in the regulatory controls established for the later privatizations of water and electricity. More recently, in November 1991, the government introduced new legislation—the Competition and Utility Regulators Bill—which aimed to further strengthen quality regulation.

Our objective in this paper is to consider the appropriate role of quality in the regulation of monopoly utilities and to examine the issues raised in the implementation of the new regulatory controls recently

* Previously a Research Assistant at the Centre for Business Strategy, London Business School.

† Previously a Senior Research Fellow at the Centre for Business Strategy, London Business School.

The financial support of the Gatsby Foundation in carrying out the research upon which this paper is based is gratefully acknowledged. Helpful comments on an earlier draft of this paper came from Michael Beesley, Matthew Bishop, Evan Davis, John Kay, Paul Richards, and David Starkie; the usual disclaimer applies.

introduced in the UK. The plan of the paper is as follows: following this introduction, in section 2 we consider the circumstances under which a monopoly supplier will distort quality from efficient levels. In particular, we consider the circumstances in which utilities in public ownership might be expected to set quality too high and we identify that privatized companies subject to basic price-cap regulation might be expected to set quality levels too low. In section 3 we consider some of the sectors where it has been feasible to liberalize competitive entry into former state monopoly activities. We find that there is little evidence to suggest that quality under competitive supply has turned out lower than resulted under monopoly public ownership. This observation weakens the case for believing that public ownership resulted in the over-provision of quality. In section 4 we examine the introduction of price-cap regulation over the last decade in the UK associated with the privatization and the parallel shifts in the regulation of enterprises which have remained in public ownership. We show that in cases where no specific provision was made for quality regulation, there is some evidence to suggest a fall in quality following the introduction of price-cap controls. This observation reinforces the relevance of quality regulation. This is the subject of section 5; we consider the relative advantages of different types of control and in section 6 we discuss some of the issues which will arise in implementation. In the final section we draw together our conclusions.

2. PRODUCT SELECTION UNDER MONOPOLY SUPPLY

In a competitive market, consumers choose between goods and services not only on price but also on quality and service, trading-off between them. Under familiar conditions, competitive markets yield goods and services of optimum quality. An extensive literature (see, for example, Tirole 1988) has examined the consequences of these conditions not being met (in particular where producers and consumers face asymmetric information about product quality) and has also examined possible solutions, both market (e.g. quality brands) and regulatory (e.g. product standards). Whilst some of these issues arise in the utilities (e.g. drinking-water quality) our particular interest in this paper is with the distortions which arise directly as a consequence of monopoly supply.

Economic theory predicts that, under familiar but restrictive conditions, an unregulated monopolist will supply goods of equivalent quality to firms in a competitive market; in essence all monopoly profit is taken in prices (Waterson 1984). In more general circumstances, however, an unregulated monopolist may find it profitable to either oversupply or to undersupply quality, the outcome depending on demand conditions (see Spence 1975). Once the firm is subject to a (binding) price ceiling, however, then it will always be profitable for the utility to set quality below the level which is efficient, given the particular price ceiling. The price-cap regulated utility undersupplies quality because whilst an increment in quality generates additional revenues—associated with the additional units demanded as a result of the rise in quality—these do not capture (absent perfect-price discrimination) the benefits to existing (intra-marginal) consumers of the higher levels of quality.

This is illustrated in Figure 14.1. The enterprise can reduce costs by reducing quality and this is worthwhile in financial terms if the foregone revenue (shaded area π) is less than the cost savings. However it will not be efficient in terms of resource allocation if the change in consumer surplus (shaded area S) more than offsets the financial benefits. The significance of this is likely to be greater where demand is more price inelastic, where the valuation placed on quality change by marginal consumers is low relative to the average and, related to this, where price discrimination is not feasible. When price discrimination is not possible the firm responds to the marginal individual valuation of quality changes, whereas the average consumer's valuation is the relevant quantity for welfare. A potential misallocation in the determination of the level of quality is the implication of this market failure. The implication is that effective monopoly regulation requires consideration of quality and service as well as price, an observation which remains true when the analysis is extended to consider the multi-product case (see Besanko, Donnenfeld, and White 1987 and 1988).

It is interesting to note that similar considerations apply to a cost-level

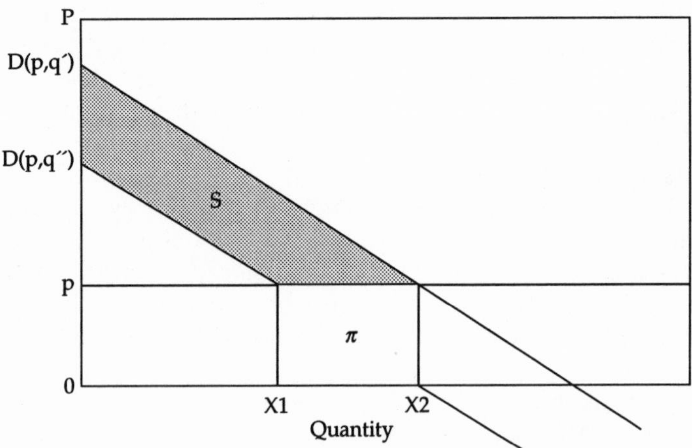

FIG. 14.1. Price-cap effects on service quality. (Source: Vickers and Yarrow 1988.)

regulated enterprise in public ownership which is subject to a regulatory ceiling on the level of average costs. This form of control has been used to regulate the UK's nationalized industries following a White Paper in 1978 which established financial performance as the industries' central objective (or constraint) and also introduced explicit targets for the levels of costs and productivity. However, in meeting a regulatory ceiling on average cost levels, incentives to underprovide quality arise in a (broadly) similar fashion to the privatized utility case illustrated in Figure 14.1.

It has sometimes been argued, however, that under traditional public ownership—prior to privatization and the parallel shifts in public enterprise regulation introduced in 1978—quality levels were set too high. That is, that specifications tended to be 'over-engineered' and capital projects 'gold plated'. The essence of this argument (which is developed systematically in Bös and Peters 1988) is that management in publicly owned firms paid insufficient attention to the costs of achieving higher levels of quality. This is illustrated in Figure 14.2. Higher levels of quality can be achieved by incurring 'costs of control'. These are effectively the costs of internal regulation—for example, monitoring and administrative costs within the organization. If managers in public enterprises are relatively indifferent to higher control costs—because, for example, they are familiar with bureaucratic structures and consensual

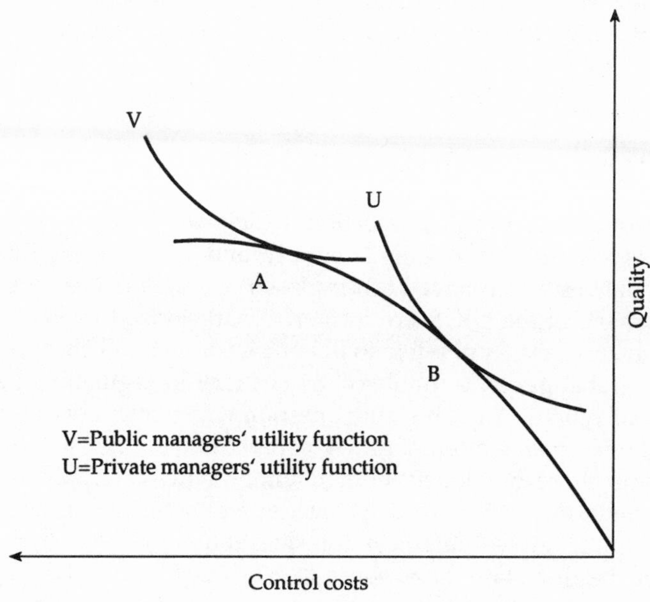

FIG. 14.2. Quality and control costs. (Source: Bos and Peters, 1988.)

decision-taking—then they will tend to set quality at relatively high levels (at point A in Figure 14.2). If privatization—or a shift toward more commercial objectives under public ownership—results in greater recognition of the relevance of control costs then the result will be that quality is set at lower levels (at point B in the figure). In Bös and Peter's terms this is a 'price which has to be paid for the reduction of excessive bureaucratization, a price measured in terms of the quality of supply'.

Thus we have identified two quite distinct processes through which privatization—or parallel shifts in public-enterprise regulation—would be expected to result in quality levels being reduced. They have very different implications, however. The first reflects a price-capped firm reducing quality below efficient levels in order to meet financial constraints. The second reflects an unwinding of the too generous provision for quality which, it is suggested has been made under public ownership.

That this concern about quality is not a wholly theoretical one is exemplified by results from a survey of the business priorities of senior management in recently privatized companies in the UK (see United Research 1990). Interviews with top management in enterprises showed that concern for product quality and for customer service rated tenth and eleventh in a listing of priorities, with far fewer executives regarding these as important business issues compared with, for example, 'competition', 'regulation', 'productivity', or 'culture change'. This observation suggests that quality, and its regulation, is a potentially important issue in practice and it is to consideration of this that we now turn.

3. LIBERALIZING COMPETITION AND PRODUCT SELECTION

The distortions in product selection which we have discussed arise directly as a result of monopoly in supply, and interactions with the regulatory controls which have been imposed in consequence. But in some sectors which, in the UK, were formerly characterized by state monopoly supply, it has been possible to liberalize competitive entry—either as a result of changes in technology, or changes in regulatory policy, or more usually, both. An interesting question which then arises is whether the levels of quality offered under competitive supply are higher, or lower, than those previously offered under state-monopoly supply. In this section of the paper, we will consider a number of cases which provide some qualitative findings on this question.

One of the first state monopolies to be deregulated by the incoming Conservative government was long-distance coach services. The 1980 Transport Act removed all direct controls on entry, except those which related to the safety of the vehicles and the competence of their drivers. Extensive entry following deregulation was followed, initially, by significant product differentiation which, in turn, led to a more general enhancement to the quality of in-vehicle facilities and associated services. It has been estimated that consumers' value these enhancements, on average, by an amount equivalent to a 10 per cent premium on price levels (see Thompson and Whitfield 1991). Figure 14.3 shows that there have also been quite large changes to both frequency of service and point-to-point journey times following deregulation. Whilst there are some circumstances in which markets in scheduled transport services set frequency above efficient levels (see Evans 1990) this is less likely where services are time-tabled and pre-booked. Taken together it is difficult to believe that this data is consistent with the view that quality was set too high under monopoly public ownership; the reverse seems more likely to be true. Essentially similar results arise if we consider the liberalizations of entry into Europe's scheduled air services (see, for example,

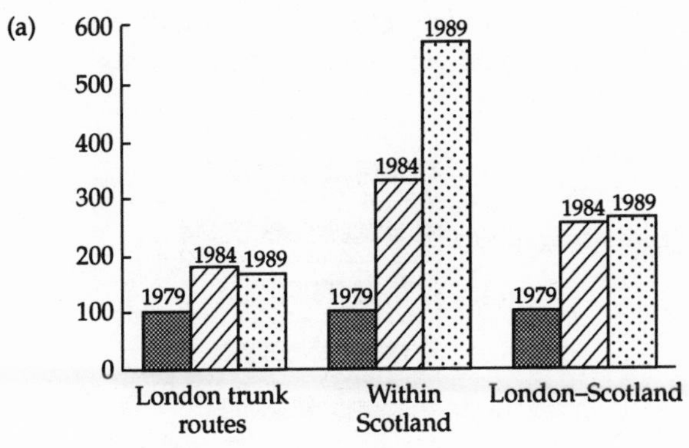

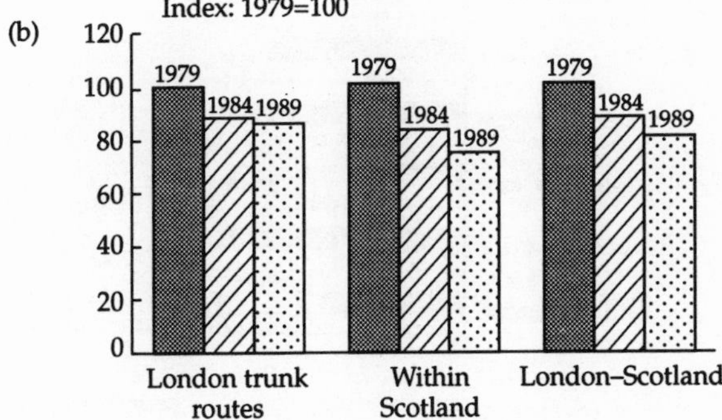

FIG. 14.3. Coaches: (a) Average service frequencies; (b) Average scheduled journey times. (Source: Thompson and Whitfield 1991.)

Abbott and Thompson 1990) or local bus services in the UK (Glaister 1990; Bannister and Mackett 1990).

The second case we consider relates to the licensing of Mercury (in 1982) in competition with BT. The nature of Mercury's network makes it a more ready alternative for large corporate users of telecoms services. Figure 14.4 shows some qualitative data from a survey carried out in 1990 of a small number of such intensive telecoms users. Survey respondents had an average expenditure of £3.8 million per annum and most of them are dual-sourced. It can be seen that they rated BT and Mercury broadly equal over a range of quality dimensions, although each company had a lead on particular quality dimensions. Most of the respondents considered that BT's service quality had increased relative to that of Mercury following the latter's entry (see Figure 14.5). Essentially similar results arise if we consider the liberalization of entry into the supply of handsets and exchanges (see Gist and Meadowcroft 1986).

The final case we consider relates to phone boxes. Concern that reliability had fallen following BT's privatization prompted a survey by OFTEL which showed disappointing data on phone box serviceability; 17 per cent of phone boxes were out of order in 1986 and over 23 per cent in 1987, with a peak of 38 per cent for Greater London.

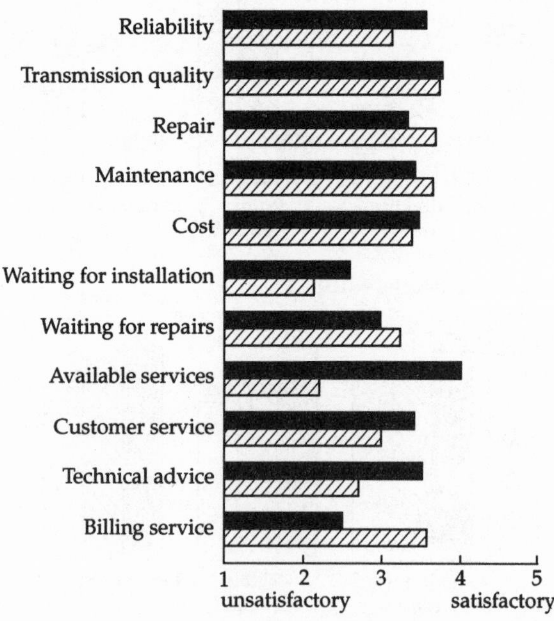

FIG. 14.4. Perception of BT (solid) and Mercury (shaded). (Source: Cohen, Dopudis, Jhunjhunnala, and Tamara 1989.)

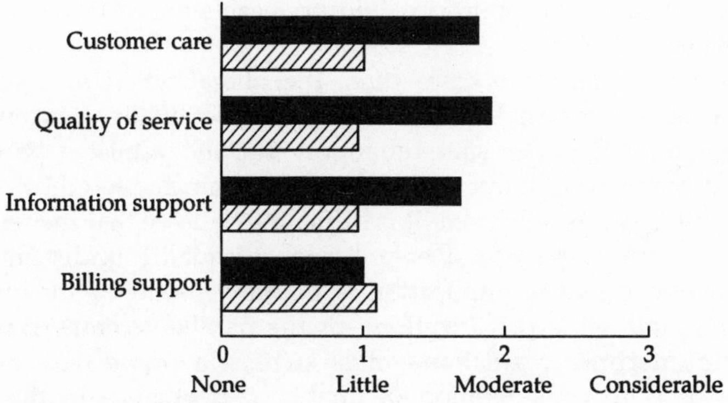

FIG. 14.5. Perceived improvements.

The Director General issued a statement in 1987 which concluded:

> I believe that BT's performance can be improved by greater managerial effort and a tightening up of procedures. Two lines of action need to be considered by me in carrying out my duty to promote the interests of users as regards the quality of service. First, the introduction of competition needs to be considered, since others may be able to do better than BT; and secondly, increased regulatory action is needed to monitor BT's performance on a continuing basis and bring further pressures for improvements.

The first option was followed to improve public phone box quality: in 1987, Mercury was authorized to provide a competing call-box service and the market for payphone apparatus was liberalized. The effects of this competitive spur can be appreciated by looking at Figure 14.6:

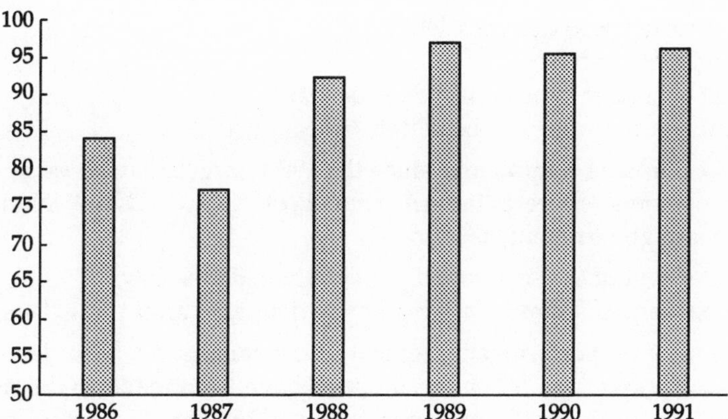

FIG. 14.6. Percentage of call-boxes in working order (BT). (*Source*: British Telecom Quality of Service Reports.)

within two years the proportion of unserviceable phone boxes had fallen below 5 per cent.

In each of these three cases then, the liberalization of competitive entry has been associated with enhanced product quality by comparison with that offered under state-monopoly supply. Whilst a part of the observed changes no doubt reflect the opportunities offered by underlying technological development it is difficult to believe that the results are consistent with systematic over-provision of quality under traditional public ownership. The implication is that any tendency for quality to deteriorate following privatization—or the parallel 'commercialization' of public-enterprise regulation—must suggest a prima facie cause for concern. It is to consideration of quality performance in the natural monopolies which we now turn.

4. QUALITY REGULATION AND PERFORMANCE

We will consider three groups of enterprises: first those still in public ownership (taking postal services as an illustration); next the first round of privatizations (taking BT as an example); and finally the more recent privatizations (considering the case of electricity).

Postal Services

The nationalized industry with probably the longest history of quality regulation is the Post Office. Although statutory duties specify only in very general terms the type of service to be provided, an operational specification of various aspects of letter-service quality has been determined by the Post Office. This relates, in particular, to:

- the time taken to deliver a letter;
- siting of letter-boxes;
- latest collection times from letter-boxes;
- number and timing of postal deliveries.

The first of these is central, and since the 1970s targets have been agreed with consumers representatives (the Post Office Users' National Council) and government, as follows:

1. 90 per cent of first-class mail to be delivered next day;
2. 96 per cent of second-class mail to be delivered after three days.

Measurement of performance against these targets over the last two decades is complicated by changes which have been made to the methods used to measure performance in 1980 and in 1988. The latter change is of particular significance. Up to that time performance had been measured from the date at which mail was received from collection (and date stamped) to the date at which preparation for delivery was completed. It was frequently argued by consumer groups that this measure underestimated the 'true' end-to-end delivery time; for example the Mail Users' Association argued in 1988 that the proportion of mail achieving next-day delivery would be 20 per cent lower if an end-to-end measurement system was used. From 1988, however, performance has been measured on an end-to-end basis. Comparable data using the two measurement systems is unfortunately not available but using the results of surveys carried out by the Consumers' Association we estimate that the change in measurement system has reduced measured performance for the first-class post by 4 per cent. This assumption provides the basis for the performance record set out in Figure 14.7. For much of the 1970s performance oscillated around the target level of 90 per cent. Towards the end of the decade performance deteriorated, associated with high labour turnover under the then current incomes policy, prompting the first of a series of 'efficiency audits' by the Monopolies and Mergers Commission (see MMC 1979, and 1984 in particular). Whilst there was some recovery in the early 1980s, through most of the decade performance ran some 3–4 percentage points below target. Over the last two years, however, performance has turned sharply upward.

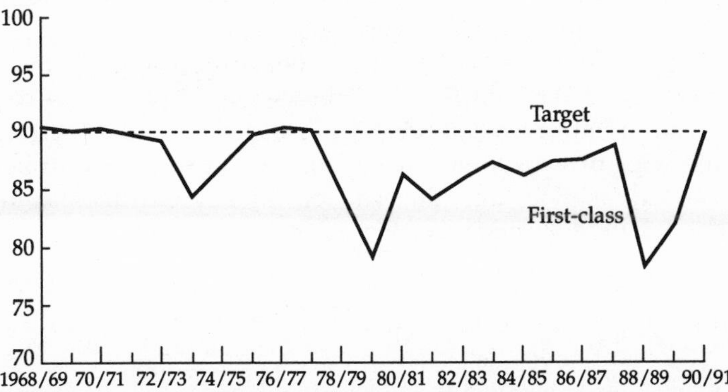

FIG. 14.7. Speed of delivery of first-class letters. The 88/89–90/91 figures have been adjusted. (*Source*: Post Office Annual Reports.)

British Telecom

No formal targets for the quality of telecoms services were specified whilst the company was in public ownership. Nevertheless the rapid pace of technological change meant that the reliability of phone services increased rapidly during the 1970s; Figure 14.8 shows that the incidence of failed calls fell by over a half.

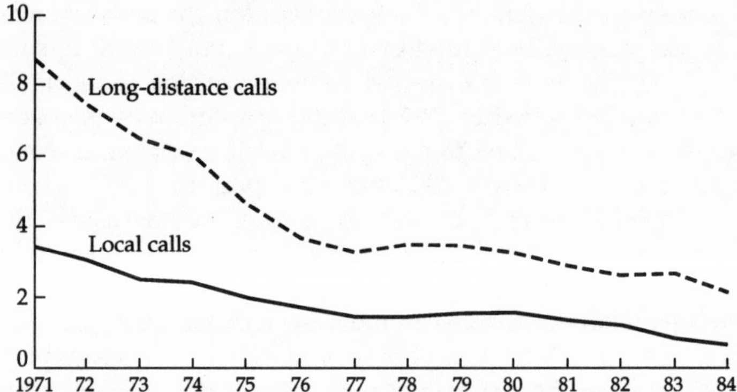

FIG. 14.8. Percentage of call failures due to the system (1971–1984). (Sources: Post Office and BT Annual Reports)

On privatization, no specific provision was made for quality regulation in BT's licence, although quality is included amongst OFTEL's objectives. Indeed the most immediate consequence of privatization was that BT ceased publishing data on its performance. Public sentiment—in the absence of hard data—suggested that quality declined in the years following privatization. A highly critical report by the Consumers' Association supported this view. The consequence was an investigation by OFTEL in 1986 which carried out its own survey on performance as well as collecting data from BT. The results—see Figure 14.9—confirm that the trend in improved call-reliability was halted in the years immediately following privatization. An engineers strike in 1987 contributed a part of the explanation, and this had an equally detrimental impact upon the speed of fault repair (see Figure 14.10).

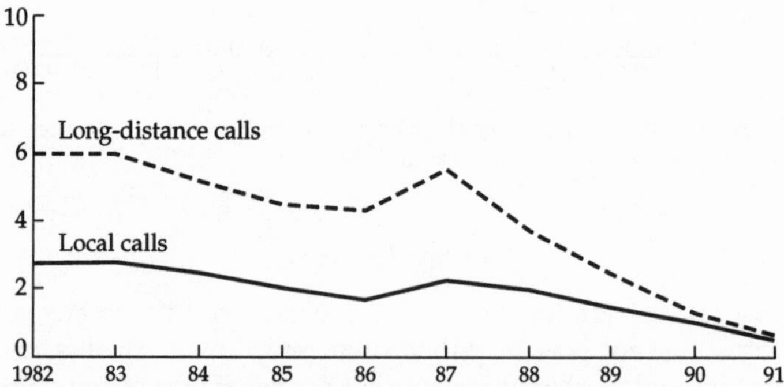

FIG. 14.9. Percentage of call failures due to the system (1982–1991) (measuring base is different from the one used in Fig. 14.8.)(Source: BT Reports on quality.)

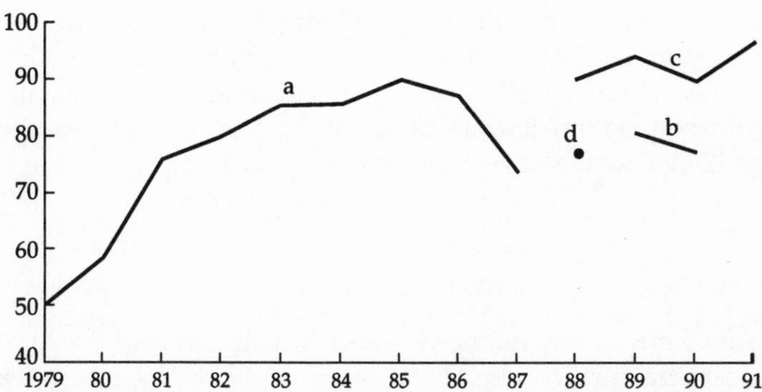

FIG. 14.10. Percentage of faults cleared by: (a) next working day; (b) 1 working day; (c) 2 working days; (d) 1 working day—estimate. (*Source*: OFTEL, BT reports.)

We have already discussed OFTEL's policies in licensing entry to rectify a perceived quality shortfall in call-box reliability. Where direct regulation was considered necessary in order to act as a substitute for market pressures, the Director-General identified two options which could be followed in re-setting BT's price control in 1988:

> A decision must be made whether to include any element for quality of service in the price-control formula. I am considering the incorporation of key indicators of performance in the price-control arrangements. Each day's delay in providing service or repairing faults, for example, could be associated with a fixed reduction in the revenues BT is permitted to raise from the price of its main services. A [second] possible solution is to require BT to accept some limited financial liability for failure to provide a service.

In the event, the second option was followed. No specific provision for quality of service was made in the revised price-control formula. Instead OFTEL obliged BT to publish performance information and to accept financial liability to individual customers for failure to meet certain agreed standards of service. Thus from April 1989, in relation to the installation or repair of a public-exchange line, BT has agreed that the customer is entitled to claim £5 for each day of delay beyond the second working day if, through its own fault, an agreed installation appointment is not met or, in the case of repair, it does not restore service. In addition, when it can be proved that money has been lost as a result of the quality failure, the customer can claim material damages (up to £1,000 if residential, and £5,000 if business). In the period October 1990–March 1991, 48 per cent of consumers entitled to compensation for fault repairs have actually claimed; the percentage for failure in meeting installation targets is only 12 per cent, however.

Data on the speed of fault repair (Figure 14.10) shows that performance has improved in the most recent years. Installation time has also been reduced: while in 1987 only 18 per cent of residential installations were performed within 8 working days, in 1991 this percentage was more than 83 per cent. Network reliability has also improved (see Figure 14.9).

Electricity Supply

In the case of electricity, unlike BT (also British Gas and BAA), provisions concerning quality regulation were explicitly introduced at the time of privatization.

The 1989 Electricity Act provides that the Director-General (DG), with the consent of the Secretary of State, may make regulations prescribing overall standards of performance, after consultation with the Regional Electricity Companies, and also prescribes guaranteed service standards for individual consumers. Any failure of the company in achieving one of the guaranteed service standards renders it liable to make a predetermined payment in compensation to the person affected by the failure.

Regulation of guaranteed source standards came into force on 1 July 1991. The DG has specified ten such standards which the public electricity-supply companies must provide to their customers (see Table 14.1). These relate, for example, to the restoration of supply after a failure. The amount of compensation is also set out (e.g. failure to restore supply within 24 hours results in payment of £20, for domestic customers, with £10 for each further 12 hours). The DG will monitor the companies' performance and the results will be published annually. Most compensation payments are made automatically; this contrasts with the compensation schemes in telecoms and gas where customers must make an application for compensation.

5. ALTERNATIVE MECHANISMS FOR QUALITY REGULATION

Both theory and practice suggests that where an enterprise is able to exercise market power, quality can be detrimented to achieve financial and commercial objectives. Against this, effective regulatory methods have got to be found and implemented. The Utility Regulators Bill—introduced following the Citizens' Charter—proposes more extensive regulation of quality for four of the privatized industries (telecoms, gas, water, and electricity, but not airports). In this section we consider some of the key advantages and disadvantages associated with various alternative regulatory systems.

Most of the public utilities are, in many respects, natural monopolists.

TABLE 14.1 Guaranteed standards[a] of performance for electricity distribution

Service	Performance level	Payment
1. Restoring electricity supplies after faults	24 hours	£20 domestic customers £50 non-domestic customers £10 for each further 12 hours
2. Notice of supply interruption	2 days	£10 domestic customers £20 non-domestic customers
3. Company fuse failures	Within 4 hours of notification during working hours[b]	£10
4. Providing a supply and meter	Within 5 working days (3 in some areas)[b]	£20 domestic customers £50 non-domestic customers £10 for failing to agree a day to call
5. Estimating charges for connection	Within 10 working days for simple jobs or 20 for most others[b]	£20
6. Voltage complaints	Visit or reply within 10 working days	£10
7. Meter problems	Visit or reply within 10 working days	£10
8. Charges and payment queries	A substantive reply within 10 working days	£10
9. Appointments on supply business	All appointments to visit on a day must be kept	£10

[a] In addition to these guaranteed standards, the DG has introduced eight 'overall standards' of performance (e.g. percentage of supplies reconnected following a fault within 3 hours, see Table 14.2). Different targets have been established for each company to reflect the different conditions of the geographic area in which each company operates and its service performance prior to privatization.

[b] Figures shown are those set for most companies, the precise performance level will differ for some companies.

Source: OFFER.

However, scope exists for the introduction of competition in at least some of the activities carried out in these industries and we discussed some specific examples in telecommunications in section 3. But in other sectors (in particular the distribution networks for gas, electricity, and water) entry is infeasible and here the regulatory task is to simulate competitive incentives.

We will consider, in turn, four alternative mechanisms and discuss their advantages and disadvantages, particularly as these relate to the

TABLE 14.2 Description of the overall standards of performance* set by OFFER for the electricity companies

1. Minimum percentage of supplies to be reconnected following faults within 3 hours and minimum percentage within 24 hours.
2. Minimum percentage of voltage faults to be corrected within 6 months.
3. Connecting new domestic-tariff customer's premises to electricity distribution system: minimum percentage of domestic customers to be connected within 30 working days, and minimum percentage of non-domestic customers to be connected within 40 working days.
4. Minimum percentage of customers who have been cut-off for non-payment to be reconnected before the end of the working day after they have paid the bill.
5. Visiting to move meter when asked to do so by customer within 15 working days in minimum percentage of cases.
6. Changing meters where necessary on change of tariff within 10 working days of domestic customer's request in minimum percentage of cases.
7. Ensuring that customers get a firm reading of the meter at least once a year in minimum percentage of cases.
8. Minimum percentage of all written customer complaints and enquiries to be responded to within 10 working days.

* The precise definition of the standards is set out in a formal determination made by the Director-General. Whilst only limited data is available on the quality levels achieved by the companies before and after their privatization, the results published by OFFER in its 1990/1 report on system performance (OFFER 1991), show no systematic variation in performance following privatization.

Source: OFFER.

incentives which are provided to companies to set quality at efficient levels, the costs of monitoring and enforcement, and economy in the revelation of information.

Publication of information on quality performance

This is a simple regulatory measure since no decisions need to be made on quality standards nor do any significant costs need to be incurred in enforcement. However, there are few incentives to the company to change its quality performance, provided it retains a dominant position, other than those which result from public and media pressure associated with demonstrated poor quality. Where entry is feasible, however, publication of information might act to reduce certain costs of entry—those associated with the quality assurance provided by incumbents' well known product brands.

Adjusting the Price Cap

In competitive markets, suppliers are constrained by financial incentives in product selection: thus a quality detriment will have a direct effect on the level of prices and/or market share which can be sustained. Therefore, explicitly incorporating a quality-sensitive factor in the price-control formula is seen by many (see, for example, Vickers and Yarrow 1988) as the most straightforward way to regulate quality.

This approach has several advantages. First it is an automatic incentive mechanism: once set up it works without the need for explicit intervention. As a result, transactions costs for both consumers and firms are negligible, at least in the periods between review of the formulae. Secondly, the enterprise is free to select one of a range of different quality/price combinations by trading-off the alternatives which can be achieved under the formula. Thus, the regulator does not need to acquire information about the company's incremental production costs in supplying different levels of quality: maximization of profits under the price and quality constraint is left entirely to the company.

One disadvantage, however, is that whilst this mechanism will affect the regulated price level it does not specifically compensate the individual consumer who has received an inferior service. Besides this, the main disadvantage lies in the regulatory costs incurred in establishing the mechanism. Such a method would require: first the definition of a quality index, which implies identifying quality dimensions and weights; second a judgement as to the appropriate relationship between price and quality in the regulatory formula; and finally an independent monitoring of quality performance. None of these issues will be straightforward or easily agreed.

Customer Compensation Schemes

As we have seen, arrangements to compensate individual consumers for poor service have been introduced for most UK utilities. When a certain standard is not met, the utility agrees that the customer is entitled to obtain compensation. The first advantage of such a mechanism is that it ensures consumer-specific compensation: the individual customer who has suffered the loss in quality will be compensated. Second the company is provided with more precise management information since it can spot the location of the quality failure. Third, with such a scheme the company is allowed to trade-off changes in quality against the incremental costs of achieving these. Thus the regulator does not fix a unique level of quality and the company can choose whether to improve service quality or pay out more compensation. As with RPI-X + Q the regulator does not need to investigate the company's costs of supplying higher (or lower) levels of quality performance.

The main disadvantages of this approach are twofold. First of all the scheme can only work when the detriment is consumer-specific and quality failures can be easily verified. For instance it would not be practicable to compensate individual consumers for failures such as noisy telephone lines. Second, transaction costs—both to the company and to the consumer—will be higher than under other mechanisms.

Minimum Quality Standards

A fourth approach is the specification of minimum quality standards: the company is penalized for failure to meet minimum levels of quality. This approach has the disadvantage that if both the price cap and minimum quality standard are binding then the company has no choice in product selection. Thus in order to determine the efficient level of quality the regulator must have information on both the company's production function as well as data on consumers' preferences. Further problems arise in fixing the correct amount of the fine and determining the way to redistribute it to consumers; in the absence of redistribution, this system does not compensate those who have experienced poor service.

Fixing minimum quality standards may nevertheless be an attractive option in presentational terms (it appears to guarantee a particular level of quality), and in circumstances where there are severe non-linearities in the consumer-benefit function, or where there are information asymmetries between producers and consumers.

6. QUALITY REGULATION

Whatever regulatory mechanism is adopted—and the preceding discussion suggests that this should be tailored to the particular characteristics of the product—there are several important issues which will arise in implementation. The first relates to how, in the absence of a market test, quality standards should be determined.

The origins of the various standards which we have discussed are far from clear. In the case of letter delivery, for example, the 90 per cent next day delivery standard seems to have been established on the basis that it was the maximum feasible at the price offered. In principle, of course, efficient resource allocation requires that standards be established with reference to consumers' valuation of a quality improvement and the corresponding costs of achieving it (see Spence 1975; and Rovizzi and Thompson 1991) for an application in relation to consumer compensation schemes). This observation raises two important methodological issues. The first, noted by Spence, is that whilst analysis of revealed preferences provides data on the valuation of quality changes on the part of marginal consumers, it tells us little about the valuations of intramarginal consumers. This suggests a role for stated preference techniques or indeed for the unbundling of prices on the basis of quality variations. Several of the regulators have started to implement surveys aimed at collecting information of this sort. The second relates to circumstances where the costs of verifying the actual level of quality delivered are high; this is a particular example of the general issue of regulation under imperfect information (see Laffont and Tirole 1991).

A second important issue relates to the appropriate degree of disaggregation of quality regulation. For example, should the regulation of letter reliability focus only on aggregate performance—across the UK as a whole—or should it disaggregate by geographic area? Is the appropriate measure the proportion of letters arriving next day, or should distinction be made between those arriving in the first delivery and those in the second delivery? It will be clear that the cost-benefit calculus required to address questions of this kind is quite complex. On the benefit side are the net benefits which arise from the introduction of a particular regulatory instrument; these net benefits comprising the difference between (changes to) consumer valuation and the costs of supply. On the cost side are the incremental control costs—to both the regulatory authority and the company—which result from implementation. Where there is scope for these latter being undervalued (as suggested by Bös and Peters 1988) then there are dangers that too detailed and wide-ranging regulatory intervention will result.

A third issue relates to how the regulation of quality fits with the regulation of prices (in the case of enterprises still in public ownership, on the regulation of financial performance). The Utility Regulators Bill envisaged that both prices and quality are regulated by the same authority (e.g. OFTEL in the case of telecommunications) and this seems the most natural solution. Whilst it might be argued that this would give insufficient weight to consumers' interests—the regulators also, generally, have a duty to the financial health of the regulated enterprise—the alternative of independent quality regulation carries the danger of inconsistency and an absence of credibility. This certainly seems to have been true, for example, of the quality targets for letter delivery, which were established by a postal users' group, but not formally integrated with government financial targets.

A more specific issue is whether quality controls are set and re-set as part of the same process in which the RPI-X price cap is adjusted. Again this would seem the most natural solution, although the Utility Regulators Bill makes no specific provision for this. Nor does it make provision for (quasi) arbitration by the Monopolies and Mergers Commission where there is dispute between the regulator and utility—as is the case where disputes arise in resetting price caps.

7. CONCLUSIONS

We began this paper by observing that whilst economic theory predicts that a monopoly supplier can generally be expected to distort both prices and product quality from efficient levels, the regulation of public utilities in the UK has largely concentrated on prices. The particular form of price regulation adopted for utilities which have been privatized—the RPI–*X* price cap—could be expected to result in quality being set below efficient levels (given the level of price cap). This result, due to Spence (1975), arises because under a price cap firms which improve product quality can only capture incremental revenues from the additional units of demand which arise; benefits to intra-marginal units of consumption cannot, absent perfect price discrimination, be expropriated. In consequence, profits are maximized when quality is set below the level which is socially efficient, at the regulated price. Similar considerations apply to cost-level regulated enterprises in public ownership. As a result it has sometimes been argued that the regulatory reforms of the last decade have paid insufficient regard to quality issues and that—in consequence—financial and commercial goals would be achieved at the expense of quality decline. However, a second, and conflicting, view frequently expressed is that public enterprises in the UK tended, at least under the methods of regulation in force prior to the 1978 White Paper, to set standards of quality too high. In essence, the argument is that under traditional public ownership insufficient regard was paid to the monitoring and control costs necessary to enhance quality and, as a result, too high a level of this expenditure was incurred. Privatization—or the commercialization of public enterprises' objectives—would again be expected to result in quality decline but in these circumstances the interpretation would be altogether more favourable. Quality reductions would be the quid pro quo for a beneficial reduction in excessive costs.

In section 3 of the paper we looked at some qualitative results from sectors where it has been feasible to liberalize competitive entry into former state monopolies. These results did not suggest that product selection under (quasi) competitive conditions was yielding lower quality levels than had been offered under state monopoly. These cases thus provide little support for the view that publicly owned utilities in the UK systematically set the quality of their products at too high a level.

The implication is that where privatization—or the commercialization of public enterprise goals—is associated with a decline in quality then this suggests a prima facie cause for concern. In section 4 we examined this question by analysing some measures of quality performance. These findings suggested that where shifts in regulation (privatization or the commercialization of public enterprise objectives) had not included direct provision for quality regulation then there was some evidence to suggest a tendency for quality to decline. Thus, in the case of letter delivery (where quality targets are set by the users' group but not directly included in government financial controls) quality performance has run at a lower level during much of the 1980s, by comparison with the period prior to the shift in regulatory controls in the 1978 White Paper. Essentially similar results arise for BR (see Bishop, Rovizzi, and Thompson 1992). Similarly, in the case of BT—where no direct provision for quality was made in the controls established on privatization—quality performance turned down in the years following privatization; some similar results arise in the case of gas (again, see Bishop, Rovizzi, and Thompson 1992).

This suggests an important role for quality regulation and we discussed the explicit provisions which have been made in the more recent privatizations of electricity (and similarly water). The legislation, introduced in November 1991—the Utility Regulators Bill—provided for more extensive quality regulation for four of the privatized industries—telecoms, gas, electricity, and water—as well as for the Post Office and British Rail. Our discussion of quality performance suggests that this is desirable. Nevertheless several important issues remain to be resolved. Even if we have been generally unpersuaded by arguments which suggest that control costs have been undervalued under traditional public ownership, nevertheless this significant widening in regulatory powers raises the dangers of excessive intervention.

The first issue relates to how the regulators determine the levels of quality which are to be achieved; the legislation makes this essentially discretionary, subject to the regulators' general duties. To achieve efficient resource allocation, consumers' valuation of higher (or lower) levels of quality should be the reference point. Given the significant information asymmetries which exist between regulator and utility on the costs of supplying incremental quality, this suggests powerful advantages to regulatory mechanisms which allow the utility to select its preferred level of quality from a range of options. For example, if the utility is confronted with a range of financial rewards for raising quality (or vice versa) pitched at levels which (broadly) equate to consumers' valuation then the product selection which maximizes profits will also be efficient. Formidable data problems will arise in measuring such valuations but there is no requirement to investigate the utilities' cost structure.

The second issue relates to which dimensions of quality should be regulated. Consumers' valuation clearly provides a first sift here—there is no point in regulating aspects of service which the customer does not care about and there should be a presumption in favour of regulating those aspects which are of deep concern. Nevertheless, there is a tricky cost-benefit calculus in weighing the costs of regulation against the benefits which might result from regulatory intervention.

Third, there is the issue of how quality regulation should fit with existing regulatory controls on prices or profits. Again the legislation makes this essentially discretionary. We see a good case for integrating the controls; that is, setting and resetting any quality controls at the same time—and in the same framework of evaluation—that price-cap controls (for the privatized utilities) or financial controls (for those in public ownership) are set and reset.

Absent this, there is a danger both of inconsistency but also of the principle of periodic intervention—with enterprises facing a stable control framework in the periods between reviews—being progressively undermined. Each of these issues remain to be resolved as the regulation of quality in the utilities is developed; and in each case successful resolution will be important to the effectiveness of the regulatory regimes which result.

References

Abbot, K., and Thompson, D. J. (1991), 'Deregulating European Aviation: The impact of bilateral liberalization', *International Journal of Industrial Organization*, 9: 125–40.

Bannister, D. J., and Mackett, R. L. (1990), 'The minibus: Theory and experience and their implications', *Transports Review*, 10/2.

Beesley, M., and Littlechild, S. (1989), 'The regulation of privatized monopolies in the UK', *Rand Journal of Economics*, 20/3: 454–72.

Besanko, D., Donnenfeld, S., and White, L. J. (1988), 'The multiproduct firm, quality choice and regulation', *Journal of Industrial Economics*, 36: 411–29.

Bishop, M., and Kay, J. (1988), 'Does Privatization Work?', Centre for Business Strategy Report, London Business School.

—— and Thompson, D. (1992), 'Regulatory reform and productivity growth in the UK's public utilities', *Applied Economics*, 24: 1181–90.

—— Rovizzi, L., and Thompson, D. J. (1992), 'Price and quality control: Regulatory reform and public utilities performance' in M. E. Beesley (ed.), *Lectures on Regulation 1991*, CBS Report, London Business School.

Bös, D. (1988), 'Recent theories on public enterprise economics', *European Economic Review*, 32: 409–14.

—— and Peters, W. (1988), 'Privatisation, internal control, and internal regulation', *Journal of Public Economics*, 36: 231–58.

Byatt, I. (1990), 'The regulation of the water industry', Occasional Paper No. 16, The David Hume Institute.

Cave, M. (1991), 'Recent development in the regulation of former nationalised industries', Treasury Working Paper No. 60, HM Treasury.

Cohen, M., Dopudi, A., Jhunjhunwala, S., and Tamura, A. (1989), 'Review of impact of telecommunications liberalization', London Business School.

Evans, A. (1990), 'Competition and the structure of local bus markets', *Journal of Transport Economics and Policy* (Sept.), 255–81.

Gist, P., and Meadowcroft, S. A. (1986), 'Regulating for competition: The new liberalised market for private branch exchanges', *Fiscal Studies*, 7/3: 41–66.

Glaister, S. (1990), 'Bus deregulation in the UK', London School of Economics.

Laffont, J., and Tirole, J. (1991), 'Provision of quality and power of incentive schemes in regulated industries', in J. Gabszewicz and A. Mas-Colell, *Equilibrium Theory and Applications*, Cambridge: Cambridge University Press, 161–3.

Littlechild, S. (1983), *Regulation of British Telecommunications Profitability*, London: HMSO.

—— (1991), *Letter to Public Electricity Suppliers* (26 June), Birmingham: OFFER.

MMC (1980a), *The Inner London Letter Post*, HC 515, London: HMSO.

—— (1980b), *British Railways Board: London and South East Commuter Service*, Cmnd 8046, London: HMSO.

—— (1984), *The Post Office Letter Post Service*, Cmnd 9332, London: HMSO.

—— (1987), *British Railways Board: Network South-East*, Cm 204, London: HMSO.

Moore, J. (1983), 'Why privatize?', HM Treasury Press Release 190/83.

Ouseley, R. J. (1988), 'An analysis of gas disconnections', Gas Consumer Council.

Rovizzi, L., and Thompson, D. J. (1991), 'Price-cap regulated public utilities and quality regulation in the U.K.', Centre for Business Strategy, Working Paper No. 111, London Business School.

Spence, M. (1975), 'Monopoly, quality, and regulation', *Bell Journal of Economics*, 16: 417–29.

Tirole, J. (1988), *The Theory of Industrial Organisation*, Cambridge, Mass.: MIT Press.

United Research (1990), *Privatisation: Implications for Cultural Change*, Morristown, NJ: United Research.

Veljanovski, C. (1987), *Selling the State*, London: Weidenfeld & Nicholson.

Vickers, J., and Yarrow, G. (1988), *Privatisation: An Economic Analysis*, Cambridge, Mass.: MIT Press.

Waterson, M. (1984), *Economic Theory of the Industry*, Cambridge: Cambridge University Press.

15

RPI-X Price-cap Regulation

RAY REES* AND JOHN VICKERS†

1. INTRODUCTION

The most distinctive feature of monopoly regulation in Britain is the RPI–X method of price control. RPI–X price control is a type of price-cap regulation. In its basic form, it requires that the price index for a defined 'basket' of the firm's regulated products and services should increase by no more than the rate of retail price inflation minus X per cent per annum for a period of years. In short, average price must fall by at least X per cent in real terms, or rise by at most $-X$ per cent if X is negative. Following the Littlechild Report (1983), RPI–X price control was introduced for BT, and the general method, albeit with important variations, has since been adopted in other privatized industries with monopoly power—gas, airports, water, and electricity.

Much of the discussion of RPI–X price control has focused on the extent to which it differs from traditional US methods of rate-of-return regulation.[1] The first purpose of this chapter is to draw out the underlying differences between modes of price regulation using the perspective of incentive theory (Section 2). We address the incentive problems arising from asymmetric information between regulator and firm, credibility problems that can give rise to underinvestment, and the danger of

* Professor of Economics at the Department of Economics, University of Guelph, Guelph, Ontario.

† Professor at the Institute of Economics and Statistics, University of Oxford.

The paper is part of the project on 'The Regulation of Firms with Market Power', and financial support from the ESRC and from the Office of Fair Trading is gratefully acknowledged. We thank Mark Armstrong, Simon Cowan, and Colin Mayer for their helpful comments and suggestions. Of course the views expressed are entirely our own, and we are responsible for any errors. This chapter was completed in mid-1992. For a more recent account, see chapter 6 of C. M. Armstrong, S. Cowan, and J. S. Vickers (1994), *Regulatory Reform: Economic Analysis and British Experience*, MIT Press.

[1] Forms of price-cap regulation were not unknown in the USA before 1983—for example they were adopted by Michigan Bell Telephone Co. in 1980—but the development of the RPI–X rule and its application to British Telecom has greatly stimulated interest in price-cap regulation there. Price caps have replaced rate-of-return regulation for AT&T, and also for some of the regional telephone companies. They are also under active consideration for other regulated industries, such as electricity utilities and gas pipeline companies.

regulatory capture. We discuss cost passthrough, regulatory lag, the setting of *X*, quality control, the scope of regulation, multiproduct pricing questions (including price discrimination and non-linear pricing), and some interactions between price regulation and competition.

This list indicates that price regulation is unfortunately a rather more complex topic than the simple form of RPI–*X* might suggest. The second aim of this chapter is to describe the variations within the theme of RPI–*X* that have been adopted in different industries and over time (Section 3). We shall argue that price control has tended to become tighter and more involved, contrary to initial hopes that 'regulation with a light touch' would suffice.

Our third aim is to emphasize that the explicit terms of price control in the licences of the regulated firms are but one aspect of price control. In addition there is much implicit and informal regulation, which is of great practical importance. Indeed, the institutional structure of regulation in Britain is conducive to a kind of 'regulation by negotiation'.

Needless to say, the literature on RPI-*X* price regulation is large and growing. More detailed discussion is contained in the Littlechild Reports (1983, 1986) on telecommunications and water, Vickers and Yarrow (1988), and the Rand Journal (1989) symposium on price-cap regulation, especially the paper by Beesley and Littlechild (1989).

2. THE REGULATORY PROBLEM

Objectives of regulation

In assessing a system of regulation it is sensible first to consider the objectives of regulatory policy and the underlying elements in the regulatory situation which create problems in attaining them. In his report on the regulation of British Telecom, Littlechild listed five criteria on which regulatory systems should be compared:

- protection against monopoly;
- efficiency and innovation;
- burden of regulation;
- promotion of competition;
- proceeds and prospects.[2]

'Protection against monopoly' has two aspects. One is the *distributional* concern that may exist about the level of monopoly profits. If this were the only concern, an elaborate system of regulation would not be

[2] The last of these objectives relates to the revenues from privatization. Thus it is not relevant to a discussion of the regulation of a firm that has already been (wholly) privatized. This is not to say that decisions made at the time of privatization are irrelevant to subsequent regulatory policy—see below on commitment.

necessary, since the profits could simply be taxed away, for example by a levy (such as that which used to be imposed on commercial television companies), or the monopoly could be auctioned off (as with commercial television now). The second and deeper concern is with the economic *efficiency* of the monopoly: its sheltered market position allows it to become inefficient in production, so that costs are not minimized; and it may use its market power to raise prices above levels of marginal costs, causing welfare losses. The achievement of the standard objectives of productive and allocative efficiency is indeed an important criterion by which different regulatory systems can be compared.

The criterion of 'efficiency and *innovation*' introduces an important dynamic element into the discussion. In industries such as telecommunications, the allocation of resources to research and development, innovation, and technological change is arguably at least as important an aspect of economic efficiency as the static consideration of productive efficiency and price-marginal cost relationships just alluded to. Indeed in the economic analysis of patents it has long been recognized that there may be a conflict between the requirements for static short-term economic efficiency and the requirements for investment in innovation. Similar issues can arise in discussing systems of price regulation.

Regulation itself absorbs resources. There are costs directly incurred by the regulator and firm operating and complying with the regulatory process, and indirect (though none the less important) costs resulting from 'rent-seeking' and other behaviour by private parties designed to influence regulatory outcomes. Many of these costs have to do with imperfect information. If information were costless a large part of the 'burden of regulation' would disappear. There may then be an implicit trade-off between the costliness of the regulatory system, particularly in relation to its informational demands, and the acuteness of the problems created by the lack of the relevant information. One claim for RPI–*X* regulation as opposed to rate-of-return regulation is that it involves lower regulatory costs both in terms of its need for information and its vulnerability to 'capture'. We examine this claim critically below.

Competition is of course not an end in itself, but rather a means to the end of achieving economic efficiency. Full and effective competition in a market would make regulation unnecessary.[3] The extent of competition possible in the five industries with which we are primarily concerned—telecommunications, airports, electricity, gas, and water—is however problematic. In electricity generation and telecommunications there is now a degree of (essentially duopolistic) competition, but the prospects for any competition in, say, water supply or electricity distribution are

[3] Conversely, regulation by an omniscient, benevolent, and powerful regulator would make competition unnecessary. Experience with state-owned monopolies suggests that these conditions are not always fulfilled.

bleak. Clearly the regulatory process and government policy more generally should seek to encourage whatever possibilities there are of genuine competition and consequential efficiency gains. Although regulatory pricing policy *per se* is but one determinant of the development of competition, there are several important interactions between price regulation and competition, and we shall discuss these below.[4]

We conclude then that the aim of regulatory pricing policy is to achieve economic efficiency in both its static and dynamic aspects, taking into account the resource costs associated with the regulatory system and any effects it might have on the development of genuine competition in the market concerned.

We now turn to the factors which present constraints to the achievement of this objective. We discuss these in terms of a sequence of three successively richer models: single-product pure monopoly; multiproduct pure monopoly; and finally a dominant firm faced with some competition. The first model provides a simple context within which to discuss the three fundamental problems of *information, commitment,* and *capture*. We then identify additional problems that arise when we introduce multiple outputs and competition.

Single-product monopoly

We begin with the textbook case of a monopolist supplying one product of given quality in the complete absence of actual or potential competition. If the regulator possessed complete information and unlimited powers of precommitment, and if there were no risk of regulatory capture, then maximal productive and allocative efficiency could be achieved and the economics of regulation would be straightforward. Under constant or diminishing returns to scale, marginal-cost pricing could be implemented and the firm's costs would be at least covered by its revenues. Investment in innovation could be carried out up to the point at which its marginal social return just equalled its marginal cost. If returns to scale are increasing, on the other hand, marginal-cost pricing would lead to losses. A comparison would then have to be made between average-cost pricing, optimal two-part or non-linear pricing, and marginal-cost-based pricing with subsidies to cover losses, to find the second-best optimal pricing policy. In practice however, there are three types of problem which rule out a theoretically ideal solution.

[4] The RPI–X formula was essentially devised with pure monopoly in mind. In some regulated industries there is now some competition, but it would be naïve to suppose that, say, duopoly necessarily does away with the need for regulation (see for example Rees 1992), and the impact of regulation on (possibly very asymmetric) duopoly needs to be considered. For a theoretical analysis of some interactions between competition and regulation, see Caillaud (1991).

The information problem

The problem of information stems from the fact that the firm's managers are typically much better informed than the regulator about cost and demand conditions in the industry, and about the firm's own choices, for example of its level of effort to cut costs. Thus, in the language of principal-agent theory, there are problems of both adverse selection and moral hazard.[5] The asymmetry of information blocks the simultaneous attainment of productive and allocative efficiency, and leads to a trade-off between them, as a simple example suffices to illustrate. Suppose that the firm's (constant) average cost level, which is uncertain *ex ante*, turns out to be c. If price control takes the cost-related form $p = c$, then allocative efficiency is achieved but the firm has no incentive to minimize c. This is the incentive problem of cost-plus regulation. If, on the other hand, price is fixed by the regulator in a way that is insensitive to c, for example by setting *ex ante* $p = \bar{c}$, where $\bar{c}$ is some expected benchmark cost level, then incentives for cost reduction are good (because the firm keeps any gains from them) but price and cost may turn out to be far apart. This is a simplistic and extreme form of price-cap regulation.[6]

It highlights a further difficulty. If we want to ensure that the firm always at least breaks even, the price cap p must be set at the level of the highest possible c, and as a consequence, in addition to the allocative inefficiency, the firm will generally make supernormal profits. If on the other hand we simply want the firm to break even on average, we would set p at the expected value of c, but then there will be a good chance the firm will make a loss *ex post*. The firm will therefore have to precommit to produce even when its costs turn out to be higher than the allowed price. This then raises the issue of renegotiation of the terms of the 'regulatory contract', and commitment to these terms by both parties, which we consider more fully below.

A general form of price control that bridges between the two extreme cases above is expressed by the formula $p = c + \gamma(\bar{c} - c)$. The parameter γ measures the power of the firm's incentive to reduce cost. Cost-plus reg-

[5] A classic paper on regulation when the regulator does not know the firm's given cost level—an example of adverse selection—is Baron and Myerson (1982). Laffont and Tirole (1986) analysed the problem when the regulator can observe the firm's cost level, but not the firm's cost-reducing efforts—an example of moral hazard. The literature on regulation when there is asymmetric information has since become vast (see Baron 1989 for a survey).

[6] If the regulator could make lump-sum transfers to the firm, as in much of the theoretical literature, such as Laffont and Tirole (1986), then incentives for cost reduction could be provided independently of price, which could be set equal to marginal cost. In practice, however, such transfers are generally not feasible, perhaps because of the danger of regulatory capture (see Laffont and Tirole 1991). Schmalensee's analysis of 'good' (as opposed to hypothetically optimal) regulatory regimes assumes that lump-sum transfers are impossible. The fixed element of two-part pricing schemes may be similar in effect to a transfer—see further below.

ulation has $\gamma = 0$ and the simple form of price cap regulation has $\gamma = 1$. In this static single-product setting, therefore, the parameter γ is a way of capturing a major difference between types of price regulation. The determination of the optimal level of γ has been an important topic in the theoretical literature on regulation (see Laffont and Tirole 1986; and Schmalensee 1989).[7]

Put another way, $(1 - \gamma)$ measures the extent of cost *passthrough* in the formula above. In practice it is often possible to distinguish between different categories of cost. Suppose that unit cost c is the sum of two independently observable components: $c = c_1 + c_2$. There could be different degrees of passthrough for each cost component. For example the scheme $p = (c_1 + \bar{c}_2)$ would involve the full passthrough of c_1 (which could be appropriate if c_1 were completely exogenous to the firm) but no passthrough of c_2.[8] In this way, we can obtain some measure of 'state-contingency' of the regulated price, which reduces, though does not eliminate entirely, the problem of ensuring financial viability of the firm when price is insensitive to costs, while leaving it with an incentive to reduce those costs that are under its control.

The discussion so far has been in static terms. Dynamics introduce a second distinction between types of price regulation, namely that of *regulatory lag*, the length of time T between price reviews.[9] Thus suppose that costs are changing, possibly stochastically, over time. The firm can however influence this process by incurring expenditures which affect the rate at which its costs change. These expenditures are not observable by the regulator, or cannot be made the subject of agreement in the 'regulatory contract'. If prices are reviewed frequently, i.e. T is short, then, as with cost-plus regulation, the incentives for cost reduction are weak, since price tracks actual costs closely. If on the other hand T is long, incentives for cost reduction are good, especially in the early part of the period, because in the short term the firm retains any profit it can generate by keeping costs down. However, allocative efficiency may be poor towards the end of the period if price gets out of line with costs, and incentives for cost reduction also weaken as the next price review approaches. The optimal value T then has to trade-off the gain in the incentive to incur expenditure to reduce cost against the loss of allocative efficiency, both of which increase with T. It can be shown that there is a tendency for optimal T to be shorter the smaller is the sensitivity of costs to cost-reducing expenditure (since the incentive effect is smaller then), and the higher is the elasticity of demand (since the resource misallocation effect from having price out of line with marginal cost is

[7] The general analysis also embraces non-linear schemes.

[8] A more general formulation is $p = [c_1 + \gamma_1(\bar{c}_1 - c_1)] + [c_2 + \gamma_2(\bar{c}_2 - c_2)]$.

[9] The following discussion is based on the analysis in Armstrong, Rees, and Vickers (1991).

larger then). It can also be shown that, quite apart from considerations resulting from technological progress, it may be beneficial to have a price cap that changes over time, which happens with RPI ± X regulation (unless $X = 0$).[10]

One simple way to characterize rate-of-return regulation is that it requires price to be reset in each period, i.e. $T = 1$,[11] which will only rarely be optimal, with price-cap regulation generally having $T > 1$. With this characterization, price-cap regulation is essentially equivalent to rate-of-return regulation with longer lags.

Placing the problem of asymmetric information in a dynamic setting also raises the issue of the so-called 'ratchet effect'.[12] Suppose that the regulator would tighten price control if he discovered that the firm was intrinsically low-cost. Then a low-cost firm might try to hide its efficiency by slacking somewhat as a review approaches in order to obtain higher prices over the next review period.

Note that the use of regulatory lag adds another dimension to the earlier discussion of cost passthrough. If the price cap can be linked to exogenous cost components by means of a passthrough formula, this allows a longer period between price reviews, and so a smaller burden of regulation and greater incentives for reduction of those cost components that are under the firm's control.

Finally, there is the question of how to regulate *quality*. Without quality regulation, price regulation may be rendered ineffective. As elsewhere, information is a prerequisite for effective regulation. Means of quality regulation include the setting of standards backed up by a system of financial penalties payable to the public purse or, preferably if it is feasible, as compensation to affected consumers. Another method is to incorporate quality measures explicitly into the price-control formula, or to say that a price review is triggered in the event of quality, in its various dimensions, falling below some preset level(s). Alternatively, it may be implicit that quality will be a factor taken into account when price reviews occur. Whereas some aspects of quality, for example timely connections and repairs, are largely determined by current expenditures, others depend chiefly upon investment expenditures, for example in

[10] Economies of scale together with growth in demand are another reason for having $X > 0$. If there are economies of scale, demand growth causes average cost to fall even if the cost curve is stationary. Let $\hat{a}$ and $\hat{q}$ respectively denote the rates of change with respect to time of average cost and demand, and let α and η respectively be the elasticities with respect to output of average cost and demand. Scale economies imply that $\alpha < 0$. The value of X that keeps price equal to average cost is $X = -100\ (\hat{a} + \alpha\hat{q})/(1 + \alpha\eta)$. For example, if average cost is falling in real terms at 2% per year, demand is growing at 6%, $\alpha = -0.25$, and $\eta = 0.4$, then X should be about 5.55%. See Vickers and Yarrow (1988, 214–15).

[11] Under rate-of-return regulation, price reviews often occur when profits appear to have become unduly high or low, rather than at fixed intervals. For a model of endogenous and stochastic regulatory reviews in this spirit, see Bawa and Sibley (1980).

[12] See for example Freixas, Guesnerie, and Tirole (1985).

network infrastructure, adequate capacity and modern technology. The question of regulatory incentives for quality is therefore inseparable from that of regulatory incentives for investment.

The commitment problem

A feature of many economic relationships is the 'hold-up' problem that may occur when it is (i) efficient for one party to make sunk cost investments *ex ante*, but (ii) irrational for the party to make those investments without some guarantee that the other party will not opportunistically exploit the situation *ex post*. Such a guarantee is often provided by long-term contracts, which commit the second party not to exploit the first, and which therefore facilitate the efficient investment.

A similar issue arises in regulation, and we now need to consider the nature of commitment in the 'regulatory contract'. Part of that 'contract' is explicit, for example in the legislation and licences of regulated firms, which are nevertheless not immutable in the long run, and part is implicit or discretionary. If the regulator and regulatory process lack the ability to commit to future prices, the concern arises that, after the firm has made sunk-cost investment expenditures, regulatory policy will be tightened with the result that the firm does not recover its cost of capital. If investors anticipate this, then the cost of capital will be increased to include a premium for regulatory risk, and the firm may be deterred from investing efficiently in the first place. Unless commitment not to 'expropriate' can somehow be achieved, there is a danger of underinvestment, especially in industries where sunk costs are important. Note that this is the reverse of the Averch-Johnson (1962) overinvestment problem emphasized in the traditional literature on rate-of-return regulation.

A possible argument for US rate-of-return regulation is that it entails a commitment, which has judicial backing and historical precedent, that a fair return on investment (or at least 'used and useful' investment) will be earned, while at the same time allowing desirable regulatory discretion subject to that commitment.[13] On this view, then, the regulator is not an independent player but is constrained not to act opportunistically by a credible commitment to be fair to investors. (Thus there is a kind of principal–agent hierarchy, with the legislature and courts as principal, the firm as the ultimate agent, and the regulator as an *intermediate* agent). In practice this commitment cannot be absolute, however, and since the mid-1970s the rates of return achieved by a number of US utilities have been eroded as a result of inflation coupled with regulatory lag in adjusting nominal prices, and by regulatory decisions to disqualify

[13] See Greenwald (1984) for a discussion of this view. For recent analyses of the regulatory commitment problem that use a repeated game approach, see Gilbert and Newbery (1988), and Salant and Woroch (1992).

some assets (e.g. nuclear power-stations) from the rate base on the grounds that they were not 'used and useful'.

What are the characteristics of RPI–*X* regulation, and its surrounding institutional structures, in relation to the commitment problem? Regulators are generally required by the legislation to ensure that the firms can finance the services needed to meet all 'reasonable demands'. Moreover, to the extent that the regulatory lag in RPI–*X* limits regulatory discretion between price reviews, there is some check on opportunism in the short term. However, as we shall see, considerable regulatory discretion remains.[14] At least as important is the possibility of major changes in regulatory policy as a result of action by government, perhaps following the election of a new government. Parliament being sovereign, in principle there are few limits to its ultimate discretion. In this regard the commitment problem may be more serious in Britain than in the USA, because judicial restraints, historical precedent, and political consensus about appropriate regulatory policy are all weaker here. In Section 3 below we shall examine the seriousness of the commitment problem in the light of British regulatory experience so far.

The capture problem

Finally, there is the problem of 'capture'—collusion between regulator and firm.[15] Again it is useful to view the regulator as part of a three-layer principal–agent hierarchy in which the government (or the general public) and the firm are respectively the ultimate principal and agent. In these terms collusion between regulator and firm is likely to frustrate the government in achieving its objectives. The danger is that the regulatory authority, far from controlling and diminishing the monopoly power of the regulated firm, instead becomes the firm's advocate, and maybe even an instrument for the maintenance of monopoly power by preventing new entry.

At first sight RPI–*X* regulation, and the British regulatory institutional structure more generally, may appear to have little vulnerability to capture, because the business of checking that annual price increases comply with the formula involves little regulatory discretion.[16] However, regulators have had a good deal of discretion with RPI–*X* regulation in practice, and the regulatory process in Britain is not open to public scrutiny—the regulator does not have to explain or justify his decisions or publish the evidence on which they were based. Nevertheless, as we

[14] To be precise, the discretion does not belong to the regulatory body (e.g. OFTEL) independently, but in conjunction with the Monopolies and Mergers Commission, whose agreement is required for regulatory changes that the regulator cannot agree with the firm in question. The need for MMC agreement is some check on potential opportunism.

[15] See Stigler (1971), and Laffont and Tirole (1991).

[16] The Littlechild Report (1983, 20) regarded low vulnerability to capture as an advantage of RPI–*X* regulation on these grounds.

shall see later, there is little evidence so far that regulatory bodies have been subject to capture since privatization.[17]

Multiproduct monopoly

In reality every regulated monopoly supplies a number of different products, for example: local, national and international telephone calls, and network access; water for domestic and industrial use, and sewage disposal; domestic, commercial, and industrial electricity and gas; and so on. As well as these obvious differences, it is essential to recognize that, when peak-load demand characteristics are important, as they are in all regulated industries, peak and off-peak services must be treated as distinct products.

If the marginal costs of the different outputs could be identified, and if marginal-cost pricing yielded sufficient revenue to cover total costs, including joint and other fixed costs, then nothing substantial would be added to the previous discussion of the single-product case. If, however, marginal-cost pricing leads to inadequate revenues to cover all costs, then there is the problem of devising a regulatory incentive system, possibly including a subsidy scheme, that leads to some appropriate price structure that does cover costs.

One approach is Ramsey pricing, in which the mark-up of price over marginal cost for product i is inversely related to the elasticity of demand for that product, and is related also to cross-elasticities of demand between products.[18] In practice, however, the regulator is unlikely to have enough information to implement Ramsey pricing, and an alternative is simply to regulate some *average* price and to leave the firm some discretion over *relative* prices, rather than regulating each price individually. A notable feature of price-cap regulation in Britain is that regulated firms have been given more discretion of this kind than, say, US utilities subject to traditional rate-of-return regulation.

What are the pros and cons of allowing the firm discretion over relative prices, and what is the best way to regulate 'average' price? A merit of permitting flexibility is that the firm can then respond to cost changes. If, for example, the cost of product i turns out to be lower than expected in relation to the cost of product j, then the firm may tend to lower the price of i and increase the price of j relative to the situation where the firm has no discretion. On the other hand, the firm's private incentives will not necessarily coincide with what is socially desirable, especially if

[17] These regulatory bodies include the Monopolies and Mergers Commission and the Office of Fair Trading, as well as bodies like OFTEL and OFGAS. Not being industry-specific, the MMC and OFT may be (even) less prone to capture.

[18] In the case of independent demands, these cross-elasticities are zero, and mark-ups are simply proportional to inverse own-elasticities of demand. On the theory of public utility pricing, see Brown and Sibley (1986).

there is actual or potential competition in some markets (see below). Even in the pure monopoly case, incentives may be out of line, depending on the average price index used.

Let w_i be the weight accorded to the price of product i in the price control formula. In other words, the average price cap takes the form: $\Sigma_i w_i p_i \leq \bar{p}$. It can be shown that if the w_i's are fixed, and if they happen to be proportional to demands at Ramsey prices (given the profit level implied by the cap on average price), then the profit-maximizing firm will choose Ramsey prices. But only by fluke would the (imperfectly informed) regulator happen to set the weights proportional to Ramsey demands. If, on the other hand, the weights are endogenous, then strategic behaviour becomes relevant, and there might be a systematic tendency towards inefficient price structures. For example, under 'average revenue regulation' the weights are proportional to output shares—that is, assuming that outputs are commensurable, $w_j = q_j/(\Sigma_i q_i)$. In that case the firm has a profit incentive to distort the price structure away from Ramsey pricing by expanding the demand of products with lower than average prices (which will tend to be those with low marginal cost or relatively elastic demand) and reducing the demand of products with higher than average prices.[19]

A simple way to regulate the structure of prices of products that are commensurable (for example therms of gas) is to ban price discrimination. However, if costs differ greatly by time of day or year, for example because of peak-load considerations, then uniform pricing is inefficient. (Uniform geographical pricing may also be inefficient.) In the absence of such cost differences, the desirability of banning price discrimination depends on the form of price constraint. With fixed weights in the index, price discrimination benefits consumers on average as well as the firm in the pure monopoly case. But if the cap applies to average revenue, consumers lose from price discrimination and the overall welfare effect is ambiguous.[20]

A related policy question is whether to allow non-linear pricing such as two-part tariffs and other types of quantity discount. This issue, which can also arise in single-product settings, is related to price discrimination because large and small users pay different average prices. The benefit of two-part pricing when there are economies of scale is that the revenue from the fixed charge can contribute towards fixed cost, thereby allowing the variable charge to be reduced, and so bringing marginal price closer to marginal cost. Under some circumstances, each consumer's benefit from consumption is so large at marginal cost prices that a lump-sum charge (for connection, line rental or standing charge) can be set that covers the revenue shortfall from marginal cost pricing

[19] See Bradley and Price (1988), and Vickers and Yarrow (1988, 103–7).

[20] See Armstrong and Vickers (1991).

without causing any consumer to stop using the product or service. While this may be approximately true for water and electricity, it is probably not so for gas and telephones. If, on the other hand, the number of consumers decreases as the fixed charge is raised, then exact marginal-cost pricing in a two-part tariff is not optimal.[21] It can be shown however that giving consumers the *option* to choose between the existing uniform tariff and a two-part tariff can benefit everyone, provided that there is no competition and that the product is a consumer good and not an intermediate good (Willig 1978). No consumer loses from the new option being available,[22] the large users who take up the option gain, and the two-part tariff is constructed in such a way that those large users yield a larger surplus of revenue over variable cost—and hence a larger contribution to fixed cost—than in the original situation with uniform pricing.

Some of the most controversial problems in regulating multiproduct firms have to do with 'cost allocation' and determining when there is cross-subsidy between activities. Consider, for example, the problem of 'allocating costs' between telephone-call charges and exchange-line rentals, or between the activities of a firm that is regulated in some of its activities but not in others. Clearly it is in the interest of the regulated firm to allocate, however spuriously, as many joint costs as possible to its regulated activities. (Under rate-of-return regulation this involves including as much capital as possible in the 'rate base'.) Disputes about cost allocation, which are likely to be all the greater if information asymmetries are large, are a good illustration of the 'burden of regulation'. This point leads to questions about policy towards structure: should a regulated firm be allowed to diversify into other unregulated activities, or indeed should it be divested of unregulated activities? If diversification worsens the regulator's asymmetric information problem discussed above, then it may hamper the effectiveness of regulation—to the benefit of the firm and to the detriment of welfare.[23] This suggests that regulatory policy should be prepared to place some constraints on diversification by regulated firms.

For a monopolist that is regulated for all products, the question of 'cost allocation' is an unnecessary one in economic terms. With Ramsey pricing, for example, there is no need to say which costs are attributable to product i and which are attributable to product j. Optimal prices

[21] This is especially undesirable if there are positive 'network externalities' between users, as in telecommunications.

[22] Note that this need not be true if the product is supplied to firms rather than final consumers. A small firm that does not take up the option might lose out if its larger rivals do (see Ordover and Panzar 1982).

[23] See Braeutigam and Panzar (1989) for an analysis of private and social diversification incentives. Vickers (1990) examines some consequences of vertical integration for price regulation when the monopolist supplies an input to potential rivals.

depend on *marginal* costs and demand elasticities. Cross-subsidy could be defined with respect to Ramsey prices—product *i* being cross-subsidized if p_i is below the Ramsey price level, and cross-subsidizing other products if it is above that level.[24] On this tight definition, cross-subsidy is absent only when there is Ramsey pricing.

A very different definition of cross-subsidy comes from contestability theory, where the test is whether there would be vulnerability to entry if no entry or exit barriers existed. On this view prices are subsidy-free provided that the revenue from each set of products is no greater than their 'stand-alone' cost of production (the cost of producing that set of products in isolation) and no less than their 'incremental' cost (the extra cost of producing that set of products in addition to the other products).[25] Under some conditions no such prices exist, but this definition typically gives a large range of 'subsidy-free' prices. It is unclear why this hypothetical free-entry test is appropriate for industries with massive entry barriers and sunk costs, as in major parts (but not all) of the utility industries, and we therefore prefer the spirit of the Ramsey approach. However, information problems prevent its precise implementation. The cross-subsidy question is of most concern when there is competition.

Actual and potential competition

A number of the issues just discussed become all the more acute when there is (actual or potential) competition. If there is 'enough' competition in an industry, then regulation is unnecessary. But if the situation is that a dominant incumbent faces some small entrant(s), then regulation will be needed—not only to protect consumers against monopolistic abuse by the dominant firm, but also to protect the entrant(s) against anti-competitive behaviour.

In the single-product case the dominant firm's price can simply be capped. A cap has the advantage of allowing downward flexibility to meet competition, but a price floor might also be needed to check predatory pricing. If the product is homogeneous, or if the scale of entry is small, then explicit regulation of the entrants' prices is unnecessary because they will not be able to charge more than the dominant firm in any case.

In the multiproduct case, however, there is the danger that average-

[24] Laffont and Tirole (1990) call this 'demand-side cross-subsidization'. In their analysis adjustment is also made for cost-reduction incentive effects.

[25] Consider a two-product example. Suppose that it costs 2 to produce each product in isolation, and that it costs 3 to produce both together (there are economies of scope). Then the stand-alone cost is 2 and the incremental cost is 1 for each product. Prices p_1 and p_2 such that $p_1 + p_2 = 3$ and $1 < p_i < 2$ are 'subsidy-free'.

price regulation might actually encourage anti-competitive behaviour unless individual prices are monitored by the regulator. Suppose that the dominant firm serves two markets, one of which is captive, the other being open to competition. If price control applies to an average of the prices charged in the two markets, then the loss from reducing price in the competitive market can be partly recouped by charging a higher price in the captive market. If the dominant firm has discretion over price structure, entry into the competitive market might be deterred.[26] Separate control of price in the captive market can therefore be an important element of policy to promote effective competition.

Regulation of the prices of intermediate products supplied by the dominant firm to rivals—such as access to local telecommunications networks or gas pipelines—is another necessary part of regulation for competition. Without proper access the competitive challenge of rivals could be thwarted altogether, but there is much debate about what constitute 'fair' terms of access. This important topic is discussed in more detail in Chapter 12 (this volume) on telecommunications by Armstrong and Vickers.

The scope for competition to play a valuable role is not confined to industries where head-to-head product market competition occurs. If the industry has a regional structure,[27] as do water supply and electricity distribution in England and Wales, then *yardstick regulation*, or 'competition by comparison', may be feasible. The idea of this is to induce competition in cost reduction between monopolists in separate areas—for example the water companies or the electricity distributors in England and Wales—by means of the regulatory system (see Shleifer 1985). Thus the allowed price in one area is related to cost performance not only in that area but also in others, perhaps simply to an industry yardstick of costs. This could be done by incorporating yardstick elements explicitly into price-control formulas. Cost passthrough formulas of the kind discussed above can easily be extended to contain yardstick elements—for example the allowable price for the firm in region i could have the form $p_i = \alpha c_i + (1 - \alpha)c_j$, where c_i is the cost level of firm i and c_j is the average cost level of the firms in the *other* regions. In this case α would be the degree of passthrough of the firm's own costs and $(1 - \alpha)$ would be the degree of passthrough of average costs in the rest of the industry. Alternatively, less formal cost comparisons could be made at times of price review.

Under ideal conditions, when the firms in question face highly

26 For an analysis of this question, see Armstrong and Vickers (1992).

27 Whether or not an industry has a regional structure depends on government policy at the time of privatization and on subsequent competition policies. For example, interregional mergers could deprive the regulator of valuable comparative information (see MMC 1990).

correlated uncertainties, yardstick regulation can overcome the fundamental dilemma in price regulation—the difficulty of reconciling incentives for productive efficiency with allocative efficiency. But in practice there are region-specific influences that must be allowed for, and this is no easy matter. Thus although principal–agent theory has established that comparative information is generally valuable in designing incentive schemes, the problem is to develop a practical means of doing this efficiently. This is one of the most important challenges facing the economics of price regulation.

3. BRITISH EXPERIENCE WITH PRICE REGULATION

The explicit rules of price control for regulated utilities in Britain are found in the licences granted to them under Acts of Parliament. In practice, however, price control goes further, because regulatory bodies can exert various informal powers. It is important in this regard to understand the institutional structure of regulation in Britain. It differs markedly from traditional US regulatory methods.

The British pattern was set when British Telecom was privatized. Under the 1984 Telecommunications Act, regulatory powers are divided between three bodies. The Secretary of State for Trade and Industry is empowered to grant licences to BT and other firms. The Director General of Telecommunications (DGT), who heads OFTEL, has the duty of monitoring and enforcing licence conditions. He advises the Secretary of State on licensing, and may have some licensing authority delegated to him. The DGT can also chance licence conditions, either by agreement with the firm in question or by making a successful reference to the Monopolies and Mergers Commission (MMC), the third element in the regulatory trio. The DGT's informal regulatory authority derives from this ability to seek licence changes. A similar institutional structure exists for gas, water, electricity, and airports.

The Scope of Price Control

Table 15.1 summarizes the main aspects of (explicit) price control in five industries. The first two rows indicate the scope of regulation by listing the main regulated and unregulated activities respectively. The regulated activities include natural monopolies such as electricity distribution and water supply, and also activities where there is some competition, for example long-distance telecommunications services. Two developments over time are worth noting. First, because of regional and vertical separation, price control in water and electricity is much more disaggregated than in earlier privatizations. Each regional water authority has its own K factor, and similarly there is an individual X factor for the wires business of each regional electricity distributor. In electricity, unlike gas, transmission, distribution and supply to small users are regulated separately.

Second, there has been a tendency for the scope of price control to increase over time. In telecommunications, services that are now formally regulated, but which used not to be, include connections, leased lines, and international calls. OFTEL (1992*a*, 9) reports that price regulation now covers about 70 per cent of BT's business compared with 50 per cent in 1989. (This despite the view in Littlechild (1983) that regulation should be a stop-gap until sufficient competition arrives.) The scope of regulation has also been extended by informal means. For example, the price level for gas supplied to large users is formally unregulated, but intervention by OFGAS in 1991 persuaded BG to reverse most of a 35 per cent price increase to electricity generators. A notable exception from the list of regulated activities is electricity generation—notable because industrial characteristics and structure suggest that National Power and PowerGen have substantial market power. The threat of regulatory intervention—by MMC referral to change licence conditions—may be an important factor discouraging its exercise. If so, this is another major example of price regulation taking place by informal means.

Definition of price index

Two broad approaches have been used to construct the index of prices of regulated services. In telecommunications the weight in the index given to the price of service i in year t is proportional to outputs in period t–1. This is called the 'tariff basket' method. It has also been adopted in the water industry. The second method, which is used in the gas, electricity, and airports industries, is the 'revenue yield' method. Here the cap is simply applied to average revenue—the total revenue derived from the regulated activities divided by the sum of their outputs. This approach can be used only when the output can be added up, as with therms of gas or kilowatt hours of electricity. By contrast, with telecommunications services—which include calls, exchange lines, etc.—there are no equivalent natural units.

From the point of view of economic efficiency, the incentives for pricing structure implied by the index construction are of interest. As was discussed in Section 2 above, average revenue regulation can create incentives that distort pricing away from Ramsey pricing, whereas fixed weights, though difficult to determine, cannot be manipulated by the firm. The tariff basket approach lies somewhere in between these cases: last year's weight is given in the current period, but this year's decisions

TABLE 15.1. RPI–X regulation

	British Telecom	British Gas	British Airports Authority	Water-Supply companies	Electricity transmission (NGC)	Electricity distribution (RECs)	Electricity supply
Regulated	Inland calls International calls (since 1991) Line rentals Leased lines	Supply to small (<25K therm) users	Airport charges at South-East airports	Water and sewerage charges Infrastructure charges Trade effluent	All transmission	All distribution	REC customers
Unregulated	Apparatus supply Mobile services VANS	Supply to larger users	All other services (retail, parking, etc)	All other activities			
Price index	Weighted by quantities in previous year	Average revenue per therm	Average revenue per passenger	Weighted by quantities in previous year	Average revenue per KWh	Average revenue per KWh	Average revenue per KWh
Choice of X (or K)	$X = 3$ (1984–9) $X = 4.5$ (1989–1991) $X = 6.25$ (1991–)	$X = 2$ (1986–91) $X = 5$ (1991–)	$X = 1$ (1987–92) $X = 8, 8, 4, 1, 1$ (1992–7)	K varies by firm and over time Average is RPI+5.5	$X = 0$	Each REC has its X Range is from RPI+0 to RPI+2.5	$X = 0$

Price structure[1]	RPI+2 for rentals and connections RPI–0 cap on median user's bill RPI–0 for leased lines	X = 0 cap on fixed charge (1991–)	Same cap applies to Heathrow and Gatwick individually	RPI–0 for infrastructure charges			Additional cap for franchise customers (< 1 Mw)
Cost passthrough		All gas-supply costs (1987–92); GPI–1 (1992–) Energy efficiency factor	75% of extra security costs (1987–92) 95% of extra security costs (1992–)	Costs of new environmental and quality regulations			Costs of power purchase, transmission, and distribution
Quality regulation	Fixed penalties for delays in repairs and connections Contractual liability	Compensation scheme being organized		EC and UK standards for drinking-water and bathing-beaches Threat of price cuts if standards not met			Fixed penalties for performance failures (capacity element in pool price promotes supply security)
Regulatory lag	Initially 5 years now 4 years Next review 1993	5 years Next review 1996	5 years Next review 1997 MMC involved	10 years (2000) or 5 years at OFWAT's or firm's request	3 years (1992)	4 years (1993)	4 years (1993)

[1] In addition there are some provisions against cross-subsidy and undue price discrimination.

affect next year's price constraint. An advantage of the tariff basket approach over the revenue yield approach is that it may be less open to strategic manipulation.

The choice of X

Price regulation could apply both to the initial level of prices and also to their permitted rate of change over time. The level of prices inherited from the past has generally been adopted for newly privatized firms, and this has been the tendency at times of regulatory review. As to the rate of change of prices, the choice of *X* has varied from industry to industry, and from region to region within the water and electricity industries. As one would expect, the highest original value of *X* was set in telecommunications, where technological advance is great (and there is considerable demand growth). The water industry, where substantial real price increases are allowed, is at the other end of the range—large infrastructure investments are necessary to meet quality standards.

In the industries where price reviews have occurred, *X* has been tightened markedly. (At the end of this Section we briefly discuss the influence of rate-of-return considerations in these price reviews.) Thus in the telecommunications price review *X* was raised from 3 to 4.5, and a year's price freeze was required (OFTEL 1988). When international calls were brought under price control in 1991, *X* was increased to 6.25, and in the 1992 price review, *X* was increased further to 7.5. In the 1991 gas-price review, *X* was raised from 2 to 5, and the extent of passthrough of gas costs was limited (see below). For south-east airports, following an original proposal by the Civil Aviation Authority (CAA) that *X* be increased from 1 to 8, and an MMC review which recommended RPI–4, the CAA finally determined that *X* in the five years from 1992–7 should start at 8 and decline to 1.

Price structure

The same is true of the regulation of price structure. In the mid-1980s BT greatly altered the balance between its local and long-distance call charges. Nothing in the formal rules of price control prevented these changes, but OFTEL was concerned that they should not be excessive, especially since Mercury's challenge was principally in long-distance services. A review by OFTEL concluded that the rebalancing up to 1986 was justified by costs, but further changes were discouraged. Pricing structure was also an important aspect of the 1988 and 1992 price reviews and the 1991 Duopoly Review in telecommunications (see Chapter 12 (this volume) by Armstrong and Vickers for further details). OFTEL's threat of making a reference to the MMC was very important in its negotiations with BT, though so far it has not been exercised. The parties came close to the brink in 1991 over a dispute concerning the balance between call charges and exchange-line rentals (BT wanting more discretion than OFTEL allowed) and rivals' terms of access to BT's network. BT finally agreed to OFTEL's terms, thus avoiding an MMC investigation. The agreement included two measures of non-linear pricing—BT was given a degree of freedom to make quantity discounts to large users, and a low-user scheme was introduced.

An important measure of price structure regulation was introduced in the gas industry in 1988, two years after privatization, when an MMC inquiry into BG's behaviour in the industrial market, which is not subject to RPI–*X* price control, recommended that BG should not be allowed to engage in price discrimination. Price structure is already on the regulatory agenda in electricity too, where OFFER has asked the National Grid Company to come forward with proposals for the structure of its transmission tariffs.

The conclusion from this experience is that in practice, as well as in theory, it is not always safe to give private firms with market power autonomy over pricing structure even when there is regulation of average price levels.

Cost passthrough

The first example of cost passthrough in British regulatory policy was British Gas, which was allowed to pass through (to consumers taking less than 25K therms per annum) all changes in the average cost of obtaining gas supplies. Passthrough also exists for BAA with respect to most additional airport security costs, and for electricity supply to smaller users, where 100 per cent passthrough of power purchase, transmission, and distribution costs is allowed (though initially there is a subsidiary RPI–6 cap which reflects existing coal contracts).

In principle, *full* passthrough should apply to costs that are entirely beyond the control of the firm, because there are no cost reduction incentive issues in this case. With BG, however, although its gas-supply costs are greatly influenced by exogenous events such as movements in world oil prices, this is not entirely so. From 1986–91 British Gas was allowed full passthrough, but in the recent price review (OFGAS 1991), an incentive for British Gas to purchase gas supplies more efficiently was introduced by restricting passthrough to the change in a gas-price index (GPI), which is based on BG's existing contracts, minus 1 per cent. There is also an energy efficiency factor, *E*. Thus the new formula takes the form: (RPI–5) + (GPI–1) + *E*. The BAA price review changed the provisions for the passthrough of additional security costs required by government, increasing the proportion recovered by BAA from 75 to 95 per cent.

Since the water and electricity distribution industries were privatized with a regional structure, they both raised the opportunity for yardstick regulation. This is a kind of cost passthrough because the price faced by consumers in one region reflects the costs achieved in other regions. The Littlechild (1986) report on price regulation in the water industry emphasized the possibility of yardstick regulation, and it appeared at one stage that yardstick components would be explicitly included in the price control formulas for electricity supply to smaller users. But in neither case did that happen. Nevertheless comparative cost data will be available at the times of price review in these industries. How the comparative data will be used in framing future price control is unclear, but its availability is likely to be an additional spur to efficiency in the interim even so. Thus there is a degree of implicit yardstick regulation.

Quality and investment

Quality regulation has generally been implicit rather than explicit. As discussed above, a broad distinction exists between components of quality that depend mainly on current expenditures (e.g. telephone installations and repairs) and those that require major capital investment expenditures (e.g. water quality and reliable electricity supplies). The quality of telecommunications services became a controversial issue in 1987. Rather than incorporating quality factors into the price-control mechanism, OFTEL asked BT to accept contractual liability for damages caused by poor performance, with standard compensation terms for late repairs, etc. In addition there always existed the threat that OFTEL would go to the MMC to seek a licence amendment to regulate quality in the event of poor quality performance. Likewise for electricity supply, there are standard compensation terms for slow repairs to restore service, for example.

The water industry provides an excellent example of regulatory promotion of investment to enhance quality. (Quality improvements are needed to meet European Community standards for drinking- and bathing-water.) The *K* factors in the RPI+*K* formulas for the privatized water supply companies were set so as to finance the prospective investment expenditures required in each region, and there is provision for OFWAT to disallow the full extent of permitted price increase if a company fails to meet its prescribed investment objectives. Most significantly, the 1989 Water Act requires the regulator to ensure that the regulated firms earn a reasonable rate of return on capital employed. This is a reflection of, and offers a degree of protection against, the commitment problem described above.

Investment issues, and the question of a new terminal at Heathrow in particular, figured in the BAA price review. In suggesting RPI–8 for

1992–7, the CAA had it in mind that a regime such as RPI+7 might be needed for 1997–2002 in order to finance the new investment (see CAA 1991). The MMC suggested making *X contingent* on the investment taking place (which is an interesting indication of a perceived underinvestment problem) but the CAA did not take up the idea, partly because of the problem of identifying the trigger point. In any event, the investment will mostly occur in the period after the next price review, and can be catered for then. These measures may be viewed partly as an attempt to overcome the underinvestment problem discussed in Section 2 above. In electricity generation, incentives for supply security—a key aspect of quality—depend on the 'capacity element' paid to generators for making capacity available, a regulated component of the otherwise unregulated pool price for bulk power (see Vickers and Yarrow (1991) for further detail). The capacity element is equal to the calculated probability of there being insufficient capacity multiplied by the estimated loss caused by a capacity shortage. Regulatory policy can affect investment incentives by adjusting this number.

Regulatory lag and price reviews

As Table 15.1 shows, regulatory lag (the time between price reviews) is typically four or five years. In the water industry the lag is ten years, but a review can be instigated after five years, and OFWAT has already indicated that it intends to do this.

For airports, where the regulatory body is the CAA rather than a new body in the OFTEL mould, the MMC is automatically involved with price review.[28] The various recommendations made by the CAA and MMC in this review have been described above. In the telecommunications and gas-price reviews, MMC involvement did not occur because agreement was reached between regulator and firm—a regulatory bargain was struck. This avoids the cost and delay of an MMC enquiry, and is perhaps to be expected in so far as the regulator and firm do not have to share power with a third party. But regulation is less open as a result, which is disadvantageous and, as we argued above, could be dangerous if there were regulatory capture, though there has been little sign of that in Britain so far.

It will be quite apparent from this discussion that regulation, and the threat of MMC reference, does not only occur at times of formal price review, but is an ongoing activity. There is no guarantee that the regulator will not intervene for the fixed period of years, and in a sense, therefore, regulatory lag is shorter than it appears to be. A clear case in point

[28] In 1987 the MMC made recommendations on RPI–*X* regulation for Manchester Airport (which is not owned by BAA) (see Beesley and Littlechild 1989). This is the first example of price review by a regulatory body in Britain.

is the fact that the 1991 review of entry conditions in telecommunications, which occurred midway through the price-review cycle, nevertheless contained important new measures of price control.

Rate of return

To end this section we return to the initial question of RPI–*X* and rate-of-return regulation. The importance of return calculations in price reviews should be emphasized. (For a fuller account see Cave (1991) and Chapter 16 by Grout in this volume.) The implicit use of rate-of-return in price reviews, and in setting *X* at the time of privatization, has been widely acknowledged (see Littlechild 1986). The capital-asset pricing model (CAPM) and the dividend growth model (DGM) have been used to estimate the cost of capital.[29] Rate-of-return considerations were important in the 1988 review of BT's pricing, but OFTEL did not state publicly what it regarded as a fair return.[30] In the 1991 gas-price review, OFGAS concluded that a real rate of return of 5–7 per cent was reasonable for the tariff market. In the airports review the CAA initially proposed that a 7 per cent real rate of return was appropriate for BAA's regulated activities, but the new price formula is expected to yield 7.5 per cent. For the water industry, OFWAT (1991) issued a consultative document on the cost of capital, which estimated that the cost of equity is 5–7 per cent in real terms and that the risk-adjusted cost of debt is 3–5 per cent in real terms, giving a weighted cost of capital of 5–6 per cent given long-run gearing levels.

Once the cost of capital has been estimated for the regulated services, the next task in a price review is to determine and measure the capital devoted to the provision of the services. This is no easy task, especially if the firm also supplies unregulated services, in which case there may be difficult cost-allocation problems. A view must also be taken about the likely scope for cost reduction and demand growth in the period ahead.

[29] The CAPM provides a risk-adjusted rate of return on equity as follows. Take a 'risk-free' rate such as the interest rate on index-linked gilts, and add the average market risk premium multiplied by the contribution to market risk by the firm in question. This latter contribution, which is called the firm's *beta*, is equal to the covariance between the return on the firm's equity and that of the stock market as a whole, divided by the variance of the return on the market. OFTEL (1992*b*) reports that BT's beta has been about 0.74, which is lower than that of British Gas (0.8) and higher than that of the water industry (0.6 on average). The DGM, which assumes a constant expected-growth rate of dividends, says that the expected return on equity equals dividend yield plus expected dividend growth. The CAPM has theoretical advantages but may be hard to rely upon in practice if, for example, short data runs mean that beta is difficult to estimate with confidence. A difficulty with both approaches is that the cost of capital for the firm's *regulated* business, which is what matters for price regulation, may be different from its *overall* cost of capital, for example, because of differences in risk.

[30] OFTEL (1992*b*, 7) derives a weighted cost of capital for BT of 17–20% in nominal terms before tax.

Finally, the parameters of the price regime—*X*, any one-off price changes, cost passthrough elements, and so on—are set so that the firm's expected rate of return is in line with the estimated cost of capital. Naturally this cannot be done with total accuracy—out-turns will generally differ from expectations for a variety of reasons.

Rate-of-return calculations are obviously central to this process. How its incentive effects compare with traditional rate-of-return regulation depend on the length of regulatory lag, the extent of cost passthrough, and particularly the way that the scope for future cost reduction is assessed (see Section 2 above). If the firm has an effective monopoly of relevant information, then incentive effects will be poorer than if comparative information can be used to establish performance benchmarks that are not so much under the control of any one firm. In this regard the price reviews for water and electricity distribution, both of which were privatized with a regional structure, will be particularly interesting.

4. CONCLUSIONS

A system of price regulation must be judged in terms of the incentives it gives the regulated firm to achieve economic efficiency—allocative, productive, in static terms and over time. There are fundamental problems inherent in the regulatory situation—arising from information asymmetries, commitment issues, and collusion possibilities—and there are no easy escapes from them.

At first sight the RPI–*X* method of price control looks simple, different from, and superior to rate-of-return regulation, with good incentives for cost efficiency, minimal regulatory burden, and low risk of capture. However, a number of parameters have to be set and from time to time reset: the coverage of the price cap; construction of the price index; whether and how much cost passthrough to allow; the level of *X*; the extent to which *individual* prices are made subject to regulation; the frequency of price reviews; and controls on quality, to name only the most obvious. This is not to say that the RPI–*X* system is the same as rate-of-return regulation. It does however mean that RPI–*X* price regulation is more complex and problematic than its original advocates appeared to believe.

RPI–*X* can be operated in various ways. 'Passive RPI–*X*' would involve the regulator simply checking that the formula was complied with year after year, leaving the firm discretion over such matters as price structure, and resetting the parameters at review times. Incentives for cost reduction would vary over the review cycle, being better just after a review than when one was imminent, and the regulatory burden would indeed be modest. But pricing efficiency, quality and competition, could all suffer greatly in the process.

'Active RPI–*X*' involves continuing regulatory vigilance backed up by the threat of an MMC reference to seek the imposition of tougher regulation. Price structure, quality, and perhaps even investment, are all under scrutiny. The regulator presses for better quality information, including relevant comparative information, from the firm(s) so as to diminish the asymmetric information gap that limits regulatory effectiveness.

The British pattern, set first by OFTEL, has been one of fairly active RPI–X. The explicit rules of price control have been supplemented by much implicit regulation. Moreover, price regulation has broadened and tightened over time largely as a result of the efforts of regulatory bodies. This has happened most notably at times of formal price review, as with those of BT, BG, and BAA, but also between price reviews, as with BT's rebalancing and the MMC inquiry into the industrial gas market. Every indication is that price regulation was too lax initially, because other objectives of privatization, including revenue raising and the political desire to privatize speedily, conflicted with effective regulation, and it is good that the effectiveness of price regulation has since been increased. The effectiveness of government policy towards competition in the regulated industries has also increased somewhat in recent years, as is evidenced by the breakup of the Central Electricity Generating Board before privatization and the ending of the BT/Mercury duopoly policy in telecommunications.[31]

These developments can be related back to two of the problems of regulation discussed at the outset, namely those of capture and commitment. The fact that British regulatory bodies have generally opted for active rather than passive RPI–*X* suggests that they have not been captured. Ironically, passive RPI–*X*, although involving a low regulatory burden, *would* have been a sign of capture. In so far as capture is reflected by weakness of policy towards competition and regulation, it appears to have been more a feature of government decision-making in the run-up to large privatizations, especially in the mid-1980s, than of behaviour by regulatory bodies, including the MMC, since then.

The tightening of regulatory policy has led to vigorous complaints by regulated firms that the rules of the game are being changed *ex post*, that they represent breach of faith with investors, and that regulatory risk jeopardizes investment plans, particularly where long-lived sunk assets are involved. There is also the political risk that a government with a less favourable attitude to private utilities may be elected. Some share-price movements have been consistent with these concerns. In our view the changes in regulatory policy have been adjustments from a situation

[31] See Vickers (1991) for a review of government regulatory policy over the past decade.

that was unduly favourable to the utilities, and not necessarily a sign of *ex post* opportunism. In short, the original regimes were not credibly sustainable.

Whether or not a more stable 'regulatory bargain' can develop from now on is an open question. RPI–X, compared with rate-of return regulation, may help in so far as it involves commitment to non-intervention for a period, but it does so very imperfectly and may carry less of a promise that there will be an adequate return to investors. However, the decisive influence probably has more to do with the structure and behaviour of institutions, both regulatory and political, than with the form of price regulation *per se*.

Price regulation in Britain has not operated as was expected at the outset of RPI–X. Rather, RPI–X and its institutional setting have provided a broad structure within which both explicit and implicit regulation can evolve in various ways, for example to include yardstick elements. Price regulation, like other aspects of private monopoly regulation in Britain, is in its early days. It will remain a central element of industrial policy in the years ahead.

References

Armstrong, C. M. and Vickers, J. S. (1991), 'Welfare effects of price discrimination by a regulated monopolist', *Rand Journal of Economics*, 22: 571–80.

—— —— (1992), 'Price discrimination, competition and regulation', mimeo, Institute of Economics and Statistics, Oxford.

—— Rees, R., and Vickers, J. S. (1991), 'Optimal regulatory lag under price-cap regulation', mimeo, Institute of Economics and Statistics, Oxford.

Averch, H. and Johnson, L. (1962), 'Behavior of the firm under regulatory constraint', *American Economic Review*, 52: 1052–69.

Baron, D. P. (1989), 'Design of regulatory mechanisms and institutions', in R. Schmalensee, and R. D. Willig (eds.), *Handbook of Industrial Organization*, Amsterdam: North-Holland.

—— and Myerson, R. B. (1982), 'Regulating a monopolist with unknown costs', *Econometrica*, 50: 911–30.

Bawa, V. S. and Sibley, D. S. (1980), 'Dynamic behaviour of a firm subject to stochastic regulatory review', *International Economic Review*, 21: 627–42.

Beesley, M. E. and Littlechild, S. C. (1989), 'The regulation of privatized monopolies in the United Kingdom', *Rand Journal of Economics*, 20: 454–72.

Bradley, I. and Price, C. (1988), 'The economic regulation of private industries by price constraints', *Journal of Industrial Economics*, 37: 99–106.

Braeutigam, R. R. and Panzar, J. C. (1989), 'Diversification incentives under "Price-Based" and "Cost-Based" regulation', *Rand Journal of Economics*, 20: 373–91.

Brown, S. J. and Sibley, D. S. (1986), *The Theory of Public Utility Pricing*, Cambridge: Cambridge University Press.

Cave, M. (1991), 'Recent developments in the regulation of former nationalised industries', Working Paper No. 59, London: HM Treasury.

Caillaud, B. (1991), 'Regulation, competition and asymmetric information', *Journal of Economic Theory*, 52: 87–110.

Civil Aviation Authority (1991), *Economic Regulation of BAA South East Airports*, CAP 599, CAA: London.

Freixas, X., Guesnerie, R., and Tirole, J. (1985), 'Planning under incomplete information and the ratchet effect', *Review of Economic Studies*, 52: 173–91.

Gilbert, R. J. and Newbery, D. M. (1988), 'Regulation games', CEPR Discussion Paper 267, London.

Greenwald, B. C. (1984), 'Rate base selection and the structure of regulation', *Rand Journal of Economics*, 15: 85–95.

Laffont, J.-J. and Tirole, J. (1986), 'Using cost information to regulate firms', *Journal of Political Economy*, 94: 614–41.

—— —— (1990), 'The regulation of multiproduct firms (Parts I and II)', *Journal of Public Economics*, 43: 1–36.

—— —— (1991), 'The politics of government decision-making: A theory of regulatory capture', *Quarterly Journal of Economics* (Nov.) 1089–1127.

Littlechild, S. C. (1983), *Regulation of British Telecommunications Profitability*, London: HMSO.

—— (1986), *Economic Regulation of Privatised Water Authorities*, London: HMSO.

Monopolies and Mergers Commission (1987), *Manchester Airport plc*, Report MMC 1, London: Civil Aviation Authority.

—— (1988), *Gas*, Cm 500, London: HMSO.

—— (1990), *General Utilities plc, The Colne Valley Water Company and Rickmansworth Water Company: A Report on the Proposed Merger*, Cm 1029, London: HMSO.

OFGAS (1991), *New Gas Tariff Formula*, London: OFGAS.

OFTEL (1988), *The Control of British Telecom's Prices*, London: OFTEL.

—— (1992a), *The Regulation of BT's Prices*, London: OFTEL.

—— (1992b), *BT's Cost of Capital*, London: OFTEL.

OFWAT (1991), *The Cost of Capital: A Consultative Paper*, Birmingham, OFWAT.

Ordover, J. and Panzar, J. (1982), 'On the non-linear pricing of inputs', *International Economic Review*, 23: 659–75.

Rand Journal (1989), 'Symposium on price-cap regulation', *Rand Journal of Economics*, 20: 369–472.

Rees, R. (1993), 'Collusive equilibrium in the great salt duopoly', *Economic Journal* (July), 833–48.

Salant, D. and Woroch, G. (1992), 'Trigger price regulation', *Rand Journal of Economics*, 23/1: 29–51.

Schmalensee, R. (1989), 'Good regulatory regimes', *Rand Journal of Economics*, 20: 417–36.

Schleifer, A. (1985), 'A theory of yardstick competition', *Rand Journal of Economics*, 16: 319–27.

Stigler, G. (1971), 'The theory of economic regulation', *Bell Journal of Economics*, 2: 3–21.

Varian, H. (1989), 'Price discrimination', in R. Schmalensee and R. D. Willig (eds.), *Handbook of Industrial Organization*, Amsterdam: North-Holland.

Vickers, J. S. (1990), 'Competition and regulation in vertically related markets', mimeo, Institute of Economics and Statistics, Oxford.

—— (1991), 'Government Regulatory Policy', *Oxford Review of Economic Policy*, 7/3: 13–30.

—— and Yarrow, G. K. (1988), *Privatization: An Economic Analysis*, Cambridge, Mass.: MIT Press.

—— —— (1991), 'The British electricity experiment', *Economic Policy*, 12: 187–232.

Vogelsang, I. and Finsinger, J. (1979), 'A regulatory adjustment process for optimal pricing by multiproduct monopoly firms', *Bell Journal of Economics*, 10: 157–71.

Willig, R. D. (1978), 'Pareto-superior non-linear outlay schedules', *Bell Journal of Economics*, 9: 56–69.

16

The Cost of Capital in Regulated Industries

PAUL GROUT*

1. INTRODUCTION

The cost of capital is the risk-adjusted return that investors in a company should expect to receive in a competitive market and, in an attempt to replicate long-run competitive returns, regulatory policy typically employs a cost of capital as one of the major determinants of either the rate of return or the price cap in regulated companies. It is no surprise, therefore, that the figure for the cost of capital is of enormous importance to regulators and regulated firms, and that large sums hinge on the cost of capital number. For example, Table 16.1 shows for a series of UK regulated firms and groups of firms how much additional profit is involved if shareholders are allowed to earn an extra 1 per cent return on equity. Despite these large figures it has taken a considerable time for the cost of capital to rear its head in the public perception. To some extent the cost of capital has not been perceived as part of the traditional everyday economic jargon and its presence in public debate was always likely to be low profile until sufficient history of profits arose to attract

TABLE 16.1. Additional profit if extra 1 per cent return earned on equity

Firm	£m.
BT	205
British Gas	107
National Grid	18
Regional Electricity Companies (E. and W.)	76
Nat. Power and PowerGen	45
BAA	29
Water and Sewage Companies (10)	82

Source: Author's calculation.

* Professor of Economics, University of Bristol.

the obvious question—is the profit level justified? The fact that a sufficient history began to develop just at the time of a deep recession pushed the cost of capital to the fore in the regulatory debate in the 1990s.[1]

In many ways this sudden focus on the cost of capital has proved frustrating for the non-specialist. To begin with, the precise role of the cost of capital in the regulatory process can be confusing and is different from its role in a conventional firm. Furthermore, there are various methods of estimation that do not always marry together particularly well. Indeed, the concept 'cost of capital' can mean a whole series of different things and the terminology requires a precise description before one can be sure that any discussion is not being confused by talking across definitions. There are also a series of quite deep technical issues that can sometimes appear almost impenetrable to the uninitiated.

In one sense there is nothing unique in this complexity. It is an unfortunate feature of economics that apparently quite simple economic concepts can become extremely difficult once the surface is scratched. For example, the well-defined notion of marginal cost is often an exceedingly knotty problem to understand and model in practice. However, the cost of capital is particularly complex and it is an impossible task to try to cover all of the issues in this simple introduction. Instead what will be attempted in this chapter is a discussion of the concept, its use in regulatory policy, and consideration of some of the most practical confusions that may have important policy implications. The layout of the paper is as follows. The following Section provides a general discussion of the role of the cost of capital in regulated industries, shows that this role is very different from that played in non-regulated industries and explains why conflict developed over the appropriate cost of capital in the years immediately following privatization. Section 3 considers, in the UK context, the measurement of the cost of capital. Section 4 discusses risk issues, particularly changes in risk that arise from the privatization of assets, and the issue of regulatory risk. Section 5 contains brief conclusions and update on recent developments.

2. THE COST OF CAPITAL AND REGULATED INDUSTRIES

It is helpful to begin with a brief introduction to the concept of the cost of capital (details are left to the next Section) and to outline the role that

[1] The paper was written in Spring 1992. There have been some minor additions to this first draft, notably a brief up-date in Section 5, but basically it stands as originally written. A particularly interesting feature of the period since 1992 has been the change in attitude to the cost of capital in the regulatory arena. At the time of writing the notion was well understood only by a small section of specialists but in the intervening two years the focus of attention on the concept has been so strong that, while considerable confusion remains, it is now recognised as a central concept in the regulatory process.

it plays in a conventional business. This provides a useful background to discuss its role in regulation and privatization. The cost of capital is the rate of return that suppliers of funds to a business require the business to provide on those funds. Any company that cannot achieve these returns will not be able to attract new funding. In contrast, any industry where returns are greater than the cost of capital will, in the absence of entry barriers, attract new investment. With free entry the new investment will drive down the rate of return and this will continue until the firms in the industry earn no more than the cost of capital. This required return is determined as part of the equilibrium in the economy and will differ between companies and projects according to the riskiness of the activity. The more risky the business then the greater will be the cost of capital since suppliers of funds will require a higher return to compensate them for holding greater risk. Of course, the actual return achieved will generally differ from the cost of capital since the latter reflects an expected return and it is most unlikely that the actual returns will be equal to the expected returns. In a conventional, non-regulated business the cost of capital is typically used as an opportunity cost of funds. For the given risk of the firm the cost of capital can be thought of as the opportunity cost of the funds invested in the business since it is the rate of return that is provided in the market on funds invested in assets of similar risk. Since it is the opportunity cost of funds then it is the appropriate rate of interest to use to discount future profits in the company. If the money invested in a project earns this required rate of return then the project will have a zero present value when discounted at the cost of capital. If it earns more than the cost of capital then the project will have a positive present value, and if it earns less then the present value will be negative. Investors are seeking investments and activities that have positive present value and in this sense the cost of capital is a benchmark to assess the performance of the company. For example, such an approach can be used by shareholders to assess the performance of management within companies, to assess the performance of subsidiaries, or to assess the viability of new or ongoing investments. The cost is capital is a hurdle rate for the business. At its simplest the role of the cost of capital in a non-regulated company is one where the management quality and external forces determine the future prices and profit, and the cost of capital is used to dictate whether the activity is worth investing in.

In the arena of regulation the above process is usually conducted in reverse. The problem is not one of deciding whether the telephone, gas, water, or electricity industry is a 'good project' that is worth funding. These industries are obviously going concerns and the real problem is to offset the market failures that arise from their natural monopoly characteristics. It is usually argued that the beneficial incentive properties of private-sector ownership are sufficient to make it the sensible mode of ownership providing that the firms can be successfully prevented from abusing their monopoly power. The regulatory role is to control the prices of the major firms in these industries in order to mimic a price structure that would occur if the companies faced competitive forces. As we have indicated, competition should imply that a company cannot make long-run returns that are in excess of the cost of capital for the appropriate risk class of the business since, if it did make excess returns, then entry would drive down the rate of return on the company's capital. Thus the cost of capital is directly used as the bench-mark to determine the prices within the regulated industry. That is, prices are pegged at a level sufficiently far below the monopoly price level that the shareholders can only receive a return on the capital in the business that is equal to the cost of capital.

As indicated, within the regulatory arena the viability of an industry is basically taken as given and the cost of capital is used to determine the price level, i.e. the relevant cost of capital is determined and then the prices of the regulated products are fixed to allow firms to achieve that cost of capital. This is the exact opposite of the use in a conventional firm where prices are independent of the cost of capital and the cost of capital is used to determine the viability of the activity. Although there are variants to the regulatory process this basic distinction between the role of the cost of capital between regulated and unregulated companies always holds.[2] This difference in emphasis is very important. For a non-regulated activity prices are not directly dependent of the cost of capital. Firms aim to maximize profit and the precise value of the cost of capital, since it is used as a hurdle rate, will only affect the marginal projects. If the cost of capital is mistakenly set too high then some marginal projects that are good are rejected and if it is too low then some bad projects are accepted. However, almost all will be unaffected by the exact value that is attached to the cost of capital. In contrast, for regulated activities almost all regulated prices will be affected by the cost of capital. If the cost of capital is over-estimated then the price of all these activities will be set too high, and if it is under-estimated then all prices will be too low. Obviously, the relationship will be stronger and more direct for rate of return regulation than price cap regulation, but the general principle holds good. The economic implications of errors in the cost of capital are far greater in the regulated sector than in the private non-regulated sector and, not surprisingly, the pressure to provide precise estimates is greater both from the regulators and those within the regulated industries than in the private non-regulated sector.

At the time of privatization the pressure to provide exact estimates of the cost of capital was much weaker. Political pressures to achieve a

[2] The effect will be much greater in a rate of return environment than in a price cap situation where many other factors will also enter the determination of the price cap.

wide range of objectives, pressure to privatize within specific timetables and the absence of shareholders to force the issue meant that the cost of capital did not receive great weight in the overall privatization process. In contrast, we are now seeing the negotiation processes focus strongly on the cost of capital debate. This can lead to an apparent conflict as newly privatized industries begin to address issues that should really have been fully discussed and agreed upon at the time of privatization. Nowhere is this more clear than in the water industry. In this case the regulatory body, OFWAT, produced a consultative document (OFWAT 1991) outlining the proposed approach to the cost of capital almost two years after the privatization had taken place. Furthermore, this document does not simply outline agreed policy at the time of privatization but argues that the cost of capital is lower than previously suggested. This has been heavily criticized by the water industry (Water Services Association 1991), both for the methods employed and the assumptions used. In marked contrast to the situation in water, within the telecoms sector, where the major player has been privatized since 1984, there appears to be far more agreement between regulator and industry on the methodology behind the cost of capital.

Of course, the regulatory system itself will affect the role of the cost of capital. Although there are several possible regulatory models the two most common are direct rate-of-return regulation and price-cap regulation.[3] Traditional rate-of-return regulation allows companies to earn an acceptable rate of return on assets in each year and it is common for the rate to be changed as conditions change. For example, in the US suppliers can request rate reviews at any point. There are examples of rate-of-return regulation, however, that do not have this flexible property. For example, the regulation of the electricity industry in Hong Kong fixes a constant nominal rate of return for 15 years. An obvious disadvantage with rate of return regulation is that it has limited incentive effects. Profit arises from increasing the capital base since this attracts the rate of return. This favours 'gold plating' (excessive employment of capital) and excessive costs. To some extent the effects on incentives can be mitigated by yardstick competition but this is difficult to institute in practice.

In a deliberate effort to avoid these incentive difficulties a system of price-cap regulation has been adopted in the UK. For a period of time, usually five years, the real upper bound on prices is fixed. For example, BT's upper bound on prices is set at RPI–X (i.e. real prices fall), British Gas and the electricity industry have price caps of RPI–X+Y where Y depends on costs that are outside of the utilities' control and in the water industry prices follow RPI+K, i.e. real prices are rising significantly. It is normal for the X factors to be constant over the five years but this need not be the

[3] This section only offers a brief discussion. A far more detailed consideration of price caps is contained in Rees and Vickers (1992).

case. Indeed, the recent agreement between BAA and the Civil Aviation Authority has set an RPI–8,–8,–4,–1 and –1 as its five-year price cap.

With simple rate of return regulation, where it is conventional for the rate of return to be set equal to the cost of capital for that period, the role played by the cost of capital is straightforward. On the other hand, the cost of capital should only be one factor in the determination of the price cap, and the influence of the cost of capital should be less when compared to a rate-of-return environment. In practice, regulators have given considerable weight to rate-of-return cost of capital comparisons and it is generally agreed that the price-cap regulation in the UK has turned out to be a more incentive-compatible form of rate-of-return regulation rather than a radical departure from more traditional regulatory techniques. However, there are still different relationships between the cost of capital and the price cap. For example, the price cap can be chosen so that the discounted future value of the company is equal to the asset value. This process can be conducted by discounting the future cash flows of the company or by comparing the cost of capital to the accounting rate of return in each period. (It can be shown that if this is conducted carefully then the approaches will be equivalent, for example, see Edwards, Kay, and Mayer 1987; and the 'Byatt Report' (HMSO) 1986.) On the other hand, a price cap can be chosen to bring the rate of return on the assets in line with the cost of capital by the end of the five-year period. There appears to be no common procedure across utilities for relating the cost of capital to the price cap. For example, the water industry appears to be closer to the former model whereas OFTEL appear to favour the latter.

Assuming the regulated industry would not be 'unprofitable' 'in an unregulated market, shareholders will wish to replace the industries' assets if they are deprived of them. It follows that a natural economic valuation of these assets is the replacement cost. If a simple RPI–*X* price cap is employed then the cost of capital applied to this asset base fully determines the price level for the period of the price cap.[4] This is the simple theoretical relationship between regulated prices in a price-cap situation and the cost of capital. A particular attraction of such an approach is that the regulatory process is not backward looking. If within each price-cap period the company is expected to earn the required cost of capital on the replacement cost of its assets then each price cap can be set without reference to past asset values.

This simple model will not apply, however, if the regulated utility is not allowed to earn an appropriate return on its assets at the time of privatization. Then major problems arise. For example, if it is known at the time of privatization that a utility will not be allowed to earn the cost

[4] This is not to say that this fully determines all prices since in a multi-commodity industry there is still the problem of the determination of the relative tariff structure.

of capital on the replacement cost of its existing assets then the market value of the utility will be less than the replacement cost of these assets. At this point the cost of capital does not determine the pricing policy. Indeed, the basic relationship becomes circular. The proposed regulatory policy determines the market value of the assets, i.e. potential investors will insist on earning the cost of capital on funds invested in the utility and this will produce an economic value below the replacement cost. If this value is taken as the measure of the valuation of the company then it is obvious that the regulatory policy is indeed the one that allows shareholders to earn the cost of capital on the utilities' assets. Thus, in a trivial sense, the regulatory policy is acceptable (in terms of allowing shareholders to earn the appropriate cost of capital on the value of the utility) regardless of the cost of capital and regardless of the implied tariffs. This fixes a value for the assets (market- or model-based) and it is possible to use this value as the base for setting future prices. The result is that the pricing policy is now tied together across time in the sense that prices chosen in subsequent price caps are not simply a function of the cost of capital but also depend on the initial prices that were chosen by the regulatory authority and the price path that the regulator intended to be followed in the future.

This somewhat unusual process is precisely the situation in several sectors in the UK, including gas and electricity, but the most dramatic is the water industry where the market value of assets (debt plus equity) is approximately £15bn. while the current cost value is in the order of £140bn. For many years the rate of return on assets in the water industry was held artificially low and at the time of privatization the *K* factors in RPI+*K* were chosen in such a way that the industry would never cover the replacement cost of existing assets, although the *K* factors were chosen to provide a sufficient return on all new investment. The proposed pricing policy and the consequent returns, discounted at the cost of capital used at the time of privatization, created a predicted value for the companies. This value is referred to as the indicative value of the assets. It is significantly below replacement cost of the assets but above the ensuing market values. This raises difficulties that have not been fully resolved. In a conventional model the replacement cost of assets will respond to changes in the economy and industry. Indicative values or past market values do not adjust over time, indeed there are very good reasons for not attempting to construct such a change, but then a degree of inflexibility in the regulatory process is introduced. The difference between indicative values and market values may indicate that the market's perception of the cost of capital is a number greater than that used at the time of privatization.

The fact that market values may be used as the base for future remuneration introduces a degree of circularity to the process although once a market value is fixed at a point, history cannot be rewritten so it will not change in the light of its future use as a base for reward. This is not true for future privatizations. If market value is used as a base there will be problems for future privatizations which will be floated in the knowledge that the future market base will determine future tariffs. Of course, in the long run, as new investment replaces old, the importance of the market or indicative values may diminish providing all new assets earn the cost of capital. Then the process will converge on to a more sensible framework in the long run. On the other hand, if the price cap covers all current cost depreciation then the low value of assets will remain, creating a permanent need for regulatory vigilance.[5]

3. MEASURING THE COST OF CAPITAL

The weighted average cost of capital

An obvious but important point to note is that there is no reason to suppose that all suppliers of funds will be paid the same amount, indeed in general they will not. The reason is that different funds will have different claims on the return from a firm and those with the least risky returns will be happy to supply funds at a lower rate than others. The supply of funds typically comes from two sources—equity finance and debt finance. The feature of debt finance is that the return is fixed and this has prior claim on the profits of the company. Equity (the share holdings in the firm) has residual claims, i.e. receives what is left once debt has been paid. Associated with each of these types of funds is a cost of capital—the cost of debt capital and the cost of equity capital. For many regulated firms the cost of debt capital is close to the rate of return on government gilt-edged stock. This reflects the fact that, since debt is paid before equity and the regulated firms are thought to be unlikely to default on their debt, loans to such companies are perceived as very safe investments. Not surprisingly, equity is viewed as far more risky and the cost of equity capital is far greater than the cost of debt.

The overall cost of capital for the firm is the weighted average of the two costs of capital. This is usually referred to as the weighted average cost of capital, the weights being the proportion of the total value of the firm that is debt and equity, i.e.:

$$\text{Weighted average cost of capital} = \text{cost of debt} \times D/(D+E) + \text{cost of equity capital} \times E/(D+E),$$

[5] An excellent introduction to the cost of capital in a finance context is given in Copeland and Weston (1984). For an introduction to the cost of capital in a US regulatory context see Kolbe, Read and Hall (1984).

where D is the market value of debt in the firm and E is the market value of the equity.[6]

The determination of the cost of debt for the firm is relatively straightforward. For the typical large UK regulated firm the cost of debt will be about 0.5–1 per cent above the redemption yield on government gilt-edged stock. There will be an issue about the time period that is relevant (this will be discussed later) but in general the cost of debt capital is not a controversial issue. It is unanimously agreed that almost all of the major practical difficulties associated with the estimation of the cost of capital arise with the measurement of the equity cost of capital.

Given that the cost of capital relates to the required rate of return then it is essential to be precise about the rate that is being measured. Two immediate distinctions come to mind. One is whether the return is in real or nominal values and the other is whether the return is being measured before or after tax. The distinction between the real and nominal cost of capital is the exact analogue of the distinction between real and nominal interest rates. There are different views in the academic field as to the advantages of each and there is no single approach that is commonly employed in the UK regulatory field, e.g. OFWAT and OFFER use real rates while OFTEL uses nominal values. One of the main advantages for using nominal values is that the raw accounting numbers relate to nominal earnings and almost all of the rates of interest in the economy are set in nominal returns. Converting both of these to real values will not help in this process and, because of the tax issues, may introduce errors. Therefore, for comparisons of present performance it makes sense to concentrate on nominal values. On the other hand, when data is projected into the future it is most convenient to work in constant currency values. There appears to be no gain in calculating estimates of inflation and it is common to use a real cost of capital in this case.

A much bigger problem is the pre- or post-tax debate. There are two main issues that enter at this point. One is whether it matters whether one looks at an after tax or pre-tax cost of capital. The other is that there are several taxes and different marginal rates of tax and thus even the decision to look at after-tax returns involves a choice of alternatives. Taking these points in reverse order, an after-tax cost of capital could mean considering the rate of return in terms of the net dividend payments that the firm could make. That is, after corporate tax and individual tax if the individual is a basic-rate tax payer. Given the imputation tax system in the UK, this is equivalent to an after-corporation-tax payment where the corporation tax includes advanced corporation tax. If we are willing to assume dividend irrelevancy then this particular return has the advantage of being easy to observe. An alternative definition is that we consider

[6] There is a major issue relating to term structure that is not considered here. See, for example, Schaefer (1981) and references therein.

after-tax returns in terms of the return after corporation tax but treating advanced corporation tax as income tax. Given that dividend payment levels are known, then it is always possible to move from the latter to the former. Of course, there is no reason to suppose that the marginal rate of tax for the marginal investors that determine the prices in the market will be the basic rate of tax. Thus, when looking at the cost of capital after all taxes, it will be the amount that the firm must pay to marginal holders that is the relevant figure. The difficulty is that such an approach requires knowledge of the set of marginal investors and their tax rates.

The choice of pre- or post-tax is somewhat difficult. Investors will be interested in maximizing the after-tax returns and it is the after-tax values that should be equalized in equilibrium. For this reason the after-tax cost of capital is a relatively well defined concept. The pre-tax cost of capital can be thought of as the pre-tax return that is necessary to give the required after-tax return. The problem is that there is no unique relationship between the pre-tax and the after-tax cost of capital. For a given after-tax cost of capital the pre-tax cost of capital can take on different values depending on several factors including the time-frame of the investment programme and the writing-down allowances. This causes a problem because regulatory authorities tend to prefer to conduct the debate in terms of pre-tax figures. This is unfortunate since discussions about the value of the tax wedge can be complex and obscure far more important issues.

The cost of equity capital

We have indicated that this is more complex than the cost of debt finance. To a large extent these difficulties arise from the fact that there are several ways of approaching the estimation problem. Of course, the existence of several different ways of looking at the same issue need not be an obstacle if the approaches tended to provide similar answers. Sadly they often deliver different estimates for what is supposedly the same value. The problem would be somewhat mitigated if one technique clearly dominated the others in every respect. Unfortunately, although it is possible to make a strong case for one approach over the others, each has its difficulties. We will consider three approaches here. The first is the capital-asset pricing model (CAPM) which is the most favoured approach. The second main route is the dividend-growth approach which provides a useful cross-check against the CAPM number. Finally, sometimes it is useful to compare accounting returns.

The capital-asset pricing model

The first approach is to begin with a theoretical, structured model of the capital market and to use the structure of such a model to estimate the cost of capital. There are two main candidates that could be adopted—the capital-asset pricing model and arbitrage-pricing theory. The former imposes rather strong assumptions on the structure of the market but has the enormous advantage of providing an extremely precise and simple form for the cost of capital. It identifies exactly what factors determine the risk and return for any asset. The model is used extensively on both sides of the Atlantic to estimate the cost of capital for both regulated and unregulated firms. In contrast, arbitrage-pricing theory requires far less restrictive assumptions. This advantage is bought at some cost in that, although the model is able to provide a precise mathematical form for the influence that risk factors have on the cost of capital, it does not identify what these risk factors are. There are techniques to identify the factors but these are not straightforward and the approach is not used by companies in the UK. It has been used to some extent for regulatory purposes in the US but the CAPM is still by far the dominant model.

The intuition behind the CAPM is relatively straightforward. At the heart of it lies the beta of the share which captures the riskiness of the share (within the framework). The risk associated with owning a share comes from uncertainty surrounding the returns from the share. Changes in these returns can be separated into two types—those movements that are related to movements in the market (i.e. systematic movements) and those movements which are specific to the company and as such unrelated to movements in the market. The risk associated with the former is called systematic risk and the risk associated with the latter is called specific risk. Specific risk is independent of the overall risk in the market and investors are able to minimize their exposure to the specific risk of any share by holding a well diversified portfolio of assets. In the limit as the portfolio becomes as well diversified as possible then changes in specific risk will have no effect on the portfolio. For this reason an investor does not need reward for holding the specific risk associated with any share since the investor can protect himself against such risk.

The implication of the argument above is that when it comes to analysing reward for risk-holding it is the systematic risk of any asset that determines the rate of return that the asset must pay. Since investors cannot diversify away the risk associated with movements of the whole market then the contribution that any particular share makes to the movement in the market portfolio will be crucial. For example, suppose on average that a particular share rises (falls) by 10 per cent whenever the market rises (falls) by 10 per cent. The addition of this share to the market will neither increase nor decrease the overall movement in the market and investors will be indifferent to adding this share to a well diversified portfolio providing the expected return on this asset is the same as the expected return to the market as a whole. In contrast, consider a share that on average falls when the market rises and rises when the market falls. The addition of such a share to the market portfolio will reduce the riskiness of the overall portfolio because falls (rises) in the market portfolio will now be less on average with the addition of the new share. Such a share will be attractive to investors because it has an element of insurance associated with it. Investors would like a large proportion of their portfolio to be in such an asset but competition for the share will bid up the price, this having the effect of reducing the expected return. The price will settle at the point when investors are indifferent to holding the share or not and this will occur when the expected return on this share is less than the return on a risk-free asset, i.e. shareholders will be willing to pay a premium to hold such a share because of the insurance feature. Clearly, the correlation between the return on a share and the return on the whole market is critical for the determination of the required rate of return on the share. The beta of a share captures exactly this relationship. (Specifically, the beta is the covariance of the returns of an asset and the market return divided by the variance of the market). The capital-asset pricing model shows that the expected return on any share has two components. One is that the share must pay an amount equivalent to the return on risk-free assets and the other is compensation for holding risk, i.e. the risk premium. The risk premium for the share consists of the product of the risk premium on the whole market times the beta of the share. The market-risk premium is the amount that the market must pay above the risk-free rate, this being the compensation for holding the risk in the market. That is, the market risk premium is equal to the expected market return minus the risk-free rate. Denoting the risk-free rate by R_f, the expected return in the market by $E(R_m)$, the expected return on the share in question by $E(R_i)$ and the beta of this share by β_i, the rate of return can be written as

$$E(R_i) = R_f + \beta_i[E(R_m) - R_f]. \qquad (1)$$

(1) is probably the most famous formula in finance. Part of the enduring attraction of the CAPM approach follows from the fact that, despite being a full equilibrium model with a well established technical pedigree, the exact structure for the cost of equity capital is both simple and straightforward. For a share with a beta of one (as is the case with the share mentioned above that, on average, matched the movement in the market return one for one) then it follows immediately from (1) that the return must be equal to the expected return on the market. There are no theoretical bounds on beta but the beta for almost all shares in the UK lies between zero and 1.5. Standard examples of companies that have low betas (and hence lower than average costs of capital) are breweries and food retailers. Examples of companies that have high betas (and higher than average costs of capital) are producers of durable goods and property companies. There has been a tendency for many commentators

to come to the analysis of betas for regulated companies with the prior expectation that the beta should be significantly below one and that any other finding is technical error. This traditional view stems from the theoretical and practical experience of rate-of-return regulation, particularly in the USA. When prices are adjusted to achieve (short-term) rate-of-return regulation then the risk associated with such a share is much reduced and it is reasonable to anticipate that betas will be small. The US experience backs up this conjecture. For example betas of 0.5 are common in the telecoms industry with betas of 0.2 appearing in the electricity, gas, and water industry. However, outside of a regulatory system of this sort, then there is no reason to suppose that this basic intuition carries through to other regulatory policies. Two simple examples will be given here to provide a flavour of the problem.

The first follows from the fact that in a price-cap relationship of the kind that we have in the UK, price caps are reset infrequently. During the period of the price cap, except for specific exceptions such as 'pass through' in water and the 'Y' factor in gas, prices cannot adjust to factors other than the RPI. There is no reason to suppose that this reduced flexibility will reduce the variability of profit, indeed it is very easy to think of examples where the inability to respond to economic changes will increase the volatility of profits and hence the beta of the shares. Thus outside of a rate-of-return regime there is no a priori reason to suppose that regulation will have a major downward impact on the beta of a company.

The second example arises from the presence of fixed expenditures that increase the riskiness of equity much in the same way as the presence of debt increases risk. Most privatized companies have to meet many obligations in terms of quality and provision and so there is little flexibility over future investment. This implies that the firms will have many fixed expenditures that cannot be moved across time. In contrast, private unregulated firms can postpone investment expenditures, and reduce quality and provision if they wish. The fixed commitments for regulated companies increase the risk of the shares in the company so one would expect regulated firms to be more risky for this reason.

The theoretical discussion above indicates that betas of UK regulated utilities will probably be greater than their US equivalents but, since long-term expected returns are regulated, the betas are likely to be in the bottom half of the distribution, i.e. less than or equal to one. This is exactly the situation in practice. The lowest betas occur in the water industry. Figures of about 0.5–0.6 are typically found. The betas for the main regulated utilities that have been privatized for some time (British Telecom, British Gas, and British Airports Authority) lie somewhere between 0.75 and 1.0, depending how one treats the stock-market crash of October 1987. If one introduces a dummy to deal with the crash then betas of 0.9 to 1.0 arise whereas ignoring the dummy provides betas of

0.75 to 0.85. For example, BAA argue that the effect of the crash should be excluded when estimating the beta of BAA. This changes the beta value from 0.78 to 0.95 (MMC 1991). A sensible answer for most utilities probably lies somewhere in between but much nearer to the value with the dummy employed. The argument against omitting the crash data point is such crashes do occur at intervals but, on the other hand, it is reasonable to suggest that the last five-years data probably attaches too much weight to the crash. Figures of around 0.8–0.9 are probably reasonable estimates.

To obtain a more precise estimate of the cost of equity capital it is necessary to introduce tax. The exact formulation depends on the tax system and features of the market but a reasonable form for the UK is to replace (1) with:

$$E(R_i) = R_f(1 - t) + \beta_i\,[E(R_m) - R_f(1 - t)] \quad (2)$$

where t is the basic rate of tax (more generally the imputation rate). The observed market risk premium, $R_m - R_f(1-t)$, varies dramatically over time and the average is not constant. For example, over the period of time 1919–92 the average risk premium, adjusted for tax, is 9 per cent using Treasury Bills as the risk-free rate and 8 per cent using gilts. This falls to 8.8 per cent and 7.6 per cent respectively for the period 1930–92 and 10 per cent and 7.3 per cent for the period 1980–92. It is difficult to conclude from this what the precise risk premium should be. The picture is also clouded by suggestions that inflation expectations may have distorted these figures. Overall a risk premium of 7 per cent is a conservative figure with 9 per cent being an upper bound. Thus if the nominal risk-free rate is 3.5 per cent the model predicts that the after-tax cost of equity capital for a utility with a beta of 0.75 will be about 8.6 per cent (using 8 per cent risk premium and 25 per cent imputation tax). If the company has a (market) debt over equity value of 0.33 then the after-tax weighted average cost of capital would be 7 per cent.

Dividend-growth model

The dividend-growth models and CAPM are based on stock-market information but whereas the latter utilize a full equilibrium notion the former make extremely simple assumptions and apply these to the data. The most common model assumes that the company pays a dividend that increases at a constant rate. The price of the share is equal to the discounted value of the dividend stream which, since dividends are assumed to be certain (or have a very limited form of uncertainty) and increasing at constant rate, is equal to:

$$P = D(1 + g)/(R + g), \quad (3)$$

where P is the price of the share, g is the (assumed constant) growth in dividend, D is the past dividend per share and R is the cost of capital for the firm. (3) is referred to as the Gordon growth model and can be rewritten as

$$R = D(1 + g)/P + g, \tag{4}$$

which provides a formula for the cost of equity capital of the firm. The attraction of the approach is that it is very simple and with the exception of g contains numbers that can be picked up from any newspaper.

There are two obvious problems. One is that the assumption of constant growth of dividend is clearly unrealistic. The effect of this is that the formula tends to underestimate the cost of capital. Although it is a theoretical issue that can be tackled, this is rarely done because this problem is dwarfed by the second difficulty. This follows directly from the role of the estimate of growth. The nominal number for the (after-tax) cost of capital will normally be in the order of 10–15 per cent. A quick check in the newspaper shows that the typical (net) dividend yield will be somewhere between 3–6 per cent. Consequently, the bulk of the estimate of the cost of capital comes from g which is the one variable that is not available explicitly. There are various methods to estimate g. One is to look at recent history (say the last 5–8 years) and to apply simple estimates to this data. This is often a reasonable first stab particularly in the case of regulated industries. An obvious case where this approach fails very badly is if the firm is very successful or has a very poor recent history. In the former case the cost of capital appears very high and in the latter case g can often be negative over the period. An alternative is to use introspection or to poll analysts and experts of various types. The danger with the latter is that the whole process can become circular since there is a tendency to use an informal guess at the cost of capital and to delete the expected dividend payout to arrive at some idea of what scope there is for increases in dividends. One cannot claim to be using any market information to arrive at an estimate of the cost of capital in such circumstances.

Despite all these difficulties one can conduct such an exercise for regulated utilities in the UK. The dividend-growth estimates of the cost of capital provide numbers which compare reasonably closely with the CAPM figures but tend to be slightly higher when we would expect them to be slightly lower.

Accounting comparisons

The final approach that can be used to arrive at a figure for the cost of capital for a company is to consider what returns are being earned elsewhere in the economy. There are theoretical arguments that can be brought to bear to suggest that the accounting rate of return, appropriately measured, in the regulated company should be in line with the return in a group of companies that are similar in all respects save that they are not regulated. In practice it is impossible to find such an ideal group for comparison. One can look to the return in the industry sector but this is particularly misleading for large-scale regulated industries, in part because there are few firms in the sector that will be of similar size. Where there are similar firms in the sector, e.g. in water and electricity, then invariably these firms are also regulated making it a meaningless exercise to try to use such comparisons as a base for assessing the required rate of return for the regulated company in question.[7] There is also the problem that one must compare appropriate accounting measures if they are to make any sense when compared to the cost of capital. This requires conversion of the figures that appear in most accounts. For example, economic depreciation rather than straight-line depreciation is required. Every set of accounts for the comparator companies should be similarly treated. To do this properly for each company is a major exercise even when the number of companies is not very large.

What happens in practice is that regulatory authorities tend to look at the rate of return on capital employed averaged over quite large sectors of the economy. Clearly, the larger the group used the less likely the final number is influenced by extreme outcomes. The difficulty is that the group of companies becomes less and less a good proxy as we continue to add firms from different sectors. Furthermore, a close inspection of the extent of variability in the data does not improve one's confidence in using such an average. For example, the distribution of rates of return on capital employed for quoted firms can often have several modes within, say, the 10–30 per cent range.

The accounting approach is in a sense fundamentally different from the other approaches. The CAPM and dividend-growth approach are based on the specific features of the firm in question and, directly or indirectly, have a notion of return for risk that is either captured in the beta or the share price. The accounting approach, particularly when aggregated across a wide range of companies, makes no adjustment for any of the specific aspects of the company. Furthermore, it is exceedingly difficult to obtain measures of risk that can explain (in a significant statistical sense) almost any of the difference between firms even when each firm's return is averaged over many years. The fact that no attempt is made to incorporate the risk characteristics of the company in question suggests that this approach is ill equipped for use as the primary method of establishing cost of capital for a regulated firm.

The main conclusion that can be drawn from accounting data is that

[7] Accounting information from similar regulated companies can be useful, however, for yardstick competition (Schleifer (1985)).

this is a useful check on the figures that are arrived at using the capital-asset pricing model but that such an approach is unable to provide the degree of precision that is required for regulatory purposes. Overall, the CAPM and dividend-growth models are superior methods of getting at the cost of capital. The most sensible procedure is to use the CAPM to assess the figure and then to use the dividend-growth model and accounting comparisons as a cross-check with more weight being placed on the former. The practice is that the CAPM and dividend-growth procedures do indeed dominate accounting comparisons as the favoured technique.

4. RISK ISSUES

In this section specific risk issues that have not been covered in detail earlier but which have considerable policy significance will be discussed. Two such issues are of particular importance. One is the comparison of risk and the consequent cost of capital between the private and public sector and the other is the degree of risk created by the underlying political and regulatory process and how this influences the rate of return and its comparison with the cost of capital.

The rate of return that is presently employed in the UK public sector (6 per cent real, pre-tax) is far smaller than the cost of capital that we have been considering for the regulated firms within the private sector. Given that the majority of the regulated industries were recently in the public sector does this imply that they should now be rejecting projects that were previously acceptable, or is it the case that either the cost of capital for the privatized companies, or the required rate of return for the public sector is incorrect? The low required rate of return for public-sector investment is based primarily on the notion that society does not require any significant risk premium since the returns from the investments are spread across the whole population (see Spackman 1991). Although it is difficult to justify almost a complete absence of risk premium in the public-sector figures there does seem to be an argument for a diminished risk premium. Note that the social pooling of uncorrelated risks across society is not sufficient to argue for a wedge between public and private required rates of return. This is because uncorrelated shocks to companies create specific risks and as we have seen specific risks require no compensation in the CAPM model. The critical point is whether the relevant covariance of a company's returns is different if it is in the private sector rather than in the public sector. There does seem some justification for this view. Assuming that the costs and benefits of public projects are distributed optimally, then for an industry in the public sector the covariance that is relevant for the investors (i.e. the general public) is the covariance with the returns on the set of all projects in the economy. In contrast, if the company is in the private sector then, if finance is supplied by a limited set of individuals, it is the covariance of the company's returns with the set of assets that these investors own (i.e. something close to the stock-market portfolio) that is relevant. It is quite likely that the covariance of the company's returns with their wealth is greater than the covariance with all projects in the economy and so privatized companies can indeed face higher costs of capital in the private sector than they did in the public sector. This can have important policy implications if there are no efficiency gains from privatization. If there are no gains then it may well be the case that there are some projects that were optimal in the public sector that are no longer optimal now that the finance comes from a subset of the population. It is difficult to believe that the difference is likely to be as large as indicated by present public sector required rates of return so it is reasonable to assume that providing the gains from privatization are moderate then there is an overall gain to privatization and regulation even though the companies face higher costs of capital. Where this problem may be more important is at the interface between the private and public sector.

A second risk issue that has important implications for the rate of return in regulated industries is political and regulatory risk. Political risk can be thought of as arising from potential radical changes in general government policy and regulatory risk as arising from uncertainty surrounding the regulatory rules and regulatory environment. In some countries the difference between these two is very strong but at a theoretical level there is probably little useful distinction between them. Indeed in the UK the two notions are closely intertwined and, at this level of discussion, best lumped together. These type of phenomena appear in all regulated industries. For example, in 1991, only two years after privatization, OFWAT wrote to several water and sewage companies suggesting that they limit their price increase on account of the unexpected gains that appeared to have arisen in the industry since privatization (the so called MD61 letter). Although the price cap had several years to go before renegotiation, all companies chose to heed the regulator's suggestion and did not increase their prices as far as the agreed formula allowed. In this case the real life of the price cap, and by implication the real rules that companies operate under, are shown to be hazy. A good example of an unforeseen major change in environment occurred in the Gas industry in 1991. British Gas operate in a regulated market but also operate in the unregulated market for large contracts, the latter being more profitable than the former. In mid-1991 the company agreed a new price cap with the regulator, to be instituted later. At the same time the Office of Fair Trading was investigating the industry to ensure that pricing policies were consistent with principles indicated in a Monopolies and Mergers Commission report in 1988 aimed at promoting competition. They found that the pricing policies satisfied this criteria but, going beyond this brief, argued that competition was developing very slowly and made further dramatic proposals. Essentially British Gas were required to reduce their share of the contract market to 40 per cent by 1995 and to operate as two separate units, one covering transportation and the other trading. The central point is that British Gas were held to the future price cap despite the fundamental change in the environment induced by regulatory action. Finally, the suggestions made by the Labour Party throughout the 1980s with regard to renationalization are obvious examples of political risk.[8]

The key question in the light of these risks is whether regulated industries should be compensated for holding such risk and whether this affects the investment policies of the industry. The argument suggesting they should not be compensated is that these risks, while almost unique to regulated companies, are basically similar to other firm-specific risks borne elsewhere. Given that the CAPM model indicates that shareholders do not require compensation for holding specific risk then regulated companies should not receive special treatment and be compensated for such risk. This interpretation is only partially correct and it is useful to think about this more carefully. It has been pointed out earlier that the cost of capital is an expected rate of return. In this expected sense the cost of capital for regulated industries is indeed not affected by the presence of regulatory risk. However, a particular feature of regulatory and political risks is that they are not usually symmetric around the expected return. The market perceives the risks as being mostly of a negative nature, as indeed the three examples above are. That is, shocks tend to reduce the rate of return without there being equivalent offsetting upward shocks. The effect of this is clear. If the expected return is to equal, on average, the cost of capital and, at the same time, the regulatory, and political processes are likely to deliver negative shocks at rare intervals, then it must follow that in normal times the rate of return must be above the cost of capital to compensate for these occasional negative shocks. As long as the market believes that these risks exist then there will have to be compensation in the form of a higher rate of return in normal periods if funds are to be available to the company. The effect is that the companies will earn the cost of capital in the long run but may require returns above the cost of capital in the short run.

Now this higher return can be thought of as a higher cost of capital or a wedge between the rate of return and the cost of capital. In some circumstances it may be acceptable to increase the cost of capital and in others it is more appropriate to try to identify the risks explicitly and incorporate these in the expected return in the relevant years. The for-

[8] This type of risk has probably receded in recent years.

mer approach is more suitable to ongoing forms of political and regulatory risk whereas the latter is better suited to deal with specific shocks that do not have constant probability of occurrence across time. Precise interpretation of the problem shows that the 'compensation' for such risk is neither inconsistent with the underlying theory nor a sign of favourable treatment.

5. RECENT DEVELOPMENTS AND CONCLUSION

Recent Developments. Regulatory policy is changing rapidly in the UK and there have been some significant changes in the topic at hand that require comment (see fn. 1). There are three features that are worth mentioning. One is that the regulatory authorities appear to be adopting a lower cost of capital. Notably, in the now completed MMC investigation of British Gas, in the ongoing *K* negotiations in the water industry and in the ongoing distribution review of the regional electricity companies (RECs), costs of capital of 6–7 per cent pre-tax have been suggested by the regulators. This is based on three factors. One is a reduction in risk as perceived by the regulator, notably in the water industry. Another is the decline in the suggested risk premium. The final one is the use of a very small tax wedge (based on simple static models) when converting from a post-tax to pre-tax cost of capital. The combination of these effects is to increase the difference between the industry and regulatory perception of the cost of capital.

The second main development has been the use of market value as the asset base rather than replacement cost as measured by CCA. This has been explicit in the MMC investigation of British Gas, and is being mooted for the RECs and in the water industry. It is clear why this is so important. As indicated earlier a regulator sets a price cap so that an efficient company will on average achieve the cost of capital on the assets employed in the business, so any change in the notion of asset value will feed immediately into the prices and impact significantly on the profitability of the company. A shift from current-cost values to the lower historical market values (share value plus debt) will reduce profits significantly. For example, it is suggested that application of OFFER's implied cost of capital to a historical market value appears to leave the regional electricity companies with almost no profit on a current-cost basis. The case of the RECs is particularly important. Unexpected use of an early market value instead of CCA or later market values as an asset base does not allow shareholders to retain legitimate unexpected returns caused by unexpected market returns, unanticipated efficiency gains, or changes in discount rates. Regulatory policy will then be retrospective, clawing back gains and reducing incentives to be efficient. Such a strategy will be a regressive step for UK regulatory policy and one that should not be taken lightly. There are also implications for pricing. If early market value is employed then share-price values close to privatization will affect pricing for many years. Pricing policy will be driven by the host of factors that impact on the share price at a particular time. For example, such factors as the Gulf War, how much the government were keen to promote wider share ownership, the role of the ERM and the market sentiments on particular days, will all help determine the relative pricing structure of the energy sector in the next century. The electricity industry plays a major role in the UK economy and it is not obvious that pricing policy in the industry should be dictated in such a random manner. Additional problems arise with future privatizations. The problem stems from the circularity issue discussed earlier in the paper. At privatization if market value is used to determine future price caps then the expected returns in the short period after privatization fully determine the share price. Any minor change in expectations, even for a single year, will be magnified enormously since it will enter the market value and lie there for decades, perhaps forever, affecting the returns and prices of the company long into the distant future. Thus the privatization of new assets if it is known market value will be used is quite difficult. The solution appears to be the use of CCA for the RECs and indicative values for the water companies. Whether this will happen remains to be seen.

Conclusions. Returning to the main thrust of the paper, we have shown that the role of the cost of capital in regulation is roughly to provide a bench-mark of the required rate of return that shareholders should receive on capital employed in the business. This enables the regulatory authority to determine the level of prices to restrict the return to this rate. Because of this regulatory procedure the cost of capital affects all prices in regulated industries whereas in the private sector the cost of capital does not determine a firm's prices but the choice of projects. The result is that the cost of capital has far greater significance in the regulated sector, and the almost inevitable result is that the cost of capital becomes a hotly disputed number in an industry in the years immediately following privatization.

We have indicated how the cost of capital can best be determined but also, I hope, shown that the process is extremely complex and not always as precise as those involved would prefer. Indeed, during the privatization process there is frequently too little consideration of the cost of capital with this giving way, post-privatization, to a position where there is almost too much pressure to produce absolutely precise figures. Furthermore, the cost of capital itself is not independent of the type of regulatory process. For example, we observe lower costs of capital in the

US than in the UK because of the regulatory structures. Indeed, the presence of regulation itself may introduce risks that drive a wedge between the cost of capital as derived from conventional formulae and the usual required rate of return and that this causes additional difficulty when trying to assess the suitability of returns. At the moment there is no standard approach that is employed to relate company returns to the cost of capital and unless all of the regulatory bodies happen to be brought together under one roof (something that looks very unlikely) one imagines that the process of convergence is likely to be slow. A similar problem arises over the question of the appropriate asset base. At privatization no details existed as to what asset base would be used for negotiation of the next price cap. It seems clear that investors were not expecting market value to be used although while it is probably reasonable to assume that investors thought CCA values would be used in the case of the RECs it is not clear what was expected in the case of water. The present problems in water and electricity would have been reduced had proposals existed at privatization. Now that these difficulties have been faced it is essential that they are explicitly considered for all future privatizations and the policy expressed quite clearly at the time of privatization. Anything less will be harmful to the UK regulatory process.

References

Copeland, T. E., and Weston, S. F. (1984), *Financial Theory and Corporate Policy*, Addison Wesley.

Edwards, J., Mayer, C., and Kay, J. (1987), *The Economic Analysis of Accounting Profitability*, Oxford University Press.

HMSO (1986), *Accounting for Economic Costs and Changing Prices*, HMSO.

Kolbe, A. L., Read, J. A., and Hall, G. R. (1984), *The Cost of Capital: Estimating the Rate of Return for Public Utilities*, MIT Press.

MMC (1991), 'BAA Plc: A report on the economic regulation of the South-East airports companies', Monopolies and Mergers Commission.

OFWAT (1991), *Cost of Capital*, vols. 1 and 2, Office of Water Services.

Rees, R. and Vickers, J. (1994), 'RPI-X price cap regulation' (this volume).

Schaefer, S. M. (1981), 'Measuring a tax-specific term structure of interest rates', *Economic Journal*, 91.

Schleifer, A. (1985), 'A theory of yardstick competition', *Rand Journal of Economics*, 16.

Spackman, M. J. (1991), 'Discount rates and rates of return in the public sector', G.E.S. Working Paper, No. 113, HM Treasury.

Water Services Association (1991), *The Cost of Capital in the Water Industry*, vols. 1–3, Water Services Association.

17

Law and Regulation: Current Issues and Future Directions

JOHN MCELDOWNEY*

INTRODUCTION

Privatization of the major nationalized industries has created a number of new regulatory agencies and a fresh legal framework to oversee the development of the newly formed Company Act companies post-privatization. A wide range of statutory powers, contracts, licences, and conditions provide the main legal mechanisms which govern the relationship between regulator, the company, and the consumer. Largely discretionary, but also of great importance to the future of each industry is the role of the relevant Secretary of State and the complex legal powers which are devoted to the relationship between the regulator and the Secretary of State. Future directions for the newly privatized industries may be determined by the political policies which the Secretary of State may pursue and this may prove more controversial than at first appreciated during the early privatization debate.

This chapter examines the legal powers of the main regulators such as OFTEL, OFGAS, OFWAT, and OFFER who, respectively, regulate the telecommunications, gas, water, and electricity industries. Also relevant is the role of the Monopolies and Mergers Commission (MMC) and the Office of Fair Trading (OFT) which combine to investigate anti-competitive practices. The Director General of Fair Trading may make a monopoly reference to the MMC or a reference covering an anti-competitive practice. Statutory authority for such a reference is included in the legislation relevant to each of the privatized utility industries.

The regulation of the newly privatized industries and the respective legal framework which applies to each industry has provided lawyers unprecedented involvement in the technical drawing up of contracts, licences, and in the interpretation of the new regulators' authority. This has implications for the future development of the regulation and legal oversight of the various industries. Potentially there is considerable scope for the expansion in the role of the courts as an aid to interpretation and review leading to ultimate accountability over the legal powers

* Professor at the School of Law, University of Warwick.

of both regulator and utility company.[1] This chapter highlights the problems of increased reliance on judicial review to oversee and scrutinize the various industries. Also considered is the question of whether there is a need for a co-ordinated inter-regulatory agency to oversee common issues confronting the regulation and supervision of these key utility industries.

LAW AND REGULATION: AN HISTORICAL PERSPECTIVE

The characteristics[2] of the British approach to legal regulation may be shortly stated. The legal form adopted in the nationalization process was the establishment of a public corporation. Although individual statutory arrangements differed, depending on the particular industry involved, nevertheless some common features may be noted. A degree of day-to-day autonomy was granted to each industry leaving ministers overall policy and direction. Ministers could influence the membership of the boards of the industry through individual appointment and the giving of general directions. Financial control, especially over borrowing and in major development programmes, was largely dependent on ministerial discretion and sanction. Generally, the role of the nationalized industries was vague and uncertain and left to the policies[3] of successive governments. Rarely were legal powers invoked or actually used in the relationship between ministers acting as an 'arm's length' regulator and responsible to Parliament through ministerial responsibility. Financial target setting after the 1978 White Paper heralded a new break-through whereby sponsoring government departments assessed individual efficiency of each government industry through scrutiny of the financial targets of the relevant industry. The question of the annual debt of each nationalized industry and the amount of public expenditure became a key aspect of ministerial policy. Such issues gave rise to relatively few legal disputes and were subordinated to the day-to-day management of the industry and the government's overall economic policies. A common complaint of nationalization was the lack of information and knowledge of the working of the industry concerned.

Historically the regulation and scrutiny[4] of industry in Britain had developed from the nineteenth century. Legal powers were first granted through Private Acts of Parliament in return for statutory responsibilities assumed by the industries—the railways and electricity companies

[1] Gordon Borrie (1989), 'The regulation of public and private power', *Public Law*, 552–67.

[2] Paul Craig (1989), *Administrative Law*, 2nd edn., London: Sweet & Maxwell.

[3] W. Cornish, G. de N. Clerk (1989), *Law and Society in England 1850–1950*, London: Sweet & Maxwell.

[4] C. Graham and T. Prosser (1991), *Privatizing Public Enterprises*, Oxford. C. Graham (1991), 'The regulation of privatised enterprises', *Public Law*, 15–20.

are two good examples. Also relevant is the experience of the early Poor Law Commission in 1834 which struck a balance between central and local government. This early form of government regulation permitted commissioners to determine the qualification and duties of local Poor Law guardians and they, in turn, appointed paid officers to administer relief subject to the Poor Law Commission. The establishment of Boards, which acted in a quasi-ministerial manner combined administrative decision-taking and both non-political or semi-independent status. A number of examples such as railways and the factories inspectorate, illustrate the experiment of placing certain activities beyond the direct reach of political intervention. Eventually these activities succumbed to ministerial control but attempts at combining or isolating ministerial intervention with regulation were made. In the example of the railways, the Railway Department in the Board of Trade in 1840 was a department board in 1844, a Commission in 1846, before absorption into the Board of Trade in 1851.

A wide variety of powers were enjoyed by such regulators, invariably, a statutory framework would set the general shape and scope of the individual Board or inspectorate. Additionally codes of practice, circulars, directions, rules, regulations were all included as part of that legal framework. Occasionally a feature of regulation involved enforcement procedures through adjudication processes which invariably might involve a fine or criminal sanction. For example the early factory inspectorate under the Factories Act 1833 had the status of a magistrate with corresponding legal powers. Inevitably claims of partisanship and bias were made against individuals in carrying out their duties and activities. One of the characteristics of the nineteenth century was a remarkable degree of detail and openness in the reports published by the various Boards, departments, and agencies. This characteristic gradually diminished as the nationalization process took place in the post-Second World War period which was characterized by secrecy and lack of information on the actual performance of each industry.

Overviewing the activities of Boards, inspectors, and ministries the courts had a limited but important role. Various devices such as Crown immunity up until 1947 were used to prevent law suits in the case of torts and the amenability to judicial review depended to some extent on the remedy sought. In the case of mandamus, for example, a Crown servant could not be compelled to perform a duty solely owed to the Crown. As Cornish has pointed out, a wide array of legal powers was available. For example, the Poor Law Commission were advised to keep within the rules of natural justice and when they acted all their members had to be present. The courts were unpredictable in their application of rules of natural justice. Technical distinctions were the hallmark of this area of the law. At one time the courts appeared to apply distinctions based on the classification of the bureaucratic function as 'judicial', 'quasi-judicial', or 'legislative', or 'administrative'. In 1964 the House of Lords adopted a more permissive approach in the landmark case of *Ridge* v. *Baldwin* [1964] A.C. 40 and thereby abolished the technical distinctions which inhibited the development of judicial review.

In summary, the characteristics of regulation such as judicial scrutiny, adjudication of disputes, and ministerial accountability were all in place during the lifetime of nationalization. No coherent system existed to oversee and monitor the system of regulation as development was *ad hoc* and pragmatic. The legal controls that there were, seldom became the subject of litigation. Few lawyers were involved apart from internal law advisers over the Company Act provisions and the requirements of the specific statutory authority of each of the nationalized industries.

PRIVATIZATION SALES

Privatization sales[5] since 1979 have gained net receipts to the Exchequer of sums in excess of £20 billion.[6] In the case of the telecommunications, gas, water, and electricity industries the complexity of the sales involved high costs in the legal and technical advice sought in order to prepare the nationalized industries for sale. The preparation for sale, including the method of sale and the pricing of the industry, is under the scrutiny of the National Audit Office (NAO) who oversee the role of the sponsoring department and may carry out value for money (VFM) audit of the sale. This offers an *ex post facto* means of review, not into the merits of government policy, but into the departments' role in privatization. Reports prepared into the privatization sales of the major utilities such as gas and telecommunications have already been publicized. Currently water and electricity sales are under scrutiny. The NAO acts on behalf of Parliament and its reports are made to the Public Accounts Committee (PAC). The characteristics of this combination of independent audit and parliamentary scrutiny are judicial in form. Significantly the proceedings of the PAC are judicial in procedure as they involve the hearing of evidence from witnesses and cross-examination. Although the reports of the NAO and the PAC have been critical in their findings there are limits to their role in overseeing and through the assessing of value for money (VFM) in the sale activities of sponsoring government departments. VFM requires the consideration of the economy, efficiency, and effectiveness of the activities of government departments. The merits of

[5] P. Cameron (1991), 'Five years of regulating Britain's gas industry', *Utilities Law Review* (Summer), 70–7. See *Gas: The Monopoly and Mergers Commission* (1988), Cm 500, London: HMSO, and *the Gas Review* (Oct. 1991), OFT (summary version).

[6] J. McEldowney (1991), 'The National Audit Office and privatisation', 54 M.L.R., 933–56.

government policy including the desirability of privatization are excluded from the remit of the NAO reports. The *ex post facto* nature of the scrutiny also sets limits on the recommendations which may be made. Nevertheless the NAO has provided recommendations for the PAC which include competitive tendering by consultants for the work of advising departments on the sale, the steps to avoid high commission rates, and the use of 'claw-back' clauses to prevent windfall profits on assets sold as part of privatization.

Taken together the NAO and the PAC provide a significant scrutiny over privatization sales in considering whether the taxpayers receive value for the sales of state-owned assets.

THE REGULATORY STRUCTURE

The legal structure involved in privatization varied depending on the nature of the industry and the goals and objectives set by government policy. The first major privatization of a public utility was enacted by the Telecommunications Act 1984. Previously a state monopoly under the Post Office from 1912 to 1981, British Telecom was established in 1981 as a public corporation which covered telecommunications; postal services remained with the Post Office. The legal structure of the 1984 Act is significant because it set a model for future privatization. The characteristics of the 1984 Act are the use of an independent regulator (OFTEL) appointed by the Secretary of State (S.1 of the 1984 Act); the operators of telecommunications systems must possess a licence granted by the Director-General of OFTEL and the Secretary of State. There is a power to refer matters to the Monopolies and Mergers Commission (MMC) to decide if the matter referred, is in the public interest. The DG of Fair Trading has powers to supervise and investigate any possible anti-competitive practices or abuses of market power. Included in the regulation is a price formula designed to 'cap' the prices charged to consumers for services. Privatization of water (OFWAT), electricity (OFFER), followed similar principles.

The government's strategy for privatization also addressed the question of the value of the market as a regulator of the newly privatized activity. Rather than simply privatize a monopoly, some liberation was attempted both before and after privatization. This policy required legal powers to regulate the market. In the case of telecommunications, competition between Mercury and BT was created when Mercury was set up to provide an element of competition. The duopoly that resulted has itself been subject to criticism and review. OFTEL has been concerned with the terms of Mercury's network connection with BT. After delays and intervention by the courts, OFTEL ruled that the two networks should have full interconnection changes based on BT's costs and a timescale was set for the implementation of connection arrangements. This applied to both national and international calls. In March 1991 the long-awaited Green Paper on the Duopoly Review was published. Its main conclusion, that all applications for new licences for new telecommunications systems would be considered, and this would include both national and international services. This may be seen as broadening the possibilities for competition beyond the original framework of the 1984 Act.

The 1984 Act became a model for future privatizations with the exception of water where important environmental functions where shared with the National Rivers Authority, in addition to the setting-up of OFWAT. In the case of electricity (OFFER) and gas (OFGAS) the role of the Directors-General share a common identity. The Directors-General may share functions with their respective Secretary of State, they may act in an advisory capacity before the granting of licences, and give general advice and information to the Secretary of State. They are each required to publish an annual report and oversee the promotion of efficiency within their respective industry. Once a licence is issued by the Secretary of State it is the Director-General who invariably may agree changes with the licence and, where necessary, may make a reference to the MMC. Directors-General, exercise adjudicative functions in determining disputes or complaints within the licence conditions. They keep their respective industries under review and each publishes a wide variety of useful information about the industry. Post-privatization experience is that more information is available and greater openness is given to practices and understandings which were hitherto confidential and kept within the culture of the particular industry. Although there is a tendency for both government and industry to prefer secrecy and confidentiality, the legal powers of the Directors-General, coupled with referral powers to the Monopolies and Mergers Commission, may provide for greater information on matters such as pricing.

There are variations in the legal powers available to the respective Secretary of State of each industry. In the case of electricity it is noticeable how wide powers have been granted to the Secretary of State, not only in the power to licence generators, transmitters, and suppliers, but also in the use of non-fossil fuel. Directions as to the fuel stocks at generating stations, the construction, operation, and financial organization of generating stations, all fall directly within the Secretary of State's powers. Compared to the powers granted to the Secretary of State under nationalization these powers post-privatization are wider and more extensive. The Competition and Service (Utilities) Act 1992 provides additional legal powers for the Directors General of the four major utilities to improve consumer protection and standards of performance.

There is also the question of the extent to which the Secretary of State may intervene in the work of the regulator. Once a licence has been issued the Secretary of State has no power to amend the licence: such power rests with the respective regulator. There is therefore a separation of the responsibilities between the Secretary of State and the regulator. However in a number of ways the Secretary of State may influence the regulator. There is informal discussion and agreement; a variety of techniques are available depending on the legal powers involved. The Secretary of State has reserve powers in the case of electricity, to stop a proposed licence modification. In the case of gas, such modification proposals may be referred to the Monopolies and Mergers Commission. Contact between the relevant government department and the industry is therefore necessary, which may give rise in future years to questions of the openness and accountability involved in such contacts. In the case of telecommunications, the Secretary of State may give general directions to the regulator, as to matters that should be taken into account in considering aspects of the telecommunications industry which are subject to review. The powers of the four regulators have been brought broadly into line by the Competition and Service (Utilities) Act 1992 and relevant regulations made under the privatization legislation for each utility. In general the Directors General may issue licences and exemptions, set performance standards for consumers and appropriate levels of compensation when standards are not met. Directors General have powers to resolve disputes between utilities and their customers, investigate, and publish information, and generally monitor compliance with licence requirements.

The question of enforcing licence conditions lies with the respective Directors-General. Power to amend the licence may be with the agreement of the licensee or through a reference to the Monopolies and Mergers Commission. The Directors-General also enjoy a number of other powers for supervision of their respective industries which removes any potential in the legal sense for the Secretary of State to intervene in the direct general running of each industry.

In the case of gas the Director-General[7] has powers to promote competition within the contract market, i.e. over 25,000 therms per annum, but is lacking a general duty to promote competition overall. In contrast the Director-General of Electricity has such powers which are widely drawn but not easily interpreted with a precise and clear meaning. Gas privatization had resulted in a virtual monopoly for British Gas where, unlike the telecommunications industry with Mercury, no competition was established at the time of privatization. British Gas was in a strong market position post-privatization with the resultant effect that the regu-

[7] J. McEldowney (1991), 'Theft and meter tampering and the gas and electricity utilities', *Utilities Law Review* (Autumn), 122–6.

lator (OFGAS) became a surrogate competitor in its attempts to regulate the gas industry effectively. A major threat to any monopolistic conduct is the use of the Fair Trading Act 1973 (Schedule 8) in requiring the MMC to consider whether such conduct militates against the public interest. A wide range of remedial action is available including adjusting contracts, the formation or winding-up of a company, and consideration of the division of the business 'by the sale of any part of the undertaking or assets or otherwise . . .'.

In the early stages of the newly privatized life of British Gas, it was apparent that a number of grounds for dissatisfaction existed. These included: individual prices were unclear and companies had difficulty estimating future gas costs; a wide variation in prices was experienced between customers with the same or similar levels of requirement; tendering for contracts lasted for only three-month periods at a time and future gas costs were difficult to estimate, given the lack of transparency in pricing; British Gas were reluctant to quote prices for interruptible supplies and required in many cases the installation of dual-fired equipment which was costly; British Gas were also unwilling to offer supply to certain types of companies which would close down when supplies were interrupted.

Such complaints were reviewed by the MMC after OFGAS made a reference on the basis of there being a monopoly enjoyed by British Gas. The MMC upheld this view of a monopoly and concluded that greater competition was required. An additional finding was that the only effective means of remedying adverse consequences flowing from the monopoly status of British Gas was direct gas-to-gas competition. A long list of recommendations relating to the pricing and tendering of gas, third-party access to the gas transmission system operated by British Gas, and transparency in the system of gas schedules were also made by the MMC.[8]

Inevitably the MMC findings in 1988 required a reorganization of the gas market and provided the regulator with increased powers in terms of enhancing his status and in securing compliance with his objectives. Ultimately the Secretary of State's wide powers under Schedule 9 of the Fair Trading Act provide a threat hanging over the industry should the monopolistic practices be continued. As a result British Gas in February 1990 entered into a number of undertakings which included: not to purchase more than 90 per cent of gas on offer, not to require the inclusion of contract terms which could frustrate that objective; to provide common carriage quotations within a four-week period. In addition price schedules were introduced for firm and interruptible contract customers

[8] N. Lewis and I. Harden (1983), 'Privatisation, deregulation and constitutionality: Some Anglo-American comparisons', *NILQ*, 34, 207–21. Cento Veljanovski (1989), *Privatisation and Competition*, London: Institute of Economic Affairs.

to prevent British Gas from blocking market entry by a strategy of discriminatory pricing.

In July 1991 the effectiveness of the remedies applied by British Gas after the MMC report (1985) was referred to the OFT for consideration. The result of that review was published in October 1991 and concluded that although British Gas had complied with its undertakings, nevertheless the dominance of British Gas in the market had remained. British Gas, because of its size and market dominance was able to assert its influence. Thus it could cross-subsidize, act in a predatory manner on pipelines competition, and to set price levels in the indemnities market that a competition could not match. All these factors led the OFT to conclude that British Gas should consider the following:

1. releasing a significant proportion of its contracted gas and reintroducing a revised version of the 90/10 undertaking;
2. an appropriate undertaking on the tariff monopoly; and
3. the establishment of a separate subsidiary to operate the gas transmission and storage system on a non-discriminatory basis at arm's length from the rest of British Gas, and agreement to OFGAS regulation of changes.

Taken together the OFT report represents a fundamental reconsideration of the market position of British Gas.

Following further investigation two MMC reports were published on 17 August 1993. Both reports contain further recommendations leading to reorganization in the trading and transportation activities of British Gas, leading to the removal of a monopoly between the years 2000 and 2002. It is intended to see a reduction in the monopoly threshold to 1500 therms by 31 March 1997.

The above analysis of the British Gas example points to inherent structural problems in the way British Gas was privatized. Splitting up the distribution side from the production of gas supply might have avoided the problems of monopoly mentioned above. The model for such a restructuring may be seen in the Electricity Act 1989 (discussed below) where the transmission grid was separated from the production and distribution system.

However the British Gas example also shows the flexibility inherent in the legal mechanisms used to regulate the industry. The legal basis for referral to the MMC and the resultant modification of the authorization allowed gradual changes to be introduced. The existing legal framework is also sufficiently flexible to realize the creation of a separate gas transmission subsidiary. This could be achieved by British Gas voluntarily adopting the recommendations of the OFT. In the event of non-compliance the regulatory structure is sufficiently flexible to hold the threat of referral to the MMC.

The combination of regulatory supervision by OFGAS, and overview by the OFT and MMC, combines wide legal powers with oversight by the relevant Secretary of State.

In the case of electricity privatization the experience of both British Gas and telecommunications suggested that a different model should be adopted to provide increased competition as part of the legal structure for the newly privatized industry. The electricity supply industry (ESI) is a key industry in the energy field—especially in promoting energy efficiency and environmental concerns. The Electricity Act 1989 adopted a combination of licensing, contractual, and statutory powers to regulate and operate the newly created structure under the post-privatization arrangements. The Central Electricity Generating Board responsible for the generation, transmission (through a national grid), and distribution of electricity to twelve Area Electricity Boards was reorganized into four companies: two fossil-fuel generating companies, National Power and PowerGen, one nuclear generating company Nuclear Electric, and the National Grid Company which owns and operates the national grid. A licence, as is common with the other utility privatizations, is required for the first time for the generation, transmission, and supply of electricity or an exemption may be granted under the Act. Licensing is a power which combines the work of both Secretary of State for energy and the Director. Wider reserve powers are given to the Secretary of State in the case of electricity than in gas or telecommunications. Such reserve powers given to the Secretary of State (S.96) are for preserving the security of electricity supply, and the maintenance and the security of buildings or installations used for the purposes connected with the generation, transmission, or supply of electricity. The Secretary of State may set the percentage of electricity required from non-fossil fuel after consultation with the DG of Electricity and suppliers, such order subject only to negative resolution in the procedure of laying the order before Parliament.

The DG of Electricity with the consent of the Secretary of State, and after consulting public electricity supplies and affected individuals, may set individual and overall standards of performance. The DG of Electricity is required to publish information which is expedient to provide information for customers of public electricity supplies.

This wide range of statutory powers is also reinforced by licensing conditions such as the avoidance of cross-subsidization and the separation of accounts between different businesses. These arrangements are common to gas, electricity, and telecommunications.

In the case of water, ten public water authorities and twenty-nine private water companies comprised the water industry before privatization. The Water Act 1989 had to address the problem of not only the new structure under privatization but the question of merger and investment in the industry. In the run up to privatization concern among the water authorities was expressed because of the fear of predatory take-overs by French water companies. The Water Act (S.230 (3)) gives the MMC power to consider whether any proposed merger might prejudice the DG of water Services' ability to regulate the industry and whether the proposed merger was against the public interest.

A merger must fulfil the requirements that:

1. either it must not reduce the number of companies under independent control, or
2. the merger must achieve some other benefit of greater significance.

The latter may be achieved by a substantial benefit to customers. Nevertheless a large number of the existing water companies had received French investment before the Act was in force, and thus the regulatory protection appeared too late to be effective.

The Water Act 1989, however, broadly follows some of the legal characteristics of the post-privatization arrangements of the other main utilities. The main regulatory instrument is the licence which contains a regulatory mechanism which 'caps' the price which companies may charge their customer. The annual increase is restricted to the RPI, plus an additional factor *K* allocated to the companies on an individual basis for each of the next ten years. This is designed according to DG of Water Services, Ian Byatt 'to offset the significant investment programmes which have been necessary to achieve the higher standards which we all seek'.[9]

In the case of water reference to the MMC may be made by the Secretary of State for Trade and Industry following advice from the OFT. The water companies may appeal to the MMC if they wish to contest the action of the DG of Water Services in respect of determining the *K* factor in the price cap, amendments to their licences, and accounting guidelines.

The actual management of the industry is, subject to the legal framework identified above, let to the individual water companies to develop. Within OFWAT's remit is a periodic review every ten years of the company, investment programme, management plan, efficiency standards, and the regulatory regime in general.

FUTURE DIRECTIONS

Some general observations may be made from the above analysis of the operation of the legal structures of regulation post-privatization. First, reliance on the use of licences and contracts has involved legal drafting

[9] Ian Byatt (1990), 'The Office of Water Services: Structure and policy', *Utilities Law Review*, 1/2: 85–90.

in the technical side of formally operating the industry. Complex and detailed licences have required skilled interpretation and careful drafting. In the case of electricity they run to many hundreds of pages and provide in formal legal language the mechanisms of running the industry. This has given rise to a number of determinations made by the DG over the interpretation of various licence conditions and statutory powers.

Second, the use of a specialized regulatory agency for each utility has opened up the industry to greater transparency in the dealings with customers and competitors. This preserves a day-to-day operational autonomy in each industry according to the best management of each company. At the same time the statutory duties shared between OFT and the individual utility regulator combine to ensure a greater observance of the regulator's wishes than the legislative powers might have otherwise permitted. The sanction of a referral to the MMC has been effective in bringing about changes in British Gas. This combination of ministerial supervision, independent regulatory agency, and the enforcement of statutory powers is familiar to the nineteenth century evolution of regulation and its development in inspectors and Boards. Curiously the degree of openness in the publication of reports and evidence of modern regulations is strangely reminiscent of the nineteenth-century experience of Boards and their reports. This is in contrast to the marked reticence of the nationalized industries to reveal their activities.

Third, the courts have not had a major role in developing and interpreting the newly privatized regulatory structures. It is fair to say, as Graham and Prosser state, 'the role of the courts has been purely technical in the few cases where they have been called upon'. Nevertheless their potential for intervention remains. In the unreported decision of the divisional court: *R* v. *Director General of Gas Supply and Another ex parte Smith and Another* /1398/88, Mr Justice Pill applied the rules of natural justice to the investigative powers of the DG of Gas Supply in his role in determining whether British Gas was justified in using its disconnection powers where it suspected an offence was committed. Relying on the main legal authorities, such as *O'Reilly* v. *Mackman* [1983] 2 AC 237, the courts have developed the potential for intervention to review the decisions of regulators and ministers where they are thought unreasonable, procedurally inconvenient, or on some grounds of unfairness. (See *R.* v. *Panel on Takeovers and Mergers, ex parte Datafin plc* [1987] 1 QB 815.) The danger of the courts substituting its view for that of the designated authority which has been given that authority by Parliament was recognized by Lord Justice Watkins in *R.* v. *Secretary of State for Trade and Industry ex parte Lonrho* [1989] 1 W.L.R. 525. The boundary of the courts' jurisdiction would seem to be that the courts should not 'arrogate to themselves executive or administrative decisions'. Interpretation of this phrase is difficult to predict and open to narrow or broad interpretations. Courts are expensive and time-consuming; the outcome is often unpredictable and very often broad policy objectives are difficult to find communicated in legal decisions. The outcome is too often based on the principle of 'the winner takes all' which may not assist in reaching compromise and negotiation. The courts in the UK have to date only performed a limited role, indicative of the preference for self-regulation and the expense and uncertainty of any potential litigation. Despite such reservations about the shortcomings of using the courts, it is likely that litigation will provide an important element in the future of the various utilities. Courts may offer an alternative to the use of the Monopolies and Mergers Commission if their role is expanded.

Fourth, in the area of competition law the characteristics of the British system are a broad discretion within ministerial control and a limited role given to individuals or the courts. The MMC, OFT, and the Secretary of State for Trade and Industry combine with the relevant regulations to oversee anti-competitive parties. Largely left to ministerial discretion the courts have shown reluctance to challenge a refusal by the Secretary of State to make a non-referral even when no reasons are given as in the *Lonrho* case above.

Taken together the British system of law and regulation post-privatization presents the following characteristics:

1. Political policy and broad discretion are combined in ministerial decision-taking.
2. Adjudicative and investigative functions are combined in the work of the relevant regulatory agency which offers an independent dimension to overseeing the activities of the newly privatized enterprises.
3. Enforcement procedures are largely self-regulatory and negotiated between regulator and privatized utility, but subject to supervision by the tough regulatory powers of the MMC. This referral power to the MMC may act as a sufficient incentive to encouraging voluntary compliance and negotiated compromises.

To date the courts have provided a limited role in developing the regulation of the utilities.

The remaining question to be addressed is the likely future direction of legal techniques of regulation in Britain. An obvious influence is likely to be the application of EC law in the fast developing area of the environment (environmental impact assessment), energy policy, and regulation of competition practices. A recent example[10] is *Foster* v. *British*

[10] R. Nobles (1990), 'Application of EC Law to supply services', *Utilities Law Review*, 1/3: 1 27–9, B. Fitzpatrick (1991), 'Direct effect of directives', *Utilities Law Review*, 34–8. J. F. McEldowney (1993), 'Administrative justice', in R. Blackburn (ed.), *Rights of Citizenship*, Mansell, 156–78.

Gas plc, European Court [1990] 2 CMLR 833. Here the European Court interpreted a dispute concerning the implementation of an EC directive 76/207 (9 Feb. 1976) on equal treatment for men and women as regards access to employment working conditions and promotion. The case has implications for anybody that engages in supply services such as privatized industries, quangos, and Civil Servants. Under the principle of the *Marshall* case [1986] ECR 723, if the British Gas Corporation had been a public body then the corporation would have been in breach of the Directive. British Gas plc as successors would have to accept liability for the unfair dismissal. More important was the question of how EC law becomes applied by the national courts as EC directives cannot be directly applied by national courts and tribunals. But where a private individual has a complaint against a state body a Directive will be directly enforceable. The judgment of the European Court has left to the national courts their ideas of public service and the application of criteria laid down by the courts. This leaves a degree of uncertainty for the future as to the precise nature of the criteria, and the likely result is confusion in the courts as to how directly or indirectly effective directives can be applied.

A number of possibilities for the future are worth considering. Gordon Borrie argues for a Director of Civil Proceedings able to take proceedings at the instance of members of the public to redress complaints. Perhaps the role of the MMC and the different ultimate regulations requires an intra-regulatory agency to ensure consistency and long-term planning as part of its strategic functions? Borrie also suggests that private actions may be adopted as an alternative to official action in the courts against abuse of monopoly power. The comparison between the Monopolies and Mergers Commission and the courts is difficult to make. Each offers its own distinctive form of adjudication with inherent advantages and disadvantages. It is not that one is intrinsically better than the other, more than the tendency to make greater use of the courts may come from two directions. First, the interpretation of EC law and implementation may be led by the Court of Justice. Second, there is a desire for legal finality which may make courts attractive.

In comparison to courts, the MMC offers a more inquisitorial and investigative procedure. Various oral hearings may be held and its own staff may carry out investigative and technical analysis. The MMC may form its own conclusion as to 'the public interest' and proceed to adopt long-term policy approaches to ongoing problems. The MMC may be able to formulate policy considerations within its broad discretion. Implementation of its proposals, however, depends on ministerial agreement and this may leave ministerial discretion with an influence over the ultimate decision. The MMC is itself subject to review by the courts and it must carry out its task in accordance with natural justice and fairness.

Taken together the requirements of public information, overview of privatized companies, and the prevention of monopolistic abuses suggest that regulators are likely to look to a greater reliance on the courts to develop legal techniques to supervise the privatized industries. A good start would be in a code of good administration for regulators and privatized industry alike. The Citizens' Charter may encourage a greater sense of individual consumer rights with the necessary requirements of a more proactive role for regulators in supporting consumer rights. The British system of law and regulation, inherited from the nineteenth century has yet to undergo a radical transformation as the whim of government policy may change and litigation is likely to develop in importance. The various regulatory agencies have yet to fully determine their future style and the use they may have for the legal techniques available.

18

Problems of Yardstick Regulation in Electricity Distribution

THOMAS WEYMAN-JONES*

INTRODUCTION

The electricity supply industry in the UK has been substantially restructured before privatization, with the consequence that, unlike electricity-supply arrangements in virtually every other country the functions of generation, transmission, distribution, and supply have been separated. These functions now differ in ownership structure, regulation, and in entry liberalization. The functions themselves are succinctly described in the briefing of the government's lead broker, James Capel (1990) as:

- Generation: the production of electricity.
- Transmission: the transfer of electricity in bulk across the country.
- Distribution: the delivery of electricity over local networks.
- Supply: the acquisition of electricity and its sale to customers.

Other chapters in this and its companion volume analyse many of the regulatory relationships and contracting issues which are evolving in the industry, particularly in the generation and transmission functions. This chapter is particularly concerned with the distribution and supply functions, and the issue of regulating a group of strategically interdependent private companies each of which has natural and statutory monopoly power. These are the Regional Electricity Companies (RECs) in England and Wales, the successors to the former nationalized Area Electricity Boards. The particular focus of the present chapter is on yardstick comparisons of the RECs who are responsible for monopoly distribution and supply in the franchise market, and who can compete for supply contracts in the non-franchise market. The franchise market includes less than 1 megawatt maximum-demand customers to 1994, and less than 100 kilowatt maximum demand customers to 1998, after which it dissolves as the limited entry of other suppliers is extended to customers of all sizes. These other second-tier suppliers may be generation companies or other public utility suppliers of billing and metering services (for example British Gas, or the Telecommunications, or Water companies).

* Senior Lecturer, Department of Economics, Loughborough University.

The RECs will be the main target of the analysis, but we need also to understand the general principles behind the nature of the regulations and the yardstick model, and especially the measurement issues involved in making comparisons amongst groups of related organizations. Recent work in economics has paid particular attention to this issue of measuring relative efficiency, and it offers a useful basis for developing comparative performance measurements.

THE REGIONAL ELECTRICITY COMPANIES

Figure 18.1 gives a broad schematic outline of the electricity-supply industry in England and Wales in 1992, showing where the price-cap regulations impinge on different parts of the industry. The distribution and supply businesses of the RECs are to be treated separately, and distribution charges enter as one of the costs of acquiring electricity for supply to final customers. This split attempts to separate the natural monopoly aspects of meeting electricity demand, i.e. distribution through a network, from the potentially competitive aspects, i.e. metering and billing, and other customer services. At present both functions are price-capped, but the initial legislation anticipated that the need for regulation of the supply business would wither away as competitive entry evolved. Roughly speaking, generation accounts for 65 per cent, transmission for 7 per cent, distribution for 25 per cent, and supply for 3 per cent of the final retail price of electricity to customers.

Table 18.1 sets out the main statistics on the relative size of the different RECs in 1989 as the privatization programme was beginning. As the table indicates, while the different companies have relatively similar numbers of customers, they do differ markedly in several respects including the size of annual load (terawatthours, tWh), the geographical size of the network, and the structure of demand as measured by the relative share of industrial load in total units supplied. Each sector, with the exception of generation, is price-capped by the familiar RPI-X regime.

In the period following privatization, the RECs have been undergoing a learning process as they came to terms with strategic planning exercises which had all previously been the responsibility of other parts of the centralized electricity-supply industry. For example, each REC now calculates its own load and maximum demand forecasts rather than adopting a central Central Electricity Generating Board–Electricity Council forecast. Each now has complete discretion over the decentralized structure of its multiproducts tariffs, and no longer simply follows a set of central Electricity Council yardsticks. Finally, and most significantly, each REC plans its acquisition of electricity for supply largely in

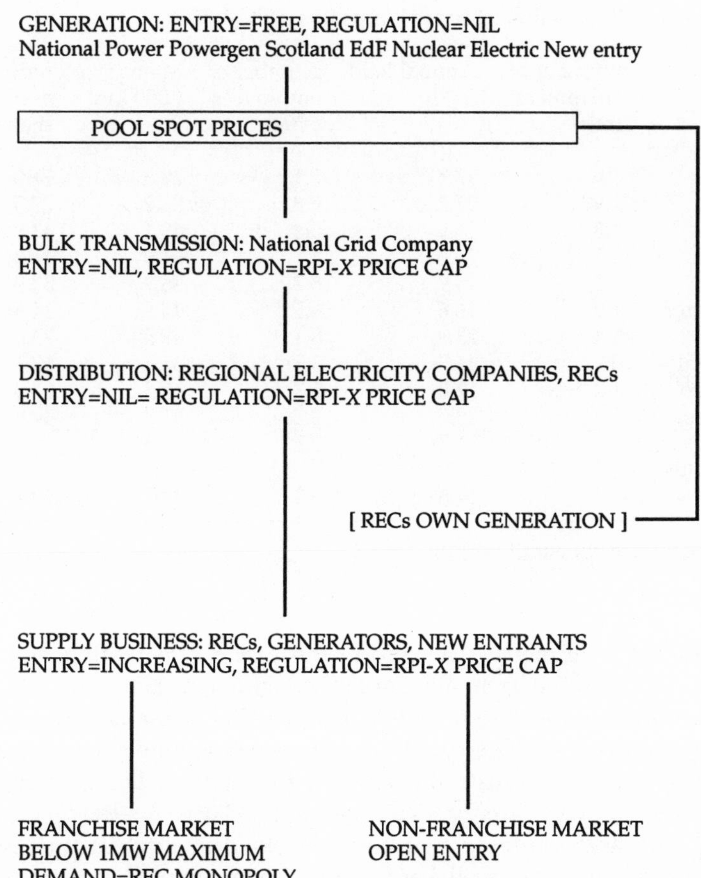

FIG. 18.1. Privatized structure of the electricity industry in England and Wales, 1992.

competition with the other supply and generation companies, and this acquisition may include its own generation as well as purchase and distribution through third-party wires. For the foreseeable future however, the RECs and their observers, critics, and customers will be most conscious of the impact of the regulatory regime under which they will operate.

REGULATORY CONTRACTS IN ELECTRICITY DISTRIBUTION

Distribution natural monopoly arises through a variety of causes, including economies of scale, scope, density and risk pooling, and

TABLE 18.1. The Regional Electricity Companies (RECs), 1989

REC	Number of customers (mn)	Annual load (tWh)	Number of employees ('000)	Mains size ('000 km)	Industrial market share (%)
London	1.9	17.8	7.1	29.5	11.0
Eastern	2.9	27.2	9.8	83.2	27.3
Manweb	1.3	16.9	5.4	43.7	43.9
Midlands	2.1	21.6	7.7	61.9	41.2
Norweb	2.1	19.9	8.2	56.9	37.9
Southeastern	1.9	16.6	6.5	45.8	24.5
Southern	2.4	23.9	8.1	69.5	23.6
South Wales	0.9	11.5	3.8	31.2	57.7
Southwest	1.2	12.0	5.7	45.8	27.0
Yorkshire	1.9	29.0	7.2	51.8	40.6
East Midlands	2.1	21.7	7.5	63.5	43.3
Northern	1.4	14.8	5.3	37.7	50.1

Source: The Electricity Council 1990.

informational asymmetry. These form the case for regulation, but also have an impact on the optimal form of the regulatory contract.

Economies of scale arise through the operation of the network which is used to deliver the industry's product to final customers in the domestic, commercial and industrial sectors of the market. The construction costs of the network are particularly large relative to the operation, maintenance, and reinforcement costs involved in electricity delivery. Consequently, there are well known arguments about the social inefficiency entailed by duplicating such a network, as would be required in a competitively organized market for electricity-distribution services. Electricity supply is storable only at very high cost, and on a small scale with technological difficulty, so that load taken at different times of the day and year in effect constitutes different products. Industrial, commercial and domestic customers may all take load at different voltages, and industrial customers may offer some reactive load facilities which ease the problem of always keeping load balanced on the system as a whole. Consequently, the supply of electricity-distribution services must be seen as a multiproduct industry offering economies of scope whereby the cost of supplying a portfolio of products is less than the sum of the costs of supplying each product separately. Economies of density and risk pooling arise through the interconnections amongst the different demand nodes on a distribution system. There will be random fluctuations at each of the different nodes, but unless these are perfectly positively correlated with each other, the risk of failing to meet demand on a system of nodes is less than the sum of the separate risks of failing to meet demand at individual nodes. Power transfers therefore make a single interconnected distribution system cheaper than a collection of individual distribution points, a phenomenon sometimes known as economies of massed reserves. Finally, and in addition to the natural monopoly power conferred by these market characteristics, there are grounds for arguing that the distribution utility will be better informed about the true nature of its cost efficiency and output productivity, the realization of the random shocks affecting demand and supply availability, and the extent of its cost reducing effort. In short, the distribution utilities exhibit all the classic conditions for viewing them as information monopolists in an asymmetric information game between the regulator as the badly informed principal, and the utility as the well informed agent. This theme, of course, runs through many of the chapters of this and its companion volume.

Prior to privatization, the distribution and supply of electricity was the responsibility of the twelve Area Electricity Boards of England and Wales which bought electricity wholesale on a predetermined Bulk Supply Tariff from the Central Electricity Generating Board. Each Board was expected to implement nationalized industry guidelines set out in a variety of White Papers (e.g. Cmnd 3437 (1967) and Cmnd 7131 (1978)) to set price at long-run marginal cost.

Since the Boards had a monopoly of information about their cost structures, this arrangement amounted to a cost-plus regulatory contract. Such contracts are known to encourage *X*-inefficient behaviour in asymmetric information games characterized by moral hazard and such inefficiency was one of the reasons for the emphasis given to the privatization programme of recent years. The game-theoretic approach to regulation suggests that an optimal regulatory contract for moral hazard problems may be one based on a price cap in which the firm is the residual claimant on profits generated by keeping costs below the price ceiling (Baron 1989).

One form of such a fixed price contract is that suggested by Shleifer (1985), in which each of a group of comparable regional monopolists has a price cap determined by the mean unit cost of the others in the group. This delivers a first-best outcome which satisfies the participation and incentive compatibility constraints on the regulated firms. When the firms differ in certain characteristics, the regulator can still obtain the first-best result by handicapping the firms according to the impact of these characteristics on the firm's unit costs.

Figure 18.2 illustrates the case of two monopolists with different unit cost curves, c_1, each of which depends on the amount of effort expended by the firm [$c_i = c_i(e_i)$]. This effort brings disutility to the firm's managers. Under yardstick regulation the firms' initial prices, p_i^* may be

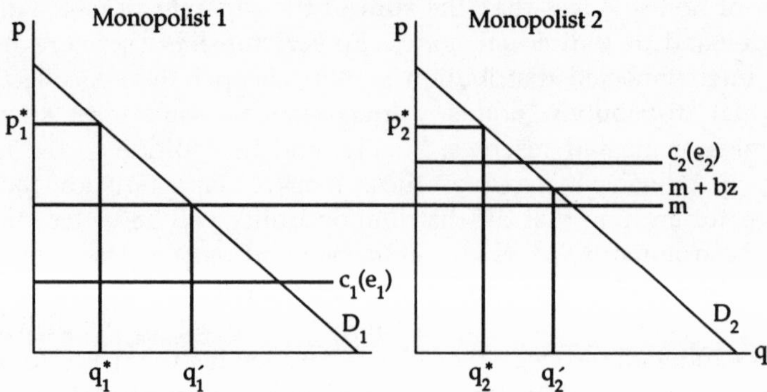

FIG. 18.2. The yardstick price-cap model.

capped at the mean observed unit cost, m. Alternatively, if the regulator believes the firms differ because of the impact of some exogenous characteristic of the operating environment, *z*, the price cap is $[m + bz_i]$ where b is the slope coefficient in a regression of c_i against z_i. In Figure 18.2, firm 1 keeps the residual profit from having its unit cost below the price cap, although it clearly must produce a higher output, an effect which is welfare improving. Firm 2 is in a more equivocal position. To beat the price cap even after allowance for the differential factor, *z*, it must increase effort to reduce costs, as well as expanding output. Otherwise it will make a loss, which violates the participation constraint in the regulator's optimization programme. Increasing effort is costly for managers, so the firm has an incentive to adopt strategic behaviour to alter the impact of z in its favour if it can. This may involve attempting to ensure that z is a variable over which it has some control. Alternatively, in the UK case, it may seek judicial review of the regulator's cost comparisons. As Besanko and Sappington (1987, 64) argue, 'When firms differ according to immutable observable characteristics, the [yardstick] incentive scheme . . . can be readily modified to effect the handicapping necessary to ensure the social optimum. When firms differ in ways that are not readily observable by the regulator, however, it will generally not be possible to implement the social optimum.' Wherever any leeway exists in the regulator's ability to impose an exogenous handicapping system, then the firm has a dimension of strategic behaviour which it may prefer to the option of reducing costs through additional effort. Hence the incentive compatibility constraint in the regulator's problem is violated, and the first-best efficient outcome does not emerge.

As is well known by now, the form of regulatory contract adopted in the UK is a price cap which does leave the utility being regulated as the residual claimant on the profits from beating the cap. In summary form, the regime consists of three parts, when we recall that each utility will have many different tariffs, $p_1, \ldots, p_n$, in its portfolio of products:

(i) the price *level* is capped;
(ii) the price *structure* is decentralized:
$P = \Sigma q_i p_i$, and $P_t = P_{t-1}[1 + RPI-X]$
(iii) the regulator determines X at regulatory review.

The index of charges, P, which is capped, is essentially an 'average revenue' index rather than a 'tariff basket'. In essence this allows the weights in the index to be partially under the control of the utility being regulated rather than being exogenous to its actions. (For more on the economic consequences of this choice, see the chapter by Catherine Price in the companion volume.) The initial choice of X factors for distribution was designed to allow the companies to raise prices above the rate of inflation represented by the Retail Price Index (RPI) in order chiefly to finance distribution network reinforcements and improvements. The distribution of these X factors, set out in Table 18.2, favours those companies with higher capital-expenditure requirements and lower load growth, both of which are partly related to the industrial market share. By contrast, all the companies shared the same X factor of zero for their supply businesses.

TABLE 18.2. The initial regulation of electricity distribution

REC	*X* factor	REC	*X* factor
London	0.00	Eastern	0.25
Manweb	2.50	Midlands	1.15
Norweb	1.40	Southeastern	0.75
Southern	0.65	South Wales	2.50
South Western	2.25	Yorkshire	1.30
East Midlands	1.25	Northern	1.55

Source: James Capel 1990.

The individual X factors were determined in the initial flotation to make the share prospectus look enticing, but are due for regulatory review after several years. One proposal for determination of X is to relate it to the firm's rate of profit over the previous years. This is analogous to the well known Vogelsang–Finsinger procedure for regulating a natural monopolist in the absence of all but historical accounting data published by the firm itself (see Vogelsang 1990). This lagged confiscation of profits is second best Pareto efficient but is open to the sort of strategic behaviour to delay the imposition of the price cap over time that was discussed above. These issues are further discussed in Besanko and Sappington (1987) and Baron (1990). Hence the *X*-efficient mechanism may be to base *X* on yardstick comparisons of the relative efficiency of firms, after allowance for environmental factors. The critical question then is how can efficiency comparisons be made that will remain incentive compatible. For example, is it clear that efficiency can be efficiently and unbiasedly estimated when firms differ in important characteristics? It would be naïve in the extreme to dismiss these differences, and base yardstick price caps on simple uncorrected financial ratios, but making the yardstick comparisons operational is not a straightforward exercise. In the case of the electricity utilities, there are large differences in the nature of their distribution networks, the type of load which predominates in their individual regions, and the customer density in each geographical area.

The proponents of yardstick regulation suggest that it may mimic actual market competition, or, more weakly, that it can economize on regulatory costs and burdens. Three critical assumptions underlie the yardstick model relating to:

- commitment
- collusion
- comparability.

Like other game-theoretic outcomes the model works on the assumption that the regulator can commit himself or herself to carrying out the predetermined regulatory contract provisions after the agent utilities have revealed the hidden information or hidden action that gives rise to the regulatory problem in the first place. Where regulators have a large public profile, and are politically sensitive appointments that may be rescinded after a general election, this necessary degree of commitment may be missing. In addition, yardstick comparisons clearly assume an absence of collusion on the part of the agents to manipulate their observed mean performance to benefit the group as a whole.

Finally, the mechanism assumes that the utilities will accept the reward or penalty outcome of the yardstick comparisons. This will fail to come about if the performance measurements used are not incentive compatible, and this will occur if they fail to account adequately for the relative performance of different monopolies with different characteristics. A critical assumption of the yardstick model of optimal regulation of a group of regionalized monopolies such as the Regional Electricity Companies is that they are directly comparable, or if not, that they can be handicapped (in the betting sense), in such a way as to make them comparable. Clearly, it is relatively easy to collect raw data which show up different aspects of a utility's financial, economic, or customer service performance. However, yardstick comparisons need measures which are independent of, or control for, the influence of exogenous variables that may have a major role in determining a utility's measured performance on a variety of indicators.

YARDSTICK AND INCENTIVE REGULATION MODELS IN PRACTICE

Yardstick models are a special case of *incentive regulation*, the basic principle of which is to decouple a utility's price structure from its own reported costs. Faced with an asymmetric information problem, this strategy is most likely to be optimal for a regulator seeking to improve cost-reducing effort, as the Schleifer model describes.

While experience with yardsticks in the UK is limited, some examples may be found in other countries, particularly the USA. Public Service Commissions in the USA have been particularly concerned to implement a variety of incentive contracts, including yardsticks featuring many different variables in the utilities' operating environments. In many cases, the utilities involved are integrated generation, transmission, and distribution companies, and the yardstick approach has taken a variety of directions. The important survey by Landon (1990) documents over sixty incentive-regulation programmes that were in use at that time by US electric utilities acting under the auspices of Public Service Commissioners, together with other discontinued and proposed programmes. Landon classifies the incentive regulation schemes in use in 1990 into ten categories according to the type of incentive which is the focus of attention. It needs to be noted, however, that the same incentive scheme may be included under several different headings. The incentive scheme categories set out in Landon's survey are:

1. Capacity availability.
2. Fuel and purchased power costs.
3. Conservation-related measures.
4. Heat-rate measures.
5. Non-ratebase plant.
6. Economy energy sales.
7. Efficient performance measures.
8. Indexed prices.
9. Line loss.
10. Construction cost cap.

Capacity-availability incentives reward/penalize a utility according to whether its capacity is available to produce output regardless of whether it is called upon to do so. There is some fixed standard of availability that the utility is expected to achieve. In most cases this is predetermined by the Public Service Commission, but, for example, in a yardstick approach, the Public Utilities Commission of Ohio compared

Centerior Energy Corporation's nuclear units' operating availability with the industry three-year average. If the availability was below the yardstick, the marginal cost of replacement power was disallowed as part of the tariff structure.

Programmes that use fuel and purchased-power costs generally reward a utility that achieves actual costs below some agreed forecast of costs, while energy conservation schemes are aimed at the idea of least-cost planning. The latter approach adopts the view that investment in energy saving is equivalent to investment in energy production if consumers maintain their real standard of living. It makes extreme assumptions about the nature of energy market failures but has had an important impact on the decisions of many of the Commissions. For example the Idaho Public Utilities Commission determined in 1989, in the context of energy conservation, that a utility that aggressively addressed the issue would be allowed a higher rate of return. Presumably the implied yardstick standard of comparison would be the other utilities in the group.

Heat-rate programmes allow utilities only to pass on a proportion of incurred fuel costs if a predetermined heat-rate (fuel efficiency) target, or forecast was not met. Out-of-Ratebase programmes mean that one (or more) plants may not be counted as part of the utility's capital stock for calculating its permitted rate of return, but the utility is allowed to keep the revenues from sales of the plant's output, either at a predetermined price, or to a third party in unregulated transactions. Similar permitted retention of revenues for off-peak sales is the basis of economy energy incentive programmes.

A few incentive programmes are specifically targeted on efficiency performance indicators, and in particular, the Iowa Utilities Board adjusts the rate of return on all Iowa utilities according to performance on the following indicators: price per unit of service, operation and maintenance costs per unit of service, customer complaints, management salaries as a proportion of total revenue, the company's bad debt ratio, innovative ideas by management, fuel cost per kWh, plant availability, company-wide load factor, and other relevant factors.

Programmes which focus on indexed rates tie a utility's tariff structure and level to externally set targets rather than its allowed cost base. The clearest yardstick example arises in the case of the Illinois Commerce Commission's regulation of Illinois Power Company. The utility's largest industrial customers are allowed to choose between a traditional tariff structure based on allowed costs, and one based on an index of twenty-four other midwestern electric utilities, on condition they stick with the choice for five years. Finally, there are a few programmes that penalize a utility for transmission losses, or put a cap on the allowed construction costs of new plant. It can be seen that many of these incentive programmes are ad hoc in nature, or focus on a very restricted dimension of the utility's activities. The target comparison is often a forecast negotiated between the utility and the regulatory commission, and in only a few cases is an explicit yardstick comparison made with other comparable utilities.

In the UK regulatory context, explicit mention of yardsticks has been limited. The draft regulations for electricity supply originally published by the Department of Energy in 1989, assumed that wholesale electricity would be sold on long-term contracts between generators and distribution companies. In determining retail tariffs, the distribution companies would take the long-term contract provisions as the base for the cost of purchased power to be passed through to customers. The draft regulations made provision for a yardstick mechanism in that each distribution company could only pass on as the cost of purchased power a weighted combination of the cost from its own contracts and the mean cost of the contracts negotiated by the other distribution companies. This was a weak provision since it opened up a strong incentive for distribution companies to collude on the long-term contracts that would be negotiated with the generators. Given the confidentiality of contract negotiations as opposed to the transparency of a spot market, this collusion incentive made the original yardstick provisions unworkable from the start.

Another area for yardstick comparisons in the UK context is the argument put forward on many occasions by OFWAT, the water regulatory body, for using quantitative estimates of utilities' relative efficiency for the setting of the price caps at the next regulatory review. Such comparisons could equally apply to the regulatory review of the RECs in 1995, and this is an area where empirical work on yardsticks is clearly essential. The rest of this chapter presents an analysis of this issue: measuring the relative efficiency of different RECs as a basis for determining price-cap X factors by regulatory review.

EMPIRICAL WORK ON YARDSTICKS

A small but significant body of empirical comparative efficiency measures exists for US and UK, and other European electricity utilities, as well as for other industries. This work seeks to compare firms within a given industry, perhaps at different points in time, by first determining which firms are performing most efficiently, i.e. constitute the *frontier* of the industry's production function, and then constructing an index of how any given firm differs from those which make up the frontier of efficient firms. This idea of frontier efficiency, and the consequent distribution of relatively inefficient firms in an industry can be traced back to the work of Leibenstein (1966) and Farrell (1957). Leibenstein argued that when constraint concern was lacking in an industry or a firm, i.e. there was an absence of pressure and competition from the external environment, decision-makers would not pursue cost-reducing or efficiency-maximizing behaviour. Such an absence of constraint concern might arise either in an uncontested monopoly, or a bureaucratic organization such as a nationalized industry. Button and Weyman-Jones (1992*a*) review some of the evidence on this.

Farrell (1957) took the presence of inefficiency in an industry as something to be measured rather than explained, and set in train a sequence of empirical work which has relatively recently attracted considerable attention. It is work in this tradition that OFWAT has referred to explicitly as a potential guide to regulatory review. In the remainder of this chapter I will review the application of this work to UK electricity distribution before and during the privatization process.

Farrell's approach to relative efficiency measurement was to construct a frontier to the firms' cost-minimizing activities, based on the best practice in the industry as a whole. Farrell's categories are best illustrated, for the case of a firm using two inputs to produce one output in the unit isoquant diagram, Figure 18.3. The isoquant yy represents all the processes (combinations of the two inputs) which can be used to make on unit of output. The firm at E is productively (or overall) efficient in choosing the cost-minimizing production process, given the relative-input prices represented by the slope of ww. A firm at Q, producing one unit of output, is allocatively inefficient in choosing an inappropriate input mix, while a firm at R, also producing one unit of output, is both allocatively inefficient (in the ratio OP/OQ) and technically inefficient (in the ratio OQ/OR) because it requires an excessive amount of both inputs compared with a firm at Q producing the same level of output, y. The use of the unit isoquant implies the assumption of constant returns to scale. However a firm using more of both inputs than the combination represented by Q may experience either increasing or decreasing returns to scale, so that in general the technical efficiency ratio OQ/OR may be further decomposed into scale efficiency OQ/OS, and pure technical efficiency OS/OR. The former arises because the firm is at an input–output combination that differs from the equivalent constant returns to scale situation that characterizes a long-run, free-entry competitive equilibrium. Only the latter represents the failure of the firm to extract the maximum output from its adopted input levels. In summary:

$$\text{productive efficiency} = \text{allocative efficiency} \times \text{scale efficiency} \times \text{pure technical efficiency}$$

$$OP/OR = [OP/OQ] \times [OQ/OS] \times [OS/OR]$$

Ignoring allocative efficiency for the moment, and concentrating on technical efficiency, Farrell suggested constructing, for each observed

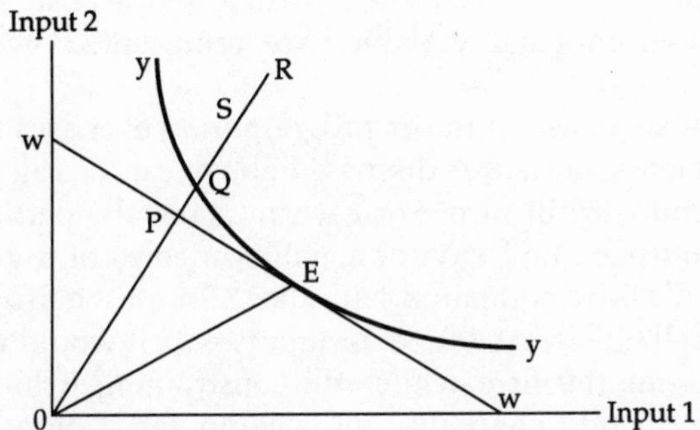

FIG. 18.3. Farrell efficiency.

firm, a pessimistic piecewise linear approximation to the isoquant, using activity analysis applied to the observed sample of firms in the industry in question. Figure 18.4 shows such a construction. Firms on the frontier, FF, are said to be efficient, while the scatter of firms above FF comprise the relatively inefficient firms in the sample. Each firm's relative efficiency can be calculated using the distance along a ray from the origin from the sample observation to the frontier, FF. The subsequent developments have extended this mathematical programming approach in several ways. The firms being compared can have several inputs ($x_1, \ldots,$ x_m), several outputs ($y_1, \ldots, y_s$), and can differ from each other due to the effect of different exogenous variables representing the external environment, ($z_1, \ldots, z_k$). These latter environmental variables correspond exactly to the factors which the Shleifer yardstick model takes into account in setting a yardstick price cap for a group of comparable

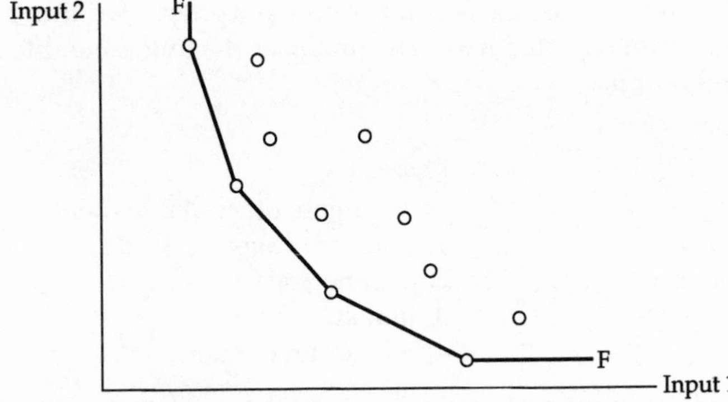

FIG. 18.4. Estimating Farrell efficiency.

utilities. If there are n firms in the industry, all the observed inputs, outputs and environmental variables are represented by the n-column matrices: X, Y, and Z.

By using a sequence of linear-programming exercises (activity analysis), the efficiency measures discussed above can be calculated for each firm in the industry in turn. For each measure the particular values of the inputs, outputs, and environmental variables of a given firm (vectors: x, y, and z), are compared with those for all the firms in the industry. For overall efficiency, the set of inputs which would minimize input expenditures for the firm while still constraining it to be part of the observed production possibility set is computed. Comparing this minimal expenditure with the firm's actual expenditure at the same input prices gives us the measure of overall or productive efficiency. For technical efficiency, we calculate the multiplicative fraction which needs to be applied to a firm's use of inputs in order to bring the firm back on to the efficient frontier while leaving its outputs and environment variables unchanged. If this fraction is unity the firm is already efficient, but if it is less than unity, it is inefficient. The latter technique is the well known Data Envelopment Analysis (DEA). The Appendix gives the full mathematical procedures used.

To gain an impression of how this model can be used to generate yardstick comparisons, it has been applied in several ways to the Area Electricity Boards in England and Wales prior to and during the privatization process (Weyman-Jones 1991; Doble and Weyman-Jones 1991; Button and Weyman-Jones 1992*b*). The results of these exercises are summarized here, and they cast light on the distribution of inefficiency in UK electricity distribution, on how that distribution changed as the privatization programme got under way, and on the difficulties of obtaining consistent yardstick comparisons among distribution companies when external economic conditions are changing.

The first consideration is to decide on the nature of the input and output variables in the analysis. For illustrative purposes, two broad categories of study are reported here. The first uses the following categories of inputs and outputs:

Study A:

Inputs	*Outputs* (kWh unless otherwise shown)
1. manpower	1. domestic sales
2. network size	2. commercial sales
3. transformers	3. industrial sales
	4. maximum demand (kW)

The second study concentrates only on short-run efficiency, but unlike the first, controls for differences amongst the utilities using a set of environmental variables ($z_1, \ldots, z_6$), which include other inputs and outputs as well as population density and market structure in the form of industrial market share:

Study B:

Inputs	*Outputs*	*Environmental variables*
1. manpower	1. number of customers	1. network size
		2. transformers
		3. total sales
		4. maximum demand
		5. density
		6. industrial share

In Study A, the choice of inputs and outputs follows well-established conventions in the empirical literature on cost studies in electricity supply. The different categories of demand reflect differences in the time incidence and duration of peak and off-peak loads, differences in the voltages at which load is taken, and differences in the provision of reactive power. These categories have relatively different impacts on costs, and partly represent the multiproduct nature of electricity supply. Similarly, the input categories reflect the standard ideas of labour and capital inputs. In Study B, the approach to input and output categorization follows the suggestion of Neuberg (1977), one of the very few empirical studies specifically directed to electricity distribution rather than electricity supply in general. Neuberg argues that electricity-distribution companies are especially concerned with delivering a service to consumers, and hence the number of consumers should be seen as the appropriate way to scale output. The choice of inputs and outputs is less narrow than it seems since the environmental controls contain the more usual input and output variables as well. The role of these latter controls is to enable us to measure relative efficiency in a way that explicitly corrects for differences in the operating environment of the different utilities being compared. Shleifer argued that this was a necessary precondition for making yardstick comparisons.

In carrying out Study A, the sample used to construct the production possibility set consisted of observations on all twelve Area Electricity Boards from 1970–1 to 1988–9 (240 observations in all). Each Board at a point in time is treated as a separate firm in order to construct the frontier. The objective in Study A was to measure technical efficiency allowing for variable returns to scale. The results of Study A are summarized in Table 18.3.

Two broad lessons appear to emerge from this set of results. The first is that inefficiency clearly has been a characteristic of the Area Boards in the twenty years leading up to privatization. On occasions some Boards have been operating more than 20 per cent away from the efficient frontier for the period under consideration. This suggests that a regulatory contract aimed at removing X-inefficiency by incentive regulation may offer real benefits to consumers. However the results also reveal a significant problem for a regulator seeking to carry out yardstick comparisons of technical efficiency. It is apparent from the results that different Boards moved on to and off the efficient frontier in different years, and a cyclical relationship with the trend of real GDP in the Board's own region was hypothesized. Table 18.3 reports the rank correlation coefficient between a Board's efficiency and the regional economic cycle as measured by the ratio of regional real GDP to its long-term trend. All of the correlations are positive, and 10 of the 12 are statistically significant at the 5 per cent significance level. The implications are critical for the nature of the regulatory review procedure. A regional electricity-distribution company's measured efficiency is synchronous with its local economic cycle, and hence the regulatory-review procedure, to remain comparable, ought to allow for this synchronicity when comparing different RECs. In short, they should be compared at similar points in their regional economic cycle, rather than at the same point in time.

TABLE 18.3. Summary results from yardstick efficiency Study A

Total number of Area Board observations: 240
Number on the efficient frontier: 45

Area board	Minimum efficiency	Mean efficiency	Correlation of efficiency with regional GDP cycle
Norweb	0.810	0.875	0.334
Eastern	0.895	0.966	0.546*
Seeboard	0.896	0.954	0.513*
MEB	0.887	0.971	0.517*
Manweb	0.875	0.960	0.541*
South Wales	0.802	0.909	0.640*
Southern	0.843	0.924	0.562*
London	0.887	0.953	0.723*
North Eastern	0.800	0.899	0.527*
Yorkshire	0.910	0.964	0.255
South West	0.734	0.838	0.544*
East Midlands	0.786	0.864	0.555*

*Rank correlation coefficient is significant at the 5% level.

Source: Doble and Weyman-Jones 1991.

Turning to Study B, a different set of questions was investigated. The observations were disaggregated into two overlapping sample windows. Sample 1 covered the Area Boards in the financial years ending:

1972, 1977, 1982, 1987, while Sample 2 covered the Boards in the years ending: 1977, 1982, 1987, 1989. In other words the second sample replaced the observations from the centre of the nationalization era with those in the year during which the Boards were preparing for privatization and the start of the incentive regulation regime. If Leibenstein's constraint concern argument (echoed in the recent developments in evolutionary economics) is valid, we might expect to see the beginnings of change in economic performance as market pressures became more pronounced. Of course these pressures were already partially being signalled in the greater financial discipline imposed in the 1980s. The objective in Study B is to measure overall cost or productive efficiency (including allocative efficiency) while controlling for the role of the environmental variables.

TABLE 18.4. Farrell efficiency results from two overlapping samples in electricity distribution

First sample		Second sample	
Mean	0.923	Mean	0.952
Minimum	0.566	Minimum	0.666
Variance	0.015	Variance	0.008
Standard Deviation	0.123	Standard Deviation	0.088

Source: Button and Weyman-Jones 1992*b*.

Beginning with Sample 1, it is the case that the mean reported figures in the table conceal a large dispersion of performance. Twenty-nine of the forty-eight sample observations showed an efficiency index of unity (or 100 per cent), but the lowest performance was that of Southern Board in 1972, at 56 per cent. The observations were chosen to reflect for each Board two years of strong economic activity, and two years of recession, since the earlier results suggested that a Board's efficiency was related to the stage of its regional economic cycle. The observations are equally split between the pre-Thatcher and the Thatcher Governments. There was no obvious pattern to the time variation of a Board's performance, although it was arguable that relative performance marginally improved in the 1980s compared with the 1970s, since only for two Boards (Manweb and Midland) was the 1980s mean score worse than that for the 1970s; for the rest it was either the same or better. This might just bear the interpretation that X-efficiency was better controlled in a political regime that was known to be less sympathetic than its predecessors to the nationalized industries.

Comparing the two overlapping samples, substantive changes in measured efficiency can be noticed. These changes take two forms. First, efficiency improves with the move towards privatization as both the mean and the minimum levels of efficiency rise. In particular, it is apparent in the detailed results that the new frontier for the industry is established largely from the 1989 cost performances, displacing the earliest nationalized observations above the cost frontier. Secondly, the variance of efficiency falls as the industry moves towards privatization. This effect may be the result of the fact that a market-constrained industry is less likely to permit the survival of particularly *X*-inefficient firms, whereas a bureaucratically organized industry may be more tolerant of extremes of *X*-inefficiency. These results reflect the inferences drawn about a wider sample of industries reported in Button and Weyman-Jones (1992*a*).

It remains true that yardstick comparisons require careful design. For example, the methodology adopted here assumes that all of the dispersion of the observations in the production possibility set is due to inefficiency. An alternative methodology could be adopted. For example, if the stochastic frontier (composed error) model of efficiency measurement suggested by Aigner, Lovell, and Schmidt (1977) is applied to the same sample to estimate a parametric cost function, very different results are obtained (see Button and Weyman-Jones 1992*b*).

The stochastic frontier model, which assumes that the distribution of performance reflects both inefficiency and random variation, found hardly any evidence of inefficiency compared with the importance of the random factors. Moreover, there was no evidence that the performance indices from the two methods were correlated. These findings can be given a policy-related interpretation. A regulator looking for yardstick inputs to the review of the utilities' X-factors might argue that the non-parametric model has indicated the need for a tight price cap to provide the incentives to reduce the dispersion of measured inefficiency. The utilities can appeal to the stochastic model to show that their different performances are due to the random factors of luck, weather, and so on, when their different characteristics are taken into account. In the UK regulatory system, this debate can be taken into a legal arena if the utilities request judicial review of the regulator's judgement, despite the intention to keep utility regulation and auditing out of the courts.

CONCLUSIONS

This chapter has reviewed a number of aspects of the yardstick model of regulation for a group of comparable utilities such as the Regional Electricity Companies. As well as setting out the theory of the yardstick model and reviewing yardstick provision amongst electric utilities in the

US, it has examined recent empirical work on making yardstick comparisons.

From this perspective, it is clear that making the textbook model of yardstick competition operational requires the specification of relatively sophisticated models and estimation methods. This, however, requires a degree of regulatory oversight and intervention which is at odds with the original intention to have 'regulation with a light hand'. In the context of the industrial organization literature, this is a reminder of the Demsetz–Williamson debate on franchise bidding. In that debate, a simple regulatory mechanism (franchise auctions) was suggested as a means of ensuring competition *for* the field as opposed to competition *in* the field, but the counter-argument was that the implied monitoring of the contingent franchise contracts and incumbent-entrant handover would impose just as heavy a regulatory burden as the original regulatory mechanism that the auction was replacing. In the yardstick case, the development of unambiguous comparisons that allow for the environmental variables affecting each firm's performance may involve the regulator in both bargaining and auditing activities the defeat the objective of designing a simple and inexpensive fixed price mechanism.

This conclusion does not undermine the case for carrying out yardstick comparisons, but, as this chapter indicates, considerable complex research remains to be done in designing models for comparative performance measurement.

APPENDIX 18.1. RELATIVE EFFICIENCY MEASUREMENT BY NON-PARAMETRIC FRONTIER METHODS

The starting point is the definition of the typical firm's cost function which depends on the firm's outputs, y, input prices, w, and environmental variables, z. The cheapest choice of inputs gives the firm's cost, C:

$$C(y,w,z) = \{\min w'x\colon x \in V(y,z)\}$$

where $V(y,z)$ is the firm's input requirement set, or set of feasible input bundles, x, that can be used to produce a predetermined output vector, y, given the levels of the environmental variables, z.

The input requirement set, or reference technology can then be represented by the free disposal convex hull of the observations, by choosing weighting vectors, λ, for each firm that show its efficiency performance in the best light.

For each firm in turn, using x, y, z to represent its particular observed inputs, outputs, and environmental variables, we proceed as follows. Overall efficiency is calculated by solving the problem:

choose $\{x,\lambda\}$ to: min $w'x$, such that:

$$\begin{aligned} x &\geq \lambda'X \\ y &\leq \lambda'Y \\ z &= \lambda'Z \\ \lambda_i &\geq 0, i = 1, \ldots, n \\ x_j &\geq 0, j = 1, \ldots, m \end{aligned}$$

The calculated productive efficiency of the firm in question is then measured by comparing its optimal expenditure using the solution vector of inputs, x*, with its actual expenditure:

$$\gamma^* = w'x^*/w'x \leq 1$$

Decomposing the problem further, pure technical efficiency is calculated by solving the problem of finding the lowest multiplicative factor, θ, which must be applied to the firm's use of inputs, x, to ensure it is still a member of the input requirements set or reference technology:

choose $\{\theta,\lambda\}$ to: min θ such that:

$$\begin{aligned} \theta x &\geq \lambda'X \\ y &\leq \lambda'Y \\ z &= \lambda'Z \\ \lambda_i &\geq, \Sigma\lambda_i = 1, i = 1, \ldots, n \end{aligned}$$

To determine scale efficiency, we solve the technical efficiency problem without the constraint that the requirements set be convex, i.e. we drop the constraint $\Sigma\lambda_i = 1$. This permits scaled up or down input combinations to be part of the firm's production possibility set. We can partition overall productive efficiency, γ, into allocative and technical efficiency indices, α and θ. Allocative efficiency can then be solved as $\alpha = \gamma/\theta$. A general reference on these techniques is Fare, Grosskopf, and Lovell (1985).

Note

This chapter draws on research carried out under ESRC grant number W102251011 in the Functioning of Markets Initiative.

References

Aigner, D., Lovell, C. A. K., and Schmidt, P. (1977), 'Formulation and estimation of stochastic frontier production function models', *Journal of Econometrics*, 6: 21–37.

Baron, D. P. (1989), 'Design of regulatory mechanisms and institutions', in R. Schmalensee and R. D. Willig (eds.), *Handbook of Industrial Organization*, New York: Elsevier.

Besanko, D. and Sappington, D. (1987), *Designing Regulatory Policy with Limited Information*, London: Harwood.

Button, Kenneth J. and Weyman-Jones, Thomas G. (1992*a*), 'Ownership structure, institutional organisation and measured X-efficiency', *American Economic Review, Papers and Proceedings*, 82 (May), 429–36.

—— —— (1992b), 'X-Efficiency in the UK: Upper and lower bounds', Economic Research Paper 92/9, Loughborough: Loughborough University.

Capel, James (1990), *The New Electricity Companies in England and Wales*, London: James Capel & Co. Ltd.

Cmnd 3437 (1967), *Nationalised Industries: A Review of Economic and Financial Objectives*, London: HMSO.

Cmnd 7131 (1978), *The Nationalised Industries*, London: HMSO.

Doble, Michael and Weyman-Jones, Thomas G. (1991), 'Measuring productive efficiency in the Area Electricity Boards of England and Wales using data envelope analysis: A dynamic approach', Public Sector Economics Research Centre Discussion Paper, University of Leicester.

Fare, R., Grosskopf, S., and Lovell, C. A. K. (1985), *The Measurement of Efficiency of Production*, Boston: Kluwer Nijhoff.

Farrell, Michael J. (1957), 'The measurement of productive efficiency', *Journal of the Royal Statistical Society*, Series A (General), 120: 253–90.

Landon, John (1990), *Incentive Regulation in the Electric Utility Industry*, Washington, DC: National Economic Research Associates.

Leibenstein, H. (1966), 'Allocative efficiency vs. X-efficiency', *American Economic Review*, 56: 392–415.

Neuberg, L. G. (1977), 'Two issues in the municipal ownership of electric power distribution systems', *Bell Journal of Economics*, 8: 303–23.

Shleifer, A. (1985), 'A theory of yardstick competition', *Rand Journal of Economics*, 16: 319–27.

Vogelsang, I. (1990), *Public Enterprise in Monopolistic and Oligopolistic Industries*, London: Harwood.

Weyman-Jones, Thomas G. (1991), 'Productive efficiency in regulated industry: The Area Electricity Boards of England and Wales', *Energy Economics*, 13: 116–22.

INDEX

Entries given in bold type indicate contributions to this volume